THE TEACHING OF ANTHROPOLOGY

THE TEACHING OF ANTHROPOLOGY

Problems, Issues, and Decisions

Edited by

CONRAD PHILLIP KOTTAK
University of Michigan

JANE J. WHITE
University of South Carolina

RICHARD H. FURLOW
College of DuPage

PATRICIA C. RICE
West Virginia University

With a Foreword by

JACK CORNMAN
Executive Director
American Anthropological Association

Mayfield Publishing Company
Mountain View, California
London • Toronto

not ref pt

Copyright © 1997 by Mayfield Publishing Company

All rights reserved. No portion of this book may be reproduced in any form or by any means without written permission of the publisher.

Library of Congress Cataloging-in-Publication Data
The teaching of anthropology : problems, issues, and decisions /
    edited by Conrad Phillip Kottak . . . [et al.].
        p.   cm.
    Includes bibliographical references and index.
    ISBN 1-55934-711-2
    1. Anthropology—Study and teaching (Higher)—United States.
2. Anthropology teachers—Training of—United States.   I. Kottak,
Conrad Phillip.
GN42.T43   1996
301'.071'—dc20

                                                                96-19790
                                                                    CIP

Manufactured in the United States of America

10 9 8 7 6 5 4 3 2 1   ACC 5781

Mayfield Publishing Company   lb
1280 Villa Street
Mountain View, California 94041

Sponsoring editor, Janet M. Beatty; *production editor,* Carla White; *copyeditor,* Patterson Lamb; *text designer,* Linda Robertson; *cover designer,* Susan Breitbard; *manufacturing manager,* Randy Hurst. The text was set in 10/12 Sabon by Archetype Book Composition and printed on 50# Text White Opaque by The Maple-Vail Book Manufacturing Group.

 This book was printed on recycled/acid free paper.

CONTENTS

FOREWORD

The American Anthropological Association (AAA) is delighted to collaborate with Mayfield Publishing Company in the publication of *The Teaching of Anthropology: Problems, Issues, and Decisions*. Affirming the value the Association places on teaching, this volume brings together the insights of more than forty contributors, who demonstrate convincingly that anthropology has timely, important, and enduring messages for students and the public.

This book is the culmination of several years of dedicated and imaginative work by the Association's Task Force on Teaching, which is supported by the Council for General Anthropology, the Council on Anthropology and Education, and the Society for Anthropology in Community Colleges, all of which are sections of the Association. The AAA also thanks the Wenner-Gren Foundation for Anthropological Research for its support. Most of these papers originated as presentations at panels featured at AAA annual meetings between 1990 and 1992.

This volume provides the first comprehensive examination of teaching issues across all the subfields of anthropology since the 1963 publication of *The Teaching of Anthropology,* edited by David Mandelbaum, Gabriel Lasker, and Ethel Albert. Both volumes focus on a range of teaching topics, issues, and audiences, but here the K–12 curriculum is also considered, along with curriculum for undergraduates and graduate students. As in the 1963 volume, the teaching of general, cultural, physical, archaeological, linguistic, and applied anthropology is broadly addressed. Neither anthropology nor the world has been static, and many of the contributors systematically address contrasts between the teaching of anthropology in 1963 and today, such as the greater diversity of contemporary students and the implications of modern technology and communication systems for teaching. The American Anthropological Association welcomes this important publication and takes pleasure in recommending the volume to teachers of and all persons interested in anthropology.

JACK CORNMAN
Executive Director
American Anthropological Association

INTRODUCTION

The Transmission of
Anthropological Culture Today

Conrad Phillip Kottak

This volume brings together the knowledge and insights of a group of scholars and teachers who share certain beliefs: that anthropology is valuable, that it has commitments, that teaching is a central part of our field, that anthropology has something to say to the public, and that we should be saying it to a wider audience. This book has emerged from several years of work and public activity by the Task Force on Teaching sponsored by the American Anthropological Association (AAA). Most of the papers assembled here were originally presented in panels held at AAA annual meetings each year between 1990 and 1992. The first panel (1990) had as its focus "Central Themes in the Teaching of Anthropology." The second (1991) explored the topic "The Incorporation of New Theory and Practice in the Teaching of Anthropology," and the third (1992) was entitled "How Exemplary Teachers Overcome Problems in the Teaching of Anthropology."

Guiding our contributors has been the goal of examining, updating, re-evaluating, and enlarging issues discussed in *The Teaching of Anthropology*, the collection edited by David Mandelbaum, Gabriel Lasker, and Ethel Albert in 1963. The focus of both volumes on teaching, especially of undergraduates, reflects our belief that college students should not be regarded as irritants but as fundamental to our professional employment. It is almost as true today as it was in 1963 that "the main sphere for the transmission of anthropological culture is the college classroom" (Mandelbaum 1963, 2).

When Herrnstein and Murray's 1994 book *The Bell Curve* can generate and publicize flawed conclusions about biology, society, and culture—similar or identical to those Franz Boas and his associates amply refuted two generations ago—it is clear that *we need to enhance public knowledge of anthropology's findings.* In our goal of disseminating such knowledge, we humbly follow a Boasian tradition best represented by Margaret Mead. In particular, we remember Mead for her success in showing anthropology's value and relevance in allowing Americans to reflect on cultural variation and the plasticity of human nature. Mead conveyed anthropology and its lessons to a broad public in a way that few if any of us do today.

Like the volume edited by Mandelbaum and others, this one surveys the teaching of general, cultural, physical, archaeological, linguistic, and applied anthropology. But several changes create contrasts between the teaching of anthropology in 1963 and today. There have been changes in students and, perhaps more important, in the settings in which anthropologists find themselves.

In his introduction to the 1963 volume, Mandelbaum noted the rapid growth of anthropology courses—for example, a 20 percent enrollment increase in a single year (1959–60) in California alone. The increase has continued, although at a reduced rate today. Contributors to the 1963 volume worried that the supply of graduate students would not keep pace with the growing demand for anthropology courses. Bernard Berelson (1960, 233–260) suggested a four-year graduate program and shorter dissertations as ways of addressing the problem. In the early 1960s the supply of trained anthropologists was so low that only ten out of fifty-six introductory courses in California's junior colleges were being taught by people with advanced degrees in anthropology.

Contrast that situation with today, when advertised positions at junior colleges routinely generate dozens of applications from Ph.D. anthropologists. The number of graduate programs, graduate students, and Ph.D.s in anthropology has multiplied so that the supply of anthropologists now exceeds the demand for them as teachers. Academic jobs are much harder to get than they were in the mid-1960s, when academia and museums readily absorbed people with Ph.D.s in anthropology. Although opportunities in academia have declined relative to the number of anthropologists with doctorates, the range of potential employment opportunities available to anthropologists has increased—especially in applied anthropology.

By 1963, Mandelbaum and Conrad Arensberg could already perceive a trend toward the increasing prominence of applied anthropology—a field designed to show "how theoretical concepts are deployed empirically and how the empirical data feed back into the development of theory" (Mandelbaum 1963, 10). That trend has strengthened; possibilities for applying anthropology full- and part-time have expanded. Many of us who never considered doing applied anthropology when we were graduate students, and who received no special training in it, now find ourselves working as consultants in varied locales, foreign and domestic. Courses and programs in applied anthropology have proliferated (see selections by Chambers, Tice, and van Willigen, this volume). But many recent and new Ph.D. anthropologists will find employment in "applied" settings where an advanced degree in another field might have done just as well and where there will be frustrations about incorporating anthropological approaches into one's regular work. This volume (especially the section "Teaching Applied Anthropology") recognizes the training needs created by the increasing number of men and women (30 percent of all Ph.D. anthropologists in a 1990 survey) doing applied anthropology.

The job expectations of the modal anthropologist have changed since 1963; indeed, one is hard put to identify a "modal anthropologist." The contribution of research to teaching was an important item of discussion in the 1963 volume, when "a university faculty member typically teaches undergraduates, does research, and supervises graduate students" (14). Mandelbaum could join his volume contributors Margaret Mead and Charles Wagley in suggesting, correctly, that an ongoing research program invigorates teaching and that basic research and education should go together.

That contention reflected the nature of, and expectations about, anthropologists' employment at a time when there were many fewer trained anthropologists than there are now. Contributors to the 1963 volume assumed that most anthropologists were and would be men (used generically there and then, but not here and now) working in universities, many with graduate programs, or in museums. *People, especially men, who earned Ph.D.s in anthropology in 1963 expected to have graduate students and research support.* The best graduate students from the major programs—especially the males—could expect tenure-track positions in good universities. They would use case material from their fieldwork and their ongoing research to invigorate their teaching of undergraduates and their training of graduate students. Junior college courses would be taught by part-timers and generalists with no advanced degree in anthropology necessary. In 1959, in the entire United States only 433 college students identified themselves as anthropology majors; 81 of them were in California (Mandelbaum 1963, 11). In the 1994–95 AAA Guide, University of California, Berkeley, lists 340 anthropology majors; University of California, Los Angeles, 339; and University of California, Santa Barbara, 262. Three California universities had more than twice the number of majors in the entire country in 1959. When I graduated in 1963 from Columbia College—a traditional hotbed of anthropology—I was one of just two or three anthropology majors compared with eighty-five there today.

Even as anthropology courses, students, and majors have expanded, the teaching prospects for anthropologists have changed dramatically. *Many, perhaps most, Ph.D. anthropologists will never train a graduate student.* Today, academic anthropologists routinely work in institutions where teaching schedules are heavy (for example, three courses a quarter, three or four times a year) and where research is not only unsupported but discouraged. And increasingly, universities (like other organizations) are cutting costs by hiring "temps" and part-timers to do the work of the generalist, which in this case means undergraduate teaching. The resulting system has two or three tiers (when graduate student teaching assistants are added in). The "regular," tenure-track

faculty get the research grants, the graduate students, the enhanced reputations, the TIAA-CREF and health care packages, and other benefits. The part-
timers get the undergraduates who use anthropology to satisfy a plethora of
curricular requirements (traditional ones like social science and natural science
distribution as well as newer requirements for courses on race, ethnicity, gender, non-Western cultures, multiculturalism, or diversity) and few perks.

Many anthropologists feel isolated as "temps" in large departments or as
regular faculty in small departments (or agencies) where there are only one or
two anthropologists on staff. Karin Tice's comments (in "Teaching Applied
Anthropology") apply to hundreds of anthropologists now working in junior
colleges, small colleges, and nonacademic settings. Tice points out that faculty
at major universities "are expected to attend and present at professional meetings, participate in the AAA, and in general contribute to the growth of the
discipline." But, normally there are different expectations outside of academia.

Anthropologists in small academic settings face similar conflicting obliga-
tions. Among students, colleagues, and clients unfamiliar with anthropology,
we must constantly explain its scope and relevance.

Compared with the collection edited by Mandelbaum and others, this
volume (see "Teaching Anthropology to Precollegiate Teachers and Students")
pays greater attention to the need for reaching beyond academia, museums,
and agencies to high schools, even grade schools, to spread anthropological
knowledge to as large a public as possible. Norah Moloney's paper considers
ways of teaching archaeology to young readers. Ruth Selig's contribution
describes new opportunities for disseminating anthropology throughout the
American educational system. She notes that within the field of education, increased anthropology-related subject matter in the curriculum and the growing
ethnic diversity of American classrooms favor the infusion of anthropological
concepts and subject matter into the precollege curriculum. Dennis Cheek provides strategies for doing this. Within the AAA, Selig detects a growing recognition that increased public awareness of anthropology could benefit the
discipline. She cites the association's new division overseeing outreach efforts,
including those toward public education. This could help correct a deficiency
noted by Jane White—that an increasingly monocultural population of American teachers does not know how to teach about diverse cultural, ethnic, and
racial groups. Gloria Ladson-Billings specifically addresses this issue by discussing the teaching of children who are African Americans.

The effective teaching of anthropology entails recognizing and dealing
with profound changes in students and society. Today's students are more diverse (for example, in age and ethnic background) than were those of the
1950s and 1960s. As White observes, we live in a world that by comparison
with those decades must seem overwhelmingly filled with alien peoples, cultures, and objects. L. B. Breitborde's paper comments on an "intensifying of
identity and culture in our classrooms." Many of our beginning students
are already well aware of cultural differences: promoted as matters of pride
and passion by segments of their communities, taught through courses in the

public schools, and enunciated as organizing principles by competing voices in the public policy arena. The variety in institutions, social relations, and customs about which anthropologists teach is no surprise for many students. As White reports, students may initially react negatively, both emotionally and intellectually, to examples of cultural differences. We need to be aware that they may have encountered "diversity" as a disruptive political force in their communities and in relation to their own schooling. The Spindlers, Friedl, Moses and Mukhopadhyay, Marcus, Nanda, Foster, Ladson-Billings, Rubin, and Heider all describe ways in which students can be engaged to rethink their own cultural identities, respect diversity, negotiate cultural boundaries, and question conventional ways of thinking as they establish relationships and construct knowledge in a rapidly changing interconnected world.

As some of our contributors emphasize, not only do we teach, *we also learn from our students*. We do this as we plan and revise the courses we teach and the textbooks we write. William Haviland's paper rightly describes student preconceptions and biases that anthropology should and does confront. But our challenges and confrontations must be laced with humility and respect. Many readers will agree with Mandelbaum (1963, 8, 13) that even thirty years later, the central problems of American higher education include student boredom, indifference, and hostility to learning, and that most college students are more concerned with their grades and social networks than with the cultivation of intellect. Still, "every student comes into a beginning anthropology course already equipped with some ideas about the subjects to be discussed . . . about the nature of culture and society—at least his own" (Mandelbaum 1963, 10–11). Robert Borofsky notes that more than in the past, students and faculty may not share important understandings about what needs to be learned and how to learn it because of their differing backgrounds. As we strive to combat ethnocentrism and provincialism, we also need to think more about how to use and channel the knowledge and experience that our students bring to the classroom. As we contemplate ways of "studying up" in our research, we should also think about ways of "empowering students" (Borofsky) by "studying down" in the classroom. That is, our teaching can be enhanced by learning more about our students' actual understandings and experiences.

Carol and Melvin Ember speak of the tentativeness of what we teach; they caution that we not regard students as blank slates on which we have to write a lesson. Norma Gonzalez and Cathy Amanti describe an experiment in which teachers learned how to build systematically on their students' backgrounds and prior knowledge to facilitate more formal learning. David McCurdy stresses what he has learned from his Macalester students' fieldwork and ethnographic writing. George and Louise Spindler report that they intentionally draw on the different social and ethnic backgrounds of their students in the ethnography courses they teach.

Contemporary students grow up in a high-tech, mass-mediated world. Many of them are more comfortable with modern technology than we are, and they force us to use it in our teaching. As Aaron Podolefsky observes, the pace of changes in computing technology, knowledge development, and communications pathways is driving a transformation in our approach to education. We use e-mail to communicate with students and colleagues worldwide. Computers and word processing software permit us to prepare and revise our own syllabi and to churn out the endless stream of letters of recommendation generated by the profusion of anthropology students. Mosaic and Netscape permit us to "surf" the "web" and the "net." Via modem, we do library research and database searches from our homes. New audio and video technology enhances our classroom presentations and permits us to offer new courses. Easily available software for data entry and statistical analysis leads to more and better courses on research methods.

With reference to ways of presenting ethnographic knowledge, Ernestine Friedl notes (with some concern) that visual images as a means of learning have become prominent if not predominant. In his discussion of teaching anthropology through film, Karl Heider stresses the impact of the video explosion (including the availability of films about other cultures made by people from those cultures) on the teaching of anthropology.

The contributors to this volume sample a wide range of experience and perspectives in teaching anthropology—general, cultural, linguistic, biological, archaeological, and applied. (We are delighted to include a new paper by a contributor to the 1963 collection—George Spindler, writing with Louise Spindler.) Our authors have designed varied teaching strategies and techniques to use with today's students. Some, for instance, require their students to experiment in professional practice, whether in ethnography (McCurdy), archaeology (Rice), or applied anthropology (van Willigen).

The Spindlers, well known for their series of case studies in cultural anthropology, tell us that they make minimal use of "anthropological theory" in their introductory course. They characterize such theory as "phrased in ways that are entirely out of the cultural framework of undergraduates" and "known and circulated within small, esoteric professional cliques." The Spindlers insist that the primary purpose of anthropology is education. They fault faculty who become "so puffed up with research and theory building that we often do not see the imperatives of our call to duty." McCurdy disputes the contention (by some of his colleagues) that "college students can't do ethnography because they don't know enough theory." He knows that undergraduates *can* do ethnography—perhaps *because* they don't spend too much time worrying about "theory."

One problem with incorporating *theory* in the college curriculum is that there is less consensus now than there used to be about what the term means and encompasses. The contributors to the 1963 volume used *theory* in two senses: as "a coherent group of general propositions used as principles of explanation for a class of phenomena" and as "the branch of a science or art that deals with its principles or methods, as distinguished from its practice" (*Random House College Dictionary,* rev. ed., 1982, 1362). In the second sense, some of those anthropologists distinguished between *theoretical* and *applied* anthropology. And with respect to the first meaning, in 1963 *ethnological theory* meant an established set of "isms": evolutionism, diffusionism, historical particularism, functionalism, structuralism, and so on. By contrast, in some recent discussions *theory* has become little more than the name dropping that is characteristic of literary criticism. It sometimes seems that someone is distributing a set of "theoretically correct" citation cards (facilitating the ritual invocation, across academic fields, of "the usual suspects"—a too limited set of voguish names and works).

Anthropological theory and knowledge rest on much more than name dropping. The Embers emphasize anthropology's body of *cumulative knowledge*. They stress that anthropology is a *science*—a "systematic field of study or body of knowledge that aims, through experiment, observation, and deduction, to produce reliable explanations of phenomena, with reference to the material and physical world" (*Webster's New World Encyclopedia*, 1993, 937). Given new discoveries and expanded knowledge, anthropologists test hypotheses, modify hypotheses, and revise theories. Fifty years ago, Clyde Kluckhohn observed, "Anthropology provides a scientific basis for dealing with the crucial dilemma of the world today: how can peoples of different appearance, mutually unintelligible languages, and dissimilar ways of life get along peaceably together?" (Kluckhohn 1944, 9).

Linguistic variation is one aspect of cultural diversity that confronts us and our students on a daily basis. The anthropological study of language (linguistic anthropology) is not the same as linguistics, as Breitborde stresses (See "Teaching Linguistic Anthropology"). The links between language, culture, and society and the relation of linguistic anthropology to broader anthropological issues are considered in the papers by Eastman, Hickerson, and DeBernardi. Carol Eastman describes three areas of current anthropological concern for language: (a) the focus on discourse, that is, language as a kind of behavior through which individuals negotiate social position; (b) a focus on the "cultural logic" reflected in the structures of particular languages; and (c) the relationship between language structure and the communicative uses to which it is put. Nancy Hickerson suggests ways of better integrating linguistic anthropology in the general anthropology curriculum, and Jean DeBernardi shows how language-focused questions may illuminate broader cultural issues.

Anthropology is a science, but through linguistic, cultural, and archaeological anthropology it also has key links with the humanities. Indeed, I see anthropology as the most humanistic of the sciences because of its fundamental respect for human diversity and its goals of eliciting, hearing, recording, and (re)presenting views and voices from a multitude of times and places. Mandelbaum (1963, 5) offers an enduring endorsement of the approach of the field anthropologist—the intent to discover and observe what people are actually doing, to listen to what they say they are doing and to what others say about them—"taking leads from what is important to them, the observed, rather than with what may be important to the observer." Through such an approach, anthropology can provide a "better understanding of diversity and similarity among cultures, and of cultural stability and change"—opening "the way to a deeper appreciation of their [students'] own culture" (Mandelbaum 1963, 7).

Today as in 1963, "humanities scholars find themselves in close accord with the ethnologist's attempts to understand and translate a people's own view of their lives" (Mandelbaum 1963, 6). As I note in my essay on central themes, anthropology applies a comparative and nonelitist perspective to the study of forms of creative expression and cultural texts, interpreted in relation to their meaning within a particular cultural context. Another link between anthropology and the humanities is the study of anthropological accounts as forms of written, visual, or auditory representations of other cultures and experiences.

As teachers and publicists of anthropology we should also remember something so basic as to risk eluding attention: anthropology is interesting. James Deetz argues that at the introductory level, the most important goal is to present material that will engage students' interest so they will want to take additional courses to amplify their knowledge. Because of this, he contends, an introductory course in archaeology should attempt to convey certain understandings about the field, with a strong unifying theme, but not attempt a comprehensive treatment of archaeology. The Spindlers also limit the scope of their introductory course in cultural anthropology, using ethnographic studies. They suggest that "culture cases" are intrinsically interesting to nearly everyone; they demonstrate the diversity and commonality of human lifeways. I agree with the Spindlers and McCurdy that students like to read ethnographies. Often they also enjoy personal accounts, including ethnographers' reactions to what goes on in the field. However, as a teacher, I have found that the most useful ethnographies are careful to describe and analyze aspects of human existence *beyond* the "ethnographic me."

Anthropology has foundations, significance, and substance—an impressive body of knowledge, on which our textbooks build (many of their authors are contributors to this volume). New knowledge is constantly added. Comparing writings in the 1963 volume edited by Mandelbaum and others with the articles here, and focusing on physical and archaeological anthropology, Patricia Rice notes changes in subject matter, teaching techniques, and perceived student needs.

> Physical anthropology in the 1960s was consistently and "traditionally" taught; "what to teach" was not an issue. All authors agreed that human evolution and "race" were the two main subjects of teaching concentration. Many modern physical anthropologists would find Lasker's suggested sixteen-week syllabus in 1963 to resemble what they do in their classrooms in 1994, though most would not spend a week on the "question of racial differences in Upper Paleolithic man," . . . but disagreement about the use of the word "race" remains an important topic. (Rice, this volume)

Race continues to be one of those topics for which anthropology's four-field approach makes a key difference. The articles by Alice Brues and by

Leonard Lieberman and Rodney Kirk stress that race has different meanings for different people, including anthropologists. Several of our contributors focus on the amount of new knowledge that has emerged since 1960—for example, epidemiology, acquired immune deficiency syndrome (AIDS), and sociobiology (Poirier, Cohen). Philip Stein wonders whether today's introductory courses adequately represent the research interests of today's professional physical anthropologists, especially such areas as growth and development, molecular evolution, demography, dermatoglyphics, forensic anthropology, health and nutrition, and biochemical genetics.

Mandelbaum could proclaim in 1963 that "in all branches of anthropology there is exemplified the careful, systematic collection of evidence, the construction of concepts, and the continuous testing of theory which are the bases of scientific method" (6).

The primacy of science in cultural and archaeological anthropology has been challenged by interpretive, reflexive, postmodern, and postprocessual critics. However, most of the articles in the physical-archaeology section still acknowledge the scientific nature of paleoanthropology (Stein, Lieberman and Kirk, Rice, Poirier). Others focus on the relevance of the subject matter to the everyday lives of students (Cohen, Poirier). According to Ernestine Friedl, anthropologists need to stress the evidence supporting the unity of humankind as a species and the human capacity to negotiate across diverse cultures. Anthropology teaches that all people "have ways of life which are worthy of serious study, and in the lives of all there is, and has been, an interplay of biological and cultural forces" (Mandelbaum 1963, 7). Mark Nathan Cohen notes, especially among biological anthropologists, expanded interest in the interaction of culture change and human genetic evolution and in applying Darwinian theory to human culture (that is, "sociobiology").

Just as most physical and archaeological anthropologists tend to agree about the value of the scientific method, most archaeological anthropologists might also agree with Fred and Stephen Plog about the centrality of the five "big questions" they pose:

1. After millions of years of adaptation as generalists—hunters and gatherers—why did humans choose to specialize by relying on farming?

2. After millions of years of living in small settlements, why did humans come to live in large ones?

3. After millions of years of considerable mobility throughout the yearly cycle, why did humans begin to reside permanently in villages?

4. After millions of years of consensual leadership, why have humans come to submit to authoritarian patterns?

5. After millions of years of living in simple societies, why did humans come to live in complex ones?

For Mandelbaum and his associates, the scientific, holistic approach to such "big questions" was a common thread in the teaching of anthropology.

"The ideas which are repeatedly emphasized in these papers have to do with the whole of human behavior, as viewed in the context of reality, and as studied in the manner of science" (Mandelbaum 1963, 4). In a useful update and clarification, Marvin Harris's contribution to this volume notes that when anthropologists use "holism," they differ in what they have in mind. He distinguishes between metaphysical holism, functionalist holism, topical holism, and processual holism. Functional holism (stressing sociocultural integration) and topical holism (stressing anthropology's breadth) predominate in the 1963 volume. To illustrate functional holism, Harris uses Beals and Hoijer's textbook (1971, 110), which defines holism as meaning that "the various aspects of culture are interrelated . . . they form systems whose parts or activities are directly or indirectly related to and affect one another." After a "rapid perusal" of current texts, Harris concludes that topical holism is gaining ground at the expense of definitions focusing on sociocultural integration. He cites Nanda's (1991, 5) holistic approach, which includes the interaction of biology and culture, health and illness in the human body, speeches, and everyday conversation. And Harris quotes my discussion of anthropological holism (which he finds closest to "the famous four-field approach") as "anthropology's unique blend of biological, social, cultural, linguistic, historical, and contemporary perspectives" and its interest in "the whole of the human condition: past, present, and future; biology, society, language, and culture" (Kottak 1991, 13, 17).

As I point out in my paper on central themes, there are certain constants, especially in the teaching of introductory, four-field anthropology. (Note, however, that the number of anthropologists well trained to teach such a course may be declining.) Borofsky's paper makes the same point: "Despite three decades of 'isms'—structuralism, cultural materialism, Marxism, feminism, interpretivism, and postmodernism, to name some of the more prominent ones—the goals for teaching introductory anthropology seem to have remained relatively the same."

Still, there does seem to be less agreement on the core of anthropology today than when Mandelbaum noted that discussions at the symposia on which the 1963 volume was based "revealed a considerable basis of agreement about objectives in teaching anthropology." Postmodern critiques have challenged disciplinary canons as well as our ideas about appropriate units of study. George Marcus emphasizes changes in both the objects of anthropological inquiry and in "anthropologists' own sense of their practices, their professional constituencies, and to whom the knowledge they produce is addressed."

By 1963, both Mandelbaum and Arensberg could perceive a trend away from the tribal toward greater attention to world civilizations. (Unlike its predecessor, the present volume lacks a separate section on regional and civilization courses.) As the world has changed, so have anthropological units and orbits. Along with classes on China, Japan, India, and the Middle East, courses are now routinely offered on the anthropology of the United States and Canada (the basis of a recent addition to the roster of societies within the AAA). Hundreds of anthropologists now specialize in the study of multiculturalism, diasporas, transnationalism, and identities (multiple, situational, negotiated, manipulated, and contested). Gender, race, ethnicity, and class enjoy new favor in anthropology textbooks and curricula. Deborah Rubin discusses the impact of feminist perspectives on the teaching of anthropology, illustrated by changes in textbooks and syllabi and by the proliferation of courses specifically dealing with gender.

Several of our contributors demonstrate how students can use anthropological knowledge to question and critique their own American culture (Haviland, the Spindlers, Friedl, Moses and Mukhopadhyay, Nanda, Foster, Rubin, and Heider). Serena Nanda shows us how she manages to teach cultural anthropology as cultural critique. Related to globalization and the expansion of multinational corporations are concepts of "development" and "modernization," which cultural anthropology has usefully critiqued, not only from the point of view of failures in practice but also for unilinear evolutionary assumptions about "progress" and the nature and desirability of certain kinds of change. Greater attention to issues of power, including the differentials that marked colonialism and its effects on native peoples, has influenced what we teach. As Nanda notes, an important part of culture change derives from efforts by Western nations to eliminate practices in other cultures that contradicted their own values and threatened efforts to build national states and maintain the colonial order.

Anthropology has a crucial role to play in promoting a more humanistic vision of social change, one that respects the value of cultural diversity. As we continue the transmission of anthropological culture, it can be as exciting today as it was for our intellectual ancestors and their students to discover in our field a better way of understanding self through the study of others

Contemporary global culture is driven by flows of people, technology, finance, information, and ideology. Business, technology, and the media have increased the craving for commodities and images throughout the world, creating a global culture of consumption. Still, it is likely that vigorous cultural differences will continue to pose resistance to what some social scientists see as a bland convergence in the future. Compared with prior generations, the young men and women of today are far more likely to travel beyond their own society and to encounter representatives of other cultures abroad or "at home." Anthropology's continuing legacy remains the exploration, understanding, and appreciation of human diversity.

Note

Acknowledgment: We acknowledge the generous financial support of the General Anthropology Division, the Council on Anthropology and Education, the Society for Anthropology in Community Colleges, and the Wenner-Gren Foundation for Anthropological Research.

References

Beals, R., and H. Hoijer. 1971. *An Introduction to Anthropology*. 4th ed. New York: Macmillan.

Berelson, B. 1960. *Graduate Education in the United States*. New York: McGraw-Hill.

Herrnstein, R. J., and C. Murray. 1994. *The Bell Curve: Intelligence and Class Structure in American Life*. New York: Free Press.

Kluckhohn, C. 1944. *Mirror for Man: A Survey of Human Behavior and Social Attitudes*. Greenwich, Conn.: Fawcett.

Kottak, C. P. 1991. *Anthropology: The Exploration of Human Diversity*. 5th ed. New York: McGraw-Hill.

Mandelbaum, D. G. 1963. "The Transmission of Anthropological Culture." In *The Teaching of Anthropology*, edited by D. G. Mandelbaum, G. W. Lasker, and E. M. Albert, 1–21. Berkeley: University of California Press.

Nanda, S. 1991. *Cultural Anthropology*. 4th ed. Belmont, Calif.: Wadsworth.

TEACHING THE INTRODUCTORY COURSE

Central Themes in the Teaching of Anthropology

CONRAD PHILLIP KOTTAK

No competent introduction to anthropology—book or course—can ignore certain central or basic themes. Central themes in the teaching of general anthropology include adaptation, change, comparison, holism, and variation or diversity. Also indispensable is discussion of anthropology's nature and some of its primary roles: as a science, as a humanities field, and as a mirror for humanity.

Central Themes

Adaptation

In the 1960s, ecological anthropology became an important field of study for biological, cultural, and archaeological anthropologists (and, through links with ethnoscience and ethnotaxonomy, for linguistic anthropologists). The 1990s have witnessed a resurgence of ecological anthropology—now focusing on issues of global change, population-environment dynamics, deforestation and other forms of resource degradation, and environmental risk perception. Although the prominence of ecological anthropology (particularly the 1960s focus on negative feedback and adaptive functionalism) declined in the 1970s and 1980s, mechanisms of biological and cultural adaptation have continued to be explicated in introductory anthropology courses.

In discussing human adaptation (the processes by which we cope with environmental stresses), we explain that cultural and biological adaptation and evolution have been interrelated and complementary, and that humans continue to adapt both biologically and culturally. Human adaptation involves an interplay between culture, heredity, and biological plasticity. Much of the diversity we see in cultures, as in nature, reflects adaptation to varied environments and circumstances. As hominid history has unfolded, social and cultural means of adaptation have become increasingly important. In this process, humans have devised a plethora of strategies for coping with the range of environments and social systems (local, regional, national, and global) they have occupied in time and space.

Our discussions of human adaptation should make clear that people creatively manipulate their environment; they are not just determined by it. Recognizing this, John Bennett (1969, 19) has defined cultural adaptation as "the problem-solving, creative or coping element in human behavior" as people get and use resources and solve the immediate problems confronting them. This first dimension of adaptive behavior involves "goal-satisfaction: if coping is successful, the people realize their objectives" (Bennett 1969, 13).

Besides the satisfaction of individual goals, a second and equally important dimension of cultural adaptation is conservation of resources. "An economy that realizes economic gain but does so at the cost of exhausting or abusing its resources may be adapting in one dimension (the first) but can be said to be maladaptive along the other." In other words, behavior that benefits individuals may harm the environment and threaten the group's long-term survival. Societies "must attempt to balance conservation of resources against economic success if they hope for a permanent or indefinite settlement [of their environment]" (Bennett 1969, 13). This, of course, is a lesson with increasing relevance for the modern world.

Change

A second central theme is change—for biological, archaeological, linguistic, cultural, and applied anthropology. Anthropology deals with change in all the following: biological evolution, major shifts in economy and society documented through the archaeological record, historical linguistics, collaboration between anthropologists and historians, longitudinal research, and ethnographic study of the perturbations and rapid social upheavals so evident in today's world. All these are central topics for anthropology; they belong in our introductory courses.

We know that the rate of cultural change has accelerated, particularly during the past 10,000 years. After millions of years of hunting and gathering, early humans in only a few thousand years had replaced foraging with food production in most places. People in local settings must cope with forces generated by progressively larger systems—region, nation, and world. State organization and, much more recently, industrial production and capitalism have profoundly influenced people throughout the world. Today's global economy and communications link all contemporary people, directly or indirectly, in a world system. The study of such contemporary adaptations generates new challenges for anthropology: "The cultures of world peoples need to be constantly rediscovered as these people reinvent them in changing historical circumstances" (Marcus and Fischer 1986, 24).

Comparison

The third theme is comparison, intrinsic to and distinctive of anthropology among sciences that study human beings. Anthropology is much more than the study of nonindustrial peoples. It is a comparative field that considers all societies, ancient and modern, simple and complex. The other social sciences tend to focus on a single society, usually that of the United States. But anthropology has a distinctive cross-cultural perspective, constantly comparing the customs of one society with those of others. Adopting this comparative perspective, anthropology examines biological, psychological, social, and cultural universals and generalities. It also considers unique and distinctive aspects of the human condition. In examining cultural elaborations on the fundamental biological plasticity of *Homo sapiens*, anthropology shows that one cultural tradition— no matter how powerful or dominant—is no more "natural" than any other.

Anthropologists, unlike scholars in other fields, do not usually talk about human nature without recognizing the impact of culture. Comparison is necessary because one culture cannot be used to make conclusive inferences about "human nature." Cross-cultural comparison is basic to anthropology. Ethnology, archaeology, and linguistics have made important contributions to the identification and explanation of cultural differences and similarities.

Holism

The fourth theme is holism and the links between the subdisciplines. Introductory students are often surprised by the breadth of anthropology—its attention to the whole of the human condition: past, present, and future; biology, society, language, and culture. Holism is the key to why American anthropology is a four- or five-subdiscipline field, with biological, archaeological, linguistic, cultural, and applied anthropology. This holism also makes us unique among fields that study human beings.

There are both historical and logical reasons for the inclusion of these subdisciplines in a single field. American anthropology arose a century ago mainly out of concern with understanding and recording the history and cultures of the native populations of North America. Interest in the origins and diversity of Amerindians brought together studies of customs, social life, language, and physical traits. (Such a unified anthropology did not develop in Europe, where the subdisciplines tend to exist separately.) The unity of American anthropology is also based on the fact that each subdiscipline considers variations in time and space. The subdisciplines continue to influence each other as anthropologists talk to each other, read some of the same professional books and journals, attend meetings and conferences together, and associate in professional organizations.

General anthropology explores the basics of human biology, psychology, society, and culture and considers their interrelationships. Anthropologists continue to share certain key assumptions. One is that sound conclusions about "human nature" cannot be derived from observation of a single culture. Anthropology offers answers to many of the "nature-nurture" and "genetics-environment" questions we hear so often, for example, about gender differences, race and intelligence, and the range of human sexuality. By examining diverse cultures, anthropology shows that race, gender, and kinship are socially constructed and that human sexuality is determined by cultural training as well as biology.

Variation or Diversity

The last theme is variation or diversity. We should let no one forget that *anthropologists are the experts on cultural and biological diversity*. We have been writing about diversity for generations, long before diversity and multiculturalism became fashionable. Cultural anthropology focuses on the cultural diversity of the present and the recent past. Archaeology reconstructs variant social, economic, religious, and political patterns, usually of prehistoric populations. Biological anthropology relates biological diversity in time and space to variation in environment—revealed in the fossil record, human genetics, growth and development, bodily responses, and nonhuman primates. Linguistic anthropology documents diversity among contemporary languages and studies the ways in which speech varies in different social situations and over time. Applied anthropology uses anthropological knowledge and methods to identify social problems and to suggest culturally specific and appropriate solutions for those problems in North America and abroad.

We must work to ensure that anthropology's long-time "ownership" of diversity is not forgotten as colleges and universities increasingly institute requirements for courses on diversity and multiculturalism. At the University of Michigan, I've noticed that many of the people who have been most active in advocating a diversity requirement know little about anthropology. We need to get our perspectives and cumulative knowledge across to such people. Anthropologists at Michigan worked hard to ensure that introductory anthropology and other appropriate anthropology courses be allowed to satisfy the university's recently created diversity requirement. Some people who advocate a diversity requirement only want to have other *American* voices represented, not voices from around the world—voices anthropologists have been heeding for years.

Science, Humanities, and Mirror for Humanity

In addition to these five themes, any introduction to anthropology should include a discussion of anthropology's nature and some of its primary roles: as a *science*, as a *humanities* field, and as a *mirror for humanity*.

As a Science

First, anthropology is a *science*—a "systematic field of study or body of knowledge that aims, through experiment, observation, and deduction, to produce reliable explanations of phenomena, with reference to the material and physical world" (*Webster's New World Encyclopedia*, 1993, 937). Clyde Kluckhohn (1944, 9) called anthropology "the science of human similarities and differences," and his statement of the need for such a science still stands: "Anthropology provides a scientific basis for dealing with the crucial dilemma of the world today: how can peoples of different appearance, mutually unintelligible languages, and dissimilar ways of life get along peaceably together?" (Kluckhohn 1944, 9).

Let me emphasize one aspect of science that Carol and Melvin Ember discuss in their chapter in this volume: *cumulative knowledge*. Anthropology has amassed an impressive body of knowledge on which all our textbooks build and which forces them to change as knowledge increases. Given new discoveries and expanded knowledge, anthropologists test hypotheses, modify hypotheses, and revise theories.

As a Humanity

Anthropology is also a *humanities* field—for several reasons. Anthropology applies a comparative and nonelitist perspective to the study of art, narratives, music, dance, and other forms of creative expression. Anthropology influences and is influenced by the humanities. For example, adopting a characteristic anthropological view of creativity in its social and cultural context, current "postmodern" (Jameson 1984, 1988) approaches in the humanities are shifting the focus toward mass and popular culture and local creative expressions. Another area of convergence between anthropology and the humanities is the view of cultural expressions as patterned texts (Ricoeur 1971; Geertz 1973). Thus "unwritten behavior, speech, beliefs, oral tradition, and ritual" (Clifford 1988, 39) can be approached as a corpus to be interpreted in relation to their meaning within a particular cultural context. A final link between anthropology and the humanities is the study of ethnographic accounts as forms of written, visual, or auditory representations of other cultures and experiences (Clifford 1988; Marcus and Fischer 1986).

I view anthropology as the most humanistic of the academic fields because of its fundamental respect for human diversity. Anthropologists listen to, record, and represent voices from a multitude of nations and cultures. We strive to convince our students of the value of local knowledge, of diverse worldviews and perspectives. We can promote humanistic goals in various ways—by recognizing the value of our students, the value of ourselves, and the value of the "other" perspectives we inform our students about. We have to teach respect while ourselves respecting the various kinds of people we habitually encounter, including undergraduates, graduate students, other faculty, professional colleagues, and, of course, the people we study.

As a Mirror for Humanity

A final basic role is anthropology as a *mirror for humanity*—a term derived from Clyde Kluckhohn's metaphor.

> Ordinarily we are unaware of the special lens through which we look at life. It would hardly be fish who discovered the existence of water. Students who had not yet gone beyond the horizon of their own society could not be expected to perceive custom which was the stuff of their own thinking. *Anthropology holds up a great mirror to man and lets him look at himself in his infinite variety.* (Kluckhohn, 1944, 16—his emphasis)

In making this point, I also want to invoke the almost mythic name of one of my teachers, Margaret Mead. Although Kluckhohn wrote the popular book called *Mirror for Man*, we will always remember Mead for her unparalleled success in demonstrating anthropology's value and relevance in allowing Americans to reflect on cultural variation and the plasticity of human nature. Mead conveyed the anthropological perspective to a broad public in a way no contemporary anthropologist does. We need to remember and revive her example.

Mead represented anthropology so effectively because she viewed it as *a humanistic science of unique value in understanding and improving the human condition.* I contrast Mead's persuasive advocacy of anthropological knowledge with a letter a prominent cultural anthropologist wrote to the *New York Times* a few years ago. The writer is said to have asserted that although he had been studying the culture of a certain country for many years, he knew less about it now than when he began. This statement may have been intended as profound and/or paradoxical, or as commenting on the complexity of the world or the rapidity of changes in it. But such pronouncements run the risk of calling anthropology's value and expertise into question. How much respect is due a profession that claims to know less now than it did when it began? Margaret Mead was an excellent and effective writer and advocate who did not doubt anthropology's cumulative knowledge.

What Has Changed and What Has Remained the Same?

In the teaching of American anthropology over the generations, some things have changed and some have remained the same. There have been changes in the students we teach and in what and how we teach them. Students seem more diverse (for example, in age and ethnic background) than ever before, yet they have grown up in a mass-mediated world, and many of them are more comfortable with modern technology than we are.

To explicate the culture(s) of the contemporary world for these students, we teach new courses and use new teaching styles, methods, and tools. For example, I regularly teach a course called "Television, Society, and Culture"—mainly for seniors and graduate students in anthropology, American culture, area studies, and communication. The course objectives are these:

- To develop the ability to analyze television (content and impact) using perspectives from cultural anthropology
- To consider the social/cultural context of (a) creation, (b) distribution, (c) reception, and (d) impact of TV messages
- To apply the anthropological perspective within a single culture (for example, that of the United States) and across cultures (for example, the cultures of Brazil and the United States)

As the world and our ways of understanding it change, new courses proliferate (such as "Ethnography as a Form of Writing," "The Culture of Postmodernity"), replacing old ones with antiquated titles like "Peoples and Cultures of the Soviet Union" or "The Mind of Primitive Man."

Many of us use modern technology in our teaching. Access to a television set and a videocassette recorder (VCR) by students and in the classroom is indispensable to my "Television, Society, and Culture" course. The students produce their own videos for projects analyzing aspects of television in a cultural context.

I also use new technology (computers) in my course on research methods—an increasingly important course as anthropologists are forced to learn more about formal methods and statistics in a world of growing numbers. I teach statistics and data analysis, using appropriate hardware and software, including programs and packages for word processing, data entry, spreadsheets, and statistical analysis. We work directly with my data sets, doing quantitative analyses in one minute that would have taken days when I was a graduate student. Changes in technology allow us to ask and answer an array of new questions.

What hasn't changed is some basic lessons and perspectives—the central themes and roles of anthropology discussed above. Today's teachers still present anthropology as a mirror for humanity: by looking at people in other cultures we can learn more about ourselves. The centrality of discussions of race, language, culture, and mind is part of the Boasian foundation of American anthropology. Marvin Harris has publicly commented at American Anthropological Association meetings that his introductory textbook (and mine) have their roots in the introductory anthropology course we both took, almost a generation apart, at Columbia University. This course can be traced back to Franz Boas—in Harris's case through Charles Wagley, his teacher; in mine, through Lambros Comitas. The framework of that course (and its transformations at Berkeley, Pennsylvania, and Yale) has remained remarkably constant and continues to serve as the framework for most textbooks in introductory general, four-field, anthropology.

Most introductory anthropology teachers seem to feel, even if they don't fully articulate it, that their task is to present certain basics of a reasonably systematic, distinctive, and useful field of study. We introductory (four-field) teachers feel comfortable with what we take to be a basic set of issues and an agreed-on content in general anthropology. Because of this, textbook authors have learned—through numerous revisions—that certain chapters have to be included (although they should be as independent of each other as possible so that instructors can assign them out of order).

Although particular instructors want new and different features and use textbooks differently, the basic course has remained remarkably stable. The organization and content of the most-used textbooks reveals a basic notion of what anthropology is about. Experimental textbooks don't usually do very well. To stray too far from the familiar is to be overinnovative and to risk poor sales. Constant updating is fine, particularly the inclusion of new fossil or archaeological finds, or discussions of "hot topics" such as gender and ethnicity, but only when those topics are clearly related to anthropology's traditional subject matter. New or "innovative" chapters should be added with care; anthropologists may be miffed when a chapter is added that they don't see as part of the core (like the chapter on American culture I added to my second edition, which I now include only as the appendix. Many anthropologists still regard American culture and modern life as outside the core).

Although much remains the same, some important changes in anthropology—and in the introductory course—reflect differences in the world. Two such changes are the increasing focus on diversity within nations and on gender issues. Reflecting requirements being implemented at many colleges and universities, anthropologists now pay much more systematic attention to all facets of diversity and multiculturalism. Ethnicity, for example, grows more prominent as a field of study, as the United States becomes increasingly cosmopolitan and internally diverse.

Given anthropology's historic and enduring focus on diversity, we have much to contribute to discussions of multiculturalism. In one example, at a session of the 1992 AAA meeting, Sydel Silverman commented on a current tendency in the United States for "culture" and "ethnicity" to acquire an essentialist, racelike immutability in the context of discussions of multiculturalism. Anthropologists know that ethnicity is often negotiated, situational, and political. It is dangerous (and anthropologically inaccurate) to see cultural identity, or ethnic identity within a multicultural society, as an invariably ascribed status that cannot possibly change.

Anthropologists need to do more to correct naive and false impressions about culture, ethnicity, and multiculturalism. Many Americans (even academics and intellectuals) rely on a Disneyesque "Small World" model of cultural diversity. I refer to an attraction at Florida's Walt Disney World and California's Disneyland in which visitors take a boat ride through an exhibit consisting of hundreds of "ethnically correct" dolls from all over the world, dancing and singing "It's a small world after all." The exhibit is a relentlessly commercial welding of globalization, multiculturalism, and postmodernism.

Many nonanthropologists think of culture in terms of curious customs and colorful adornments—clothing, jewelry, hairstyles, dancing—like the dolls at Disney World. This bias toward the exotic and the superstructural (often recreational or musical—a minstrel show view of culture) even shows up in anthropological films. Many ethnographic films start off with music, often drum beats: "Bonga, bonga, bonga, bonga. Here in (supply place name) the people are very religious." The (usually unintended) message is that people in nonindustrial societies spend most of their time wearing colorful clothes, singing, dancing, and practicing religious rituals. This feeds into the current commercial manipulation of culture as exotic superstructure—costumes, jewels, crystals, lost arks, temples of doom that are mysterious, inexplicable, and ultimately unserious—to be appreciated, appropriated, and sold in ethnic fairs and boutiques that are oh-so-carefully quaint. In their ethnographic accounts—whether spoken, written, or visual—anthropologists can do more to spread the word that culture is something that ordinary people live each day. Attention to anthropology's core themes and lessons can help correct deficiencies and make anthropology's role more central in college teaching and public awareness.

References

Bennett, J. W. 1969. *Northern Plainsmen: Adaptive Strategy and Agrarian Life.* Chicago: Aldine.

Clifford, J. 1988. *The Predicament of Culture: Twentieth-Century Ethnography, Literature and Art.* Cambridge: Harvard University Press.

Geertz, C. 1973. *The Interpretation of Cultures.* New York: Basic Books.

Jameson, F. 1984. "Postmodernism, or the Cultural Logic of Late Capitalism." *New Left Review* 146:53–93.

———. 1988. *The Ideologies of Theory: Essays 1971–1986.* Minneapolis: University of Minnesota Press.

Kluckhohn, C. 1944. *Mirror for Man: A Survey of Human Behavior and Social Attitudes.* Greenwich, Conn: Fawcett.

Marcus, G. E., and M. M. J. Fischer. 1986. *Anthropology as Cultural Critique: An Experimental Moment in the Human Sciences.* Chicago: University of Chicago Press.

Ricoeur, P. 1971. The Model of the Text: Meaningful Action Considered as a Text. *Social Research* 38:529–562.

Webster's New World Encyclopedia. 1993. College edition. New York: Prentice-Hall.

Anthropology Needs Holism;
Holism Needs Anthropology

Marvin Harris

An article of faith long held among anthropologists is that our profession derives its claim to a distinctive space in academia because of its holistic approach. Robert Borofsky (1994, 12–13), for example, claims that the proposition, "cultures need to be studied as wholes, not as fragmented pieces," forms part of the "shared traditions" that "hold cultural anthropology together." Who among us has not assured our introductory students that they have done the right thing in taking ANT 1001 because unlike the heathen sociologists or historians, anthropologists possess the holy grail of holism? Unfortunately, as with so many precious gifts of the intellect, anthropologists do not agree on what holism is. There seem to be not one but at least four kinds of holistic approaches available to the social sciences. Before examining their strengths and weaknesses, permit me to name them as follows: metaphysical holism; functionalist holism; topical holism; and processual holism.

Metaphysical Holism

Metaphysical holism has its roots in the late nineteenth century neo-Hegelian arguments against the spread of mechanistic materialism (Phillips 1976). The neo-Hegelians (like many of today's postmodernists and postprocessualists) held that phenomena such as organisms and human societies could not be studied by the methods that were appropriate for the study of inorganic phenomena. Although this theme is historically linked to metaphysical holism, it is not an intrinsic component of the latter (contra Phillips). One might, for example, wish to apply holistic metaphysical principles to all branches of science, not merely to organisms and societies.

At the core of metaphysical holism, there are three propositions:

1. The whole is more than the sum of its parts and cannot be reduced to them.
2. The whole determines the nature of its parts.
3. The parts cannot be understood if considered in isolation from the whole.

Metaphysical holism is too vague and confusing to merit inscription on the tattered banners of our beloved but beleaguered profession. Any priority given to the whole over its parts founders on the question of how the whole is to be discerned and described. As a consequence of natural selection, we experience the world in terms of disjunctive macrophysical entities such as a chair, a tree, or a person; anyone can see these things as wholes; but no one has ever seen an institution, a society, a culture, or a sociocultural system as a whole. Sociocultural wholes are necessarily knowable only through a process of logical and empirical abstraction from the observation of their parts, the smallest of which are the activities and thoughts of individuals (Harris 1964). It is illogical to assert that the whole of society and culture is more than the sum of its parts because the only way we can get to know the sociocultural whole (as distinct from trees, chairs, or individuals) is to add up its parts and analyze their relationships.

On the other hand, turning to the second point, the proposition that the whole sociocultural system determines the nature of its parts would be quite acceptable if it were accompanied by an equal emphasis on the determination of the whole by the parts. For if we mean by "determination" some causal process such as evolution, then it is clear that selection operates on both the whole and its parts, which therefore determine each other.

Similarly, the proposition that the parts cannot be understood if considered in isolation from the whole is again reasonable but capriciously incomplete. For we must add that the whole also cannot be understood in isolation from its parts. One cannot understand an automobile without looking under its hood. But this emphasis on mutual interdependence and determination is the hallmark of functionalist rather than metaphysical holism.

Functionalist Holism

Fortunately, there are alternative conceptions of holism that define the relation between parts and wholes without committing anthropology to the defense of a neo-Hegelian worldview. In this alternative, a holistic approach is simply one that emphasizes, in the words of Webster's third edition, "the organic or functional relation between parts and wholes." If we change this slightly to read "between parts and parts, and parts and wholes," we get a definition of holism that has enjoyed considerable popularity among anthropologists for many years. Borofsky (1994, 13) identifies this genre of holism as seeing cultural elements "as inter-related and interdependent." Beals and Hoijer's textbook, *An Introduction to Anthropology*, states that holism means ". . . the various aspects of culture are interrelated . . . they form systems whose parts or activities are directly or indirectly related to and affect one another" (1971, 110). A similar definition of holism appears in William Haviland's (1993, 13) popular introductory textbook: "Only by discovering how all cultural institutions—social, political, economic, religious—relate to one another can the ethnographer begin to understand the cultural system. Anthropologists refer to this as the **holistic perspective**" [bold in original].

If we suppose that "relate to each other" includes "affect each other," then Haviland's definition of holism is very close to that of Beals and Hoijer. (There are additional ingredients in Haviland's and Beals and Hoijer's definitions that I discuss later in the chapter).

Functional holism does not require us to accept any of the dubious propositions that characterize metaphysical holism. The whole is not greater than the sum of its parts; the whole does not determine the nature of its parts more than the nature of its parts determine the whole; and neither the parts nor the whole can be understood in isolation from each other. Best of all, one does not have to abandon the logical and empirical foundations of science in order to conduct research concerned with sociocultural phenomena. There is only one problem: functionalist holism is not the invention of nor the special preserve of anthropology.

In the history of the social sciences, the notion that all parts of sociocultural systems relate to and affect each other is a paradigmatic stance that originated with Spencer's *Principles of Sociology* and Durkheim's *Rules of the Sociological Method*. Given these founding auspices, functionalist holism can scarcely be passed off as a contribution uniquely anthropological. Indeed, the argument has been made that all the social sciences necessarily rest on a foundation of functionalist premises (Davis 1959).

Topical Holism

Topical holism refers to the breadth of topics (aspects, subjects) that anthropologists study. Logically, functional and topical holism are not mutually exclusive; in fact, many anthropologists apparently see functional holism as the source of the uniquely wide breadth of holistic anthropology. As noted by Beals and Hoijer (1971, 110), "in contrast with more specialized disciplines, [anthropologists] stress study of the whole society. This position is possible because the various aspects of culture are interrelated." Similarly, Haviland's functionalist definition quoted earlier refers to holism as a matter of paying attention to how "*all* cultural institutions [emphasis added] relate to each other." In a sidebar definition (1993, 14) Haviland defines holistic perspective topically but minus the reference to "all cultural institutions." Instead, holistic perspective is the "principle that things must be viewed in the broadest possible context."

Both Haviland and Beals and Hoijer are the authors of excellent four-field texts. It is somewhat surprising, therefore, that in defining holism in terms of topical coverage, they omit any appeal to the archaeological, biological, and linguistic contexts that have traditionally added topical breadth to the teaching of anthropology. Perhaps the explanation for this omission lies in the conceptual priority bestowed on sociocultural systems by the social sciences. Functional analyses traditionally lie in the domains of institutions; the inertia of this position makes it difficult to reconcile functional holism with a topical holism that does justice to archaeological, linguistic, psychocultural, and biocultural studies.

A rapid perusal of additional introductory texts suggests that topical-breadth definitions of anthropological holism are gaining ground at the expense of metaphysical and functionalist definitions that focus on sociocultural integration. Nanda's (1991, 5) "holistic approach," for example, includes the interaction of biology and culture, health and illness in the human body, speeches, and everyday conversation. For Howard and Dunaif-Hattis (1992, 4), holism involves all aspects of the human condition, including a society's physical environment and its past as well as its present. Ember and Ember's (1990, 3) holistic approach includes the physical characteristics of our prehistoric ancestors and the biological effects of the environment on a human population. Kottak (1991, 12; 19) defines the thrust of anthropological holism as "anthropology's unique blend of biological, social, cultural, linguistic, historical and contemporary perspectives," and further, "Holistic: Interested in the whole of the human condition: past, present, and future; biology, society, language, and culture."

Note that Kottak here comes close to defining anthropological holism as the famous four-field approach. True, the word *archaeology* gets slighted, but one can easily interpret "historical" and the "past" as indicative of an archaeological component.

A troubling aspect of topical definitions of holism is that they are based on laundry lists of topics or subdisciplinary perspectives. These lists lack any internal or external logic suitable for explaining why one item is on the list and another is not. In the case of the four fields, for example, we know we are dealing with a convention that reflects the outcome of various battles over academic turf at the beginning of the century. The absence of psychology, ecology, and demography seems especially egregious in speaking of the "whole human condition." Furthermore, there is the question of the allocation of time and space to the various components. Haviland writes that we need to provide a broad view of culture "without emphasizing one of its parts to the detriment of another." But is this even theoretically possible, given the different professional experiences and paradigmatic commitments of authors and teachers? True, most popular textbooks cover a similar range of topics (allowing for the distinction between cultural and general versions) and they even display a considerable amount of similarity in emphasis. But this is not a vindication of the topical definition of holism; rather it merely signifies that one of the first things textbook publishers do is to make sure that all the topics that are prominent in the most popular texts are included in their own authors' works.

Processual Holism

The escape from laundry lists, insipid functionalism, and Hegelian mystification lies through the relation between holism and holistic processes. Anthropology does not seek holistic perspectives as an end in itself. Rather, anthropologists use that perspective because it has been found to be crucial for solving the major riddles of human existence. In broadest terms, these riddles have to do with the origins and spread of the hominids; the origins and spread of Homo sapiens; the causes and effects of human biological polymorphisms; the origin of human linguistic capacity and the origin and spread of human languages; the emergence of human consciousness; the origin of human society and culture; and the causes of the divergent and convergent evolution of human sociocultural systems.

It is impossible to advance our understanding of these holistic processes without relying on the findings of the traditional four fields plus many other subfields and sister disciplines. Inevitably, broadening the intercourse with other disciplines raises questions of competence and authority. Publishers can help here by sending texts for review by appropriate specialists. But anthropologists who are committed to holism must come to terms with the risks of making mistakes. In this connection, warning students that the findings of science are provisional and subject to various distortions and biases may help to relieve some of the *angst* associated with holistic perspectives. Another point to be kept in mind is that the misinformation transmitted through a holistic text or introductory class is not likely to be as remote from current expert opinion as the usual sources of knowledge about biocultural evolution, such as creationism and New Age necromancy. Bear in mind that only a very small percentage of students take introductory courses in anthropology in order to prepare for graduate school. The great majority are only "passing through" and one anthropology course is all they will ever take. Indeed, *that* one anthropology course may be the only course in the social sciences they will ever take. Given the fact that anthropology has more to say that is vital for our ability to live as informed and responsible citizens of the world than any other discipline, with so little time and space in which to say it, our students deserve to have us try to give them the broadest view possible.

In addition to its concern with the grand theory of human and cultural evolution and its open-ended multidisciplinary scope, processual holism implies a commitment to a definite set of epistemological and methodological options.

Mental/Behavioral

Activity, defined as body part motions with environmental effects, as well as thoughts or internal cognitive events, enters the data sets of processual holism. Anthropological paradigms that opt for restricting the field of cultural studies to mental events (such as those of Robarchek 1989; Geertz 1973) fall outside all definitions of holism, not merely outside the definition of processual holism.

Emic/Etic

Both emic and etic stances are requisite to processual holism. Given the current ascendancy of paradigms that define culture in purely mental and emic terms, it seems likely that the commitment to holism is in decline. Paradigms that confine culture to emic and mental components cannot be regarded as holistic.

Globally Comparative

Processual holism requires the use of the comparative method to test causal hypotheses about general processes. Samples drawn from global databases such as the Human Relations Area Files are a regular feature of the development of globally applicable holistic theory.

Diachronic/Synchronic

Processes unfold through time, giving rise to convergent and divergent biocultural and sociocultural systems. The latter can therefore be viewed in a slice-of-time as well as a developmental perspective. Processual holism requires the use of both diachronic and synchronic methods. In the synchronic mode we have ethnography, human biology, medical anthropology, and descriptive linguistics; in the diachronic mode, we find archaeology and prehistory, history, paleodemography, paleontology, historical linguistics, and many other time-oriented approaches.

Much of the appeal of anthropology to its practitioners and students formally derived from the traditional image of anthropology as a holistic discipline. As we have seen, however, what the textbooks and the teachers mean by holism is not necessarily holistic or distinctive of anthropology. In fact, some constructions of holism deliberately exclude major aspects of anthropological knowledge (such as the four fields or etics). Processual holism is more inclusive than the alternatives and certainly has never been popular outside of anthropology. It remains to be seen whether anthropologists are ready to broaden their commitment to the goals of truly holistic paradigms.

References

Beals, Ralph, and Harry Hoijer. 1971. *An Introduction to Anthropology.* 4th ed. New York: Macmillan.

Borofsky, Robert, ed. 1994. *Assessing Cultural Anthropology.* New York: McGraw-Hill.

Davis, Kingsley. 1959. "The Myth of Functional Analysis as a Special Method in Sociology and Anthropology." *American Sociological Review* 24:757–773.

Durkheim, Emile. 1938. *The Rules of Sociological Method.* 8th ed. Chicago: University of Chicago Press.

Ember, Carol, and Melvin Ember. 1996. *Anthropology.* 8th ed. Upper Saddle River, N.J.: Prentice-Hall.

Geertz, Clifford. 1973. *The Interpretation of Cultures.* New York: Basic Books.

Harris, Marvin. 1964. *The Nature of Cultural Things.* New York: Random House.

Haviland, William. 1993. *Cultural Anthropology.* 7th ed. Orlando, Fla.: Harcourt Brace Jovanovich.

Howard, Michael, and Janet Dunaif-Hattis. 1992. *Anthropology: Understanding Human Adaptation.* New York: HarperCollins.

Kottak, Conrad Phillip. 1991. *Cultural Anthropology.* 5th ed. New York: McGraw-Hill.

Nanda, Serena. 1991. *Cultural Anthropology.* 4th ed. Belmont, Calif.: Wadsworth.

Phillips, Denis. 1976. *Holistic Thought in Social Sciences.* Stanford, Calif.: Stanford University Press.

Robarchek, Clayton. 1989. "Primitive Warfare and the Ratomorphic View of Mankind." *American Anthropologist* 91:903–920.

Spencer, Herbert. [1876] 1896. *Principles of Sociology.* Reprint, New York: D. Appleton.

Science in Anthropology

Melvin Ember and Carol R. Ember

We believe that the most important thing to transmit to students in anthropology is the tentativeness or uncertainty of our knowledge or understanding. But even if understanding is always tentative, we believe that it can be improved over time, particularly if our pursuit of it involves the testing of hypotheses. Textbooks in anthropology may generally try to convey what anthropologists have achieved in the way of understanding as well as appreciation for the evolution of humans; but we think that textbooks should also teach students how to distinguish between theory and evidence, and how possible explanations can be and have been tested (see Ember and Ember 1996, 227–240). To be sure, not all anthropologists would agree that testing is necessary, but we are convinced that it is if we are to believe anything with any objective, or intersubjectively shareable, degree of confidence.

We think it is not productive when textbooks are viewed as authorities and are ingested and regurgitated unquestioned. We think that textbooks should communicate the uncertainty as well as the results of scientific investigation and understanding. So, at the risk of either preaching to the already converted or seeming to scold the resistant, we try here to outline what it means to *understand* in science, what it means to test possible explanations, and why there is always uncertainty in what we think we know.

Explanations: Associations and Theories

In science, to understand is to explain—to show how what is to be understood is related to other things in some objectively ascertained way, even if the supposed relationship is deemed only tentatively confirmed (Hempel 1965, 139). There are two kinds of explanation that researchers try to achieve—associations and theories. An association is an observed relationship between two or more measured variables—things, attributes, or quantities that vary from one instance or example to another. A theory is more general, suggesting or implying associations and therefore possibly explaining them.

Let us consider the associational kind of explanation first. We say that an observation or instance of something is explainable if it conforms to a general principle or relationship. So, for example, to explain why the water left out in the basin froze last night, we say that the outside temperature was quite cold last night and that water freezes at 32 degrees F. The statement that water solidifies (becomes ice) at 32 degrees is a statement of a relationship or association between two variables: variation in the state of water (liquid versus solid) and variation in the temperature of the air (above versus below 32 degrees F). The truth of the relationship is suggested or confirmed (tentatively) by repeated observations. In the physical sciences, such relationships are called laws when they are generally accepted by scientists. We find such explanations satisfactory because they allow us to predict what will happen in the future or to understand something that has happened regularly in the past. In the social sciences, associations are usually stated probabilistically: we say that two or more variables tend to be related in a predictable way, which means that there are usually some exceptions (due to measurement error, cultural lag, other unmeasured predictors). For example, to explain why a society has a long postpartum sex taboo (for a year or longer), we can point to the association or correlation that John Whiting (1964) found in a worldwide sample of societies: those societies with apparently low-protein diets tend mostly to have long postpartum sex taboos. Technically, we call the apparent relationship between low protein and the sex taboo a statistical association, or one that is unlikely to be due to chance.

Even though laws and statistical associations explain by relating what is to be explained to other things, we usually want to know more—why those laws or associations exist. Why does water freeze at 32 degrees F? Why do societies with low-protein diets tend to have long postpartum sex taboos? Therefore, scientists try to formulate theories that will explain the observed relationships, the laws and statistical associations (Nagel 1961, 88–89). It is difficult to be very precise about what a theory is. By way of example, let us return to the question of why some societies have long postpartum sex taboos. We have already seen that a known statistical association can be used to help explain such taboos: generally (but not always), if a society has a low-protein diet, it will have a long postpartum sex taboo. But most of us would ask why. What might be the mechanism by which a society with a low-protein diet develops the custom of a long postpartum sex taboo? John Whiting's (1964) theory is that the taboo may be adaptive, that natural selection may favor it, under certain conditions. Particularly in tropical areas where the major food staples are low in protein, babies are vulnerable to the protein-deficiency disease called *kwashiorkor.* Whiting's theory is that if a mother delays having another baby for a while, the first baby might have a better chance to survive because it can be fed mother's milk for a longer time. Whiting suggests that parents may be unconsciously or consciously aware that having another baby too soon might jeopardize the survival of the first baby, and so they might decide to abstain from intercourse for more than a year after the birth of the first baby.

As this example of a theory illustrates, we can identify differences between a theory and an association. A theory is more complicated, containing a series of statements. An association usually states quite simply that there is a relationship between two or more measured variables. Another difference is that although a theory may mention some things that are observable (such as the presence of a long postpartum sex taboo), parts of it are difficult or impossible to observe directly. For example, with regard to Whiting's theory, it would be difficult to learn whether people had deliberately or unconsciously decided to practice a long postpartum sex taboo just or mainly because they recognized that babies would thereby have a better chance to survive. Then too, the concept of adaptation—that some characteristic promotes greater reproductive success—is difficult to verify because it is difficult to discover whether different individuals or groups have different rates of child survivorship just or mainly because they do or do not practice a supposedly adaptive custom. So, some concepts or implications in a theory are unobservable (at least at the present time). In contrast, statistical associations or laws are based entirely on observations (Nagel 1961, 83–90). But—and this is very important to remember—both associations and theories could be wrong: the measurements (in the case of an association) might be generally incorrect or all the implications (in the case of a theory) may not have been tested and confirmed. In short, whether we are dealing with associations or theories, our understanding is always uncertain to some (usually unknown) extent.

Just consider how much less vitriolic our controversies might be if all of us realized that any of us could be wrong!

Why Theories Cannot Be Proved

The unprovability of theories deserves some further discussion. An association can be retested many times, and if it is confirmed or replicated those many times we may consider it proved. But we cannot ever say the same thing about any theory, even though many people think the theories they learned in physics or chemistry classes have been proved. Unfortunately, many students may get that impression because their teachers present the so-called lessons in an authoritarian manner. Nevertheless, scientists and philosophers of science generally agree that even though theories may have considerable evidence supporting them, their truth is not established with certainty. This is because many of the concepts and ideas in theories are not directly observable and therefore not directly verified. For example, scientists may try to explain how light behaves by postulating that it consists of particles called "photons." But we cannot observe photons, even with the most powerful microscopes. So, exactly what a photon looks like and exactly how it works remains in the realm of the unprovable. The photon is a "theoretical construct," something that cannot be observed or verified directly. All theories contain such ideas, and for this reason alone theories cannot be proved entirely or with absolute certainty (Nagel 1961, 85; see also McCain and Segal 1982, 75–79).

Why should we bother with theories, then, if we cannot prove that they are true? Perhaps the main advantage of a theory as a kind of explanation is that it may lead to new understanding, albeit tentative. A theory can suggest or imply new possible relationships that might be supported or confirmed by new research. For example, Whiting's theory about long postpartum sex taboos has a number of implications that could be investigated by researchers. Because the theory discusses how a long postpartum sex taboo might be adaptive, we would expect that certain changes would result in the taboo's disappearance. Suppose people adopted mechanical birth-control devices or began to give supplementary high-protein foods to babies. With birth control, a family could space births without abstaining from intercourse, so we would expect the custom of postpartum abstinence to disappear. So too we would expect it to disappear with protein supplements for babies, because kwashiorkor would then be less likely to afflict the babies. Whiting's theory might also prompt investigators to try to learn whether parents are consciously or unconsciously aware of the problem of close birth spacing in areas with low protein supplies.

Although theories cannot be proved, they, like hypothesized associations, are rejectable. The method of *falsification* (showing that a theory seems to be wrong) is the main way that theories are judged (McCain and Segal 1982, 62–64). Scientists derive implications or predictions that should be true if the theory is correct; those implications or predictions should withstand tests that could falsify or disconfirm them. Theories that are not falsified are accepted for the time being because the available evidence seems to be consistent with them.

What Is Evidence?

In determining what is acceptable evidence that a hypothesized association or a theory is probably true or not true, the word *probably* is the key. No discussion of single cases purposively selected and no analysis—statistical or other—of a number of cases personally selected by the investigator can provide an acceptable test of a hypothesis or theory. There is just too much possibility of investigator bias in such assessments. Ideally, then, we should test our ideas against samples of cases that have been randomly selected from some statistical universe; we should measure the variables of interest validly and reliably; and we should evaluate the strength and significance of the results in the ways that have been developed by mathematical statisticians. If we want to reduce the uncertainty of our understanding, we must test that understanding scientifically; and to test our hypotheses and theories scientifically, we must have training in research design and statistical inference. (For a brief discussion of scientific research design, see Ember and Ember 1996, 235–240.)

In sum, we think the most important thing we can transmit to students is the uncertainty of knowledge. This can be done in a number of ways. One is to teach a little philosophy of science, statistics, and research design, all of which convey the uncertainty in all knowledge and in all testing. A second way is to present theories as tentative ideas and to indicate the kinds of evidence that might be used, or have been used, to test them. A third way is not to be afraid to say "I don't know" or "We don't really have a good answer to that question" when students ask "why" questions. Fourth, we need to let our students know that they may very well be able to think of possible answers to our currently unanswered questions, and that they may be able to collect evidence in the future that falsifies some of our currently accepted, even cherished, theories. If we want our students to go on to do creative work in anthropology, we need to communicate more than we ordinarily do that anthropology is open to new ideas. When we communicate the uncertainty that is inherent in the pursuit of understanding, we encourage the pursuit to continue. The outcome can only be what most of us wish—a better understood world!

References

Ember, Carol R., and Melvin Ember. 1996. *Anthropology*. 8th ed. Upper Saddle River, N.J.: Prentice-Hall.

Hempel, Carl G. 1965. *Aspects of Scientific Explanation*. New York: Free Press.

McCain, Garvin M., and Erwin M. Segal. 1982. *The Game of Science*. 4th ed. Monterey, Calif.: Brooks/Cole.

Nagel, Ernest. 1961. *The Structure of Science: Problems in the Logic of Scientific Explanation*. New York: Harcourt, Brace and World.

Whiting, John W. M. 1964. "Effects of Climate on Certain Cultural Practices." In *Explorations in Cultural Anthropology: Essays in Honor of George Peter Murdock*, edited by Ward H. Goodenough, 511–544. New York: McGraw-Hill.

Cleansing Young Minds, or
What Should We Be Doing in
Introductory Anthropology?

WILLIAM A. HAVILAND

Before we can answer the question, What does anthropology know that should be transmitted to students in the introductory course, we need to consider the nature of undergraduate students in general and why they are in our class. At my own institution—which I have no reason to believe is atypical in this respect[1]—most students are in our introductory course not because they want to become anthropology majors but for one of two other reasons. One is that they need to satisfy a distribution requirement for a course in social science or one in "non-European" culture (the latter requirement was instituted at the University of Vermont a few years back, and a number of other colleges and universities either have implemented or are in the process of implementing similar requirements). The second reason is that they have an elective slot to fill, and having encountered "exotic peoples" through such sources as *National Geographic Magazine* or films and videos of the "Indiana Jones" variety, they have decided to sign up for a course that they think will be all about strange people living in bizarre ways in mysterious places. If the course is given at a convenient time so they don't have to get up too early, wait too late to eat lunch, or miss out on any afternoon activities, so much the better. But whatever the motivation, rare is the student who has more than a vague idea of what anthropology really is all about.

On top of this, students bring with them all the biases, misconceptions, and stereotypes of their own culture that they have absorbed over their entire lifetimes thus far. Included among these, of course, is the idea that anthropologists are exclusively in the business of recovering the bones of extinct human ancestors, discovering lost civilizations, or describing present-day peoples whose supposedly "ancient ways" are on the verge of extinction. Few have any inkling of what anthropologists are really trying to accomplish or that they have anything important to say about the contemporary world or the problems that beset humanity today. Far more serious, though, is the cultural insularity and ethnocentrism they display. For example, most students have never even thought to question the notion that human history amounts to a "ladder of progress" leading predictably and inevitably to "ourselves." They take for granted that the institutions of Western society in general and U.S. society in particular—however imperfect they may be—represent the most "advanced" known, and the more people differ from us, the more "backward" or "less

may affect those living in another. It is especially important for them to realize how people living in the Third World are affected by the lifestyles of people living in the industrialized countries of the globe, with their concentration of wealth and power. My own favorite way of dealing with this is through the concept of "global apartheid," showing how the world system today is like apartheid as it has been practiced in South Africa. At the same time, students need to realize that the worldwide spread of such things as Coca-Cola, blue jeans, and transistor radios doesn't mean that cultural differences are disappearing, or even that they should disappear. As Bernard Nietschmann (1987) has pointed out, the majority of the approximately 120 wars being waged today, many of which have been going on for years and even decades, are being fought over the right of people to remain true to their own institutions rather than being forced to adopt those of some other society.

In concentrating on the things that anthropologists have learned, we must of necessity forgo devoting much time to many of the theoretical debates that so often engage us. For one thing, involved debates over such issues as whether ethnographies are no better than fictional accounts of other cultures require a great deal of background that first-year students and sophomores simply do not have; also, in their eyes, such debates make it appear that we do not know what we are doing. Issues that may seem terribly important to us may seem silly or incomprehensible to the average undergraduate. Furthermore, these topics are apt to be about as interesting to our students as theological arguments over how many angels can dance on the head of a pin, and lengthy discourses on method and theory are likely to trigger huge yawns. To lower-level college students, this is "the big turnoff." What they want to know is what we have discovered, and this they frequently find quite fascinating.

In concentrating on what we have learned, we must of course try to convey some sense of how we discover and how we operate as anthropologists. We can find ways to do this, however, without its getting in the way of our primary mission (that is, without letting the tail wag the dog). We should also convey a sense of the importance of the scientific approach in anthropology, although here we must be careful. We must not slight the humanistic side of our discipline, for our somewhat "schizoid" nature is, after all, one of our strengths. The other social sciences are adept at dehumanizing people through their great emphasis on quantitative methods. Although such methods have their place, they too easily reduce real flesh and blood people, with all their feelings, hopes, and aspirations, to mere ciphers. As such, they become too easily subject to manipulation, with little regard given to their own needs and wishes. Of all the social sciences, anthropology has a particular obligation to get beyond numbers to real people, to recognize the humanity of those we study.

Just as we should not slight the humanistic side of our discipline, neither should we slight the scientific side. But I do not think we should get into lengthy discourses on the nature of science. After all, students will inevitably get a lot of this in other courses, but they *won't* get much anthropology elsewhere. We must remember that for many students the introductory course is the only real exposure to anthropology that they will ever get, and it is better that they be exposed to the "bottom line"—what we've discovered—rather than just how we got to the bottom line. And if we do this well, we may entice more students back for a second and third dose than otherwise would have come. That is where we can get more heavily into matters of method and theory, but we won't get them for another time if we turn them off in the introductory course!

Note

1. Although many students at the University of Vermont are from in state, often from rural areas, many are drawn from out of state, in large part from the major metropolitan areas in the Northeast.

References

Allen, Susan L. 1984. "Media Anthropology: Building a Public Perspective." *Anthropology Newsletter* 25:6.

Geertz, Clifford. 1984. "Distinguished Lecture: Anti Anti-Relativism." *American Anthropologist* 86:263–278.

Nietschmann, Bernard. 1987. "The Third World War." *Cultural Survival Quarterly* 11(3):1–16.

Shaw, Dennis. 1984. "A Light at the End of the Tunnel: Anthropological Contributions toward a Global Competence." *Anthropology Newsletter* 25:16.

Anthropology's Challenge:
Disquieting Ideas for Diverse Students

L. B. Breitborde

As teachers, we often like to think of ourselves as introducing students to a "world of ideas." This enterprise, however, sometimes seems directed to students with little idea of the world. The challenge this creates for us as teachers of anthropology is formidable, for among the social scientists, it is we who are most committed to engaging the whole range of cultural complexity—in customs and social organization—that represents persisting and dynamic features of the human experience. And it is we who go beyond the simple documentation and inventorying of differences to ask, "What is the *significance* of these differences?"

How can we engage our students with such ideas?

Here, I wish to explore one aspect of this challenge: namely, the increasing impact of the diversity of our students on their understanding of our subject matter. That cultural diversity, the subject matter of anthropology, should itself constitute a challenge to effective teaching is not simply an irony; it is the logical outgrowth of the fact that the elements accounting for that diversity— and the differing perspectives and experiences of our students—are themselves the subject of our study. If ever any introductory cultural anthropology instructor gave simple lip service to the notion that culture shapes our feelings, emotions, and perceptions, many of us now utter these words with renewed respect and frustration—as we struggle to help students constrained by their culturally shaped feelings, emotions, and perceptions to understand realities radically different from their own.

Students, Identity, and Culture

In a number of ways, the attention students give to their own cultural context(s) affects their ability and willingness to cross cultural boundaries, which is the *modus operandi* of our discipline. As Ernestine Friedl (this volume) has noted, students of the 1990s represent a transition from the "individuality" and "unconnectedness" associated with their counterparts of the 1980s. Today, students often see themselves as persons "sheathed" in a particular culture or identity—an ethnic or gendered or social identity that is not simply fundamental but also constraining, one that separates them from others sheathed in other kinds of cultures or identities, making communication and understanding each other's ideas difficult if not impossible.

This intensifying of identity and culture in our classrooms is a reflection of changes in wider American society. Many students come from diverse communities. Many will have encountered diversity as an increasingly dissonant feature of their own precollegiate classrooms. They have been exposed to cultural differences as competing perspectives, promoted by various segments of their communities, on the content of the history and other subject matter taught in the public schools and as competing voices in the public policy arena. The variety in institutions, social relationships, and customs about which we anthropologists teach does not come as news to many students, but they may have encountered them as disruptive forces in their communities and in relation to their own schooling.

This culturally based cacophony is already a serious challenge to our colleagues teaching social studies in elementary and secondary schools. How does one teach, for example, about political values when there is no consensus on many of those values in wider society? The efforts of social studies teachers to explore the human condition—the full range of human social institutions, systems of social relationships, and customs—are viewed by some as alienating students from the social institutions, social relationships, and customs of their own communities. Even the character of the various communities to which students belong—neighborhood, city, state, national, regional, and global—is subject to different political and economic points of view. In our college and university classrooms, the intensifying of attention to identity comes at a time of unprecedented expression—and disruption—of the communities that are the immediate social context of our schools.

A further technological element has complicated the construction of identity, forcing us increasingly to redefine what we have long taken for granted in our curriculum. Traditionally, precollege social studies education prepared our students to understand their place in the world through a decades-old sequence of concentric spheres of orientation. "Home-neighborhood-city-country-world" may continue to describe the broadening scope of "space" and "place" in kindergarten through twelfth grade social studies texts. But these spheres are increasingly being reshaped. Television and other media provide alternative communities, free of spatial constraints, in which students interact. Other technology—especially computers, phones, and fax machines—create still additional social networks in which students participate. In the late twentieth century, through CD-ROMs and the Internet, students have access to data and information that can originate anywhere in the world. Most important, new communities of people with shared interests and common values develop among individuals separated by large expanses of space but in instant communication with each other through technology. "Downloading," "GIS," and "virtual reality" are not simply the jargon of a new educational technology but may signal the emergence of new social processes, relationships, and identities freed from spatial limitations. Shared experience is now possible with persons from whom one is separated by thousands of miles. "Community" is no longer isomorphic with "place."

Ideas That Disturb

A recent commentator in the American debates on multiculturalism has implicitly made anthropology's case:

> The future of America . . . in a globalized economy without a Cold War, will lie with people who can think and act with informed grace across ethnic, cultural and linguistic lines. And the first step in becoming such a person lies in acknowledging that we are not one big world family, or ever likely to be; that the differences between races, nations, cultures and their various histories are at least as profound and durable as their similarities; that these differences are not divagations from a European norm, but structures eminently worth knowing about for their own sake. In the world that is coming, if you can't navigate difference, you've had it. (Hughes 1993, 96)

Preparing our students for "gracefully navigating" in a world of difference presents special obstacles if those students view "difference" as a barrier to understanding. How do anthropological ideas fall on the ears of students whose sense of themselves is bound with new, unprecedented notions of community and for whom, increasingly, such identity may inhibit their understanding of others not like them? The best anthropology will help students grasp more deeply the complexities of the various communities in which they take their place. But awareness of such complexity is as likely to disturb as it is to comfort students. As we teachers guide them in the exploration of the human cultural record, students will begin to realize their own complicity in larger social and cultural processes of which they may not have been aware or which they may have taken for granted. We may help raise their consciousness about colonialism, or raise their consciousness about the social construction of the idea of race. Our classes may implicate our own students in global economic and cultural forces. Our reading assignments and discussions may situate students themselves in the "global ethnoscapes" resulting from massive movements of people and transmission of ideas (Appadurai 1991). They may change students' understandings of some of the more canonical examples of Western civilization by revealing their culturally heterogeneous sources (Wax 1993). They may result in students' despair of their own embeddedness in the effects on Mexican emigration of the North American Free Trade Agreement, or the impact of video arcades springing up in West African cities, or the implications of sales of the latest Madonna CD in Southeast Asia.

Such things make the world in a very real sense a more complicated, difficult, and troubled place to live in than would otherwise be the case, that is, if such information were not transmitted in the classroom. Anthropologists, then, are in the business of disturbing, of raising consciousness, of making people uneasy—*of doing this deliberately.*

The Culture of Students and the Teaching of Anthropology

The best anthropology educators struggle to find a way to engage their students *constructively* with the disquieting ideas of our discipline. But this is no mean trick.

Our students may be not only disturbed by our ideas but also confused by their own lack of knowledge of how to grapple with the different perspectives that generate those disquieting notions. When one's cultural identity is closely tied to perceptions, experiences, and ideas, tolerance is a necessary tool to promote mutual respect and harmony. But in an academic context, when one's perceptions and ideas should be subject to productive questioning, criticism, and debate, tolerance alone is not sufficient. Tolerance may silence students with "different" opinions because they are not equipped to engage openly and intellectually with such differences, and silence is inimical to the goals of education. Our schools probably do a better job of promoting tolerance than of providing students with tools with which to engage intellectually with the ideas diversity generates.

Robert Hughes refers to a related phenomenon in American culture generally, but especially in our schools, where emotions and feelings have replaced logical argument:

> For when the 1960s' animus against elitism entered American education, it brought in its train an enormous and cynical tolerance of student ignorance, rationalized as a regard for "personal expression" and "self-esteem." Rather than "stress" the kids by asking them to read too much or think too closely, which might cause their fragile personalities to implode on contact with college-level demands, schools reduced their reading assignments, thus automatically reducing their command of language. Untrained in logical analysis, ill-equipped to develop and construct formal arguments about issues, unused to mining texts for deposits of factual material, the students fell back to the only position they could truly call their own: what they *felt* about things. When feelings and attitudes are the main referents of argument, to attack any position is automatically to insult its holder, or even to assail his or her perceived "rights"; every *argumentum* becomes *ad hominem*, approaching the condition of harrassment, if not quite rape. "I feel quite threatened by your rejection of my views on [check one] phallocentricity/the Mother Goddess/the Treaty of Vienna/Young's Modulus of Elasticity." (Hughes 1993, 66)

If our students are affected both by the heightened salience of their cultural identities and the privileging of feeling over reasoned argument, then our classroom endeavors are even more complex! How do we shape an environment in which academic enterprise and intellectual inquiry can be conducted with concern for feelings but without the silencing, stultifying, or constraining effects that considerations of feeling are quite able to generate? Conversely, how do we construct an environment in which the concern for reason does not become a convenient rationale for dismissing feelings, of trampling on part of the humanity of our students (and of ourselves) in the name of reason and logic?

There is without question some dissonance, or even silent confusion, in our classrooms. But the social, political, and economic factors that account for such uncertainty are themselves part of the subject matter of anthropology, as are the factors responsible for the transformations of the "communities" from which our students draw their identities. Here, then, is a clue: one guide for our enterprise as educators lies in explicitly recognizing the increasing salience of diversity in the identities of our students, and in the suggestion that those differences may shape students' predisposition to understand new and different ideas. Such an awareness of our students' identities is not a new idea for teachers, but the insulating power of some contemporary social identities makes this task more difficult. Effective teachers of anthropology will need to engage in a renewed ethnography in their classrooms, to see the process of learning as interactive, and to attempt to incorporate information about all the "actors" involved. As ethnographers, we should ask how race, ethnicity, gender, age, values, and other qualities shape the way students respond to us and condition our mutual expectations. We need to bring our own identities, and those of the authors we assign, to bear openly and explicitly in our classrooms.

These are issues faced by all serious teachers in late twentieth-century American classrooms, but they are especially poignant ones for anthropology. It is the special responsibility of anthropological educators to help students recognize that they have a stake in the very communities and institutions characterized by vibrant, often cacophonous, voices around them. As we lead our students through the study of sociocultural phenomena, we have the potential to help them understand the reasons for and power of alternative realities and perspectives, including those that affect their own communities and lives. In this way, anthropology continues to have the potential to realize what has always been its goal: the understanding of the self through the examination of the other. Perhaps more than any other enterprise conducted by our colleges and universities, anthropology is less compartmentalized and less insulated from the larger society we are helping our students to enter. This is both its special challenge—and its promise.

Note

Acknowledgment: The ideas in this article were developed initially while I was a discussant in the symposium, "How Exemplary Teachers Overcome Problems in the Teaching of Anthropology" at the 91st annual meeting, American Anthropological Association, San Francisco, 1992. Subsequently, several ideas were developed through discussions at the spring 1993 meeting of the Social Studies Advisory Committee of the Wisconsin Department of Public Instruction, and through a presentation on "Engaging Differences" to the 1993 fall faculty conference at Beloit College.

References

Appadurai, Arjun. 1991. "Global Ethnoscapes: Notes and Queries for a Transnational Anthropology." In *Recapturing Anthropology: Working in the Present,* edited by Richard G. Fox, 191–210. Santa Fe, N.M.: School of American Research Press.

Hughes, Robert. 1993. *Culture of Complaint: The Fraying of America.* New York: Oxford University Press.

Wax, Murray. 1993. "How Culture Misdirects Multiculturalism." *Anthropology and Education Quarterly* 24:99–115.

Empowering Students at the Introductory Level

ROBERT BOROFSKY

An introductory course is one of the easiest courses to give badly.

Mandelbaum 1963c, 56

Then and Now

Some Striking Similarities

It is intriguing to reread Mandelbaum, Lasker, and Albert's 1963 book, *The Teaching of Anthropology*. The comparison of teaching's "state of the art" then and now provides much food for thought. Interestingly, the teaching goals enunciated in that 1963 book and in the present 1996 volume are surprisingly similar. Despite three decades of "-isms"—structuralism, cultural materialism, Marxism, feminism, interpretivism, and post-modernism, to name some of the more prominent ones—the goals for teaching introductory anthropology seem to have remained relatively the same. Based on a survey of anthropology departments, Bruner and Spindler (1963, 142) noted in 1963, for example,

> the primary goal of the introductory course is to enlarge the horizons of undergraduates. . . . [I]n rank order, the specific purposes . . . [are] to communicate (1) a sense of the wide range and variability of human culture, (2) an appreciation of culture as a holistic and integrated system, (3) a respect for other ways of life and an understanding of ethnocentrism, (4) a perspective on one's own culture and insights into modern life through the application of anthropological concepts, (5) an awareness of the continuity of [human beings] . . . and culture in long-term evolutionary perspective, and, finally, (6) some conception of anthropology as a discipline.

Mandelbaum (1963, 7) summarized the goals for teaching anthropology as follows:

> It should give students a wider acquaintance with other peoples, a better understanding of diversity and similarity among cultures, and of cultural stability and change. It should open the way to a deeper appreciation of their own culture, and should provide incentive and intellectual equipment with which they will continue to develop their knowledge after they leave the classroom.

Haviland's concern (in this volume) with "combating provincialism and ethnocentrism" is paralleled by Du Bois's (1963, 35) suggestion in the 1963 volume that the viewpoints "professional anthropologists hope for in their students are empathy, curiosity, and objectivity."

As in the present book, many of the authors in the earlier one stressed broad, intellectual goals over specific points of content. Quoting Bruner and Spindler (1963, 142) again, anthropologists indicated "they are attempting to communicate a point of view rather than any particular set of concepts or body of data. Specific cases and problems are simply media for the expression and transmission of the anthropological point of view." And lest we think the current concern for anthropology's integrative role in a fragmented world of knowledge is new (n.b. Rappaport 1994), we should note that in 1963, Mandelbaum (1963b, 556) asserted, "Anthropology tries to conjoin, rather than fragment, knowledge of man." Mead (1963, 596) likewise emphasized anthropology's role in "integrating the diversity of our existing knowledge."

Some of the educational problems faced in 1963 are quite similar to problems faced today. Paralleling our present concern with encouraging a multicultural perspective, for example, a 1961 Ford Foundation Report asserted: "During their undergraduate years, all students should get at least an introductory acquaintance with some culture other than their own" (J. Morrill and others 1961, 17, quoted in Mandelbaum 1963a, 11). And in 1963 there was the problem of "student boredom." Boredom? Here is how Mandelbaum (1963a, 8) phrased it: "The central problems of American higher education, according to one extensive study, are not those of talent, expansion, or money. 'Rather the central problems are student boredom, their indifference and hostility to learning, and the irrelevance of their associations and relationships with other students to their education' (Clark and Trow 1961)." A dedicated teacher such as French (1963, 172)—an individual who in fact has been given a special American Anthropological Association (AAA) award for his commitment to teaching—had this to say:

> By and large, the aims of students are antithetical to those of teachers . . . they hope to graduate and to gain the opportunities and privileges they regard as deriving from this attainment. . . . In general they choose and participate in courses in such a way as to minimize effort and maximize rewards, especially grades. For them, a good course is one which facilities this "economizing" process. If at the same time the course is "interesting" or "stimulating," then so much the better.

Part of the concern expressed in the 1963 volume regarding student interest relates, of course, to the fact that nonmajors predominated then, as they do now, in introductory anthropology courses (see Mandelbaum 1963a, 11; 1963c, 57; Stein and Haviland in this volume). But it also relates, as French indicates, to differences in perception between students and teachers regarding what undergraduate education is about.

Some Key Differences

There are two themes, however, that in a cumulative way, critically distinguish the present teaching context from that of 1963. First, the gap between students' and teachers' perspectives of the educational process has, if anything, become wider today. Over the past three decades, the undergraduate student population has become much more diversified than in the past—in terms of background as well as age. On the positive side, this broadening of the student body means that a greater range of people now take advantage of the college experience than ever before in our nation's history. But it also means that students and faculty, because of their differing backgrounds, may not share important understandings regarding what needs to be learned and/or how one is to learn it. Beyond a motivation gap there is often a large perception gap regarding the meaning of the undergraduate experience, especially in respect to what and how students learn.

And second, there appears to be a "watering down" of intellectual standards. There are references in Mandelbaum, Lasker, and Albert (1963) to the "gentlemen's C." (For readers unfamiliar with the term, it refers to the grade one got for not educationally straining oneself too much.) Today, this "C" has often turned into a "B" as a result of grade inflation. And with this higher grade for comparable (or perhaps less) work has come a sense among both academics and the general public that students—despite their good grades—are not necessarily learning what they need to be effective in today's world. There are cries, both inside and outside the university, about graduates not being able to analyze ideas, read critically, or write effectively.

The goals of an undergraduate course today, especially at the introductory level, run parallel, then, to those of 1963. But the value an introductory course has now—in terms of what students gain from it—seems more open to question. One can find, as French implies, earlier concerns about undergraduate education. But the breadth and intensity of the concerns seem to have increased significantly. What was taken somewhat for granted in 1963 was the value of the undergraduate experience. That no longer can be (or is) assumed. The crucial challenge facing us today is not the quality of our vision. It is how to implement that vision in a classroom that differs in significant ways from the classroom of 1963.

Two Suggestions

One might propose a range of solutions to this problem. As possibilities, I want to suggest two that have generally worked for me. The first focuses on modeling anthropological forms of analysis. The second deals with skill development.

Modeling Anthropological Forms of Analysis

There is an obviousness to having students actively involved in the learning process. It not only reflects John Dewey's approach to education, but it resonates with our own development as anthropologists—our moving from reading texts as graduate students to conducting independent fieldwork, to teaching the subject matter and writing about it. French (1963, 177) phrases it perceptively: "A good student can learn and forget almost anything; sound educational methodology would expect *permanently* useful insights to be derived only from some degree of participation in the role activities of the discipline." In a smaller-sized class—say, under forty students—this might seem far easier to do than in a large class. Yet in some ways, the same principle is involved with both groups.

Students can learn the excitement of anthropology by being anthropologists, by sharing the process of intellectual discovery. They can explore—first with a teacher and then on their own—how to frame and solve anthropological problems. I find a problem orientation works best when it is not added as the frosting on a cake of anthropological content but is embedded in the very organization of the course and frames the selection of readings. Let me explain.

My introductory course progresses through three stages of cognitive development. The course moves from (1) presenting a summary of the types of problems that concern anthropologists to (2) providing models of how anthropologists solve these problems to (3) providing students with the opportunity to solve similar problems themselves. The course begins with a short introductory textbook that presents an overview of the questions anthropologists ask and the types of answers offered by them. It is important for students, I feel, to have this overview. It not only presents students with a "snapshot" of cultural anthropology but also provides a framework for analyzing the ethnographies that follow. I have tried different texts in this regard, but whichever one I choose, students tend to find it the most boring book in the course for the reason French (1963, 174) cites:

> In anthropology, or in another field, the kind of reading matter provided by the average textbook increases the probability that students will remain students. Anthropologists may write textbooks, but they don't read them. The digested facts contained in most texts are as conveniently forgotten as they are conveniently learned—in part because the very consistency in the point of view of a single book eliminates the tantalizing discrepancies that can encourage students to become involved in the current problems of the discipline.

After the introductory book, students read six ethnographies as illustrations of the anthropological approach. I have used a range of ethnographies over the past decade involving some combination always of Western and non-Western groups. I am constantly evaluating these ethnographies—asking students which they like and why—and when it seems reasonable, replacing one with another, or simply out of curiosity, experimenting with a new one. Part of the reason I use a range of texts is so students are drawn into comparing various groups, especially their own with others. Comparison, I stress, is critical to the anthropological process. But there is another important reason for the six ethnographies. It provides a number of *models* regarding what good ethnographies are like. Students see the range of problems anthropologists deal with and the types of data anthropologists use to solve these problems. By way of illustration let me note the ethnographies I currently use, not because they are necessarily the only, or even the best, ones for others but because they provide an idea of what I mean: Martha Ward's *Nest in the Wind,* Barbara Myerhoff's *Number Our Days,* Colin Turnbull's *The Forest People,* Lila Abu-Lughod's *Veiled Sentiments,* Marjorie Shostak's *Nisa,* and Elenore Bowen's (that is, Laura Bohannan's) *Return to Laughter.*

The introductory text and the six ethnographies set the stage for students to conduct their own fieldwork, applying what they have learned in their readings to carrying out actual fieldwork projects. They often find the process both scary and exciting. To help students get started, I pass out descriptions of ethnographies done in previous classes and then, a week later, have a class discussion regarding who is planning to research what topics. I also place on library reserve high-quality ethnographies done in previous classes so students have models to guide them. I am continually intrigued by the diverse challenges students set themselves. These range from conducting fieldwork at a public art museum, junior high school, drug center, college dorm, or nudist colony to working with zookeepers, the homeless, military families, prostitutes, or small businessmen selling shell necklaces to tourists. Some students stay relatively close to home in the sense of working with something they already know a bit about. Others perceive it as an opportunity to do something daring, exploring a group they have wondered about but knew little of. Students focus in on a particular issue, problem, or paradox they discover during their research. They analyze it and write up their data on it in much the same manner the anthropologists did in the ethnographies they read. The papers tend to run to fifteen or more typed pages.

At the same time the course assignments are progressing from a broad overview of the field to modeling ethnographic analyses to the students' development of their own ethnographies, I focus on a related pedagogical process in class lectures. I provide a different overview from that of the introductory text, focusing on problems and concerns that currently exist in the field. I often phrase issues in personal terms—in relation to my own fieldwork, writing, or professional experiences—so students can see how I, as an individual they know, am grappling with these problems. And I continually ask students questions during lectures. As introductory classes at Hawaii Pacific average twenty-five to thirty students, I know each one's name and randomly call on most of them during a class lecture. Students may at first feel shy about responding, but they soon realize there is relatively little penalty for getting the wrong answer. (Although some responses are obviously more correct than others, I try to be positive about all of them, encouraging students to keep exploring for a better answer.) At times it proves helpful to give students a hint regarding what I am looking for, such as providing the first letters of key words in the answer. In respect to how a surplus of food does (or does not) relate to increases in population density and warfare in certain societies, for example, I might simply write "p. d." on the board for population density. Within a very short time—as I clarify the issue, as I explore with students how anthropologists tend to investigate such a relationship—some student will often call out the answer, having thought through the issue to its logical conclusion. Students compare the process to a TV quiz program. But there is no mistaking their involvement. As a teacher, you can perceive students, again and again, analyzing problems in an anthropological manner. They start thinking like anthropologists as they answer questions and, as you might expect, ask me questions in turn. The banter adds excitement to the class. Most students appear involved, and for those who begin to fade out, I simply call on them by name to keep their attention from flagging. The stick (calling individual names) and carrot (fun) process keeps students active participants in the lectures. A contagious enthusiasm (and even laughter) often pervades classes.

Before turning to skill development, I should add one point. Fitting with Edward Tylor's assertion that anthropology is a "reformer's science," students are encouraged to reflect on how various cultural patterns might be changed for the better. They are encouraged to bring up problems of everyday life, and we, as a class, discuss possible approaches to them. I take seriously, and I ask the class to take seriously with me, Boyer's statement in *College: The Undergraduate Experience* that "students must be inspired by a larger vision, using the knowledge they have acquired to . . . advance the common good" (1987, 284).

Reinforcing and Refining Skills

What perhaps is most striking about the 1963 volume *The Teaching of Anthropology,* in my view, is its limited focus on skill development. One might wonder if the volume's authors were dealing with a better prepared group of students than many teachers face today. Could advanced reading, writing, and analytical skills be assumed for students in 1963? That certainly is not the case today. Yet, I wonder if the limited focus on skills does not convey something else as well. It could also mean that many teachers in 1963 did not see refining various intellectual skills as critically important in anthropology courses. (I remember one study from this period indicating that graduating seniors had poorer writing skills than entering freshmen, largely because students did relatively little writing during their four years in college.) But whatever the explanation, my second suggestion emphasizes—as many teachers in many disciplines stress—reinforcing reading, writing, and analytical skills in every course one teaches.

Skill reinforcement works best, I believe, when it is embedded in the very structure of a course. Skill development should not be viewed as simply an "add-on" to a course's requirements. It should be seen as basic to a course's intellectual goals—basic to encouraging the critical, analytical thinking that is central to being an anthropologist.

The first day of the introductory class, when I introduce the course, I discuss with students how to *read* the seven required books effectively. I show them the type of essay exam I give and explain, as well as I can, how they need to read to do well on an exam. (This past year, I began handing out drafts of Borofsky, 1994, xiii–xix, that summarize the points involved.) Essentially I focus on three themes: (1) selecting an effective reading strategy, (2) reading each book by paragraphs and sections rather than word for word, and (3) constructing the author's meaning for each chapter read. I emphasize that different types of exams require different reading strategies. For essay exams (such as the exams in this course), reading for broad ideas is critical. I stress that simply reading lines on a page (and occasionally marking a passage in yellow), without trying to understand what a section is about, is self-defeating in the course. It wastes effort. Students must focus on what the author's perspective is and how she or he constructs it. Students must "read for meaning."

Most students are intrigued by my suggestions. Few, however, initially follow them. Many find it more comfortable to continue their old reading habits. They see their inability to summarize two or three hours of reading as simply a regrettable fact of life.

What makes students change their approach to reading are elements embedded in the structure of the course, especially the organization of class tests. The format for class tests is always the same. Students must summarize and evaluate the major themes in a selected set of chapters. The course assignment sheet groups the chapters of each book into specified sets. For *Nisa* this might involve A (the introduction and chapters one through three), B (chapters four through seven), C (chapters eight through eleven), and D (chapters twelve through the epilogue). Out of perhaps ten possible sets of chapters that students are responsible for on an exam—involving usually two or three books— I choose one set of chapters to test them on (such as chapters four through seven of *Nisa*). I write these chapter numbers on the board. Students then have to write lengthy essays summarizing and evaluating these chapters. Because remembering the themes involved in various chapters can prove difficult, I allow students to bring in five words per chapter to help them recall what the chapters of each book deal with. Realizing they need to know themes rather than details, students spend considerable time going through the material searching for and evaluating broad ideas in preparing their word lists for an exam. In preparing for the exam, in other words, students go through the very intellectual processes that are required in effective reading: separating out themes from details and constructing an author's meaning as well as evaluating it. Casually finding out from a friend what is in a chapter rarely helps if one has not done the reading. The essay exam is too long for that. And of course, trying to "bull" one's way through an exam without having done the reading is nearly impossible. The alternative to following the suggestive steps in reading is so overwhelmingly self-defeating that most students not only do the reading but use the "reading for meaning" strategy.

Students are also drawn to this strategy if the reading assignments each week are fairly long. Some students persist with reading the books word by word. But most give up in exhaustion after a few weeks and turn to a more conceptual type of reading that focuses on evaluating how an author develops his or her theme.

Let me add two notes. First, for students to have even a reasonable chance of doing well on this type of exam, they need to go through the kind of critical analysis that one encourages in anthropology students. Critical analysis is not some frosting on a cake. It is basic to passing an exam. And it is done before the exam, often with friends, in a relatively relaxed, thoughtful manner. Second, having a photocopied form for students to write on—with set spaces for the themes and supporting points to be made in an argument—makes it relatively easy for me to grade students' essays. Before using such forms, I at times found myself confused regarding what points a student was developing where in an essay. But these forms make that relatively clear. The result is that I am able to read essay exams and type up comments for each student in a relatively short time—often not much longer than correcting a fill-in-the-blank or short-answer exam. And reading the exams can be intellectually intriguing. Seeing how students conceptualize a particular set of chapters can be quite interesting. Many offer rather thoughtful syntheses.

Analytical *writing* is also embedded in the curriculum. The above noted ethnography accounts for 30 percent to 35 percent of a student's grade. A rough draft is *always* submitted prior to the final paper. Because students spend considerable time on this paper, I have found that a good practice is to have it due well before the final rush of papers at the end of the semester. (I often require it two-thirds of the way through the term.) Then, following Brown University's Writing Fellow's program, an advanced anthropology student goes over the paper with the introductory student for twenty minutes or so, pointing out both conceptual and mechanical areas to work on. Talking with another student seems to work better than talking with the teacher in this regard. Students feel less eager to please and, as a result, talk through their problems more honestly. The ethnographies are graded on three criteria: (1) the cogency of the descriptive data, (2) the student's ability to conceptualize cultural patterns within the group studied, and (3) the ability to relate such patterns critically to broader contexts within American society.

I feel an uneasy sense of pontificating in these last paragraphs. I do not mean that the techniques I use work best in all situations or with all students, but I do want to suggest that they illustrate a key point: it is critical, with today's students, that the refining and reinforcement of reading, writing, and analytical skills be embedded within a course's basic structure. This is essential to helping students develop the skills they need after graduation. Passing off skill development to remedial teachers or simply blaming high schools for the problem will not do. If we are interested in teaching broad, conceptual anthropological perspectives, we need to encourage the effective reading, analyzing, and writing of anthropological material. That is both the burden and the privilege of teaching anthropology in today's undergraduate environment.

Conclusion

Teachers today often deal with students who lack important intellectual skills on entering college; if a serious effort is not made to help them, they will very likely graduate without these skills. Teaching, in this context, means beginning where students are. But it does not mean ending there. It means stretching students, exciting them. And in the process of demanding much, it also means helping students develop and/or refine the tools they need to achieve much.

From this perspective, an introductory anthropology course should empower students with the tools that will allow them to continue empowering themselves intellectually long after the course is over. This is what I think Mandelbaum (1963a, 7) meant when he suggested that teaching anthropology "should provide [the] incentive and intellectual equipment with which . . . [students] will continue to develop their knowledge after they leave the classroom." It is an important goal to aim for in any introductory class. And it is, I believe, a quite achievable one.

References

Borofsky, Robert. 1994. "A Personal Note to Undergraduates." In *Assessing Cultural Anthropology*, edited by Robert Borofsky, xiii–xix. New York: McGraw-Hill.

Boyer, Ernest. 1987. *College: The Undergraduate Experience in America*. New York: Harper and Row.

Bruner, Edward, and George Spindler. 1963. "The Introductory Course in Cultural Anthropology." In *The Teaching of Anthropology*, edited by David Mandelbaum, Gabriel Lasker, and Ethel Albert, 141–152. Berkeley: University of California Press.

Clark, B. R., and Martin Trow. 1961. "Determinants of College Student Subculture." To appear in *The Study of College Peer Groups*, edited by T. M. Newcomb and E. K. Wilson, New York: Social Science Research Council.

Du Bois, Cora. 1963. "The Curriculum in Cultural Anthropology." In *The Teaching of Anthropology*, edited by David Mandelbaum, Gabriel Lasker, and Ethel Albert, 27–38. Berkeley: University of California Press.

French, David. 1963. "The Role of Anthropologist in the Methodology of Teaching." In *The Teaching of Anthropology*, edited by David Mandelbaum, Gabriel Lasker, and Ethel Albert, 171–178. Berkeley: University of California Press.

Mandelbaum, David. 1963a. "A Design for an Anthropology Curriculum." In *The Teaching of Anthropology*, edited by David Mandelbaum, Gabriel Lasker, and Ethel Albert, 49–64. Berkeley: University of California Press.

———. 1963b. "Introduction." In *The Teaching of Anthropology*, edited by David Mandelbaum, Gabriel Lasker, and Ethel Albert, 555–557. Berkeley: University of California Press.

———. 1963c. "The Transmission of Anthropological Culture." In *The Teaching of Anthropology*, edited by David Mandelbaum, Gabriel Lasker, and Ethel Albert, 1–21. Berkeley: University of California Press.

Mandelbaum, David, Gabriel Lasker, and Ethel Albert, eds. 1963. *The Teaching of Anthropology*. Berkeley: University of California Press.

Mead, Margaret. 1963. "Anthropology and an Education for the Future." In *The Teaching of Anthropology*, edited by David Mandelbaum, Gabriel Lasker, and Ethel Albert, 595–607. Berkeley: University of California Press.

Morrill, J. L. and others. 1961. *The University and World Affair*. New York: Ford Foundation.

Rappaport, Roy A. 1994. "Humanity's Evolution and Anthropology's Future." In *Assessing Cultural Anthropology*, edited by Robert Borofsky, 153–166. New York: McGraw-Hill.

Teaching and Learning Anthropology in the Twenty-First Century

AARON PODOLEFSKY

Since there is little prospect for a general decrease of classes, the lecture will necessarily be the major vehicle of undergraduate teaching. A lecture can be a powerful instrument; it can—as was said of a lecture by Sarte—plough up the minds of the listeners as a tractor ploughs up a field. But Sarte did not attempt to sustain that effect through the American semester pattern of three lectures a week for fifteen weeks.

Mandelbaum, 1963

The swirl of political and economic events can at times evoke and enliven the passion with which we academics approach our calling. A bit over a decade ago, on the first day of fall classes, something on the radio made me want to talk to students about contemporary social and economic conditions and the importance of anthropology. I didn't want them to copy down the reasons I think anthropology is critical; I wanted them to think about it.

Over 200 students filled a lecture hall waiting to hear their professor's introductory remarks, collect a copy of the syllabus, and learn what books to buy for the course. As they sat passively, I began with a question: "Tell me," I said, "what do you think are the biggest problems confronting America today?" Rather than follow the typical two-second delay with the answer to my own rhetorical question, I waited. Slowly the hands went up and the answers came, then more quickly—crime, poverty, discrimination, pollution, environmental degradation, racism, inflation, intolerance, international conflict, and stress were some of the students' responses.

Much to my satisfaction, the students identified social and cultural problems as the most pressing and the most intractable. However, they had not previously made the connection between these current events and the social science disciplines. We spent the rest of the hour talking about the nature of the social sciences and why they are important. We discussed the relationship between basic and applied research and the benefit of informed policy. Students began to understand that learning about past and present cultures and societies is fundamental to perceiving the cultural components of everyday events.

This attempt to create an interactive setting in a large lecture was a pivotal point in my attempts to *engage* students in the learning process. I realized that even in large lecture halls I could release absolute control of the learning environment with positive results. While the lecture format is still necessary to educate masses of students, we are increasingly moving away from the notion that teaching is telling and learning is listening.

Engagement of students in their own educational experience is a key concept in numerous educational reforms—for example, active learning and co-operative education—but it is not a new idea. Confucius is reported to have said, "Tell me and I will forget. Show me and I will remember. Involve me and I will understand."

As we look forward to changes in teaching anthropology over the next thirty years (during which time today's new faculty will become the senior faculty), we must briefly examine the environmental context of education and how it might change from 1993 to 2023. Beyond pedagogical theory, the revolutionary pace of changes in computing technology, knowledge development, and communication pathways is driving a transformation in our approach to education. What was a good idea in the days of Confucius is a necessary development as we approach the twenty-first century.

The Information Explosion

The notion that we are moving from the industrial era to the information era will be news to no one. At present, knowledge doubles every five years. By the year 2000, 97 percent of what is known will have been discovered during my lifetime. By 2020, knowledge will double every seventy-three days. A decade ago, in *Megatrends* (1982, 17), John Naisbitt declared that "we are drowning in information but starved for knowledge." In the future, without changes in education, we will be drowning in knowledge but starved for understanding.

Technological changes transform the strategic value of particular resources, as shown in the following chart. During the agricultural era, land was the primary strategic resource. The rise of the machine in the industrial era led to the increased importance of capital. Predicated on computing technology, knowledge is the capital of the information age.

	Agricultural Era	*Industrial Era*	*Information Era*
Dominant Technology	Plow	Machine	Computer
Strategic Resources	Land	Capital	Knowledge

Anthropologists are used to studying such revolutionary shifts, but how have we adapted? During 1979, Chris McCarty and I drafted a paper on the use of computers for processing qualitative field data (Podolefsky and McCarty

1983). My favorite review came from an anthropologist who suggested reject-ing the paper because "anthropologists are not interested in computers." Things have changed, indeed.

During the 1940s and 1950s, the number-crunching capabilities of comput-ers transformed the face of modern sociology and psychology while cultural an-thropology, because of its fieldwork orientation, continued to rely on textual data. Recent changes in computing capabilities for handling text have made word crunching a reality, and this is having a major effect on data collection and management. Anthropologists take computers to the field to record textual and numeric forms of data. We can easily copy digitized data (disks), or store these data on a file server that is network accessible, creating unprecedented opportu-nities to share data among scholars and students. H. Russell Bernard and his col-leagues have provided computers to native speakers, allowing these individuals to produce their own ethnographies (Bernard and Salinas 1989) and more re-cently to create written text in what were previously unwritten languages (Bernard 1992). Qualitative texts, Human Relations Area Files, and many other data sources can be made increasingly available to students as well as scholars.

The use of visual media has a long history in anthropological teaching. Visual images can now be digitized and stored on laser disc or compact disc (CD) and managed (randomly accessed on command) through computers for classroom or research use. Not many years ago, J. Jerome Smith of the Univer-sity of South Florida was pioneering efforts to bring together students, com-puters, and video discs. Students responded to questions, and their response called up video clips stored on laser disc. Today, multimedia software allows a seamless integration of laser disc, CD-ROM, videocassette recorder, and data stored on hard drive in either lecture or laboratory settings.

Anthropologist James Chadney is making creative use of multimedia tech-nology. Chadney teaches a large introductory anthropology class to over 200 students and is employing multimedia as an auditory and visual accompani-ment to his lectures. His computer-based applications (based on a slide show metaphor) integrate sound, video images, and text. His current plans are to continue developing the lecture format around multimedia and then expand his efforts into a more interactive mode where students attend multimedia lec-tures two hours every week and then spend time at a computer terminal delv-ing more deeply into the assigned topic.

The digitized, random access world of laser disc and CD-ROM, as com-pared to the linear world of audio- and videocassettes, allows faculty and students to navigate through data in ways that more closely model the process of exploration and learning. Lectures can become data/information-based conversations.

Hot on the heels of the information explosion is the revolution in commu-nication, bringing with it a host of terms unfamiliar to the average faculty. Satellite downlinks and mobile satellite uplinks, microwave, and fiber optics are providing information-sharing opportunities of unprecedented magnitude.

This revolution in communication further compounds the effects of the doubling rate of knowledge.

A thousand years ago, if you wanted to learn something, you sought out a wise person. A hundred years ago, you went to a library. Today, we and our students can communicate electronically and access databases around the world. It seems that each day a new service (such as gopher or LIBS) turns up on my screen. Each leads to new dimensions of opportunity and at the same time an endless source of frustration as I find myself lost in cyberspace.

As well as accessing data, there are additional opportunities to make creative use of communications technology in teaching. Roy Sandstrom, a historian at the University of Northern Iowa, has been using e-mail as a supplement to his normal office hours. Although Sandstrom kept eight office hours a week, one-third of his students had schedule conflicts that prevented them from meeting with him during office hours. Sandstrom logs on to e-mail four times a day (including early morning and late at night), which means that he answers most student inquiries within a couple of hours of their posting. This is a significant improvement over the normal twenty-four to forty-eight hours that elapse before an office visit is possible.

Students who at first resisted the idea of using e-mail often became hooked after a short time. Most students logged on with questions about course mechanics, study tips, or sources for further reading. Sandstrom and several students developed "electronic friendships," sending humorous anecdotes or setting up appointments for coffee at the student union. He still gets e-mail from some of these students asking both personal and professional questions.

Starting in the summer of 1992, Sandstrom put all his classes, from lower division to graduate courses, on an electronic bulletin board (BBS—sometimes called a "notes conference"). He posted the syllabus, study tips, reminders of special assignments, and items designed to encourage use of the BBS, such as tips on using e-mail (how to forward, print, extract, and so on). He provided class notes from previous days' lectures for students who missed class or who wanted to improve their note-taking skills. These were an especially great help to lower-division students.

Advanced students made good use of the BBS by responding frequently to one another. Less advanced students engaged most often in student-instructor only contacts. For the more advanced students, the BBS became an electronic meeting place where they could share substantive discussion of course topics. Sandstrom believes that electronic contact is less threatening than class participation for shy students who will offer more blunt comments and questions over e-mail than in class. He found their openness "a bit surprising."

Sandstrom believes that contacts with students tripled as a result of e-mail. He got many inquiries on a daily basis. This, of course, is not without cost. During a semester in which he taught about 110 students in three classes, he reports spending five to ten additional minutes responding to students each time he got onto e-mail—twenty to forty minutes per day.

As anthropologists, we are particularly interested in expanding students' horizons by exposing them to other cultures. This past January (1993), Leigh Zeitz, instructional technology coordinator at the Malcolm Price Laboratory School, University of Northern Iowa, found an intriguing message in an Internet discussion group. Akira Taniguchi, a high school English teacher in Osaka, Japan, was looking for students from other countries with whom his twelfth-grade students could correspond about the murder of a sixteen-year-old Japanese exchange student, Yoshihiro Hattori, in Louisiana on Halloween night, 1992. Dr. Zeitz answered Mr. Taniguchi's message and proposed the project to Mary Beth Kueny, a seventh-grade social studies teacher at the Lab School.

The Japanese students composed four letters expressing shock at the exchange student's murder. They asked why Americans do not ban the possession of guns by citizens, as is done in Japan, and how the American students felt about gun control. They expressed their fears about coming to the United States. Some of the Iowa students agreed that guns should be banned while others argued that in America owning guns is a nonnegotiable right. The students from Osaka and Iowa continued the exchange of personal descriptions of themselves and their schools, their friends, and their dreams.

This connection was extended to a link between a first-grade class in Iowa that was studying Japan and a Japanese first-grade class from Osaka. Similar projects have now been completed with students in Mexico and Australia. The faculty find that the students ask questions based on what they have learned from the cultural units taught in their school. They ask questions that emphasize the differences between cultures and are often surprised at the similarities.

The possibilities for teaching and learning in anthropology classes are obvious. The power of the Internet will extend to two-way interactive video, voice, and data. These capabilities are now being used in distance education and distance resourcing and will be expanded to allow discussions among people from around the globe.

Computing and communication technologies, in the context of an exponentially expanding knowledge base, will ultimately change the way teaching and learning take place in the twenty-first century.

Linear Models in a Random Access World

As we move toward the next century we will no longer be able to use linear models of instruction in a random access world. My son Isaac made this perfectly clear to me about a year ago, when he was thirteen. I brought home a software package and we sat down to figure out how to use it. Being a kid, he wanted to load it right onto the machine and get started. Being a dad, I said, "Let's read through the instructions carefully to learn how to operate the program." After something of a "disagreement," I headed off with pad, pencil, and instruction manual; Isaac headed for the computer—disk in hand. An hour later, I had plowed through the first fifteen pages or so and was proudly ready to explain to him how best to get started. I found Isaac surfing through the program like he'd been using it for a month. I could draw only two conclusions: either he is a lot smarter than I am (which is possible), or his way of learning was superior to mine.

I was trying to learn a very complex system in the linear fashion that I learned in grade school: start at the beginning of the book and go from A to B to C and so on. Isaac was learning the way kids always learn complex systems (such as language) outside the school/classroom setting. I realized that this is also the way I learn when, as a scholar, I begin a new research project. Isaac's learning strategy combines trial and error with access to guides such as pull-down help menus and personal friends. In other words, he follows a nonlinear path to construct his own knowledge. This helps him learn not only the particular program but also how to approach learning other programs of a similar type.

Students of the Twenty-First Century

The students who will be in our colleges and universities in the year 2000 are those who are now ten to fifteen years old, and some of them are doing some rather amazing things. Last year when I was at the American Anthropological Association meetings, Isaac got a larger hard drive for our home computer. With many reservations, I gave him permission over the phone to install the drive—if and only if he got help. He called the computer manufacturer and a technician talked him through the installation of the drive. He needed this additional space because several months before he had downloaded, over the modem, some bulletin board software and had set up his own "BBS." I don't know where he learned how to do this, but a couple of dozen kids were now routinely dialing into our computer (which runs twenty-four hours a day) to play games, leave messages for each other, or engage in two-way "talk."

When I was a kid, I spent my evenings the American way—on the couch watching Walt Disney. But Isaac is always at the computer, communicating over the modem or playing an on-line game while also talking to another kid on another phone tucked under his ear. Nowadays, one computer game at a time is not enough (nor is one phone line in a house). While many of our incoming students, like Isaac, appear unable to perform as well as we would like in the mundane skills, such as spelling and sentence construction, I suspect that many of the students who will enter the university in the year 2000 will be exceptionally sophisticated learners. I think Isaac represents one type of student we will be teaching at our universities in the year 2000 and beyond. Can we ask these students to sit in a lecture hall three hours a week while we talk at them in the guise of education?

Teaching for Tomorrow

The environmental context of teaching and learning in the twenty-first century will clearly differ from that of the twentieth. Just as education adapted to the arrival of the printing press, so must university teaching in the next century take account of the technological, information, and communication environments.

The learning needs of society are changing. Repetitive, mass production is out; creative problem solving is in. Students will need the opportunity and ability to access information and actively construct knowledge through nonlinear processes. Higher education must expand its focus on the development of *thinking* skills (critical thinking/reflective judgment). Students will increasingly hone their skills and abilities through cooperative problem solving directed at real-world problems.

The accessibility of computing and information technology to today's youth is producing a different sort of student for tomorrow's university. The question is this: can the institution change to meet the needs of twenty-first century students? In 1939, the distinguished educator John Dewey wrote: "It is demonstrable that many of the obstacles for change which have been attributed to human nature are in fact due to the inertia of institutions and to the involuntary desire of powerful classes to maintain the existing status."

The pedagogical changes made both possible and necessary by the changes in computing and communication technology provide an opportunity for higher education's rebirth, and as Bob Dylan sang three decades ago, "Those not busy being born are busy dying."

Postscript

The changes that have occurred in educational technology in the brief time between drafting this chapter and the final editing speak volumes about one of the chapter's central themes—the rapid rate of change in technology and its uses. Two years ago, faculty members were experimenting with electronic office hours and discussion groups; now, these are commonplace. Today, distribution lists for broadcasting messages to entire departments or classes of students are easy to construct. With one command, we can send letters to all faculty in our colleges or universities. Students may browse the Worldwide Web seeking out tens of thousands of sites, from anthropology departments' Home Pages to museums and databases. In fact, the next edition of *Applying Anthropology* and *Applying Cultural Anthropology* (Podolefsky and Brown 1996) will have an extensive appendix written by James Chadney, describiing how anthropology students can use the Worldwide Web. Some innovative faculty are putting courses, course notes, and syllabi on the Web. Departments have Home Pages that offer much of the information that advisers used to provide. The extent of the information accessible—often in graphic form—is astounding. There is no sign that the rate of change will slow.

While we should embrace change, we are not required to adopt every innovation technologists invent. It is up to us to assure that new technologies are used to create a deeper and more thoughtful educational experience.

References

Bernard, H. R. 1992. "Preserving Language Diversity." *Human Organization* 51(1):82–89.

Bernard, H. R., and J. Salinas Pedraza. 1989. *Native Ethnography: A Mexican Indian Describes His Culture*. Newbury Park, Calif.: Sage.

Dewey, J. 1939. "Theory of Valuation." In *International Encyclopedia of Unified Science*, edited by Otto Neurath. Chicago: University of Chicago Press.

Mandelbaum, David. 1963. "The Transmission of Anthropological Culture." In *The Teaching of Anthropology*, edited by David Mandelbaum, Gabriel Lasker, and Ethel Albert, 1–21. Berkeley: University of California Press.

Naisbitt, John. 1982. *Megatrends*. New York: Warner Books.

Podolefsky, Aaron, and Peter Brown (eds.). 1997. *Applying Anthropology*. 4th ed. Mountain View, Calif.: Mayfield.

Podolefsky, Aaron, and Peter Brown (eds.). 1997. *Applying Cultural Anthropology*. 3rd ed. Mountain View, Calif.: Mayfield.

Podolefsky, A., and C. McCarty. 1983. "Topical Sorting: A Technique for Computer Assisted Qualitative Data Analysis." *American Anthropologist* 85:886–890.

The Ethnographic Approach to Teaching Cultural Anthropology

Dᴀᴠɪᴅ W. McCᴜʀᴅʏ

It's the middle of spring semester, 1995. Macalester College junior, Joe Schreiber, has spent five evenings during the last few weeks interviewing two waitresses at a late-night restaurant. He is focusing on the part of their culture they use to handle drunks who come in after the bar next door closes. Senior, Pam Kriege, has spent hours with a worker at a half-way house for drug addicts, learning about urine checks, resident programs, and body searches. Sophomore, Shai Hayo, is on his fourth interview with a member of a Rockabilly bowling league discovering how they effect a remembered 1950s lifestyle.

These students are part of a Macalester College ethnographic fieldwork course that focuses on the study of American microcultures. They are part of a growing trend to teach cultural anthropology by doing it. For example, undergraduates at Radford University are working on a group project interviewing rural residents about what it will mean when a new power line crosses their lands. Others, such as those in introductory anthropology at the University of South Carolina, are doing short projects on focused activities, such as borrowing patterns in the dorms. In fact, undergraduates are doing ethnographic fieldwork in dozens of colleges and universities in the context of regular courses and in summer field schools.

Some anthropologists have raised objections to the involvement of undergraduates in ethnography. They feel that undergraduates lack sufficient theory to do research. They claim that fieldwork is too complex an art to teach to undergraduates in the short time typically provided by semesters and quarters. They argue that undergraduate research takes too much time to oversee, that it can only be done in small classes, and that undergraduates cannot be trusted to manage the ethical issues associated with research.

This paper argues that ethnographic fieldwork is a powerful and practical way to teach cultural anthropology to undergraduates. Ethnography is a hallmark of cultural anthropology, one that distinguishes the discipline from other social sciences and humanities. Undergraduates learn best and gain valuable perspective on what happens in the traditional classroom when they actually *do* fieldwork rather than simply read about it. This paper will look briefly at an early attempt to systematically involve undergraduates in fieldwork, the Macalester program, then review and attempt to answer some of the objections raised by critics.

A Program of Undergraduate Ethnography

The Macalester ethnography program began in the spring of 1970. That was the year James Spradley joined the faculty as a second anthropologist and when together we decided to focus the program in cultural anthropology by basing it on student ethnography. Our reasons for doing so related to the early stage of the program and its position at the college. Anthropology was a new subject at Macalester. Many students and some of the faculty in other disciplines had little idea what the discipline was about. We wanted anthropology to succeed and grow at the college. To achieve success we felt that the anthropology curriculum should be unique in some way; it should stand out as different from other social sciences and humanities. A clear focus, one unique to the discipline, might help us reach this goal.

We also wanted a program that was both interesting and useful to undergraduate students, even to those who would not major in the field or go on to graduate school. Again, we recognized that this goal would be difficult to attain. The discipline's growing specialization often seemed to ignore the more general questions that interested students. Without a broad familiarity with anthropological concepts, data, and theory, students would find it difficult to discover the discipline's explanatory power.

Student ethnography seemed to meet our program requirements. First, ethnography was visible and a fundamental part of anthropology. It promised to be useful, interesting, and fun for students. We noticed that several disciplines, including our own subfields of archaeology and physical anthropology, often involved their students in firsthand research, and that students, by doing research rather than simply reading about it, learned more about and developed greater enthusiasm for their subjects.

We also felt that ethnographic field research contributed most to our own graduate education and professional experience. Ethnography enabled us to see other people's points of view more clearly. It made the concept of culture sensible to us in a new, more powerful, way. It enabled us to look at human behavior differently from the way scholars in other disciplines viewed it. If ethnography could do half as much for our students as it did for us, we reasoned, our anthropology program would succeed.

The decision about how to proceed with an ethnography program presented its own problems, however. Both Spradley and I had already taught more typical anthropological methods courses in which we discussed a variety of fieldwork techniques. Our students read about these methods and occasionally did short, week-long, assignments. Although learning certainly took place, neither of us felt satisfied with the results. Students often seemed confused and lost. They didn't know what to observe or ask. They quickly ran out of questions and they rarely knew what to do with results.

The trouble seemed to be lack of focus. There were too many methods and too little time for students to learn them. In addition, in 1970 ethnographic methods were loosely defined at best. It was difficult for inexperienced students to acquire a sense of what fieldwork was about in the short time available in class, and they had little idea of what to look for in the field and what to do with data once they were noted down. We felt we needed a focused method that would provide more structure for students, one they could master in a semester, one that would yield original and useful data they could analyze and interpret.

We found this structure and focus in ethnoscience ethnography. Although ethnoscience had been criticized as overly ideational and a method that would yield only what should be, not what is (a criticism I hotly dispute to this day), Spradley's experience using ethnoscience ethnography during a study of tramps (Spradley 1970) and our early experience teaching it to students said otherwise. Better, we were able to translate the work on ethnoscience published in the professional literature into a structured, step-by-step method students seemed to understand (see Spradley and McCurdy 1972; Spradley 1979, 1980; McCurdy 1992).

Several properties of ethnoscience, or ethnosemantics as we called it then, made this possible. Ethnoscience included a limited, clear definition of culture: *the learned, shared knowledge that people use to generate behavior and interpret experience.* Using this definition, we could tell students what to look for when they did ethnography—the cultural knowledge of informants. Our students would now be students in a different kind of classroom, the field. Informants would teach them, not professors.

But informants were not trained teachers; students needed a systematic way to elicit cultural knowledge from them. Again, ethnoscience could provide that structure. The foundation of ethnoscience as we saw it was the idea that a significant part of culture is coded in words. If one can learn the insider's language—the folk terms used by members of a cultural group—and if the meaning of the words can be learned, then part of the group's culture can be discovered. Anthropologists always did this informally when they entered the field and learned the language of the people they wished to understand. Ethnoscience was an attempt to formalize the process.

To organize this for students, we divided the elicitation process into a descriptive phase, a taxonomic structure phase, and an attributional meaning discovery phase. The descriptive phase was designed to get informants talking about their cultural worlds and to use their folk terms in the process. The taxonomic structure phase—really a play on the idea that people, in this case informants, remember things better in the context of lists and close associations—was designed to elicit much more detail. Taxonomies are lists of closely related folk terms. They help produce a detailed inventory of things, acts, feelings, and other aspects of the human cultural experience and as part of the method, form the basis for the last phase, the discovery of meaning. This phase used the comparison of closely related terms found in taxonomies to generate detailed differences and similarities among cultural categories.

Using this structure, we were able to generate a limited number of question frames that students could ask during each phase, and we were able to work field observation, the elicitation of stories, and other anthropological field techniques into the method without too much confusion.

Objections to Undergraduate Ethnography

Many anthropologists have questioned the ethnographic enterprise over the past few years, not just for students but for all cultural anthropologists. It will not be my place here, however, to defend the enterprise as a whole. The method I have discussed assumes that most organized groups of people, despite individual variation and the uncertainties of postmodern encounters, do share conventions that organize their behavior and the interpretation of experience. In this sense it argues that culture is at least "real" for the people who hold and use it. The method also depends on the belief that it is possible to *do* systematic ethnography. It is predicated on the notion that trained observers can elicit the cultural knowledge of others and describe it to a general audience in such a way that informants will usually agree with what is said about them. This may not hold true for the ethnographer's more general interpretations of a culture, but student ethnographers rarely get to this level in their work. Finally, the method assumes that ethnography is not a form of informant exploitation, at least not in any degree greater than most social interaction.

Many critics, however, believe in the authority of ethnography but still doubt that undergraduates can or should do it. They reserve the enterprise for professionals and graduate students. Let us look at the most common criticisms.

First, some critics argue that undergraduates lack the necessary theoretical sophistication to do ethnography. I encountered this question several years ago when an anthropologist, who was also the father of a Macalester student, took his son and me to lunch. As our conversation progressed, he bluntly asserted that it was impossible for undergraduates to do ethnographic research; they simply did not know enough theory.

I could have responded to this view by simply arguing that it was wrong. Our undergraduate students had been doing ethnography for twenty years and undergraduate fieldwork was finding its way into an increasing number of anthropology departments around the country. To be sure, some of the more than 4,000 ethnographies I had read over the years were poor, but many were good and some were really first-rate. Nineteen Macalester students had published articles based on their undergraduate research, and a few others had published articles and books using studies they started while they were undergraduates.

The lack-of-theoretical-sophistication criticism should not be rejected out of hand, however, because it points to two important requirements of field research. The first is that to be manageable, ethnography needs structure and focus as I noted above. One can argue that theory is necessary to ethnographic research because it meets this need. It helps ethnographers choose what to observe and what to ask. Theory shapes the direction a study will take, giving it focus and definition. Without theory, many argue, ethnographers would founder in a sea of complexity, producing random descriptions without significance. Ethnographic research requires a purpose if it is to be significant, and theory is what establishes research importance. The second is that theory gives significance to ethnography. Ethnography should be done to test and elaborate on theory.

The problem with these arguments does not lie in the assertion that structure and purpose are necessary to ethnographic research, for they clearly are. Instead, it rests with the view that theory is the *only* way to meet these needs. On the contrary, ethnographic fieldwork, as noted above, can also be organized effectively by using one or more of the structured field techniques readily available in several methods books. Ethnoscience ethnography was our choice for this task, as I have already noted; and in partisan fashion, I believe it works best, but there are many other effective research techniques (see, for example, Bernard 1993; Crane and Angrosino 1984; Werner and Schoepfle 1987).

Evidence for the success of these techniques when they are used by undergraduates may be found in several published works that include student ethnographic papers (see, for example, Spradley and McCurdy 1972; Kottak 1982). In addition, there have been almost yearly symposia at the national meetings of the American Anthropological Association dealing with strategies to teach anthropology through research and the use of various techniques to structure ethnography.

Nor is theory required to establish a study's significance. I feel this point is especially difficult for many anthropologists to accept. Theory is preeminent in graduate anthropology, and for many anthropologists, doing research without theoretical foundation is inconceivable. Yet, I think there is ample evidence that ethnography can take on significance without an initial basis in theory. First, from the student perspective, learning to do ethnography, any ethnography, can be valuable and an end in itself; second, it can serve as a basis for the generation of theory.

The revelations one gets from doing ethnography are purpose enough for many of the undergraduates I teach. Many students come to anthropology with the assumption that human beings are really the same everywhere. Ethnographic research demonstrates the fallacy of this view. By doing ethnography, students learn that others often classify the world differently, that the same things or actions can have different meanings for people with different cultures, and that the rules of the game may not be shared. They enjoy the power that comes from viewing a seemingly familiar situation through the eyes of actors with a different cultural perspective.

For example, one student excitedly told me that she had discovered an important source of tension among employees working at a restaurant she had visited for several years: towels. She had learned from her informant that *towels*, renamed *rags* when they became wet, were always in short supply. Wait staff regularly "borrowed" towels from each other and some went so far as to hide them to ensure a ready supply. Another student found that female residents living in a retirement home have five ways to disguise nap-taking. They hide this activity because they are afraid it will be used by the staff to downgrade their level of independence.

Many students also see ethnography not as a research technique but as a skill for finding out what other people know and do. Because they expect to encounter new social situations throughout their lives, they value ethnography for its adaptive utility. This utility becomes especially clear to them if they engage in study abroad while they are students, but they also often learn to apply ethnography in situations they encounter at home.

Ethnography also enables students to generate their own theory. For example, one student discovered that the paramedics he was interviewing used three languages to convey the same information: a radio language, a technical–medical language, and slang, marked by words such as *crispy critter,* meaning a badly burned patient. He explained the existence of each language functionally, noting that the last, slang, seemed to ease the emotional stress that developed in paramedics as a result of treating seriously injured, often mutilated, accident victims.

In sum, I think that undergraduates can do ethnographic research successfully without knowing much theory, and that research appeals to their sense of discovery and the realization that ethnography can be useful.

A second criticism of teaching through ethnography concerns its practicality. "Ethnography would take too much of my time," several anthropologists have told me. "It might be practical in small classes, but not at my large university."

I have to admit that there is substance to this objection. Having students do ethnography requires more faculty supervision and feedback. It also often results in a paper, and papers are difficult to manage in large classes.

But here, too, there are some strategies for managing the load. One solution is to limit the size of the ethnographic project. For example, anthropologist Michael Coggershall at Clemson University sets small ethnographic tasks, such as having all his students ask student informants about rules for borrowing things. Jack Weatherford at Macalester College has had his students do one interview with a foreign student. In my classes, I urge students to focus on particular social situations or clearly bounded microcultures, and in introductory classes, to limit the size of papers to ten pages.

Time can also be saved by employing labor-saving devices. Fieldwork techniques can be presented to groups by lecture rather than to students individually. Detailed handouts on how to do the research project often save instructor time. So does structuring projects into weekly tasks that can form the basis of student problem-solving sessions. And of course, there are always teaching assistants and preceptors, who, with experience, can help immensely with the teaching load.

Finally, one can offer smaller courses devoted entirely to ethnographic research. These may require more faculty time and involvement, but fewer students make for a manageable work load. Courses, such as ours on ethnographic interviewing, and summer ethnographic field schools take this approach.

A personal note: using these techniques, I cannot claim to have solved all the practical problems associated with teaching student ethnography, but I have managed to send out as many as 100 students to do research in one semester with good results. Paper reading still takes too much time and I still spend more hours working with student ethnographers than I intend to, but I find that the process is so much fun that I don't mind the work.

Finally, several anthropologists have raised the problem of ethics. Can one flood a community with inexperienced ethnographers without running a risk to both informants and students? It is undeniable that ethical risk exists. Indeed, it is present for any ethnographic study no matter how well trained and experienced the anthropologist. But just as professional anthropologists must learn to deal with ethical problems, so can undergraduate students be cautioned to consider these matters.

For example, it is possible to have one's students read the statement of ethical principles and responsibilities adopted by the American Anthropological Association. One can set limitations on what can be studied as I do when I forbid students to study illegal microcultures, or interviewing style when I caution them against falsely identifying themselves or their intentions.

It is also wise to discuss common ethical dilemmas in class and to present examples of ethical problems. For example, you can ask whether students should reveal the identity of their informants. Will revealing cultural data hurt an informant or other members of a microculture? Should ethnographers show their ethnographic papers to their informants? Do informants have the right to edit papers or add to them? Clearly, a certain degree of trust in student judgment is required if one is to send them out to do ethnography, but so far, that trust seems justified by experience.

In conclusion, this paper argues that ethnographic research is a central and unique property of cultural anthropology. It claims that with clear focus and structure (here I describe our use of ethnoscience for this purpose), ethnography can be undertaken by undergraduate students without theoretical training, and they often perceive it to be fun and useful. It may actually be a helpful way to bring students to theory. Although teaching ethnography may place a strain on faculty time, adaptive measures make it practical even for fairly large classes. Similarly, although ethnography always entails ethical risk, such risk may be reduced by openly facing ethical consequences. In short, this paper argues that like chemistry, biology, archaeology, and physical anthropology, cultural anthropology can also involve undergraduate students in research, and that this research can take place in the human laboratory of everyday life.

References

Bernard, H. Russell. 1993. *Research Methods in Cultural Anthropology.* 2d ed. Newbury Park, Ill.: Sage.

Crane, Julia G., and Michael V. Angrosino. 1984. *Field Projects in Anthropology: A Student Handbook*. 2d ed. Prospect Heights, Ill.: Waveland Press.

Kottak, Conrad Phillip, ed. 1982. *Researching American Culture: A Guide for Student Anthropologists*. Ann Arbor: University of Michigan Press.

McCurdy, David W. 1992. "Teaching Ethnographic Interviewing." *Anthro Notes: Natural History Bulletin for Teachers* 14(2):5–8, 14.

Spradley, James P. 1970. *You Owe Yourself Drunk*. Boston: Little, Brown.

———. 1979. *Ethnographic Interviewing*. New York: Holt.

———. 1980. *Participant Observation*. New York: Holt.

Spradley, James P, and David W. McCurdy. [1972] 1988. *The Cultural Experience: Research in Complex Society*. Chicago: SRA. Reprint, Prospect Heights, Ill.: Waveland Press.

Werner, Oswald, and G. Mark Schoepfle. 1987. *Systematic Fieldwork*. 2 vols. Newbury Park, Ill.: Sage.

TEACHING ABOUT
CULTURAL DIVERSITY

Teaching about Cultural Diversity

Jane J. White

Why Study Anthropology?

Anthropologists are unanimous in their claim that the study of anthropology will give college students knowledge and skills useful for solving real-world problems. Thirty years ago, Mandelbaum (1963, 5) argued that

> the student, like all the rest of us, must move in an alien culture from time to time, even if it is only the unfamiliar environment of a new job or neighborhood. His movement will be facilitated and his understanding deepened if he can learn to use the approach of the field anthropologists, looking closely, clearly and dispassionately at what people actually are doing, as well as listening to what they say they are doing and learning what others say about them; gathering his information at first hand, rather than relying exclusively on documents and statistics; taking his leads from what is important to them, the observed, rather than what may be important to the observer; testing his ideas about them within a frame of ideas which has been developed out of a broad spectrum of knowledge about [human]kind, rather than one which pertains to a few cultural settings or a single civilization.

Approaching life as a field-worker, the student will be "alert to multiple potentialities in culture and behavior, ready to see and seize diverse explanatory factors" (Mandelbaum 1963, 5).

In a 1960 survey of the introductory course in anthropology, Bruner and Spindler (1963, 142) concurred that the primary goal was "to enlarge the horizons of undergraduates, to open and broaden young minds." A survey of anthropologists who teach the introductory course concludes that the purpose of the introductory course is to communicate

1. a sense of the wide range and variability of human culture
2. an appreciation of culture as a holistic and integrated system
3. a respect for other ways of life and an understanding of ethnocentrism
4. a perspective on one's own culture and insights into modern life through the application of anthropological concepts
5. an awareness of the continuity of [humans] and culture in long-term evolutionary perspective
6. some conception of anthropology as a discipline

In a similar vein, Margaret Mead asserted that anthropology is "uniquely situated" to help integrate knowledge that has been inadvertently fragmented in the specialization of other disciplines. She maintained that "anthropology will help to bridge the gap between the understanding of the past, the grasp of the present and an ability to deal with the future" as we "search for a new way of educating men and women who can both understand and cope with our intricate, just emerging universe with its tremendous contradictions, discrepancies, potentialities and dangers" (1963, 595).

Many of the same claims are still being made thirty years later. Anthropologists writing today are unanimous that the purpose of teaching anthropology is to enable undergraduate students to better *understand* the human condition (see Kottak, Harris, Embers, Spindlers, Haviland, Breitborde, Borofsky, this volume). Like Mandelbaum (1963), the authors in this volume write about students using anthropology as a way of problem solving (Kottak, Harris, Borofsky, Podolefsky), of explaining (Embers) and of acquiring "analytical and critical habits of mind" (Friedl).

Like the anthropologists writing in *The Teaching of Anthropology* (Mandelbaum, Lasker, and Albert 1963), the authors in the first section of this volume maintain that the study of anthropology can

- "allow Americans to reflect on cultural variation and the plasticity of human nature" (Kottak)
- enable students to "live as informed and responsible citizens of this world" (Harris)
- enable students to "learn what it means to understand in science, what it means to test possible explanations, and why there is always uncertainty in what we think we know" (Ember and Ember)
- "combat the provincialism and ethnocentrism of our introductory students" (Haviland)
- "engage students with significant ideas" (Breitborde)
- "empower students with the tools that will allow them to continue intellectually empowering themselves long after the course is over" (Borofsky)

- "engage students in their own educational experience" (Podolefsky)
- "use ethnography to see other people's points of view more clearly" (McCurdy)

In the second section of this volume, anthropologists further argue that students can use anthropological knowledge to question and critique their own American culture (Spindlers, Friedl, Moses and Mukhopadhyay, Nanda, Foster, Rubin, Heider). Some also maintain that students should learn to challenge the reigning conventional anthropological wisdom (Friedl, Marcus, Nanda, Foster, Rubin, Heider).

We must now investigate whether these claims are rhetorical or real, possibilities or improbabilities. Can a single course really make a difference in a student's life? The purpose of the authors in the second section is to describe how knowledge from an academic discipline can help people function in their everyday world. In this second section, the authors explicitly describe how anthropological courses and/or knowledge can be structured to engage students so that they begin to question taken-for-granted assumptions and concepts. The starting point for these authors begins with the examination of cultural differences.

Starting Where the Students Are: Teaching as Challenging the Known

Each year, teachers of anthropology courses restructure the readings, the assignments, the activities to address in the best way possible the perceived needs of their students. At first glance, the supposedly nonjudgmental and nonevaluative anthropologists/authors in the first two sections of this volume seem to render surprisingly pejorative descriptions of their students. For example, Friedl notes that undergraduate students in introductory courses are often "unsophisticated" and "naive." Nanda finds that students can be "ethnocentric"; Breitborde characterizes them as "unknowingly bound by their own cultural constraints"; and Haviland bluntly describes introductory students as insular, provincial, and functionally illiterate, "'conned' by their own culture into believing a lot of things about themselves and other people that are not necessarily true." Kottak and Friedl also rail against the messages of picturesque but essentially meaningless cultural differences perpetuated by the media and commercial interests.

On second glance, however, it is not the students but the knowledge that the students have *not* acquired as they were enculturated by their family, peers, school, and the larger American society with which anthropologists wish to take issue. Indeed, these authors are showing respect for their students by believing that they will be able to learn about ways of living that are different from their current beliefs and practices. These teachers are willing to challenge and then support their students so they can consider alternative ideas and perhaps change some of their notions about the world. Haviland argues that the purpose of the introductory course is to confront students with "biases, misconceptions and stereotypes of their own culture," to question "progress" and the belief that the "nuclear family" is always the ideal social unit.

The conventional wisdom that students bring with them about who they are and their place in the world has changed over the years (Friedl). Today, anthropology teachers characterize students as assuming that they are constrained within a single culture in a multicultural world (Friedl, Breitborde). One of the primary functions of an anthropology course is to challenge the limited notions of ethnicity that students from both middle-class and ethnic minority backgrounds bring with them. One of the biggest changes in the last thirty years is the dramatic increase in the diversity of college students, in age, ethnicity, race, class, gender, personal experience, and geographical location (Spindlers, Friedl, Moses and Mukhopadhyay, Nanda). In this section, a number of authors describe ways that students can be engaged to rethink their own cultural identities, negotiate across cultural boundaries, and challenge conventional ways of thinking as they establish relationships and construct knowledge in this rapidly changing and interconnected world. But the authors differ in how they think this can be done.

Teaching for Understanding

The Spindlers argue that "the communication that makes a difference is not happening" in many college classrooms. They do not start with anthropological theory because it is "phrased in ways that are entirely out of the cultural framework of undergraduates." Rather than a one-way linear transmission from "the experts," the Spindlers engage the students by "culture shocking" them with foreign sights and behaviors in films that the students must work hard to understand. Even though large numbers of students fill a lecture hall, the Spindlers interact with them by reacting to their written questions, carefully selecting, sequencing, and comparing culture cases so that core concepts and carefully grounded theories of anthropology can be inferred and addressed.

Like the Spindlers, Friedl also talks about how the students initially undergo confusion when they are challenged with interpreting photographs from other cultures. She too finds that students initially are confused by their confusion, not understanding that they "never see with pristine eyes."

The article by Moses and Mukhopadhyay is pivotal in this section. Like the Spindlers and Friedl, Moses and Mukhopadhyay contend that the most useful knowledge and skills they can impart are those that enable their students to overcome cultural bias. They do this by

- promoting the idea that "identity" and "self-awareness" are culturally constructed

- promoting the use of anthropological theory and cross-cultural data to explain culturally biased behavior at home and abroad

- establishing a cultural context in which to understand values

Moses and Mukhopadhyay unabashedly use the core concept of culture to help their students talk and read their way into understanding their own multicultural university setting through a series of thoughtful and lively exercises and questions for discussion.

The Moses and Mukhopadhyay article also begins to address directly concerns that are confronted in the subsequent articles: problems of representation and problems with the use of the concept of culture. Arguing that students arrive on a university campus with a "narrow" definition of self, students are asked to locate themselves in their own networks of cultural and ethnic groups, to analyze everyday situations that may seemed biased, and to develop ways "to look for individual not group representations."

Marcus clearly explains how the postmodern debate and critique that arose in the 1980s affected both the theory and practice of anthropology as a discipline. Arising out of literary studies that questioned how cultures, societies, institutions, and individuals should be written about, the postmodern condition, says Marcus, has "transformed both the objects of anthropological inquiry and anthropologists' own sense of their practices, their professional constituencies, and to whom the knowledge they produce is addressed." Marcus illustrates how central concepts of the discipline, such as primitive and contemporary, no longer capture the reality of who we are "as observers and who the peoples are we have observed." Marcus challenges all anthropologists and their students to rethink how we represent the differences that we and our students are trying to understand.

In "Close Encounters of the Third Kind," Nanda discusses teaching cultural anthropology as cultural critique. With her many years of experience teaching diverse, nontraditional students "whose backgrounds do not make them less ethnocentric," she presents the contemporary dominant American culture "as just one of the many alternatives in the world past and present." She argues that the contemporary dominant American culture, like all cultures, "is humanly constructed; thus it can be humanly changed." Nanda details a series of readings and activities that enable students to "look more carefully at central and taken-for-granted values, ideas, and institutions of our culture, such as race, gender, class, ethnicity, individualism, patriarchy, nationalism, work . . . and others." She selects readings and activities with special attention to the "role of unequal power as it shapes cross-cultural encounters." She lists provocative readings, often presenting discrepant events or coming from the margins of the American culture, that enable students to see our culture from the outside and/or to identify with other people's culture from the inside.

Foster continues the postmodern focus in looking at encounters in terms of power and race. Based on the premise that "teachers teach more than their subject; they also teach themselves," Foster describes who she is, an African American woman professor, and tells about her first nonencounters and encounters with institutional and individual racism, the settings in which she has taught, and how she challenges racism in her teaching by actively engaging students in their own learning.

Just as Foster worked with concepts of power and racism, Rubin describes the "transformative rethinking of anthropological approaches to the question of gender." She suggests that much of the work to be done is corrective: reinterpreting the body of knowledge already accumulated in anthropology. Rather than using the false generic of "man" and assuming that there is a universal nature of women, Rubin contends that differences in gender relationships should be studied in domains such as language, ritual, economics, politics, and religion.

The article by Heider that concludes this section again reflects the changes in anthropological thinking in these postmodern times. Heider describes changes that have occurred in "visual aids" from the few anthropological films available in 1954 such as *Nanook* or those made by Mead and Bateson to the thousands of films and videos available today. He describes the change from the "omnipotent narrator's voice" to the technical advance of synchronized sound "which allowed people's own voices to be heard." Heider is enthusiastic about the new technology of videotape, which can capture the same information as film now for a fraction of the cost.

Conclusion

Since the 1963 publication of *The Teaching of Anthropology*, much has changed: both the composition of the student body and their underlying assumptions about themselves, their society, and the world; the accumulated knowledge of anthropology and underlying assumptions about how to represent and use it. Even our taken-for-granted beliefs about what are real-world problems and how they should be addressed have altered. Diversity in potential teaching technologies—laser discs, CD-ROMS, e-mail, and computer applications that integrate sound, video images, and text as well as the rapid expansion of teaching materials from journals to videos—has also made selection of content and process more difficult for the instructors of introductory anthropology courses. Even as current students "surf" through new software packages, anthropologists should still be able to use carefully sequenced combinations of "classic" slides, films, and/or ethnographic texts to have students confront the "alienness" of other cultures. As well as conducting small field studies, students should actively be engaged in listening to voices of peoples who used to be marginalized in our society. Students should be invited to join discussions of local, contemporary, multicultural issues and be put in classroom situations where they may explore what it is like to be an outsider trying to "make it" in an alien dominant culture. Thus, the teaching of anthropology has moved from Mandelbaum's concern for students who moved "from time to time" in an "alien culture" (Mandelbaum 1963, 5) to helping undergraduates see multiple potentialities for action within "our intricate, just emerging universe with its tremendous contradictions, discrepancies, potentialities and dangers" (Mead 1963, 595).

As we approach the twenty-first century, Podolefsky reminds us that "we will no longer be able to use linear models of instruction in a random access world." But whether we use e-mail or office hours, seminar discussions or large lecture halls wired for sound, it is crucial for us to understand that we must engage and struggle with our students if they are to understand their options in their local and global world. Rather than merely packaging anthropological knowledge so that it is readily accessible, the anthropologists in this section have chosen to engage students in "disquieting activities and ideas" so they will learn new perspectives.

References

Bruner, Edward M., and Spindler, George D. 1963. "The Introductory Course in Cultural Anthropology." In *The Teaching of Anthropology*, edited by David G. Mandelbaum, Gabriel Lasker, and Ethel M. Albert, 141–152. Berkeley: University of California Press.

Mandelbaum, David G. 1963. "The Transmission of Anthropological Culture." In *The Teaching of Anthropology*, edited by David G. Mandelbaum, Gabriel Lasker, and Ethel M. Albert, 1–21. Berkeley: University of California Press.

Mandelbaum, David, Gabriel Lasker, and Ethel M. Albert, eds. 1963. *The Teaching of Anthropology*. Berkeley: University of California Press.

Mead, Margaret. 1963. "Anthropology and an Education for the Future." In *The Teaching of Anthropology*, edited by David G. Mandelbaum, Gabriel Lasker, and Ethel M. Albert, 595–607. Berkeley: University of California Press.

Teaching Culture Using "Culture Cases"

GEORGE SPINDLER AND LOUISE SPINDLER

We have taught introductory anthropology to about 14,000 students during the past forty years, introducing them to anthropology and culture as we conceive of it. We use "culture cases" as the vehicle for teaching and learning about culture at many levels, including the introductory course. To make the use of case materials understandable, we need to declare where we stand on larger matters concerning the purpose of doing anthropology and of doing education.

We believe the purpose of anthropology is education in the broadest sense. Anthropologists do research on diverse lifeways to better understand the human condition and to communicate that understanding to the public. This understanding is constantly enlarging and modifying. The processes of education are likewise changing. We live, study, and teach in a state of flux, but strive for continuity.

This position demands that anthropologists face their primary obligation of educating. We research, analyze, and spin webs of explanation to have something to say that will be worth communicating to others. But as college and university faculty, our pressing obligation is to teach, and the primary focus of that teaching is the undergraduates, the young males and females who will be the educated men and women of our consensual republic (and who will ultimately determine whether there is an anthropology). All the other activities of faculty are subsidiary to that obligation, including graduate training and research. Graduate training and research are not unimportant, however, because communicating, that is, teaching, is a product of research, and who does the teaching is a product of graduate training.

What, of achieved knowledge, is worth communicating to undergraduates? Some anthropologists think theory should be the focus. The trouble with theory is that it is necessarily phrased in ways that are entirely out of the cultural framework of undergraduates. Theories are also inevitably precious, known to and circulated within small, esoteric, professional cliques. When theories become more widely recognized, they do not last very long. Witness the waves of theory such as structuralism and ethnoscience that have swept over anthropology and subsequently almost disappeared. Theories matter to anthropologists, but they must be translated and they must be widely applicable to understandable problems in human life to make a difference in undergraduate education. Usually they are not, and in introductory courses dominated by theory, students are left puzzled and often hostile. The communication that makes a difference is not happening. It is our conviction that theories decontextualized from cultures should not be taught in undergraduate, beginning anthropology courses.

We use culture cases because they are intrinsically interesting to nearly everyone and because they can demonstrate the diversity and commonality of human lifeways on our little planet. Almost all freshmen need more of what these lessons have to teach. Most come from culturally limited backgrounds, particularly the sons and daughters of middle-class Americans. Ethnic minority students also bring their identities to school with them, but they are likely to have had some significant and personally meaningful experience cross-culturally in American society, much of it negative. Well-constructed culture case studies of diverse peoples and places challenge narrow personal persuasions issuing from a firm foundation of class and ethnic prejudice.

Culture cases do not come ready-made out of diversity. Behavior and sentiment must be observed, recorded, and interpreted. Behavior that is understandable in a setting foreign to the reader must be made understandable in that of the reader in order to be communicated. The processes involved are so subtle and complex that some instructors have given up, or strain observations through theory, leaving the observations unrecognizable and often quite irrelevant to the enhanced understanding of human behavior.

A useful culture case is close to the behavioral ground, observed and reported by trained observers who can acknowledge cultural and conceptual bias but not allow that bias to bend observation totally out of shape and who see themselves as part of the phenomenon being studied and interpreted. Reflexive ethnography is essential to useful culture cases; it always has been, but now we have a name for it.

There are other criteria for good ethnography and useful culture cases to be used in teaching, and we have developed a list of specific features of a "good ethnography" (Spindler and Spindler 1992). We have tried to apply relevant criteria in our selection and editorial development of the case studies in our series, Case Studies in Cultural Anthropology, but of course there are hundreds of culture case studies not in this series that exhibit the characteristics of a "good ethnography."

Culture cases are at the core of cultural anthropology and the starting point of what we teach in all undergraduate courses. All the lessons to be learned from comprehending the diversity of human behavior as well as its comforting commonality are derived from culture cases—not directly from theories of human behavior but from human behavior interpreted judiciously in the conceptual framework of anthropology and related disciplines.

There is more to anthropology that should be taught to undergraduates than cultural diversity and commonality. In addition are concepts, analytic procedures, and yes, theory. But culture cases can be used as springboards to these matters. Concepts, analysis, and theory grounded on case studies can be communicated effectively.

Teaching the Course

During the 1950s, we used, among other readings, Ruth Benedict's *Patterns of Culture* and Margaret Mead's *Coming of Age in Samoa*, and sometimes *Sex and Temperament.* There were solid ethnographies available and some classic ones as well, but often for undergraduates, they killed rather than generated interest.

At one time, we used Walter Goldschmidt's record album "Ways of Mankind." We can still hear Talestyva's soft, Spanish-accented voice in *Desert Soliloquy,* telling us that a lot of things made him happy as a child in the pueblo. The voice was that of a professional actor but the cultural materials were carefully worked out. We played those records in a hall seating over 700 students and everyone listened with rapt attention.

And we used films. One of them we still use: *Churinga,* with C. P. Mountford's "imperialist colonialism" as well as his humanity coming through, and the scenes of digging for honey ants and witchety grubs and increasing kangaroos through ritual. Brief glimpses of the Churinga open the door to the wondrous world of Arunta cosmology.

In the mid-fifties it was daring to use films, or at least to use films that were even mildly interesting. Today, we use ten films, one each week of the quarter, and require the reading of four case studies as well as various other readings. We lecture on the emergence of culture from a primate base, kinship, rites of passage, early childhood, cultural transmission, demography and subsistence, gender identities and their construction, warfare and the regulation of violence, the moral equivalent of war, "normal" and "abnormal" seen cross-culturally, colonialism, and social and cultural adaptation.

Culture cases are our foundation, springboard, trampoline, and support system. Without culture cases, we would not know how to teach. We start with cultures; we interpret and generalize from cultures; and we critique Western culture in this framework. We call this the inductive method, though at times we turn to deduction. But we start with cultures.

Lectures are not limited by or to case studies; rather, case studies serve as points of departure and as ready sources of examples and illustrations already shared, through readings and films, with the students. For example, the discussion of kinship and social organization starts with the central and western desert aborigines of Australia (Arunta and Mardu). As students have already read Tonkinson's *The Mardu* (1991), we have some confidence that certain particulars of kinship are already shared. Relationships among subsistence techniques, environment, demographics, and possible sociopolitical consequences are then compared to the Dani of the New Guinea Highlands (Heider 1991). The Hutterites and Amish (Hostetler and Huntington 1980, 1992) are used as stabilized, institutionalized, socioreligious movements. The Hutterites and Amish illustrate boundary maintenance and symbolic representation of identity and its reinforcement through cultural transmission. The Yanomamo (Chagnon 1992) along with the particularly rich film resources are used to demonstrate the genesis of control of aggression, and the Sambia (Herdt 1986) are used as a springboard for discussion of homosexuality cross-culturally. This allows students to reflect upon the problem of gender identity in their own society, particularly the extreme polarization of this identity in American culture. The Bateson and Mead films of the Balinese are used to challenge complacency about cultural interpretation, as interpretations of the Balinese contain remarkable contradictions. The case study on the Menominee (Spindler and Spindler 1984), accompanied by slides that we have taken in the field, is used as the beginning of a discussion on adaptation to catastrophic change, exploitation, and deprivation, and the psychological concomitants of that adaptation.

By using this culture case approach, we weave our way through the major problems and processes of human existence with concepts, grounded theory, and contemporary scholarship in anthropology, with some cross-disciplinary excursions, but always with reference to known, communicated culture cases. No generalizations are made without such reference. And as often as possible and reasonable, comparative references are made to our own habitat, the United States, and the problems of subsistence, sexual politics, religion, social life, and education that students face in their daily lives.

Each culture case leads into certain topics and each topic leads to exploitation of certain, or all, cases. The course proceeds through the academic quarter with a constant movement into and out of, and often back into, culture cases and topics.

The Case Study Series

In 1960, we published our first six case studies in cultural anthropology with Holt, Rinehart and Winston: *Being a Paluan* (Barnett), *Bunyoro* (Beattie), *The Tiwi* (Hart, Pilling, and Goodale), *The Cheyennes* (Hoebel), and *Tepoztlan* (Lewis); *Vasilika* (Friedl) followed shortly. These originals are still all in print. Since then, more than 150 case studies have been published with 56 currently in print, and many of those out of print having been reissued by Waveland Press.

For many teachers, the most useful case studies for instructional purposes are those that can be combined with films. The Dani, Yanomamo, Hutterite, and the Mardudjara case studies are good examples.

In 1968–69, we began badgering some of our colleagues to describe their personal experiences, their feelings, and their personal interaction with the "natives," and join this with the procedural hardware of their fieldwork. *Being an Anthropologist*, first published in 1970, was the result. The chapters in this volume have also been combined with the case studies to which they are relevant.

It is interesting that none of the critics of ethnographic writing mention the undergraduate reader. Specific mention is given to writing for colleagues and for that elusive multitude, the educated lay public, but not for undergraduates. And yet the largest, and potentially most important, readership for anthropology is the undergraduate readership. Although there is little point in trying to make them into anthropologists, we do want to make them into citizens who will think "anthropologically" about cultural differences, multiculturalism, ethnicity, imperialism, and oppression.

Conclusions

The position taken here, that the primary purpose of anthropology is education, will not be popular or even taken seriously in many quarters of the academy. We faculty are so puffed up with the self-created importance of research and theory building that we often do not see the imperatives of our call to duty. Graduate students are taught as part of an undeclared agenda that teaching is a necessary evil, to be dispatched efficiently but not with dedication and passion, so that one can turn to the real work of writing articles and books for whatever clique is regarded as the significant readership at the time. Young faculty close their doors and minds to undergraduates, for they do not offer tenure; in fact, excessive attention to them and their needs may obstruct the path to promotion and tenure. A joke going around in academic circles is that junior faculty pray that they won't get a teaching award before they achieve tenure. Heavy enrollments in classes are unwelcome as this may be seen as the result of "playing to the students" or a reputation for "easy" courses. Senior professors become so detached from teaching and the classroom that they become unavailable to even their younger colleagues, and some buy their way out of teaching with research funds so they can spend their time largely, or exclusively, on research. There are many faculty and departments to which these rather negative characterizations do not apply, but there are serious tendencies in these directions in too many colleges and universities.

APPENDIX
Commentaries: A Technique for Increasing Communication

Here, I discuss a technique that I developed for use in smaller classes. The commentary technique enhances communication with students from a wide variety of social and cultural backgrounds. Students are instructed to ask questions about the material, express their feelings of objection and agreement, and critique the material read from a personal experience point of view. The material is often a case study or short ethnographic piece about some distinctive culture. To avoid stage fright, which most students suffer, they put the critique into written form and submit it for review. Certain critiques are selected for discussion, and this becomes a basis for a part of the instructional period.

These are not "critical reviews" in the usual sense. The beginning student does not have enough background for this. It is the *reactive* aspect that reinforces the validity of the students' personal experience and observation. Many students have an ethnic background or come from rural areas and experience a form of culture shock in college or university settings. They do not understand their own confusion. And they often ask questions of their material, as read or heard in class, that add a fresh new dimension.

The commentaries permit a movement, in some degree, into the student's world. So often we teach as though students had no thoughts or feelings of their own and have only to accept and even internalize ours in order to learn.

References

Barnett, Homer. 1979. *Being a Paluan*. Fieldwork ed. New York: Holt, Rinehart and Winston.

Bateson, Gregory, and Margaret Mead. 1939. *Trance and Dance in Bali. Character Formation in Different Cultures*. New York: New York University Film Library.

———, and Margaret Mead. 1939. *A Balinese Family*. New York: New York University Film Library.

Beattie, John. 1960. *Bunyoro: An African Kingdom*. New York: Holt, Rinehart and Winston.

Benedict, Ruth. 1934. *Patterns of Culture*. Boston, Mass.: Houghton, Mifflin.

Chagnon, Napoleon. 1992. *Yanomamo*. 4th ed. Fort Worth, Tex.: Harcourt Brace.

Friedl, Ernestine. 1962. *Vasilika: A Village in Modern Greece*. New York: Holt, Rinehart and Winston.

Hart, C. W. M., Arnold Pilling, and Jane Goodale. 1988. *The Tiwi of North Australia*. 3rd ed. New York: Holt, Rinehart and Winston.

Heider, Karl. 1991. *Grand Valley Dani: Peaceful Warriors*. 2d ed. Fort Worth: Harcourt Brace.

Herdt, Gilbert. 1986. *The Sambia: Ritual and Gender in New Guinea*. Fort Worth, Tex.: Harcourt Brace.

Hoebel, E. Adamson. 1977. *The Cheyennes*. 2nd ed. New York: Holt, Rinehart and Winston.

Hostetler, John, and Gertrude Huntington. 1980. *The Hutterites of North America*. Fieldwork ed. Fort Worth, Tex.: Harcourt, Brace, Jovanovich.

———, and Gertrude Huntington. 1992. *Amish Children*. 2d ed. Fort Worth, Tex.: Harcourt Brace.

Lewis, Oscar. 1960. *Tepoztlan: Village in Mexico*. New York: Holt, Rinehart and Winston.

Mead, Margaret. [1928] 1961. *Coming of Age in Samoa*. Apollo Editions. New York: William Morrow.

———. [1935] 1963. *Sex and Temperament in Three Primitive Societies*. Apollo Editions. New York: William Morrow.

Spindler, George D., ed. [1970] 1986. *Being an Anthropologist: Fieldwork in Eleven Cultures*. Reprint, Prospect Heights, Ill.: Waveland Press.

Spindler, George, and Louise Spindler. 1984. *Dreamers with Power: The Menominee*. Prospect Heights, Ill.: Waveland Press.

———, and Louise Spindler. 1992. *Cultural Process and Ethnography*. In *The Handbook of Qualitative Research in Education*, edited by Margaret LeCompte, Wendy Millroy, and Judith Preissle, 53–92. San Diego: Academic Press.

Tonkinson, Robert. 1991. *The Mardu: Living the Dream in Australia's Desert*. 2d ed. Fort Worth, Tex.: Harcourt, Brace, Jovanovich.

Fifty Years of Teaching Cultural Anthropology

Ernestine Friedl

Someone has said that teaching, like preaching, may be described as throwing a large pail of water over a stand of narrow-necked bottles. You hope that some of the water will get into some of the bottles. In one sense, this is a true description, but more profoundly, it is not. For bottles are rigid, stay in one place, and are unresponsive. The necks of students vary in size, their bottles vary in age and capacity, they do not stand still, and they talk back. Nor are they ever empty to start with. What fills students' minds, the unsophisticated questions of naive undergraduates and the critical energy of graduate students, is a constant stimulus to our renewal as teachers. It is also the base on which the content of our anthropology courses should be built.

My realization of the importance for teaching of what is in students' minds—of their conceptions of themselves and of their relation to the world in which they live—came only after many years of watching student generations change. To convey what I wanted students to learn about anthropology and what I hoped they would remember long after they finished college, I discovered it was necessary to know, in the parlance of our day, "where they were coming from."

I wanted to imbue all undergraduates with my own fascination with studying humankind in all ages, times, and places; to see them develop respect for the methods and findings of the discipline; and to hope that a few might be inspired to devote their lives to anthropology. (Academics do like to clone themselves.) Another equally important aim was to help students, future anthropologists or not, acquire analytical and critical habits of mind. In this endeavor, anthropology, a quintessentially liberal arts subject, needs to join with other disciplines to enhance a good liberal arts education.

In the United States, in my view, a liberal arts education has the mission of helping students first to learn academic and intellectual received wisdom and then to challenge it. It is equally important to provide contrasts, historical and contemporary, with the ideas, values, and common parlance of the immediate present. A college education should enhance perspectives on the contemporary world and show that what students take for granted is not taken for granted in their own communities and certainly not in the rest of the world. Students should discover that the current conceptions of received wisdom, either intellectual or popular, have not always been canonical. They should also discover that they are not always aware of many patterns of their own culture, even though the patterns govern their actions.

The question is what kind of course content and teaching techniques might accomplish such a laudable mission. Success in conveying perspective and contrast depends on the sense of what students' knowledge, beliefs, and life experiences are. The views of late adolescent and young adults, and certainly of the mature adults attending colleges, keep changing as world political and economic events and cultural fashions affect the social contexts in which they live. The forties were not like the fifties or the sixties, nor were the seventies like the eighties. In the meantime, what anthropologists teach is influenced by the changing values, attitudes, and intellectual positioning of the discipline. It is this subject I shall turn to first.

When I began teaching, a half century ago, the one semester introductory course included paleontology and physical (biological) anthropology, archaeology, linguistics, and cultural-social anthropology. The unifying theme was the concept of evolution: the evolution of humankind physically and culturally. To reconstruct that kind of history and to account for both the similarities and variations in the practices and beliefs of peoples in contemporary human societies required integration of knowledge from the four fields. There was an intellectual question driving the evolutionary paradigm: what is the *nature* of human nature? My students memorized a considerable amount of information about fossil hominids, stone tool traditions, language families, and marriage and kinship systems. They learned some geography; they could locate the societies we studied on the map. Such a curriculum kept anthropolgists alert to developments in all four fields. At my doctoral prelims I was asked about the 1940s version of the controversy over the origin and relation of the Neandertals to Homo sapiens. After the exam, one of the examiners commented on how well I seemed to understand that question even though I was a cultural anthropologist. I thanked him but did not mention that by then I had taught fossil hominids to at least ten college classes. To introduce them to cultural variation, students were required to read one entire "classic" monograph such as Malinowski's *Argonauts!*

An evolutionary approach led to the major finding that different ways of life, varied cultures, and social systems were not the end product of single determinisms like biology, immutable tradition, or simple chance. Nor was variation in intelligence among populations a force driving history. Rather, each culture and society was a consequence of interrelations among ecological, economic, political, historical, and cultural events. These forces are in a constant state of change, sometimes slow, sometimes fast. Explanation of change was what I thought anthropology was about and explanation required comparative study.

Students were not going to remember nor were they expected to retain all the details of such diverse material for the rest of their lives. In addition to the concept of evolution as a key to my intellectual stance, however, was a conviction that anthropological findings not only contribute to knowledge but also influence attitudes and behavior. I went into anthropology at a time when fascist racist dogmas and Stalinist communism were strong and gaining influence in the world at large. The realization that categories of race as we knew them were not based exclusively on physical variation but were constructed differently in different cultural and political settings could, I thought, contribute to better race relations. Studying people in their own terms not in "ours," whoever "we" and "they" might be, could create better understandings of "others." Relativity in this sense, as a strategy for learning about ourselves and others, is a significant method of scholarly inquiry. Further, once students became aware of the intellectual and linguistic sophistication of even the technologically simplest societies, and the complex history that led to their (and our) current state, they would surely gain respect for people everywhere.

In the course of fifty years, anthropology has gone through many permutations. Theoretical positions—from evolution to functionalism, to structuralism, to political economy, to poststructuralism, to ethnography as a literary and aesthetic pursuit—wax and wane and wax again. Cultural theory as developed by literary scholars and popular culture studied by all manner of academics have added new problems for anthropologists. Issues of race and culture (and gender) in the guise of ethnicity and nationalism are back in the limelight, and anthropologists have added the study of Europe and their own European-derived cultures to the roster of their ethnographic and theoretical interests. My teaching has been based on functionalism, political economy, and the study of Europe with selected examples of other approaches. But all teachers, I believe, are obligated in both beginning and advanced courses to discuss the importance of different intellectual positions for the accumulation of knowledge, and to make explicit what they have selected from the intellectual possibilities for their teaching. For my generation it is embarrassing to discuss in class personal details of social position and ethnicity, but it may be necessary.

Among students, two changes in point of view have become important for teaching. Visual images as a means of learning have become prominent if not predominant to this generation. More startling still have been the shifts in basic assumptions about the relations between individuals and society, between themselves and the social contexts in which they live. The effort to give contrast and perspective on the perception of visual cues and the issue of the students situating themselves in a social context are discussed next.

Students have a deeply held folk belief "that one picture is worth a thousand words." In the seventies and eighties they became convinced that they could learn from visual images what is "real." What they see on television—and incidentally, on films in our classrooms—they assume gives them more direct access to information than print. To balance that view, I developed exercises in "seeing." The first day of class (before introducing myself and before handing out the syllabus), I showed the students ten slides from the Greek village I had studied. Each slide was on the screen for two minutes and they were asked to write down only what they *saw*. They were not told where, when, or by whom the pictures had been taken. The analysis of the results revealed a number of surprises. The slides were in color but only two students in a class of fifty mentioned color. The people were described as poor and hard-working. Yet there was not one single slide showing anybody working. A display of dowry linens with several girls standing behind it was described as Mexicans selling textiles in the market. There were no price tags in evidence. A picture of a street with just one or two people visible at a distance was thought to be a deserted village. It was the siesta hour. The only slide for which they actually resorted to depicting what they saw was a photograph looking down at a Turkish-style latrine. They said it was a semicircular something with ridges in it. When we reviewed the results, the point of the lesson was that we never see with pristine eyes; there is always selective perception and interpretation in terms of each person's culture and experience. I did not want to leave them with the sense that all images were suspect, but rather that for informed understanding it is necessary to analyze the cultural assumptions and overt principles of the producers of photographs and films. It is equally important for each of us to examine critically the way our social and personal experiences influence our own perceptions of the content and meaning of images.

Far more surprising than the preconceptions influencing what they saw was the class's reaction to the exercise. Many of them thought they had been made to look foolish and stupid even though there were no grades and the exercise had been handed in anonymously. I tried to reassure them, with less success than I would have liked, that they were neither foolish nor stupid but were merely doing what we all do; we see through the screens of our individual social placement and individual knowledge and experience. For so deeply held a folk belief as "seeing is believing" to be challenged simply unnerved them.

A second exercise in observation also brought its surprises. It was basketball season and, Duke basketball being triumphant at the time, it was possible to ask the students to watch a game on television. They were to record every instance they could of players touching each other. They chose a remarkable array of categories to observe and record. Some described touching as the pushing and shoving that were part of the physicality of the game. Others noted only fouls that involved touching, or the "high" fives for encouragement, or the hugging and slapping the rump for camaraderie and support, and some noticed the floor zones in which touching took place. My point to the students was that there is no explicit and conscious cultural patterning for touching in basketball; it is not in manuals nor do sports announcers mention it unless it is in violation of the rules. That leaves observers like themselves with no guides to what to look for, so they are free to make their own selections and see what interests them. The result is a greater variety of bases for observation than exist for programmed cultural forms. The exercise was also a demonstration of patterned cultural behavior, largely out of the awareness of the athletes who participated.

For me, however, the most important changes in students' minds over the years have been the changes in how students situate themselves in the social contexts in which they live. In the 1940s and into the 1950s, from classroom discussions, assigned papers, and private conversations, it was clear that the students' basic assumption was that economic and political forces, far more powerful than they, influenced their lives. They did not need Foucault to convince them of the pervasiveness of power. They felt there was little they could do, as mere individuals, to control their own fates. Some had been adolescents during the Depression; later they had lived through the Second World War and had observed the repressions of fascism and communism, followed by the passivity of the fifties. These powerful forces were overwhelming. To suggest a contrasting view, I emphasized situations in which individual striving, in spite of community pressures, made a difference. Fortunately, I had done fieldwork and historical studies of the Chippewas of Wisconsin, so I had firsthand knowledge of people whose individualism triumphed, at least for a while, over colonial forces.

By the end of the sixties and through the seventies and eighties, the zeitgeist of the United States and of college-age students had shifted from a sense of helplessness to a sense of being all-powerful. Students were seeing themselves as individuals situated in no social context at all. They thought that whatever they had accomplished or would accomplish was dependent only on their own abilities. Young women thought the gender revolution was complete and they could succeed without support from others; affluent students had little recognition of the advantages their parents had provided them; African American students were beginning to resent affirmative action programs. It was as if the community, the social world, was not there. They were living in individual bubbles like children who have no immunity to disease. They knew phrases like the baby-boomers, the Vietnam generation, and the flower children of the sixties, but they did not believe the demographic, political, economic, or cultural conditions applied to them. They were not aware that such contexts provided contraints and opportunities that influenced, although they did not fully control, their fates or anyone else's. In the universities where I was teaching, there were, until the late eighties, too few African American anthropology students to convey the force of racism, and many of those who were there were not talking about it.

To balance that outlook, to provide contrast, I chose to highlight cultures that would show the constraints under which people's lives developed. Greek rural society, where I had done fieldwork, and peasant cases in general were sources of excellent examples. Greek ideology stresses a heroic concept of the individual, yet even the Greeks I knew were not totally aware of limitations on their freedoms. A first-rate film on a Cypriot rural community made by Peter Loizos called *Life Chances* showed the fates of each child in a family of five children. Women had to have dowries to marry and much of the wealth was provided by their fathers and brothers. The more daughters they had, the harder the men had to work. By the end of the film, the students could see that the combined effects of the ratio of boys to girls in a family, the size of their landholdings, the increase in dowry expectations over the years, the differential opportunities for education as each child grew up, the conditions of national politics and economy, and to be sure, variation in individual effort and talent all contributed to the social and economic condition reached by each of the children as adults—and the fate of each was different from that of the others.

Another useful teaching device was a role-playing peasant game. Students chose a family role. They were then asked to apply what they knew about the economics, social structure, and culture in the society to negotiate marriage transactions among themselves in their assigned roles. They came straight up against the constraints and freedoms influencing the outcome of the people whose roles they were playing. To be sure, the more skillful and smarter negotiators made the best of their situations, but they could not go beyond the opportunities their circumstances permitted.

In the 1990s, because I no longer teach, what I read in the student newspapers, the public press, and the *Chronicle of Higher Education* has to suffice for my impression of students' basic assumptions. I hazard a guess that our students do not view the individual person as constrained primarily by economic and political forces, as they did in the forties, nor as rootless individuals. They feel they are already bound, or are forced to be bound, or want to be bound in a "culture," in a multicultural world. Instead of the individual bubble, they are embalming themselves in different cultural fluids that they think do not intermingle, and indeed are antithetical to each other.

The needed contrast and perspective for anthropologists to stress is the evidence supporting the unity of humankind as a species and the human capacity to negotiate across different and diverse cultures, even as those practicing each culture try to overcome inequalities and are in competition for power.

The major theme of this chapter has been that for successful learning and teaching, one must take into account how, in the course of years, student generations and faculty develop different intellectual and emotional baggage. *Students* and *faculty* have been used as if they were homogenous entities. This is manifestly not the case. Both groups vary with respect to class, race, gender, age, ethnic history, geographical provenience, and life experiences. That makes the task of ferreting out what influences the perceptions of students and of ourselves as teachers difficult but all the more important. Without the attempt to do so, anthropologists will not be able to convey the dimensions and the fascination of our discipline, nor contribute to the efficacy of a liberal arts education, nor provide an intellectual base for mutual understanding among peoples of the world.

Using Anthropology
to Understand and
Overcome Cultural Bias

YOLANDA T. MOSES AND CAROL C. MUKHOPADHYAY

Not unlike our society as a whole, university campuses are struggling with the issue of how to build communities that promote multiculturalism, cultural pluralism, and cultural diversity. All these terms, although rooted in an anthropological tradition, have been "borrowed" for use by other disciplines and audiences. It is time that we as anthropologists reclaim and make explicit these concepts by what we teach in our introductory classes. We should let students know that what they learn in our classes will be helpful in preparing them to live and work with people from diverse ethnic, gender, and cultural communities. Even in classrooms that look homogeneous it is important for students to develop the perspectives, skills, and knowledge that will prepare them to live in, work in, and contribute to a society that is increasingly multicultural and global. We as enlightened anthropologists take it for granted that what we teach will automatically be incorporated by our students for their use, forgetting that the majority of them have not been exposed to anthropology as a field of study prior to coming to college.

In addition, for many of our beginning students, being on a college campus is the first time they have had prolonged contact with students from other ethnic, cultural, and religious groups as well as with students who are gay, lesbian, or bisexual. As practicing anthropologists and teachers for over eighteen years each—and in the case of one co-author, an academic administrator for over ten years—we are convinced that many of our students do not bring to the university/college the skills necessary to understand or to overcome the kinds of cultural biases they will experience on their campuses or in their communities.

This chapter offers approaches and suggestions that can guide faculty to help students enjoy their university experience by encouraging them to be open to new ideas and points of view on what it means to value cultural pluralism and cultural diversity. The first part of the essay suggests how the introductory cultural anthropology class can be taught more effectively; the second part describes how anthropological concepts can be integrated into freshman seminars or orientation programs.

The Introductory Cultural Anthropology Course

The majority of people in our classes for the past eighteen years have not been anthropology majors. For one of us at a public polytechnic university, the students were engineering, architecture, science, and business majors who would have careers as professionals in those fields. Many of the other co-author's students were preparing to become elementary or secondary school teachers. Our approach to teaching developed out of our need to give students knowledge and skills that would be useful for them in whatever profession they wanted to pursue. So it was important not to teach the book from cover to cover but to develop a set of specific competencies and skills, including critical writing skills and values clarification skills, that would help students negotiate the various cross-cultural experiences they would have during their university years, in their professional lives, and as productive citizens.

In this section of the chapter we focus on three areas of development important to students if they are to understand and overcome cultural bias:

1. Understanding themselves in the context of their own personal and cultural identities, knowing their various roles in the university/college context, and in the larger outside world. Students should learn that they are "multicultural persons."

2. Exploring, understanding, assimilating, and using the various theories, facts, and cross-cultural perspectives of cultural anthropology to answer the cultural bias issues that may face them in their everyday lives. Among the current "hot topics" are bigotry on campus, deteriorating race relations in this country and abroad, homophobia, religious intolerance, institutionalized sexism, racism, and the persistence of poverty in our overall affluent society.

3. Clarifying their values (at least the ones they bring to campus with them) so they can see their "worldview" in relationship to other worldviews. This does not mean that we set out to *change* those values, but we do try to get students to recognize *why* and *how* these values shape the way they see different issues. We want students to acknowledge the legitimacy of other points of view. We want them to develop *tolerance,* and ultimately the desire to live in and contribute to a culturally pluralistic world.

Developing Cross-Cultural Competencies in the Cultural Anthropology Course

What concepts does cultural anthropology offer that first- and second-year students need to know if they are to gain the basic skills to understand and overcome cultural bias? We have found that the concepts of culture, ethnocentrism, cultural relativity, and application of the research methodologies of anthropology (such as ethnography and fieldwork) are the core concepts that we teach. Students come to understand that cultural behaviors are learned, are not immutable, and can therefore be changed. Students learn that ethnocentrism and cultural relativity are the two ends of the continuum of cultural responsiveness to "others," to outside stimuli, and to threats. Students also learn that the methodology of anthropology allows them personally to move beyond generalizations about "other people" and to explore in a firsthand way (through fieldwork) what it is like to "walk in another person's shoes." Our first goal is to help students realize (1) that "identity" and "self-awareness" are culturally constructed; (2) that anthropological theory and cross-cultural data can be used to explain culturally biased behavior at home and abroad; and (3) that students can establish a cultural context in which to understand values. Our second goal is to help students develop the competencies that will allow them to apply their new knowledge in their lives.

Identity and Self-Awareness: The Multicultural Self: The first area that students should explore is their own identity and self-awareness in a multicultural context. Anthropologists have had a lot to say about the subject of identity. These works range from Margaret Mead's classic *Coming of Age in Samoa* ([1928] 1961) to Ruth Benedict's *Patterns of Culture* ([1934] 1959) and her book about Japanese national character, *The Sword and the Chrysanthemum* (1946), to Abraham Kardiner's *The Individual and His Society* (1939). More recently, identity has been addressed by the cognitive anthropologists, such as Michelle Rosaldo in *Knowledge and Passion: Notions of Self and Social Life* (1980), and the postmodernist anthropologists, such as G. Marcus and M. Fisher in *Anthropology and Cultural Critique* (1986).

Students often come to our classes with a very narrow definition of self and our goal is to help them expand that definition so they understand the various levels of identity at which they function, whether consciously or unconsciously. Many students of color, for example, assert their ethnicity as primary, while European-American students, especially those on the West Coast of the United States, tend not to identify strongly with any particular ethnic group or with a particular microculture.

We have written elsewhere on the subject of multiculturalism and anthropology (see Carol C. Mukhopadhyay and Yolanda T. Moses "Anthropological Perspectives on Multicultural Education" 1994). Although the term *multicultural* emerged in the 1970s out of ethnic "minority" demands for educational equity and widespread rejection of assimilationist models of American society and institutions, we argue that anthropological perspectives incorporate, but go beyond, definitions of ethnicity. The goal is to develop cross-cultural competencies in multiple cultures, especially gender and class, and to encourage boundary crossing to promote intergroup harmony.

In 1976, after summarizing the literature, Margaret Gibson offered a useful definition of multicultural anthropology. Building on Ward Goodenough's statement that multicultural education is "part of the normal human experience," (1976) she called multicultural education "the process whereby a person develops competencies in multiple systems of standards for perceiving, evaluation, believing and doing" (Gibson 1984, 172). This definition derives from the anthropological concepts of education and culture. To anthropologists, education refers to formal and informal processes through which culture is transmitted to individuals. Whereas schooling is one example of this process, education is universal.

Culture, although variably defined, embraces all that humans create: material products (tools, clothing); social-behavioral products (families, corporations, schools, greetings); and mental products (concepts such as "holy water"; systems of thought such as Buddhism). All of these human products embody culturally created meanings or shared knowledge, enormously complex cultural knowledge structures that individuals use for interpreting, experiencing, and acting on the world. Helping students to tap these cultural *meanings*, the social behavior as well as the tangible material artifacts, becomes the route for them to begin understanding self.

We tell our students that cultures are not monoliths. Within any society there are numerous microcultures based on common religion, class, occupation, age, gender, activities, and others. (A college or university is one such microculture.) Although ethnicity is a salient category, it constitutes only one microculture in which individuals function, and ethnic "identity" is one of many cultural identities individuals acquire. We want students to understand that microcultures exist in all societies, and that their success in the university, at least partly, rests on their ability to acquire competencies in interacting in those microcultures.

This approach, as noted above, incorporates but goes beyond ethnicity. It precludes over-stereotyping ethnic groups, which vary, minimally, along gender and class lines. "It also recognizes similarities between ethnic groups rather than focusing on differences; and thus promotes crossing cultural boundaries rather than ethnic boundary maintenance" (Mukhopadhyay and Moses 1994, 3971). John Ogbu (1987) tells us that because humans are capable of multiple competencies, "culture-switching," like "code switching," need not require abandoning primary cultural group identity, which is a problem in some ethnic and cultural communities (and we would add college classrooms). Nor do we believe that culture switching will lead inevitably to the breakdown of one's own value system.

In summary, we envision multicultural education as promoting competence in multiple cultures for all students. We tell our students that the anthropological literature shows that boundary crossing has long been a method for promoting intergroup harmony in the face of potential conflict. We also tell them that in a fast-shrinking world, cross-cultural competence is one way to promote human cultural preservation and harmony.

Exercises in Identity and Self-Awareness: Activities that encourage students to locate themselves in their own networks of cultural and ethnic groups are often useful. For example, asking students to construct their own personal kin and social network, asking them to list eight to ten microcultures to which they belong, asking them to construct their own life histories or nuclear and extended family histories are productive exercises. As students share this information about themselves, they begin to discover the things they have in common. These simple exercises provide them with a personal reference point as well as some understanding of the complexity of who they are. Armed with their sense of "self" and "place," students are better prepared to understand how the resources of the anthropological literature can help them to obtain the cross-cultural literacy they need. Arvizu and Saravia-Shore (1990) regard cross-cultural literacy as the skills and perspectives that are needed to learn additional cultural competencies, to understand basic cultural processes, and to recognize the macrocultural context in which they are embedded.

Using Cross-Cultural Literacy and Literature to Understand Cultural Bias: The second area in which students should develop is their knowledge of anthropological theory and how they can use this to understand their multicultural world. Students in our classrooms are very concerned about the intolerance they see in the world, in their communities, and on their campus. One major problem they have is a lack of understanding of *why* people behave the way they do. By using the extensive ethnographic record of anthropology, we have been able to show students that culturally biased behavior is patterned and exists in cross-cultural contexts as well as in our own society. We have been able to show the circumstances under which this behavior can be mitigated. Later in the chapter we offer examples of eight different "hot topics" that can be used in the classroom. These target the pervasiveness of bias toward the "other," a concept that is universal in anthropological literature. By looking at real examples of bias and bigotry on campuses, students can apply anthropological concepts to real-life situations.

Exercises in Applying Theory to Understand Bigotry and Intolerance on College and University Campuses: Incidents of bigotry and intolerance are on the rise on college and university campuses across the country. According to the National Institute against Prejudice and Violence, more than 250 of the nation's 3,300 colleges and universities have reported acts of ethno-violence since mid 1986. By some estimates, at least half this number again go unreported (Stern 1990). These incidents often result in hostility and strained relations between students. Many administrators and faculty do not know how to address such situations. Some incidents are simple, such as an outright racist remark or hate slur. Others are more complicated. For example, a faculty member may say something in a classroom that some students interpret as bigoted while others do not. How do you use the issue to show both students and faculty that the "cultural baggage" they bring into the classroom influences their actions and reactions?

In the introduction to cultural anthropology class, students should learn how to look at and analyze these issues from their own anthropological perspective. What does anthropology tell us about the nature of bigotry, of prejudice, of mistrust of strangers, of fear of the unknown? It can teach students that contact among cultural groups who do not know each other or see each others' humanity can be full of conflict and tension. There is also the conflict of class or ethnic status that can come into play. For example, white-Asian tensions may be explained by Karl Marx's social stratification theory of the haves and the have-nots. The traditional haves (European American male university students) now have to share limited resources with the traditional have-nots (the Asian students) who are challenging the traditional high-status place that European-American males have held in the university. (These include access to scholarships, the best faculty, and prestige, particularly in areas of science, mathematics, and engineering). So "Asian-bashing" by European-American males, while certainly not condoned, can be couched in an anthropological framework for a better understanding of what may be *going on*, and more importantly, how to change it.

Following are eight of the talking points or thought pieces that Moses has used in her classes to explore students' feelings and biases on issues that call their values and cultural identity into question. Students are asked to assume the role of faculty or administrator, of perpetrator, or of victim in each of the vignettes. They are forced to "walk in the other person's shoes" by using anthropological explanations (from resource material provided to the class) in giving their responses.

1. There is no such thing as a biological concept of "Race." We should stop using the word altogether. It has no meaning.

Our note: Although anthropologists have discarded the biological concept of race as a viable concept in favor of the more accurate description of gene pools and clines, there is still a socially and culturally constructed usage of the word that is powerful and operative. Social racism remains a very highly charged issue. Unfortunately, we also see a tendency for people to ascribe biological characteristics to social race categories. For example, there is still a widespread belief in this country that African Americans are not genetically capable of learning at the same rates as European Americans and Asian Americans. We discuss the public policy implications of those beliefs in class.

2. Why is a word like *nigger* hurtful and inflammatory when a European-American student uses it to address an African-American student? When African-American students use it with each other, however, there often appears to be no friction.

Our note: In this discussion we talk about the powerful relationship between language and culture. Culture imports meaning to words that in theory are meaningless. For example, in American society, the word *nigger* has been used in very negative ways to denigrate and to dehumanize African Americans. It is tied to the history of American slavery, the Jim Crow system of discrimination that systematically, legally and illegally, shut African Americans out of the opportunity to be *full* participants as citizens in American society. We remind students (of all cultural groups) that it was only in 1964 in this country that the Civil Rights Acts and Voting Rights Acts were put in place to finally guarantee African Americans equal treatment before the law. In addition to the non-African-American students who know very little about the history of race relations in this country, an increasing number of immigrant students, first-generation Americans, and international students not only are not knowledgeable about African-American history and culture but know little of American history and culture as well. This exercise allows these students the "safe space" to ask questions of fellow students that they would otherwise not have asked. Non-African-American students want to know why, if the word *nigger* has such negative connotations for African Americans, they sometimes use it with each other? African-American students tell them that by taking a negatively charged word and appropriating it for themselves and for their *own* use, it is first neutralized and eventually comes to be used in a positive way as a "core blackness" or authenticity that African Americans reaffirm among themselves. It is taboo for a non-African American person to use it.

3. The fact that Asian-American students, African-American students, and Hispanic-American students tend to sit in groupings by themselves in the university student cafeteria bothers many faculty members and administrators. They see this as a form of self-segregation. What do you think?

Our note: We find the discussion around this issue useful at many levels. First, it allows us to talk about group identity along ethnic lines as one way for students to congregate, to find a home, a safe space in an environment (especially on predominantly European-American campuses) that does not readily create other forms of identity for students. As they get older, students may cluster based on other interests such as major, research interests, sports, and so on. We also discuss how the administrators notice students of color sitting in groups but not necessarily European-American students sitting in groups together. We discuss how the *goal* of racial integration or assimilation was strong in this country in the 1960s and 1970s. The administrators may see the groupings as segregation (or failure to achieve the goal of integration) on campus, whereas the students may see their behavior as perfectly normal.

4. A national fraternity was kicked off the college campus for holding a mock "slave auction" in which young women in chains were "sold" to the highest bidder. The fraternity members felt that the penalty was too harsh. They were just having fun; besides, it was a fund-raiser for their organization. Do you think the penalty was too harsh? What is your reaction to this event?

Our note: We use this discussion to talk about fraternal orders and the symbolism and reality of slavery—especially in the United States. We discuss the notion of women as property and chattel and how in American society it is offensive to denigrate women, especially in light of the heightened sensitivity caused by the feminist movement. The symbol of the "auction block," like the use of the Confederate flag, is also perceived by most African-American students to be a slap in the face to them and their ancestors who had to endure a history of slavery in this country.

5. A multicultural group of women students and a group of male and female Jewish students have just petitioned the president of the university to refuse permission for a speaker from the Nation of Islam to address a group of African-American male students on campus. This meeting is closed to women. There have been reports in the press that the speaker has made anti-Semitic remarks wherever he has spoken. What would you do if you were the president? Discuss why.

Our note: This example is very sensitive because it covers several major issues and sets of values that conflict. Our laws value freedom of expression very highly, even if it means the president must allow a speaker to say things on campus that may be biased, inflammatory, and untrue. Women students are sensitive to being excluded on the basis of their gender; Jewish students do not want to hear hurtful remarks against their history and traditions; the speaker for the Nation of Islam feels he has a right to profess his religious beliefs.

6. A Native-American student (Sioux) at a predominantly European-American university gets a note under her dormitory room door that says "Custer should have finished off your entire degenerative race." Although her friends and her roommate urge her to report the incident, she does not want to say anything. Why do you think she will not come forward? What would you do?

Our note: This is a good opportunity to talk with students about the diversity of Native-American culture, acculturation, gender roles, and issues of honor and shame cross-culturally.

7. The Gay Students Union has petitioned the Homecoming organizers to allow them to have a float in the annual Homecoming parade. It is the first time the organizers have received such a request. The student government gave its approval, but campus officials are concerned about the reaction of the alumni, who support the university through donations, and the city council, that gives the college the permit for the parade to use city streets. What is your reaction? Why?

Our note: This example allows discussion of civil rights and the status of gay and lesbian students on campus and in our society. It also provides an opportunity to look at cross-cultural issues of homosexuality and the pervasive homophobia in American society—for example, the current national issue of gays in the military.

8. A group of women students and women's studies faculty are outraged that an engineering professor uses examples of female anatomy in his class to illustrate certain points about buoyancy (the ability of certain objects to float). When female students objected, they were told it was only a joke and not to be such serious feminists. What would you do as a fellow professor? Do you think the women students are taking the issue too seriously?

Our note: Needless to say, the discussion around this topic is usually very lively. This example allows the class to look at gender roles, the use of sexuality in humor in our culture, the issues of academic freedom (the right of instructors to teach what they want and how they want without outside interference), and the issues of status and power.

Although these examples are not exhaustive, we have found them useful in engaging students in a dialogue using their own experiences *and* the anthropological data to understand and, we hope, eventually overcome their cultural bias.

Anthropology and Values Clarification: The third area we stress for students is learning to see values in a cultural context. We want students to leave our classes with a better understanding of who they are and what they value and why. The concept of worldview, "a culture's characteristic way of perceiving, interpreting, and explaining the world" (Kottak 1994, 417), is a useful concept here. It not only provides students a way to see why they embrace and legitimize certain behaviors in their own personal lives, but it also allows them to understand how the concept is embraced by people of other cultures, both here and abroad.

Research reveals that students change as a consequence of attending college. They usually become more culturally, aesthetically, and intellectually sophisticated, expanding their interests in the humanities, the fine arts, and social issues. In addition, exposure to cultural material and to people from other ethnic groups can cause students' behaviors to become more open and other-person oriented, more politically tolerant, and more respectful of others. Finally, the college experience tends to foster the increased use of principled reasoning in judging moral issues. People who go to college, in summary, tend to be more liberal than people in society at large (Hartel, Schwartz, Blume, and Gardner 1994); Astin 1993).

Framework for Discussion of Values: First- and second-year students who take introductory anthropology courses generally have not had to be self-reflective about these issues. Using such writings as Horace Miner's "Body Ritual among the Nacerima" (1956) and "One Hundred Percent American" (Linton 1937), students explore mainstream American values and worldview, at least from the perspective of classic anthropology. Students read works such as John Gwaltney's *Drylongso* (1980), in which he talks about "core black culture," or "The Persistence of *Le* in the Light of Japan's Modernization" by Hitoshi Fukue (1988), in which the author discusses how post–World War II modernization did not eradicate the value of the traditional *le* system that focuses on the centrality of the family lineage system. Exposure to such writings provides students with insights into the African-American worldview and the Japanese worldview, respectively.

George and Louise Spindler's *The American Cultural Dialogue and Its Transmission* (1992) provides the framework to discuss with students the shifts in American students' values from the 1950s through the 1960s, 1970s, and 1980s. It includes a chapter by Henry Trueba, "Mainstream and Minority Cultures: A Chicano Perspective" (1992), and one by Melvin Williams, "The Afro-American in the Cultural Dialogue of the United States." These authors explore the biculturality of the value systems of Latino Americans and African Americans, respectively. The book also contains a very useful Values Projective Technique exercise that students can take themselves (91) as well as a list of case studies that explore various aspects of American culture that can be helpful in class discussions (168–169).

Teaching Anthropological Perspectives in Freshman Orientation Courses

The freshman seminar or freshman orientation course is designed to introduce, new, first-time college students to the institution. In addition to basic study skills and an overview of academic programs, these courses often give first-generation college students a systematic analysis of what college is, what students can expect to get from their college experience, and how to get along with students from diverse cultural backgrounds. In this course, students should be exposed to ideas and concepts that lead them to question their frame of reference and value system.

Freshman orientation courses could benefit from teaching students the basic concepts of culture, cultural pluralism, ethnocentrism, and worldview as backdrops for (1) understanding the structure of the university and (2) developing cross-cultural communication skills.

Understanding the Structure of the University

Many first-time college students do not know what to expect from their on-campus experience. Data on the retention of students show that many students drop out in the first year of college because they are confused about what their college experience should be and are unsure of how or where to get help if they need it. They get lost in a system that is often not responsive to their needs (Green 1988; Wright 1987). If students learn the concept of culture, they can conceptualize the university as a cultural system with a set of patterned behaviors and structures. This knowledge can help them make sense of the university organization and how it works. In an article entitled "The Challenge of Diversity: Anthropological Perspectives on University Culture," Moses (1990) offers a concise analysis of university culture that can be very helpful to students. She notes that colleges and universities are like other macrocultures in two important ways: they have an ethos, or stated mission, and they are hierarchical.

The Institutional Ethos or Worldview: The ethos or worldview of the college or university is usually described in the mission and goals statement in the catalog or in publications that present the history of the college, how it got started, who started it, and for what purpose. For example, the City College of New York was founded in 1847 to provide a quality *public* (free) education for the children of immigrants in the city of New York. Only after 1951 were all units of the college finally open to women. This mission differs from those of institutions such as Columbia and Harvard, for example, that were founded to serve a different clientele in their early days.

Institutional Structure: Colleges and universities, though different in many ways, are basically hierarchical or stratified. Students who understand social stratification will have a better understanding of how the university works.

There are faculty hierarchies, program and degree hierarchies, administrative hierarchies, and student hierarchies.

- The president or chancellor has the ultimate authority for the institution.
- The provost or academic vice president usually has more status and prestige than the vice president for student affairs, who may have more status than the vice president for administration, and so on down the hierarchy.
- Middle managers—deans and department chairs—operate at a level closer to students and can often be more helpful to them than officials higher in the structure. Students need to understand the role of these managers. Frequently, students do not know whom to talk to other than the faculty if they have questions or problems.
- The faculty also has a hierarchy, and often students do not understand it. Knowing that there are full professors, associate professors, assistant professors, lecturers or adjuncts, and graduate teaching assistants gives the new students some sense of how to approach them or interact with them. It may also help them in choosing the adviser who is right for their needs.

These examples, again, are not exhaustive or comprehensive, but they give you the flavor of how understanding the concept of social stratification and hierarchy can be empowering to first-year students.

Developing Cross-Cultural Communication Skills

Using the anthropological literature on language and culture, sociolinguistics, proxemics, and verbal and nonverbal behavior, you can show first-year students the importance of developing cross-cultural communication skills. Understanding cultural differences and similarities is only part of being successful in college. Students must learn to communicate across these boundaries of difference. *Becoming a Master Student* by David B. Ellis (1988) offers some suggestions to students that we have modified and use in helping students develop cross-cultural communication skills.

- *Learn to listen to others.* Focus on what the person is saying and respond to that statement or thought. Too often we are formulating our own response while someone is talking to us; what we give back is what we want to say, not a genuine response to what the speaker is telling us.
- *Be active.* Learning implies activity. You do not learn about others by sitting passively in a classroom next to people from different backgrounds. It is not *their* responsibility to educate you.
- *Look for common ground.* Some goals cross cultural lines. Most students want to succeed in college regardless of their backgrounds. Strategies include joining study groups that are cross-cultural and cultivating friendships that are cross-cultural, or doing volunteer work with people from different cultural groups. Teachers should be conscious of balancing study groups in the classroom along gender and ethnic lines.

- *Assume difference in meaning between what speaker says and what listener hears.* When we speak, we need to be aware that what we say may have a different meaning to others from the meaning we intended. When we speak to others, we must avoid the assumption that we have been understood or that we fully understand the other person. This strategy extends to actions as well as speech. A good technique may be to ask the other person to repeat what has been said and vice versa. For example, one can say "I believe you were telling me . . . is that correct?" It shows that one is trying to understand the meaning of what is being said.

- *Look for individual rather than group representations.* Sometimes what we say tends to stereotype whole groups of people. For example, students worried about a grade in math might express concern about "all those Asian students who are skewing the class curve," or a European-American music major who assumes his African American classmate knows a lot about jazz. We can avoid such errors by seeing people as individuals rather than as spokespersons for an entire group.

- *Get inside another culture.* If a student is fascinated by or attracted to another culture, encourage him or her to explore that culture by reading books, going to movies, seeing plays, talking with students from that culture. Encourage them to educate themselves by taking an anthropology course in that area or getting a reading list from an anthropology professor.

- *Find a cultural "broker."* Diane de Anda, a professor at UCLA, speaks of three kinds of people who can communicate across cultures: *translators, mediators,* and *models.*

  Translators are bicultural—people who relate skillfully to those in a mainstream culture as well as to people from a contrasting culture. They can share their own experiences in overcoming discrimination, learning another language or dialect, and coping with stress. Translators can point out differences between cultures and help resolve conflicts.

  Mediators belong to the dominant or mainstream culture. He or she may not be bicultural, but values diversity and is committed to cultural understanding. Mediators can be teachers, counselors, tutors, or mentors.

  Models are members of a culture who set a positive example. They are students from any "racial" or cultural group who participate in class and demonstrate effective study habits (Harris 1988, 218).

- *Celebrate your own culture.* Using anthropological approaches allows you to gain a new appreciation of your own culture. You can see how your cultural assumptions and values have helped to shape your worldview. This viewpoint should help you see both the strengths and weaknesses in your own and other people's cultures.

- *Ask for help.* Be willing to speak up and ask for help when you need it. Often, your questions will be helpful to others in the class. (Note to faculty: Encourage students to ask for help with questions such as "How do you learn best?" or "None of you is asking a question; does that mean the idea is clear to you or do you need more explanation?" Questions such as these can get cultural differences out in the open in a constructive manner.)

- *Point out discrimination in your institution.* If you see people from other cultures ignored in class, underrepresented in school organizations, or ridiculed by other students, help stop this kind of bias by pointing it out. Most universities and colleges must abide by federal and state policies that prohibit discrimination. Your campus probably has to respond to these procedures. Know them and use them if necessary. (Note to faculty: Encourage students to understand that valuing diversity and fighting bias begins with them.)

In summary, the price we all pay for failure to understand other cultures is racism, prejudice, and bigotry. We believe these attitudes cannot survive when faced with the knowledge, group values, and compassion that result from learning how to communicate across cultures. Students exposed to anthropological concepts early in their college experience can develop the skills to succeed in both the classroom and society.

References

Arvizu, Steven, and Maria Savaria-Shore. 1990. "Cross-cultural Literacy: An Anthropological Approach to Dealing with Diversity." *Education and Urban Society* 22(4):364–376.

Astin, Alexander. 1993. *What Matters in College? Four Critical Years Revisited.* San Francisco: Jossey-Bass.

Benedict, Ruth. [1934] 1959. *Patterns of Culture.* New York: New American Library.

———. 1946. *The Sword and the Chrysanthemum.* Boston: Houghton Mifflin.

Ellis, David B. 1988. *Becoming a Master Student.* Rapid City: College Survival, Inc.

Fukue, Hitoshi. 1988. "The Persistence of *Ie* in the Light of Japan's Modernization." In *Toward Multiculturalism: A Reader in Multicultural Education,* edited by Haime S. Wuvzel, 123–130. Yarmouth: Intercultural Press.

Gibson, Margaret. 1984. "Approaches to Multicultural Education in the United States: Some Concepts and Assumptions." *Anthropology and Education Quarterly* 15(1):94–119.

Goodenough, Ward. 1976. "Multiculturalism as the Normal Human Experience." *Anthropology and Education Quarterly* 7(4):4–6.

Green, Madeline F. 1988. *Minorities on Campus: A Handbook for Enhancing Diversity.* Washington, DC: American Council on Education.

Gwaltney, John. 1980. *Drylongso: A Self-Portrait of Black America.* New York: Random House.

Hartel, William C., Stephen W. Schwartz, Steven D. Blume, and John N. Gardner. 1994. *Ready for the Real World.* Belmont, Calif.: Wadsworth.

Kardiner, Abraham. 1939. *The Individual and His Society.* New York: Columbia University Press.

Kottak, Conrad Phillip. 1994. *Anthropology: The Exporlation of Human Diversity.* 6th edition. New York: McGraw-Hill.

Linton, Ralph. 1937. "One Hundred Percent American." *The American Mercury* 40:427–429.

Marcus, G., and M. Fischer. 1986. *Anthropology and Cultural Critique.* Chicago: University of Chicago Press.

Mead, Margaret. [1928] 1961. *Coming of Age in Samoa.* New York: Morrow Quill.

Miner, Horace. 1956. "Body Ritual among the Nacerima." *American Anthropologist* 58:504–505.

Moses, Yolanda T. 1990. "The Challenge of Diversity: Anthropological Perspectives on University Culture." In *Cultural Diversity and American Education,* edited by Thomas G. Carroll and Jean J. Schensul, 402–412. Newbury Park, Calif.: Sage.

Mukhopadhyay, Carol C., and Yolanda T. Moses. 1994. Anthropological Perspectives on Multicultural Education. In *International Encyclopedia of Education: Research and Studies,* edited by Torsten Husen and Neville Postlethwaite. Oxford: Pergamon Press.

Ogbu, John. 1987)"Variability in Minority School Performance: A Problem in Search of an Explanation." *Anthropology and Education Quarterly* 18(4):312–334.

Rosaldo, Michelle. 1980. *Knowledge and Passion: Notions of Self and Social Life.* Stanford, Calif.: Stanford University Press.

Spindler, George, and Louise Spindler, eds. 1992. *The American Cultural Dialogue and Its Transmission.* New York: Falmer Press.

Stern, Kenneth G. 1990. *Bigotry on Campus: A Planned Response.* New York: American Jewish Committee, Institute of Human Relations.

Trueba, Henry. 1992. "Mainstream and Minority Cultures: A Chicano Perspective." In *The American Cultural Dialogue and Its Transmission,* edited by George Spindler and Louise Spindler, 122–141. New York: Falmer Press.

Williams, Melvin D. 1992. "The Afro-American in the Cultural Dialogue of the United States." In *The American Cultural Dialogue and Its Transmission,* edited by George Spindler and Louise Spindler, 144–160. New York: Falmer Press.

Wright, D. J. 1987. *Responding to the Needs of Today's Minority Students.* San Francisco: Jossey-Bass.

The Postmodern Condition and the Teaching of Anthropology

George E. Marcus

Postmodern anthropology, so-called, is part of a condition of society and academia just as postmodernism more generally is. Such a condition permeates the curriculum of anthropology and reflects a debate and a critique, arising in the 1980s, that concerned the form and meaning of anthropology as a discipline, given certain very explicit recognitions about contemporary changes in global conditions of societies and cultures. These have transformed both the objects of anthropological inquiry and anthropologists' own sense of their practices, their professional constituencies, and to whom the knowledge they produce is addressed. Conveying a sense of these transformations would mark, in varying styles and intensities, a distinctive postmodernist teaching of anthropology. Postmodernist anthropology is most certainly not merely another subspecialty in the discipline, nor another "in" theoretical fashion, as it has often been passed off. Indeed, to my knowledge, it has not been taught as such either.

The recent critique of anthropology took the form of a challenge to the rhetoric and conventions by which anthropologists had produced knowledge in the form of the ethnography. This made anthropologists very self-conscious about their methods and discourse, but it also legitimated and opened new avenues of inquiry. Further, this critique, which began with a so-called literary turn (Clifford and Marcus 1986)—the reflexive questioning of the modes of writing and rhetoric on which the discipline has unself-consciously depended—was by no means specific to anthropology. It was one case of what now appears to be a historic reevaluation of many disciplines in American academia during the 1970s and 1980s, which, indeed, spread through the stimulation of a certain crisis of literary studies trying to transform itself into cultural studies with powerful interdisciplinary resonances. Whatever postmodernism has meant in the arts and architecture, in the humanities and social sciences, it refers to this interdisciplinary ferment that has unsettled established, largely positivist models of practice.

The term *postmodern* can refer both to the conditions of knowledge or intellectual sensibility at present *and* to the actual conditions of society that require new approaches for understanding them. John Rajchman's characterization of postmodernism is particularly cogent, expressed out of his amazement that such a vague object could have become so ubiquitous and so focusing of discussions in the current interdisciplinary trend for so long. As he says (1987, 51):

> Postmodernisim is like the Toyota of thought: produced and assembled in
> several different places and sold everywhere. . . . Postmodernism is a sign
> of the loss of the colonial model of a universal culture spread out to educate
> the world at large. It is rather theory for a post-colonial world of products
> sold in different places without a center . . . it is like the *lingua franca* of
> this world. It can be made and consumed everywhere and nowhere.

It is interesting that Rajchman's, like many other characterizations of postmodernism, uses economistic metaphors like market competition and inflation
to characterize the conditions of knowledge, or else uses medical, epidemiologi-
cal metaphors that suggest postmodernism is like a virus or an infection. Either
way, what is ironic is that real conditions of postmodernity, not well understood in sociological or ethnographic terms, are used as the source of
metaphors for describing the conditions of postmodern knowledge and sensibility. That is, the great changes afoot in economy, society, and polity are the
metaphors for equally great changes in the culture and sensibility of intellectual
life. It is also irresistible to go in the contrary direction and see how cultural discourse feeds back on social, political, and economic processes. Indeed, teachers
who might be sympathetic to a so-called postmodernist influence on anthropology are less threatened by the loose, anarchic conditions by which knowledge is
now produced as postmodernism. They are much more interested in conveying
a sense of the actual social conditions of postmodernity, which are the major
stimulant of the crisis of representation within the discipline itself—the defeat
of concepts, past approaches, and rhetorics in the face of unprecedented velocity and sources of change that disrupt our notions of what a society is, what a
culture is, what an institution is, even what a person is.

The so-called crisis of representation that has spurred the recent and continuing critique of paradigms of work in cultural anthropology has taken place
within a much broader vortex that has been affecting a number of disciplines of
the humanities and more tangentially the social sciences and professions as
well. The label "crisis" is a make-do for a very complex set of initiatives that
range from the impact of academic feminism on revising taken-for-granted perspectives in many disciplines to the permeation of radical critical ideas about
the nature of language and the process of knowledge, produced during the
1960s by the French poststructuralists such as Derrida, Foucault, and Lacan,
and disseminated in the United States initially through literature departments.
In its American context, the success in provocation of these various resources
for critical ideas also had to do with the widely felt decline of American power
since the 1960s in world affairs, and the alienation of left/liberal academics
from domestic politics in the conservatives' dismantling of the welfare state.

The core of this crisis has had to do with both language and authority in
the conduct of those disciplines that produce current knowledge about society
and culture. First, there has been the bedrock sense that the concepts developed in various disciplines to describe, assimilate, and domesticate reality are
no longer adequate. The language of culture, class, sets of binary distinctions

such as modern versus traditional, individual versus society—although these might have been critiqued piecemeal at different times in the past in various disciplines—now seem en masse to capture no longer the magnitude or quality of changes occurring in the contemporary world. There is a sense, differently expressed in different disciplines, of the need for a major overhaul of ways of thinking and writing, and ultimately of questions asked. This is far from a cosmetic or partial self-critique, and it has led to a variety of productive and not so productive debates about different models of work and different objects of study in fields ranging from economics, to history, law, architecture, art, and philosophy.

With the critique of the language and the cognitive models of disciplines also came a critique of the authority of the kinds of knowledge they produced. Far from nihilistically destroying authority, the search has been for new forms of authority in reconfigured fields of knowledge production—what is now to count as knowledge? Who is to be included and excluded from having a voice or position in the development of knowledge about society and culture? On what basis can a special authority for disciplines be established once the community who receives and assesses the knowledge that they produce widens within and beyond academia?

In anthropology, the crisis of representation has taken the form of two specific predicaments that go to the very heart of its practice and the topics to which it has historically addressed itself. The idea of the primitive—however modified this concept has become—has been central to the way anthropology has conceived its object of study. Contemporary people on which anthropologists have focused have been conceptually viewed as alien to the experience of modernity—as separate in time and space, as radical exemplars of difference and alternative possibility from us. Recent critiques of this view have argued that the category of the primitive has been an integral dimension of the development of the notion of modernity itself and is inseparable from this notion at the core of our own self-identity in the Euroamerican West. This means that our own identity and those of the people that anthropologists have studied should no longer be represented or described in terms of binary us–them contrast. This merging of what was previously and fundamentally contrasted in conceptualizations at the foundation of doing anthropology requires a radical reconfiguration of what our object of study is—who we are as observers, and who the people we have observed are, if not primitives and exotics. This critique of the basic conceptual distinction at the core of anthropological work pushes us toward new objects of study and modifications in our methods.

Second and relatedly, there is a new sensitivity to the terms on which difference—cultural, racial, gender, or class—can be established and discussed. How to establish difference in a world where the object of study itself has been called into question raises additional theoretical and methodological questions for anthropology. Thinking about the nature of difference and how it emerges in social life is not just the emblematic concern of anthropology or of the emerging interdisciplinary arena of cultural studies; it is itself one of the key and widespread forms of social thought at this moment in the history of modernity, and is indeed one of the major topics for cultural analysis in anthropological research. In short, there is a certain identity or parallel between our own predicaments as a scholarly subculture and the cultures that are our subjects of study. This raises profound questions about the past forms of authority of anthropological representations and on what basis a special claim for our own creation of knowledge about others might be made.

The permeation of the postmodern condition in the anthropology of the 1980s and 1990s applies both to those who have in various ways identified with this seminal critique of the discipline *and* to those who have resisted or been ambivalent about this critique. Thus, postmodern anthropology must be defined in terms of the centrality of the recent debate and its effects on the diversity of ways that anthropology is practiced and taught, rather than as a new subspecialty or replacement paradigm as such. There is no adjectival subspecialty called postmodern anthropology, comparable to, say, symbolic anthropology, political anthropology, or interpretive anthropology. Few, if any, courses by this title are taught, to my knowledge. Rather, the way that the postmodern condition has affected the teaching of anthropology is a more complicated matter, as it cannot be (and in fact has not been) easily contained within the conventional categories by which topics within the discipline have been taught. The postmodern influence is marked by the increasing idiosyncratic phrasings of course titles and by reading lists that are a thorough mix of disciplinary and interdisciplinary sources, with the latter often playing the role of a guiding provocation or inspiration in the course.

The teaching of postmodern anthropology is therefore about the revision of the traditional anthropology curriculum under pressure of internal critique and, not unrelatedly, change in the world(s) in which anthropologists have worked. Rather than dead-ending in repetitive, endless restatements of radical critique, or winding up with what we had before with just a change in rhetoric or jargon, or ending in a pallid plea to be more self-conscious in using the usual methods, the project of critique is finally justifiable only as a difference that makes a difference. Now, those raised in the tradition of social science may be ill at ease with teaching anthropology as a discipline so strongly resting on a foundation of critiques, deconstructive methods, and the like. The latter certainly open the way to new venues and questions, but when does work settle into new paradigms of research and teaching, projects that seem more positive? First, I hope that I am making the case effectively that crises, critiques, and the like—such negative sounding words—actually do serve as the positive bases of research and teaching: they are productive and creative of new and systematic insights. Indeed, in the usual model of work, based on natural science ideals, simplicity is good and too much complexity is fruitless. Much of what I have been describing thrives on complexification—the ability to overcome the languages and finesses that refined theory for the analysis of the late nineteenth- and early-twentieth century forms of modernity but which no longer seem to work for what appears to be unprecedented in contemporary social processes. To comprehend the velocity of contemporary changes and re-organizations of culture, economy, and society both globally and locally requires a much more complex model of work and teaching, and much more complex views of what objects of study are.

Second, it cannot be emphasized enough that critiques lead not to discovering novel paradigms but to strategies of reinvention, a recreation of the intellectual capital of the past. In this sense, there is a high tolerance for the fragmentation and recombinations of past theoretical legacies.

Demystified of a world of primitives, exotic societies in which it can operate, the field of inquiry of anthropology becomes the emergent present, the contemporary. And what is the contemporary? If there is one very large issue or debate that gives structure to much of the impulse behind the crisis of representation and the positing of a postmodern condition—a sense of things happening in the world that are impervious to or not clearly seen through the available conceptual frames and rhetorics of the human sciences—it is the question of the continued viability of nation-states in the face of global reorganizations and phenomena in the not very well charted (call it post-modern) space of the transnational or transcultural. All that is local—closely observed—is at the same time global, and vice versa. How to achieve descriptions of this relation in very specific settings is our problem in both research and teaching. As one of the pioneers of British cultural studies, Stuart Hall, remarked recently, it is clear that local life is alive and well, as is the global arena, though their intimate relationships are not well understood, but the nation-state itself and the concept of civil society, to which much of what we have tried to understand as social and cultural life in modern societies has been directed over the past centuries, seem shaky at best.

I do not want to give the impression that the issue of the viability of the nation-state in the midst of emergent processes of transnationalism is decided; it cannot be, because it is happening. The nation-state seems powerful, still the focus and frame of attention about matters social and cultural. Yet, it also seems to be irrelevant to so many new initiatives in the world—from the activities of corporations to grass-roots social movements dealing wth the environment and the assertion of ethnic identity. This is probably the most interesting and global debate for the social sciences and cultural studies of the contemporary, and it is into this fray that a critical anthropology is well prepared to enter with its fine-grained descriptions of social and cultural processes from many different angles and many different places.

In the United States, this debate over the present and future of the nation-state has various manifestations. The specter of national decline is one such high-anxiety context, and it has made improbable best-sellers of such academic books as Paul Kennedy's *The Rise and Fall of the Great Powers* and Alan Bloom's *The Closing of the American Mind*. Abroad, a united Europe challenges the birthplace of the ideas that shaped the modern nation-state, and in many other countries with huge diasporas, transnational flows of people, resources, and culture reshape local agendas. What is clear about the present is that it goes far beyond mere past Utopian hopes for internationalism or slogans like the new world order, or 1960s-like impulses to act locally and think globally. Now there is a sense of the immediate presence of local-global articulations of everyday life and within the operations of major institutions. It is to the emergence of such articulations in older contexts that so much of the new anthropology is oriented. And in this orientation, we are always operating against a more conventional frame—vestigial thinking, provocatively put—and as such this is why new research and teaching in its formulation must arise from practices of critique. But why cultural?

The stakes in the debate about the viability of the nation-state exceed the understanding of the emergent world. The nation-state frame has been an implicit if not explicit framework for our thinking about society and culture. Certainly, the dominant, high-prestige forms of expert discourse on society in terms of economic interest and political value assume an economy and polity that in turn operate within variant forms of the Western evolved nation-state. As such, the crisis of representation, to which I have referred, is about the displacement of the foundational nation-state referent from the heart of our most public discourses about contemporary reality. In such reconfigurations, the role of the cultural sphere—of value, of differences among races, places, gender, and classes—has moved more toward the center of concerns.

Culture has always been comfortably domesticated on the margins of the dominant discourses, but just as the latter no longer optimistically produce knowledge about their traditional objects, so an even less manageable notion of culture moves in from the margins. In a sense, the predicaments of anthropology that I described earlier have become general predicaments for many other disciplines where the weight of attention to culture has increased—the predicaments of seeing others as now integral to us, of seeing our own traditions and present concerns as *multicultural*—a now infamous and loaded ideological term precisely because the means for thinking about cultures in new social contexts are not available. The problem is to conceive of difference not as something produced by far distant cultures—that is, assimilable to understanding by a total and thorough knowledge of that culture in its own rooted territory—but rather as produced at the boundaries of interactions and the creations of new cultural forms in emerging transnational contexts. It is just these sorts of predicaments that call for a new vocabulary and set of values pertaining to culture. This would be a notion of culture far more radical than the older liberal views pioneered by anthropology and other fields. Rather than mastering other cultures by understanding them as complete systems of language and cognition, and thus conquering, so to speak, cultural difference in the process by making the cultural other transparent, the critical study of culture confronts endless and intractable difference generated by the process of cross-cultural interpretation and understanding itself in various sociopolitical contexts.

The following are some of the general premises by which the teaching of anthropology under postmodern influence is now conceived and undertaken.

These premises are not rules or even methodological guidelines. They are new assumptions that are not necessarily easy to follow—in fact, they are each subject of various theoretical side debates themselves. But while these debates rage, they are issues that shape the presentation in courses of the postmodern condition that permeates anthropology.

1. There is an assumption of a sharp discontinuity with the past. History is of course important, and historicizing one's contemporary subjects is essential to prevent flights of Utopian fantasy. Indeed, there is a wing of cultural anthropology whose strategy is to negotiate a new relationship with historians to whom anthropology has always been close. This is valuable, but in focusing on the contemporary, historical narrative is less of a guide; the assumption is that the present is a departure from the flow of twentieth-century historical narrative, and this methodologically gives one a different set of lenses without falling into futurology. Certainly, the history built into the concepts we use to think about society in a taken-for-granted way is a main contributor to the crisis of representation. Conversely, more daring and less contiguous forms of comparative history are thought experiments that may indeed help reconceptualization of the present. For example, there are certain fascinating parallels between the end of the fifteenth century in Europe and the present. Talking about other times and places becomes sometimes a most interesting surrogate for talking about our own predicaments.

2. Relatedly, critical anthropology works in a fine-grained way to develop understandings of emergent processes in the transcultural or transnational sphere by not giving authority to any particular metanarrative. We work without the authority of a paradigm such as Marxism or structuralism, borrowing, recombining, and committing ourselves with a sense of irony from within whatever legacies of thought are available to us. In this style, a favorite move is to recover the present relevance of forgotten or near forgotten thinkers. For example, between the wars, thinkers like Georges Bataille and Walter Benjamin have been recuperated with interesting consequences in both anthropology and cultural studies.

3. There is avoidance of binarisms and dualisms that conceptually have structured most modes of theoretical thought—modernity versus tradition, individual versus society, religion versus science, history versus memory, body versus mind, oral versus literate, and of course, us versus them. Modern thought has been built on these kinds of distinctions, which in the present context has probably made invisible many of the mergings, mixings, and interreferences going on. The point is to develop an analytic and didactic discourse that is nonessentialist.

4. Relatedly, there is a taste for linking what seems incommensurable, for relating processes that seem by conventional thinking "worlds apart." This desire to merge perspectivally what has been kept apart is also signaled by the subtitle of *Writing Culture*—the poetics and politics of ethnography. The idea is that culture, aesthetics, and symbols have a renewed relevance to understanding

spheres of interest, politics, production, economics, and political economy from which they had long been separated, and vice versa. This combining of politics and poetics—juxtaposing them, blocking them together, and if lucky finding systematic relations between them—is one of the major impulses in trying to work with emerging transcultural and transnational spheres of social and cultural organization.

5. Finally, anthropology as a form of cultural critique is reflexive, which is perhaps its most emblematic feature and the one that radically separates it from the dominant tradition of work in the social sciences. Reflexivity means more than merely being aware of your assumptions. Rather, it presumes that in any study of the contemporary there are always already existing relationships of a historical, institutional, and personal nature between the scholar and an object of study, and that an embedded part of the work itself—from inquiry, analysis, and writing, to teaching itself—involves creative ways of thinking about and incorporating this connectedness of oneself, and the specific academic institutions and society that produce one's perspective, with the object of study. Rather than mere self-awareness, reflexivity requires positioning of the knowledge that one creates as constitutive of that knowledge. This of course is the cornerstone of hermeneutic philosophy and method on which anthropology and other humanist perspectives in the social sciences have historically been based. This does not lead to subjectivism, or vagueness, but rather to a reconstituted form of qualified objectivity. Indeed, it leads to a precision of concept and analysis because research and teaching are so explicitly positioned and situated—and not the product of the myth of a detached, impartial, Archimedian perspective.

The Binds and Stakes of Teaching Anthropology under Postmodernist Influence

Any course in the anthropology curriculum that is positively influenced by the array of influences discussed above, labeled postmodern, explicitly identifies itself as such. It does so by some framing presentation of the set of critiques that then operate as a didactic strategy for revising or reinventing established topics in anthropology. To some extent, feminist-inspired revisions of kinship studies and the latter's transformation into contemporary courses in gender and gender relations are an early model of this now widespread transformative and critical mode of teaching in anthropology that can be broadly labeled postmodernist. Given such a self-conscious break with the past of the discipline in the presentation of courses, it is fair to ask about the degree to which postmodernist teaching is in fact continuous with long-standing critical orientations by which anthropology has been presented. In short, how much of the above is alike or different from what anthropologists have always offered their students?

What postmodernist teaching of course shares with the established tradition of teaching anthropology in U.S. universities is a sharp critical orientation aimed at challenging cultural hegemonies in Western societies through strategies of defamiliarizing what is taken for granted. In anthropology, as in postmodernist teaching, this has been accomplished first by juxtaposing examples of distinctive difference, and then by examining more systematically the relations that difference suggests. Of course, the special anthropological mode of producing its critical, defamiliarizing juxtapositions has been through the knowledge of cross-cultural diversity that it has meticulously developed through the ethnography of people and places elsewhere.

Postmodernist teaching departs from the established tradition of teaching anthropology in that it strongly questions the concepts, rhetoric, and methods by which examples of difference can be represented in the contemporary world. Both traditional anthropology and postmodernist teaching begin with counterintuitive appeals to the experience of the student, but the postmodernist influence suggests that this move cannot be grounded as it has been in the past. In other words, the postmodernist tendency complexifies the traditional teaching task of anthropology by not only defamiliarizing cultural assumptions in the West but *also* by defamiliarizing the tools that have long been used to carry out this task. Conditions of postmodernity in the world require the reformulation of concepts and frameworks by which difference is presented to students. The notion of bounded cultures, for example, is not necessarily the foundation for considering the differences that arise from postmodern conditions of hybridity, crossing borders, creolization, and multiple subjectivities.

The debate in the discipline is thus whether older models of culture can assimilate these present conditions of cultural formation. So-called postmodernists are those who take the position that new departures, new kinds of interdisciplinary relationships, and theoretical influences are necessary to continue to pursue traditional disciplinary questions in the contemporary world.

This postmodernist concern with a more radical content to the remaking of the critical function of cultural anthropology places anthropology in a profound yet productive involvement with contemporary interdisciplinary arenas, most notably cultural studies (which has inherited much of the legacy of the 1970s' and 1980s' debate about postmodernism). This arena generally downplays disciplinary identities, and in fact encourages transgressing them. Consequently, the bind for an anthropology curriculum, then, that regularly draws its intellectual capital from participation in this arena is how to sustain ties to the disciplinary tradition in teaching—how, for example, to incorporate the teaching of Malinowski and Evans-Pritchard with Said and Spivak. In my own courses, ties to the specifically disciplinary tradition of anthropology are sustained by grounding or testing the theoretical provocations emanating from the broad cultural studies arena by the body of ethnography that anthropologists continue to produce. But there is no single or formulaic answer to this issue; it is being confronted in every course that is open to the postmodern condition in a positive way.

Why, in short, postmodernist teaching in anthropology seems different, even though it shares much with the past critical sensibility of the discipline, is that it proceeds not under some fiction of a secure, ever-progressing paradigm but rather under the provocation and stimulus of self-critique that in its most unsettling moments risks disciplinary erasure. Those who teach under post-modernist influence would say that the challenge of adapting anthropology to the changing conditions of the world and of knowledge production itself make such a risk worth taking.

References

Clifford, James, and George E. Marcus, eds. 1986. *Writing Culture; the Poetics and Politics of Ethnography*. Berkeley: University of California Press.

Rajchman, John. 1987. "Postmodernism in a Nominalist Frame: The Emergence and Diffusion of a Cultural Category." *Flash Art* 137:49–51.

Close Encounters of the Third Kind
Selected Themes, Resources, and Strategies
in Teaching Cultural Anthropology

SERENA NANDA

This chapter focuses on teaching cultural anthropology as cultural critique. My emphasis on this approach grows out of my twenty-five years of teaching experience with "nontraditional" students, and developments within and outside anthropology since the 1970s, which raise questions about the relation of our methods, theories, findings, and relevance to the unequal distribution of power in the world in which we live and work (Hymes 1969; Asad 1973; Said 1989, 1993).

Teaching anthropology as cultural critique is congruent with the major issues and interests within anthropology today: postmodernism, reflexive ethnography, the world systems and world historical approaches, symbolic anthropology, cultural materialism, applied anthropology, and Marxist and feminist anthropology. It tends toward written, visual, and exhibited/performed representations.

Anthropology as cultural critique is connected to the central anthropological understanding that all cultures are humanly constructed and that our own culture is just one of the many alternatives in the world, past and present. This theme encourages students to look more carefully at the central and most taken-for-granted values, ideas, and institutions of our culture such as race, gender, class, ethnicity, individualism, patriarchy, nationalism, work, capitalism, education, self-concepts, romantic love, the family, success, and particularly, the claimed superiority of Western culture as these patterns shape their own identity and behavior and the interactions between our culture and others.

The aim of reducing students' ethnocentrism by making them more conscious of the construction of their own culture is a long-acknowledged and widely shared aim of teaching cultural anthropology (Mandelbaum 1963, 7–8). The premise—and the promise—of cultural anthropology has mainly been to develop a respect for the diversity of humankind and to critique the notion of Western superiority. The particular anthropological contribution—teaching that culture is humanly constructed and can thus be humanly changed in more reasonable and humane directions—gives cultural anthropology its inherent potential as radical critique. Further, the anthropological emphasis on the relationship between the ability to see other cultures from the inside and our own culture from the outside is one of the most frequent justifications for teaching anthropology in a general liberal arts curriculum. That cultural anthropology has not yet, perhaps, lived up to all its promise of leaving the world a better place than we found it is a powerful incentive to try harder. This is as necessary in today's world as it was in an earlier, more frankly imperialist era.

Being taught anthropology as cultural critique is essential for all students, and no less so for the increasing numbers of "nontraditional" students we teach: students who commute to large, public, urban universities; who come to college after working or raising children, often the first of their poor or working-class families to attend college; who are frequently from ethnic or racial minorities; and who are motivated by occupational goals that rarely include majoring in anthropology. Many, if not most, of these students are among the *colonized,* as Edward Said (1989, 207) uses the expanded definition of this term—that is, from those "subjugated and oppressed" classes, which, in a world increasingly divided into "betters" and "lessers," fall into the category of lessers. Their backgrounds do not make them less ethnocentric; indeed, having sacrificed so much to succeed in college, which they see as the main avenue to upward mobility in our society, they are often even more reluctant to question society's values than students who are more privileged. But their own position—so ambiguous and contradictory, and thus full of personal tensions—leaves them open to cultural critiques, and this is a resonant theme around which to structure the teaching of cultural anthropology.

Fulfilling the promise of anthropology as cultural critique requires explicit attention to two notions: encounters and power. The term *encounter* is an apt metaphor for much of what teaching cultural anthropology is about. First, it recalls the encounter between Europe and the non-European cultures and societies of the world that have largely been the subject of anthropological inquiry, and indeed, the stimulus and the context in which anthropology as a discipline developed (Harris 1969; Stocking 1987). Second, ethnography, our major methodology, is at its heart an encounter between anthropologists and their subjects through fieldwork. Reflections on this encounter have an increasingly important place in cultural anthropology (Sanjek 1991; Tedlock 1991) and should be reflected in our teaching. Third, teaching anthropology is an encounter between ourselves and our students, for whom we largely act as interpreters of the first two encounters, that replicates some aspects of these two other encounters and to which it has more than an incidental connection. In each of these three encounters, it is essential to seek an understanding of behavior that views both parties engaged in an interactional *system,* a perspective that brings up the second important concept, that of power.

Acknowledging the disparities in power in the encounters noted above is a critical dimension in both doing and teaching cultural anthropology. By becoming more aware of the ways in which unequal power affects—or afflicts—our subjects, theories, methodology, and teaching, we are better able to recognize both resistance and creative collaboration between the parties as past actualities and future possibilities.

Certain critiques of cultural anthropology hold that it has not sufficiently acknowledged, understood, researched, represented, or taught its subject as an encounter in the context of a particular historical moment, with specific interests at work that benefit some segments of society more than others. These critiques become more trenchant in the contemporary context of the global economy and the attempts to build an international political community as well as in the domestic context of multiculturalism in academe (Perry 1992).

A focus on the role of unequal power as it shapes cross-cultural encounters, or encounters between different segments of populations within nations, leads us in two directions that are useful for teaching anthropology as cultural critique. One direction provides a closer and more multisided reading of the encounters between the West and non-Western cultures. This reading has been an important vehicle for seeing ourselves as others see us, in addition to being a more accurate rendering of the histories of those encounters (Schwartz 1994; Shohat and Stam 1994). Second, considerations of disparate power lead to a more explicit consideration of the politics of culture—that is, the role of power in creating, maintaining, diffusing, and using cultural representations. Viewing cultural representations as subject to interpretation in terms of power and interests enlivens the treatment of both current and classic anthropological resources as these are reexamined, for example, through the eyes of feminist theory (Weiner 1976; Mascia-Lees et al. 1989). A culture-of-politics perspective directs attention to anthropological representations of others and also to powerful vehicles for cultural representations of ourselves and others, such as the popular media, court opinions, or the congressional record, with which anthropological representations compete. Indeed, as the subjects of these representations write and talk back (Cesaire [1955] 1972; Fanon 1968; Ashcroft et al. 1989), the clash of representations, within our own society and on a global scale, emerges as an important theme in teaching cultural anthropology. A focus on the role of power and interests in cultural encounters and in representation of ourselves and other cultures is tied to a teaching strategy of maximum student discussion and participation as it allows for, indeed insists on, multiple readings of any text.

The focus on the role of unequal power in cross-cultural encounters (or those between dominant and subordinate segments of a national society) insists that what we think we know about ourselves and others is shaped by the distribution of power in our society and in the world. Teaching this theme requires strategies and resources that involve asking questions about the hidden power at work in interpreting, producing, appropriating, and distributing all forms of knowledge, including that of cultural anthropology.

With this consideration in the foreground, new perspectives illuminate the three encounters I noted earlier: power disparities come to their proper central location in explaining the encounter (1) between Europe and the non-European world, both in the past and in the present; (2) between anthropologists and the "other," whether in fieldwork or in ethnographic representations; and (3) between student and teacher as they question these encounters and their representations in a wide range of texts (Casey 1991; Shor 1987).

The remainder of this essay suggests some resources and strategies that may be useful in teaching the themes discussed above, based on the premise that most of our students will not be anthropology majors and that we will have only one chance, or several at most, to get their attention. These recommendations are highly personally selective and only suggestive. I have concentrated on sources that are readable, provocative, and relatively accessible and that will generate student discussion (even for students who are academically underprepared as many of our students are). Because of space limitations, many excellent references have been left out, particularly those that are suitable only for very advanced students and anthropology majors.

As noted earlier, the special qualities of cultural anthropology that make it useful as cultural critique grow out of the connection between seeing other cultures from the inside and seeing our own culture at a distance. This connection generates respect for other cultures. The same concepts used to "make sense" of other cultures—adaptation, the interrelationships of parts of a culture, the symbolic nature of human behavior, the integration of human biology and culture—can be applied to the analysis of our own culture. In this way, our culture is critiqued not in the sense of being shown to be all wrong or more hateful than others, but rather as a construction that is shaped according to the same processes involved in constructing other cultures.

Critiquing our own culture can effectively begin with a flashback process, shocking the student into consciousness by experiencing our culture from the outside. We can use representations of our culture by outside visitors (de Toqueville's *Democracy in America* [1956] is full of short, provocative, still relevant gems); studies of the United States by foreign anthropologists (Ogbu 1974); the work of American anthropologists writing about their own culture in particularly interesting, accessible ways (Harris 1974; 1981); and fiction or nonfiction writings about the dominant culture of the United States from the margins (for example, Du Bois [1903] 1989; Brown 1972; Gish 1991). In addition, we may also use what Edward Said (1993) calls "discrepant" or "contrapuntal" readings of materials on the same subject from different sources, which, when juxtaposed, provide new perspectives on our own culture and its interaction with others.

Particularly useful for introductory students are the short, well-known, provocative pieces that critique our culture in covert ways: "Shakespeare in the Bush" (Bohannan 1966), "One Hundred Percent American" (Linton 1937), and "Eating Christmas in the Kalahari" (Lee 1969). Horace Miner's now classic "Body Ritual among the Nacirema" (1956) invites comparison with Conrad Kottak's "Rituals at McDonald's" (1978). The latter is even more provocative when used in conjunction with questions about "Where's the Beef?" (Rifkin 1992a, 1992b), which demonstrates the global effect of American eating habits. Other articles that work successfully in the same way are Ruth Benedict's "The Uses of Cannibalism" (1959a) and "Counters in the Game" (1959b). In the first, Benedict makes an apparently straightforward cost-effectiveness argument for substituting cannibalism for warfare between nations; in the second, she more didactically (and therefore somewhat less interestingly) compares the Kwakiutl and the Amercian cultures as both prizing status seeking but doing so in ways completely incomprehensible to the other. As Clifford Geertz (1989) aptly points out, almost all of Ruth Benedict's work, particularly, *Patterns of Culture* (1961) and *The Chrysanthemum and the Sword* (1974), only seem to be about "them"; they are really about "us." A wide range of short articles on lessons learned from other cultures in the process of anthropological fieldwork (DeVita 1992) and a collection of anecdotal accounts of foreign anthropologists in the United States (DeVita and Armstrong 1993) also make direct hits on ethnocentrism in an accessible, provocative way, as does Bowen's longer, substantive (and very funny) classic account of fieldwork among the Tiv (1964).

"Exoticizing" culture in the United States is particularly effective in teaching when you use insightful and unusual anthropological perspectives to examine subjects that are part of our students' daily lives, such as pets (Perin 1988) or football (Dundes 1985). Carefully chosen excerpts from the films of Frederick Wiseman are also useful; his most recent, *Zoos* (1991), nicely complements the consciousness-raising work of Donna Harraway (1989) in uncovering concealed values of dominance and manipulation in science, as represented by the Western penchant for collecting and displaying live—or stuffed—animals. On the subject of display, two of the very saddest examples, which illustrate the role of anthropology in the social construction of race as well as provide an excellent description of twentieth-century racism, are *Ota Benga: The Pygmy in the Zoo* (Bradford and Blume 1992) and "The Hottentot Venus" (Gould 1985). I follow up the latter with a reading of the poem "The Venus Hottentot" by Elizabeth Alexander (1992), which imaginatively gives Saartjie Baartman her own voice. An effective way to stimulate student thinking about the construction of normal and abnormal in our society and who gets to define these terms is to discuss their reactions to the photographs of Diane Arbus (1972), which I show as slides in the classroom.

Sustained treatments of important American cultural patterns and social institutions, which raise students' consciousness about the distribution of power in their own society, include Jack Weatherford's analysis of Congress (1985) and Constance Perin's work on the cultural construction of "home" (1977). On adolescence and education, Margaret Mead's *Coming of Age in Samoa* ([1928] 1971) can be followed up by a discussion of *Coming of Age in New Jersey* (Moffatt 1989). A critical look at war can be achieved by juxtaposing excerpts from Studs Terkel's *The Good War* (1984) with sections from Lamont Lindstrom and Geoffrey White's work on World War II that provides photographic and oral historical contrapuntal memories of Westerners and Solomon Islanders (1990). The connection between war and a cultural ethos of masculinity is also highlighted by pairing readings about the fierce Yanomamo (Chagnon 1983) with even a short reading about the relationship between violence and masculinity in our own culture (Ehrenreich 1990).

As a classroom strategy, I have very successfully used juxtapositions in eliciting student participation on the topics of love, marriage, and family. I begin by asking the students to make up a "personal ad" in class. Students are not shy about reading these aloud (always eliciting much laughter), and one student lists the main criteria of the ads on the board, dividing them by gender. I then read aloud (or pass around for the students) a section of the matrimonial columns from an Indian newspaper. The contrasts between the different requirements for male/female relationships in India and the United States lead to insightful student thinking on the relationships between economics, family systems, and marriage, and to their rethinking the rather unique American idea of "romantic love" as the basis for marriage.

Deconstructing central structural concepts in American society such as race, gender, class, and ethnicity is an essential component of teaching cultural anthropology as cultural critique and most explicitly requires considerations of encounters and power. Gerald Berreman's comparative analysis of the construction of race as a social category (1988) is complemented by Virginia Dominguez's *Black by Definition*, a close, careful, examination of the cultural construction of racial categories in Louisiana (1986).

With the importance of feminist anthropology in the past three decades, resources on the construction of gender and the ways in which an androcentric anthropology has distorted its subjects are numerous; most helpful in addressing this topic is the recent American Anthropological Association publication on teaching gender (Morgen 1989). Issues about the construction of gender can also be effectively approached by a strategy of analyzing the margins to reveal the center. Readings on third or alternative genders in other cultures (Herdt 1993; Williams 1992; Roscoe 1991; Nanda 1990) raise unavoidable questions about our culture's deeply held division of the world into male and female. Ann Bolin's "In Search of Eve" (1988) also uses this strategy as she reveals core values of femininity in the United States through a study of transsexuals. An extremely provocative, short film that guarantees student thinking on gender construction and is a good way to open up this topic is *Keltie's Beard*. It is about a young woman who grows a beard and the responses she encounters in our own and other cultures.

Moving from the examination of our own culture to the ways in which our cultural ideas have shaped and been shaped by our interactions with others can begin with exploring the expansion of capitalism from Europe to other parts of the world. *Europe and the People without History* (Wolf 1982) is basic: its various chapters can also be selectively used in conjunction with more regional treatments of the encounter between Europe and the non-European world. Wolf's emphasis on the *interactional* nature of these critical encounters in human history lays the groundwork for viewing non-European cultures as more active participants in their own history. It is a good background for introducing material on the resistance of the non-European peoples through fiction (Achebe 1969; Sembene 1970; Ashcroft et al. 1989; al-Rahman 1989), theory (Fanon 1968; Suleri 1992), ritual performances (Rouche, film, 1957), litigation (Merry 1991; Norgren and Nanda 1988), secrecy (Price 1983), subterfuge (Scott 1985), and religious syncretism and communalism (Lewis 1993).

Understanding the various processes of interaction between Europeans and non-Europeans also can help students think more insightfully about the processes of constructing cultures and related issues of authenticity and tradition. Many of the cultural identities relevant in the contemporary world have been formed in the process of culture contact and European colonialism (Hobsbawm and Ranger 1983) and demonstrate that European "history" is subject to the same processes of "invention" as are histories of other societies (Sahlins 1994).

It is appropriate to begin the study of these encounters and the resulting cultural constructions as part of our own nation's imperial ambitions, with Indian oratory (Vanderwerth 1972) or with Keith Basso's Apache Whiteman stories (1979), both of which provide accessible examples of how "they" see "us." The creation of self-serving representations of Native Americans in the dominant culture is usefully conveyed in Lyman's work (1982) on the careful editing and even deception that went into many of Edward Curtis's photographs of Native Americans (which can be shown as slides in the classroom). Haunani Kay Trask's writings on Hawai'i (1993) and the film *Half Life: A Parable for the Nuclear Age* (O'Rourke 1986) are particularly provocative illuminations of the imperial excursions of the United States, because they involve places that are central to the "tropical paradise" fantasies that are such an important part of mainland Americans' construction of "the other."

Contesting representations of non-Western peoples that put questions of power in the forefront also gives new illumination to classic anthropological topics. Cole and Chaikin's account of Canadian attempts to repress the potlatch (1990) reminds us that the imperial encounter on the North American continent was itself implicated in the intensification of this Northwest Coast Indian practice; it is to the credit of the recent Kwakiutl exhibit at the American Museum of Natural History (Jonaitis 1991) that the suppression of potlatch was included. The concept, "culture change," is all too passive, making it seem as if change happens without agency. Our students need to know that an important part of culture change in the world derives from the conscious and determined efforts of Western nations to eliminate practices in other cultures (within their borders or outside them) that contradicted their own values and threatened the effort to build national states or to maintain the colonial order.

The cultural constructions of the "other" in service to Western colonial enterprise are examined in interesting ways by Todorov (1984), Alloula (1986), Torgovnick (1990), and Said (1979) through an examination of European religious ideas, popular culture, art, novels, and scholarship. Gannanath Obesekeyere's (1991) examination of the European-Polynesian encounter finds it more interesting to explore why the Polynesians had reason to think the Europeans were cannibals than whether the Polynesians were cannibals, a question Europeans obsessed over. The Comoroffs's work (1992) on the colonial era in Southern Africa sets a high standard in meticulously demonstrating how the maintenance of European national identities was intimately connected to a construction of "the other" that was used to justify an assault on every aspect of the lives of the colonized.

Two excellent (and controversial) films that attempt to give voice directly to both parties in the encounters between Europeans and indigenous peoples are *First Contact* (1983) and *Cannibal Tours* (1987). Both films are situated in New Guinea, one in the 1930s and the other involving modern tourism. Watching them in sequence raises interesting questions about what, if anything, has changed in fifty years.

It is in the context of the continued postcolonial domination of the non-West by the West that anthropological representations specifically have most come under assault. Although contemporary reflexive ethnography addresses some of the issues involved in the view of cultural anthropology as a "stepchild of imperialism," a central problem remains: even with the dismantling of the colonial empires, the power disparity between Europe and the non-European world is a salient political fact that causes, as Edward Said puts it, an "almost insuperable discrepancy between political actuality based on force, and a scientific and human desire to understand the Other . . . sympathetically in modes not always circumscribed and defined by force" (1989, 217). Not everyone will agree with Said's arguments that anthropologists must take the powerful position of the United States in the world economy and global politics into account in their research. However, the recognition of this fact, some of the problems it raises in the creation of anthropological representations of the other, and our social responsibilities as intellectuals are, in my opinion, valid questions to be raised in the context of teaching.

Three important contemporary topics in this regard are the impact of multinational corporations, the human rights movement for indigenous peoples, and the issues surrounding the appropriation of cultural artifacts and identities for commercial purposes. These topics directly concern the traditional subjects and interests of cultural anthropology. The impacts of external economic factors on local economies and cultures are central in some ethnographies (Nash 1979) and the publications of Cultural Survival demonstrate one of the more significant anthropological efforts in collaboration with cultures that are ethnographically most familiar to students, such as the !Kung and the tropical forest populations of South America.

One important perspective on the impact of multinational corporations highlights the effect of the global factory on women (Warren and Bourque 1989). The impacts of multinationals abroad (Bonsignore 1992) can be usefully compared with their related impacts at home through such films as *Poletown Lives* (1982) and *Roger and Me* (1990). These films add a visual dimension to downward social mobility in the United States (Newman 1989), an aspect of our social stratification system that is rarely considered by students in their pursuit of the American Dream. Related to the expansion of multinational corporations is the concept of "development." Cultural anthropology can usefully critique this concept not only from the point of view of its failures in practice but also as a way of better understanding the identification between change and "progress" as a Western cultural value and the ways in which a global economy interacts with local cultures.

Attempts to construct a universally applicable statement of human rights has been challenged using the argument of cultural relativity, a central concept in cultural anthropology germane to the discussion of a globally wide variety of current events. These range from the fatwah on Salman Rushdie to the suppression of female circumcision. Classroom debates and small group discussions are good strategies for eliciting student participation on a number of questions: whether economic and social rights are as basic as political rights of free speech and free press (Howard 1992; Lal 1992); whether it is acceptable to name a car, baseball team, or malt liquor after a Native-American tribe or chief; or whether it is ethical to display Native-American bones as tourist attractions (Milun 1991–92). Several years ago, a simple raising of hands in my class indicated that not one of my students who shopped at Banana Republic (and many did) knew what a Banana Republic was. Since then, I begin this section of my course by repeating that survey and then reading Pablo Neruda's poem, *The United Fruit Co.* (1961).

If we are to attract and hold the interest of the many students who are not majoring in anthropology, raising these issues of cultures in interaction in the contemporary world, in which concepts of cultural anthropology play a central role, is essential. In demonstrating the impact of the central ideas of cultural anthropology outside the ivory tower, and in organizing our teaching around the themes of cultural encounters that have contemporary relevance for our students, we can more successfully compete with other disciplines and the popular media, which, however superficially, incorporate the idea of culture into their vocabulary and analyses.

Anthropology today is competing with highly technically accomplished representations of the "other" in the media. These representations, as well as students' own encounters with the "other" through tourism, warfare, or the popular media, very frequently exacerbate the distancing with the "other" and do not generate the anthropological aim of respect for cultural diversity. Indeed, these encounters, while seeming to make other cultures more "accessible" than ever, increase, rather than lessen, the need for cultural anthropology in a liberal arts curriculum, particularly an anthropology that continues its traditional attempts to see other cultures from the inside and to see ourselves as others see us.

Note

Author's Note: An important resource for teaching cultural anthropology along the lines suggested in this essay is *Anthropology as Cultural Critique: An Experimental Moment in the Human Sciences* (Marcus and Fischer 1986), which also contains some excellent teaching suggestions. I am very grateful to the National Endowment for the Humanities, which funded my participation in the 1991 Summer Seminar, *The Politics of Culture: Perspectives from the Pacific*, led by Geoffrey White and Lamont Lindstrom, at the East-West Center at the University of Hawai'i. The seminar provided a most congenial setting for furthering my thinking on these subjects as well as suggesting a wealth of useful references. In addition, I would like to acknowledge the interdisciplinary, student-focused, Thematic Studies Program and the Department of Anthropology at John Jay College, both of which have encouraged a deep commitment to teaching at our college. My friend and colleague, Jean Zorn, was kind enough to read an earlier version of this paper and her comments were most helpful.

References

Achebe, Chinua. 1969. *Things Fall Apart*. New York: Fawcett.

Alexander, Elizabeth. 1992. *The Venus Hottentot*. Charlottesville: University Press of Virginia.

Alloula, Malek. 1986. *The Colonial Harem*. Minneapolis: University of Minnesota

al-Rahman, Abd. 1991. *The Trench*. New York: Pantheon.

———. 1989. *Cities of Salt*. New York: Vintage.

Arbus, Diane. 1972. *diane arbus*. Millerton, N.Y.: Aperture.

Asad, Talal, ed. 1973. *Anthropology and the Colonial Encounter*. New York: Humanities Press.

Ashcroft, Bill, Gareth Griffiths, and Helen Tiflin. 1989. *The Empire Writes Back: Theory and Practice in Post-Colonial Literatures*. London: Routledge.

Basso, Keith. 1979. *Portraits of "the Whiteman": Linguistic Play and Cultural Symbols among the Western Apache*. New York: Cambridge University Press.

Benedict, Ruth. 1959a. "Counters in the Game." In *Writings of Ruth Benedict: An Anthropologist at Work*, edited by Margaret Mead, 40–43. New York: Avon.

———. 1959b. "The Uses of Cannibalism." In *Writings of Ruth Benedict: An Anthropologist at Work*, edited by Margaret Mead, 44–49. New York: Avon.

———. 1961. *Patterns of Culture*. Boston: Houghton Mifflin.

———. [1946] 1974. *The Chrysanthemum and the Sword: Patterns of Japanese Culture*. New York: Houghton Mifflin.

Berreman, Gerald. 1988. "Race, Caste, and Other Invidious Distinctions in Social Stratification." In *Anthropology for the Nineties*, edited by Johnetta Cole, 485–518. New York: Free Press.

Bohannan, Laura. 1966. "Shakespeare in the Bush." *Natural History,* August–September, 28–33.

Bolin, Anne. 1988. *In Search of Eve: Transsexual Rites of Passage*. South Hadley, Mass.: Bergin and Garvey.

Bonsignore, John J. 1992. "Multinational Corporations: Getting Started." *Focus on Law Studies* 8(1). (Available from the American Bar Association, Commission on College and University Non-professional Legal Studies, 541 N. Fairbanks Court, Chicago, IL 60611–3314.)

Bradford, Phillips Verner, and Harvey Blume. 1992. *Ota Benga: The Pygmy in the Zoo*. New York: Bantam.

Bowen, Elenore Smith. 1964. *Return to Laughter*. Garden City, N.Y.: Doubleday.

Brown, Dee. 1972. *Bury My Heart at Wounded Knee: An Indian History of the American West*. New York: Bantam.

Casey, Geraldine. 1991. "Racism, Anger, and Empowerment: Teaching Anthropology in a Multi-Racial, Working-Class Environment." *Transforming Anthropology* (Special Issue: Teaching as Praxis: Race and Ideologies of Power) 2(1):9–15.

Cesaire, Aime. [1955] 1972. *Discourse on Colonialism,* translated by Joan Pinkham. New York: Monthly Review Press.

Chagnon, Napoleon. 1983. *Yanomamo: The Fierce People.* 3rd ed. New York: Holt, Rinehart and Winston.

Cole, Douglas, and Ira Chaiken. 1990. *An Iron Hand upon the People: The Law against the Potlatch on the Northwest Coast.* Seattle: University of Washington Press.

Comoroff, John, and Jean Comoroff. 1992. *Ethnography and the Historical Imagination.* Boulder, Colo.: Westview.

DeVita, Philip R., ed. 1992. *The Naked Anthropologist: Tales from around the World.* Belmont, Calif.: Wadsworth.

DeVita, Philip R., and James Armstrong, eds. 1993. *Distant Mirrors: America as a Foreign Culture.* Belmont, Calif.: Wadsworth.

Dominguez, Virginia. 1986. *Black by Definition.* New Brunswick, N.J.: Rutgers University Press.

Du Bois, William E. B. [1903] 1989. *The Souls of Black Folk.* New York: Bantam.

Dundes, Alan. 1985. "The American Game of 'Smear the Queer' and the Homosexual Component of Male Competitive Sport and Warfare." *Journal of Psychoanalytic Anthropology* 8(3):115–134.

Ehrenreich, Barbara. 1990. "The Warrior Culture." *Time,* 15 October, 100.

Fanon, Franz. 1968. *The Wretched of the Earth.* New York: Grove Press.

Geertz, Clifford. 1989. *Works and Lives: The Anthropologist as Author.* Stanford, Calif.: Stanford University Press.

Gish, Jen. 1991. *Typical American.* Boston: Houghton Mifflin.

Gould, Stephen Jay. 1985. "The Hottentot Venus." In *The Flamingo's Smile: Reflections in Natural History,* 291–305. New York: W. W. Norton.

Harraway, Donna. 1989. *Primate Visions: Gender, Race, and Nature in the World of Modern Science.* New York: Routledge.

Harris, Marvin. [1969] 1990. *The Rise of Anthropological Theory: A History of Theories of Culture.* New York: Harper.

———. 1974. *Cows, Pigs, Wars and Witches: The Riddles of Culture.* New York: Vintage.

———. 1981. *America Now: The Anthropology of a Changing Culture.* New York: Simon and Schuster.

Herdt, Gilbert, ed. 1993. *Third Sex, Third Gender: Essays from Anthropology and Social History.* New York: Zone.

Hobsbawm, Eric, and Terence Ranger. 1983. *The Invention of Tradition.* New York: Cambridge University Press.

Howard, Rhoda E. 1992. "Human Rights and the Necessity for Cultural Change." *Focus on Law Studies* 8(1). (Available from the American Bar Association, Commission on College and University Non-professional Legal Studies, 541 N. Fairbanks Court, Chicago, IL 60611–3314).

Hymes, Dell. 1969. *Reinventing Anthropology.* New York: Pantheon.

Jonaitis, Aldona, ed. 1991. *Chiefly Feasts: The Enduring Kwakiutl Potlatch.* New York and Seattle: American Museum of Natural History and University of Washington Press.

Kottak, Conrad Phillip. 1978. "Rituals at McDonald's." *Natural History,* January, 74–83.

Lal, Vinay. 1992. "The Imperialism of Human Rights." *Focus on Law Studies* 8(1). (Available from the American Bar Association, Commission on College and University Non-professional Legal Studies, 541 N. Fairbanks Court, Chicago, IL 60611–3314.)

Lee, Richard Borshay. 1969. "Eating Christmas in the Kalahari." *Natural History,* December, 14, 16, 18, 21–22, 60–63.

Lewis, William F. 1993. *Soul Rebels: The Rastafari.* Prospect Heights, Ill.: Waveland.

Lindstrom, Lamont, and Geoffrey White. 1990. *Island Encounters: Black and White Memories of the Pacific War.* Blue Ridge Summit, Penn.: Smithsonian Institution Press.

Linton, Ralph. 1937. "One Hundred Percent American." *The American Mercury* 40:427–429.

Lyman, Christopher. 1982. *The Vanishing Race and Other Illusions: Photographs of Indians by Edward S. Curtis.* New York: Pantheon.

Mandelbaum, David G. 1963. "The Transmission of Anthropological Culture." In *The Teaching of Anthropology,* edited by David G. Mandelbaum, Gabriel W. Lasker, and Ethel M. Albert. Berkeley: University of California Press.

Marcus, George E., and Michael M. J. Fischer. 1986. *Anthropology as Cultural Critique: An Experimental Moment in the Human Sciences.* Chicago: University of Chicago Press.

Mascia-Lees, F., P. Sharpe, and C. Cohen. 1989. "The Postmodernist Turn in Anthropology: Cautions from a Feminist Perspective." *Signs: Journal of Women in Culture and Society* 15(1):7–33.

Mead, Margaret. [1928] 1971. *Coming of Age in Samoa.* New York: Morrow.

Merry, Sally. 1991. "Law and Colonialism." *Law and Society Review* 25(4):891–922.

Milun, Kathryn. 1991–92. "(En)countering Imperialist Nostalgia: The Indian Reburial Issue." *Discourse* 14(1):58–74.

Miner, Horace. 1956. "Body Ritual among the Nacirema." *American Anthropologist* 58:503–507.

Moffatt, Michael. 1989. *Coming of Age in New Jersey.* New Brunswick, N.J.: Rutgers University Press.

Morgen, Sandra. 1989. *Gender and Anthropology: Critical Reviews for Research and Teaching.* Washington, D.C.: American Anthropological Association.

Nanda, Serena. 1990. *Neither Man nor Woman: The Hijras of India.* Belmont, Calif.: Wadsworth.

Nash, June. 1979. *We Eat the Mines and the Mines Eat us: Dependency and Exploitation in Bolivian Tin Mines.* New York: Columbia University Press.

Neruda, Pablo. 1961. "The United Fruit Co." In *Pablo Neruda, Selected Poems.* New York: Grove Press.

Newman, Katherine. 1988. *Falling from Grace: The Experience of Downward Mobility in the American Middle Class.* New York: Vintage.

Norgren, Jill, and Serena Nanda. 1988. *American Cultural Pluralism and Law.* Greenport, Conn.: Praeger.

Obesekeyere, Gannanath. 1991. *The Apotheosis of Captain Cook: European Mythmaking in the Pacific.* Princeton, N.J.: Princeton University Press.

Ogbu, John. 1974. *The Next Generation: An Ethnography of Education in an Urban Neighborhood.* New York: Academic Press.

Perin, Constance. 1977. *Everything in Its Place: Social Order and Land Use in America.* Princeton, N.J.: Princeton University Press.

———. 1988. *Belonging in America.* Madison, Wis.: University of Wisconsin Press.

Perry, Richard J. 1992. "Why Do Multiculturalists Ignore Anthropologists?" *The Chronicle of Higher Education,* 4 March, A52.

Price, Richard. 1983. *First-Time: The Historical Vision of an Afro-American People.* Baltimore: Johns Hopkins University Press.

Rifkin, Jeremy. 1992a. *Beyond Beef: The Rise and Fall of the Cattle Culture.* New York: Dutton.

Rifkin, Jeremy. 1992b. "Beyond Beef." *Tikkun* 7(2):28–29.

Roscoe, Will. 1991. *The Zuni Man-Woman.* Albuquerque: University of New Mexico Press.

Sahlins, Marshall. 1994. "Goodbye to Tristes Tropes: Ethnography in the Context of Modern World History." In *Assessing Cultural Anthropology,* edited by Robert Borofsky, 377–394. New York: McGraw Hill.

Said, Edward. 1977. *Orientalism.* New York: Random House.

———. 1989. "Representing the Colonized: Anthropology's Interlocutors." *Critical Inquiry* 15:205–225.

———. 1993. *Culture and Imperialism.* New York: Knopf.

Sanjek, Roger. 1991. "The Ethnographic Present." *Man* (n.s.) 26:609–628.

Schwartz, Stuart, ed. 1994. *Implicit Understandings: Observing, Reporting, and Reflecting on the Encounters between Europeans and Other Peoples in the Early Modern Era.* New York: Cambridge University Press.

Scott, James. 1985. *Weapons of the Weak: Everyday Forms of Peasant Resistance.* New Haven, Conn.: Yale University Press.

Sembene, Ousmane. 1970. *God's Bits of Wood.* Garden City, N.Y.: Doubleday.

Shor, Ira, ed. 1987. *Freire for the Classroom: A Sourcebook for Liberatory Teaching.* Portsmouth, N.H.: Heinemann.

Shohat, Ella, and Robert Stam. 1994. *Unthinking Eurocentrism: Multiculturalism and the Media.* New York: Routlege.

Stocking, George. 1987. *Victorian Anthropology.* New York: Free Press.

Suleri, Sara. 1992. *The Rhetoric of English India.* Chicago: University of Chicago Press.

Tedlock, Barbara. 1991. "From Participant Observation to the Observation of Participation: The Emergence of Narrative Ethnography." *Journal of Anthropological Research* 47(1):69–94.

Terkel, Studs. 1984. *The Good War: An Oral History of World War Two.* New York: Pantheon.

Tocqueville, Alexis de. 1956. *Democracy in America,* edited by Richard D. Heffner. New York: Penguin.

Todorov, Tzvetan. 1984. *The Conquest of America.* New York: Harper and Row.

Torgovnick, Marianna. 1990. *Gone Primitive: Save Intellects, Modern Lives.* Chicago: University of Chicago.

Trask, Haunani. 1993. *From a Native Daughter: Colonialism and Sovereignty in Hawai'i.* Munroe, Maine: Common Courage Press.

Vanderwerth, W. C., ed. 1972. *Indian Oratory.* New York: Ballantine.

Warren, Kay B., and Susan C. Bourque. 1989. "Technology and Development Ideologies: Grameworks and Findings." In *Gender and Anthropology: Critical Reviews for Research and Teaching,* edited by Sandra Morgen, 382–410. Washington, D.C.: American Anthropological Association.

Weatherford, Jack. 1985. *Tribes on the Hill.* Rev. ed. Westport, Conn.: Greenwood.

Weiner, Annette. 1976. *Women of Value, Men of Renown: New Perspectives on Trobriand Exchange.* Austin: University of Texas.

Williams, Walter. 1992. *The Spirit and the Flesh.* 2d ed. Boston: Beacon.

Wolf, Eric. 1982. *Europe and the People without History.* Berkeley: University of California Press.

Films

Cannibal Tours. Dennis O'Rourke. 1987. 77 min., color, $75 rental, video. Direct Cinema Ltd., P.O. Box 69799, Los Angeles, CA 90069.

First Contact. Bob Connolly and Robin Anderson. 1983. 54 min., color and b/w. Rental $75. Filmmakers Library, 124 E. 40th Street, New York, NY 10016; Tel.: 212/808-4980.

Half Life: A Parable for the Nuclear Age. Dennis O'Rourke. 1986. 86 min., color. Purchase $350 Video. Direct Cinema Limited, Inc., P.O. Box l00003, Santa Monica, CA 90410; Fax 310/396-3233.

Keltie's Beard: A Woman's Story. Barbara Halpern Marineau. 1983. 9 min., color. Available from Filmmakers Library ($40 rental; $150 purchase).

Les Maitre Fous. Jean Rouche. 1957. 30 min., color. Documentary Educational Resources, 101 Moose Street, Watertown MA 02172.

Poletown Lives. George Corsetti, Jeanie Wylie, and Richard Wieske. 1982. 56 min., color, New Day Films.

Roger and Me. Michael Moore. 1990. Color, 91 min., VHS, Warner Home Video, $19.95.

Zoos. Frederick Wiseman. 1991. 134 min., color, video purchase, #350. Zipporah Films, One Richdale Avenue, #4, Cambridge, MA 02140.

Strategies for Combating Racism in the Classroom

MICHELE FOSTER

It is sometimes said that teachers teach more than their subject; they also teach themselves. In this chapter, I explore what I, an African American woman professor who has worked in predominantly European American university settings, teach not only about the subject of educational anthropology but about myself as well. To do so, I first describe who I am and the settings in which I have taught. Next, I present three areas where I attempt to challenge racism and the means I employ to achieve this goal. In some cases, these means are the result of deliberate choices. In others, they result merely from who I am. Those seeking answers or a set of strategies for combating racism will be disappointed. If it does anything, this chapter raises questions about an enterprise still in the making.

Learning to Recognize Racism

I was born in 1947 and grew up in the 1950s and 1960s. This was a time during which racism was rarely discussed, if it was discussed at all. When my Pullman Porter grandfather talked about what we today know as racism, he talked as if it were the property of individuals. It existed in the visible structures of segregation: separate schools, bathrooms, and accommodations for blacks and whites.

As a "Negro" in my precollegiate years of the 1950s and in my beginning college years in the early 1960s, it never occurred to me to interpret any of my negative experiences through the lens of racism. When I encountered difficulties, I attributed them to failures on my part or to the prejudices of individuals. It was only as I came to the end of my undergraduate years when my identity had been reformed as a black person that I came to understand that some of what had transpired over my lifetime might have been the result of racism.

As I did my doctoral work at an Ivy League university, I was more aware of racism. But despite this awareness, I found little evidence that life at the university was any less racist than when I had been an undergraduate.

Since the 1950s, there have been significant changes in the way we have come to understand racism. Racism is now classified into two types—individual and institutional. But how has this new understanding influenced this generation of college students? Among my students, although they seem aware of and indeed may abhor individual acts of racism, they do not seem to recognize that institutional racism is a fact of life.

After completing graduate school, I began teaching at the University of Pennsylvania in the Graduate School of Education. Despite its location in the city of Philadelphia, the number of African American students and faculty, especially women, was low. Later, I began teaching at the University of California-Davis, which although located in a multicultural state, also has a paucity of African American students and faculty.

To illustrate the severity of the problem, I will use the University of California-Davis as an example. In 1991–92, the year I began teaching at Davis, out of approximately 22,000 students, only 785 African Americans were enrolled in all the colleges and schools on the entire campus. There were seventeen African American faculty, six of them African American women. Four were in the College of Letters and Sciences. Four of these six women were tenured and I was one of them. The percentage of all African American faculty at Davis was 1.5%; the percentage of African American women faculty was .05%.

Although these numbers may seem low, they are close to the national statistics. In 1991, 2.5 percent of the full-time instructional faculty at institutions of higher education were African American men, and only 2.2 percent of the full-time instructional faculty at institutions of higher education were African American women.[1] Put another way, this means that at Davis the ratio of African American students to African American faculty was 46:1. Assuming that about half these students were women, the ratio of African American female students to African American female faculty was 65:1, which is slightly higher than the nationwide ratio of African American female students to African American female faculty, which is 58:1.

The likelihood that African American students will encounter African American faculty is low, but even more alarming and more relevant for this article is the minuscule probability that European American students will ever face an African American faculty member. Although the ratio of any group of students to any group of faculty varies tremendously from one campus to the next, given that the ratios of European American students to African American faculty of either gender is 364:1, the odds are low that Davis students, whether European American or African American, or students at any other campus will have had the experience of sitting in the class of an African American faculty member by the time they graduate.

At the University of Pennsylvania and the University of California-Davis, I taught graduate courses in the anthropology of education, the ethnography of speaking, and cultural diversity. At the University of California-Davis, I also taught two large undergraduate general education courses of 125 students each. Students were required to take these general education courses for graduation. Many of the students enrolled in these classes were majoring in science, engineering, or preprofessional studies and a good number of them resented having to take courses they perceived as irrelevant to their major and future careers. They believed, moreover, that general education courses should not be too difficult and should not take time from subjects they deemed more important. Consequently, they were resentful if the coursework was too demanding.

Challenges to Racism

There are three areas where I confront and challenge racism in the classroom. One challenge occurs around ideological issues, another is related to curricular issues, and the third deals with process.

Challenges through Curricular Issues

The general education course, Philosophical and Social Foundations of Education, traditionally is based on the disciplines of philosophy, history, sociology, and psychology. The dominance or intellectual stranglehold that psychology has held over the field of education can frequently be seen even in their physical connections, as the two departments are housed in the same building on many campuses. Despite the lip service paid to a more inclusive multicultural focus, schools of education often disregard the very notion of culture. Although this may seem strange to anthropologists, one of the real challenges faced in education courses is trying to present the alternate view of anthropology to students accustomed to the normative framework of psychology.

A large literature has developed over the past twenty years that deals with the influence of culture on schooling. To present students with a different understanding of what could be going on in the classrooms, I introduce the work of educational anthropologists like Frederick Erickson, Shirley Brice Heath, John Ogbu, Susan Phillips, my own work, and that of other educational anthropologists.

This is primarily a curricular issue. How do we get students to understand that education and schooling are not the same thing? How do we get students to consider that there may be alternative explanations to the psychologically based explanations educators rely on to explain school success and school failure? How do we get students to unpack ethnocentric terms like *culturally deprived*? This may seem like a small matter. However, in my work with students, it has become increasingly clear that not just in education courses but in most other courses as well students rarely are presented with information about African Americans, Native Americans, Mexican Americans, and Puerto Ricans that suggests their behavior makes sense.

The course also raises the question of who is responsible for the failure of students who are not European American. In other words, an important function of using an anthropological framework for understanding education and schooling is to move students away from explanations of individual deficiencies, personal deficits, and psychological maladaptation to anthropological perspectives that highlight alternate and competing cultural values, worldviews, and participation structures, which are part of the normal human condition.

My students are similar to those Friedl (this volume) describes in the 1960s, 1970s, and 1980s, individuals devoid of social and cultural context, who subscribe to the American ideology of individualism. So moving them away from psychological to anthropological explanations is difficult.

Challenges to Ideology

When they arrive at the college campus, many undergraduates have never encountered an African American in a position of authority. Consequently, many struggles go on in the contested terrain of my classroom as students dispute my intellectual and pedagogical authority. Before the first class begins, I sit in the audience and mingle with the students to get a sense of who they think the instructor might be. Do they expect a male professor? Have they heard that the professor is African American? When I finally present myself as the professor, the reactions range from shock and disbelief to mild curiosity. Once students get accustomed to the fact that I will be the professor, there are more obstacles to be dealt with. One of them concerns my presentational style. Despite my competence in middle-class academic conventions and discourse practices, my presentational style, classroom demeanor, discourse, and interactional style have been substantially influenced by my membership in a working class African American community. This is a style that most students have rarely encountered in the classroom and they either like it or they dislike it. Those who like it do so because in large classes of 125 students, I can lecture and simultaneously engage them in a conversation. On the other hand, many students are affronted by a presentation style not typical of the erudite, dry, often unenthusiastic style that has come to be associated with the intellectual, academic setting,[2] even though that is a style many of them resent.

Another contested area concerns the expectations I place on students and the demands I make of their academic work. "Who is this African American woman," they ask, "who demands that they come to class, defend their assertions, read the course material, and write with clarity and precision?" "Who is this African American woman who refuses to acquiesce to their demand that a grade be changed merely because they question it?" "What leads this African American woman to believe that she recognizes competent writing?" In this regard, my very presence in the university classroom is a challenge to the ideology of who can be a source of authority in the classroom.

An anecdote best illustrates the issues under discussion. Most of the students who challenge my assessment of the work are young white males. One young man whose work had been evaluated by the teaching assistant, also a black woman, contested the C grade she had assigned his mid-term examination. Claiming that a graduate student could not accurately assess his work, he demanded that his examination be reviewed by the professor. I reevaluated his midterm and, convinced the teaching assistant had been generous, awarded him a C-. When he came to my office hours, he argued, "The problem with you is that you don't like my writing style." To which I responded, "You don't have a writing style for me not to like. A writing style is the deliberate choice of conventions, or the breaking of them for a particular effect and that's what you haven't done."

Challenges through Process

I have devised particular pedagogical strategies to make visible the institutional racism that surrounds students but which they fail to recognize. Like Podolefsky (this volume), I have long been aware of the need to make learning interactive and to engage students actively in their own learning. In addition to attending my lecture-discussions, students work cooperatively in small groups. To make students aware of the many manifestations of institutional racism, I require them to bring in some real evidence of the phenomenon—a document, a sign, a report of some behavior, or anything else that might represent institutional racism. Students report what they have found and observed, and we discuss these issues in class.

Students at the University of Pennsylvania brought in a photograph of a placard they discovered in a secretary's office. Designed in a New Orleans ante-bellum style, the placard read "Slave Quarters." At the University of California-Davis, several students have remarked that they often overhear people refer to women and black faculty members by their first names but rarely hear these same individuals refer to white male faculty by their first names. We spend a lot of time in class discussing whether the indicators they have found are really manifestations of racism, and what kinds of racism these instances might manifest.

In the Cultural Diversity in Education course, a methods course required for students seeking a teaching certificate, I have developed an exercise in which I take passages from a second- or third-grade basal reader. I bring these passages to class, assume the role of a primary teacher, and ask the students to assume the role of primary students in a reading group. As the students read, I correct any errors that do not conform to African American English pronunciation and grammatical rules. We then discuss what it feels like to have to intuit and publicly perform with a set of different pronunciation and grammar rules, which by the way, do not affect the meaning of what you are reading.

The major thrust of this chapter has been to illustrate the means I use to expose students to a set of experiences Breitborde (this volume) has called "disquieting." Although confronting students with disquieting ideas and experiences may have educational value, it poses dangers for those who choose to do so. This practice raises a number of issues for administrators, especially as universities start to place more emphasis on teaching in deliberations about merit, tenure, and promotion. Do undergraduates respond to comparable behaviors of black and white faculty members in a similar manner? Do they judge them in the same way? At least one study suggests that other African American women faculty also report that European American students seem to resist their intellectual and pedagogical authority (Moses, 1989). These issues are worth further investigation.

It is too early to tell whether the strategies reported here make a difference in students' attitudes. I have reason to believe that they will eventually bear fruit. And for the moment that will have to suffice.

Notes

1. The statistics in this section are adapted from a 10 February 1994 article in *Black Issues in Higher Education.*
2. bell hooks has also addressed this point. See *Talking Back: Thinking Feminist, Thinking Black,* pp. 73–83.

References

hooks, b. 1989. *Talking Back: Thinking Feminist, Thinking Black.* Boston: South End Press.
Moses, Y. 1989. *Black Women in Academe: Issues and Strategies.* Washington, D.C.: Association of American Colleges.
Phillips, M. 1994. "Black Women Academics Meet, Send Message to Clinton." *Black Issues in Higher Education* 10(25):14–16, 19.

What Adding Women Has Stirred Up
Feminist Issues in Teaching Cultural Anthropology

Deborah S. Rubin

Nothing said in this paper can be considered original or avant-garde. It is clearly not its function to debate possible breakthroughs in anthropological theory but rather to propose the kinds of concepts that should appear in an integrated and balanced curriculum.

Cora Du Bois, 1963, 27

In the mid-1970s, three now-classic works—Michelle Rosaldo and Louise Lamphere's *Woman, Culture, and Society* (1974), Reyna Rapp Reiter's *Toward an Anthropology of Women* (1975), and Ernestine Friedl's *Women and Men: An Anthropologist's View* (1975)—were published, launching the transformative rethinking of anthropological approaches to the question of gender. These books asked and then began to answer the question, "Where are the women?" in anthropological accounts of cultures near and far. It was quickly apparent that this question contained another: How have anthropological concepts and methods directed or deflected our attention to and from women's activities and beliefs and influenced our interpretations? The emphasis in feminist anthropology thus shifted from documenting women's experiences for the purpose of answering universalist questions (such as What factors can predict women's status cross-culturally?) to refining the concept of gender and then rethinking anthropology from a gendered perspective. In the years since those first efforts to "add women and stir," feminist contributions to theory in anthropology have been made in each of the four major subfields and their subspecialties.[1] The rise of feminist theory in anthropology, though not always explicitly acknowledged,[2] has played a central and critical role in redefining and reformulating many of our basic assumptions about the meanings and patterns of social life that we as cultural anthropologists investigate.

What impact has feminist thought in the discipline had on the way in which cultural anthropology is taught to undergraduates? Should feminist anthropology be incorporated into introductory level courses or is it a distinct subfield that should be left to specialists? I argue that it is not only possible but critically important pedagogically to incorporate new theory into the teaching of introductory courses in anthropology. I also argue that materials that accurately represent the fruits of two decades of feminist work are readily available and easily incorporated into an introductory cultural anthropology course.

After briefly defining the scope of feminist anthropology and the concept of gender, this chapter discusses the impact of feminist perspectives on the teaching of undergraduate anthropology, illustrated by recent changes in textbooks and syllabi.[3]

What Is Feminist Anthropology?[4]

No single characterization applies to all positions labeled feminist, either in anthropology or outside it. Feminist anthropology in the United States grows out of and is grounded in second wave feminism, that period of feminist political activism and consciousness that emerged in the 1960s and 1970s. There are several connective strands between the diverse branches of feminism, known by a host of overlapping labels: radical, cultural, liberal, bourgeois, and socialist feminism. All feminists recognize that there are biological differences between sexes but argue that these physical traits neither dictate social behaviors nor explain the cultural meanings of those behaviors. Sexual difference does not justify structured inequality of opportunity nor access to public or private power and influence. bell hooks says, "To me, the essence of feminism is opposition to patriarchy and to sexist oppression" (hooks, Steinem, Vaid, and Wolf, 1993, 34). Marilyn French writes that feminists "believe that women are human beings, that the two sexes are (at least) equal in all significant ways, and that this equality must be publicly recognized" (1985, 442). The various branches of the feminist movement disagree on how to achieve the goals of equality between the sexes. Some feminists argue in favor of a gradualist approach through education and reform: some for separatism and isolation; others for a total overhaul of our current economic and social systems.

Contemporary feminism gave birth to feminist anthropology, and the latter is as diverse as its antecedents: "The feminist anthropological project has been influenced by shifts in the larger intellectual scene and in the global political economy in which we all live" (di Leonardo 1991, 1). Feminists in the 1960s and early 1970s who were also anthropologists found that the feminist concerns of their everyday lives outside the academy—specifically, the equal treatment of women—translated into their questioning anthropological texts and research methods as well as their treatment in the academy.[5] They found that women were not being equally treated in ethnographies, in data collection, or as subjects of research, and they created the work that became known as "cross-cultural perspectives on women" or the "anthropology of women." This period of "adding women and stirring" was largely corrective work, adding to the body of knowledge already accumulated by anthropologists or reinterpreting data collected about women by researchers, male and female, whose assumptions about the unimportance of women's role in cultural production had skewed their interpretations of the data. It soon became clear that reporting on women required a new examination of the concepts anthropologists had used. Examples of this type of work include Sally (Linton) Slocum's article (1975) reworking the "Man the Hunter" model in favor of "Woman the Gatherer," Annette Weiner's work on women's contributions to the Trobriand Island economies (1976), and the work of Jane Collier (1974) and Louise Lamphere (1974) on women and politics.

Much of this early work acknowledged that there was a universal category of "woman" that could be discussed and compared. "Woman" was assumed to be a natural cross-cultural category, even as ethnographic writings reflected women's multiple responsibilities and valuation in different cultural groups. First efforts at cross-cultural comparisons struggled with questions about universal subordination (Rosaldo and Lamphere 1974) or historical stages of equality and/or complementarity (Reiter 1975; Leacock 1978; Sacks 1974).[6] By trying to make sense of the many pictures of women that were brought to light, slowly at first and then more rapidly, in older monographs and new field studies, the first feminist anthropologists quickly came to question the utility of a single category of "woman." Within a few years, the contortions needed to fit all biologically defined women within any single category made clear its problematic character and, even more, that its apparent "naturalness" was actually another cultural construction, and one from Western culture at that (Strathern 1981; Yanagisako and Collier 1990). As many authors have noted (Morgen 1989; Moore 1988; di Leonardo 1991; Mullings 1992; Spelman 1988), the dismantling of "woman" was one of similar efforts to deconstruct concepts of "women's status," "race," "class," "ethnicity," and finally gender itself.

What type of anthropological research and writing can be called feminist anthropology today? To begin with, not all anthropological research that deals with women is necessarily feminist anthropology. Nor need all feminist anthropology deal with women. Following the usage of the *American Heritage Dictionary* (3rd ed.), the term *feminist anthropologist* may be applied to a person of any sex[7] who subscribes to the beliefs of feminism—that is, "belief in the social, political, and economic equality of the sexes." Henrietta Moore says of the relationship between feminism and anthropology in her book of that title,

> The identification of feminist concerns with women's concerns has been one of the many strategies employed in the social sciences to marginalize the feminist critique. . . . [T]he basis for the feminist critique is not the study of women, but the analysis of gender relations, and of gender as a structuring principle in all human societies. (1988, vii)

Feminist anthropologists use the concept of *gender* rather than *sex* as a fundamental starting point for social and cultural analysis. Gender, however, is a contested concept, used differently by different theorists. Most commonly, "gender" labels cultural definitions of masculinity and femininity (or other categories)[8] that are presented as analytically distinct from the so-called raw facts of biology—that is, sex.[9]

Distinguishing sex from gender has yielded powerful insights about the capabilities of culture and history to characterize difference among people. Gender, according to Moore (1988, 13), may also "be seen as a symbolic construction or as a social relationship," often in complementary ways. The term *gender* may also indicate that the ethnographer is researching *both* men and women, even while relying on dichotomous sex-defined categories of "male" and "female" for this purpose.[10] *Gender* also identifies a set of relational categories rather than a unidimensional property of individuals. People, under this usage, neither possess gender nor are they members of the "male" or "female" gender, although they have a gender identity. Judith Butler (1990) reviews the difficulties involved in defining gender without also examining the attendant assumptions of concepts such as "construction," "the body," and "identity."

Analysis of the categories of sex and gender has shown that although they are not reducible to each other, they are not entirely separate. Like other dualistic conceptualizations, they are too simplistic to capture the complex relationship between cultural meaning and human biology (Yanagisako and Collier 1990). If other cultures can show us different ways to link up but not reduce human behavior to sexual categories, we need also to look at the specific cultural associations of sex and gender that are common to the intellectual heritage of the discipline of anthropology. The division of "sex" from "gender" may be better understood as a specific cultural belief; what Mukhopadhyay and Higgins (1988) suggest is the product of a Eurocentric "folk" model of reproduction-related ideologies of gender.

In the last few years, one emphasis of feminist anthropology, as in other branches of feminist theory, has been to articulate more fully the intersections of gender with other social inequalities (Collins 1991; Morgen 1989; Mullings 1992; King 1988; Spelman 1988; Ware 1992), an effort that has continued the interdisciplinary character of much anthropological work. Feminist research has pointed out previously unrecognized ethnocentric biases in American anthropology and the Western grounding of many of its analytical categories (Lamphere 1991, ix). Though certainly not the only subfield to tackle these problems, feminist anthropology has been one of the most influential.

Acknowledging the Feminist Critique in the Teaching of Anthropology

To what extent have these three elements of the feminist critique—full recognition of the diversity of both women and men in creating human society, analysis of the gendered content of anthropological concepts, and investigation of the intersection of gender, racial, and class inequalities—been acknowledged in the teaching of introductory anthropology? Introductory textbooks are one of the most important sites of curriculum reform. For this reason, the American Anthropology Association's (AAA) Gender and the Anthropology Curriculum project paired the authors of five popular textbooks with feminist anthropologists[11] to address new theoretical perspectives on gender and to incorporate more fully the wealth of ethnographic data on women recently produced or uncovered. As Sandra Morgen and Mary Moran, co-coordinators of the textbook project explain, its goal was "to help them [the textbook authors] to *improve* their texts, not to produce a list of *approved* texts" (Morgen and Moran 1990, 100). The project generated requests from other authors for advice and collaboration from feminist anthropologists in revising their works.

Comparing this new generation of volumes to their ancestors reveals significant changes in both titles and content. Nonsexist language has replaced the use of "man" as a false generic that was commonly found in anthropological writings of earlier decades. Recently published texts have moved from depicting universally defined sexual categories as the basis for a specific sex-linked division of labor toward an exploration of how cultures differently define and construct gender relations in a variety of social domains such as language, ritual, economics, and politics. New texts often feature the works of prominent anthropologists who have written about gender issues, sometimes quoting at length from their ethnographies, showing pictures of women anthropologists in the field and emphasizing the activities of men *and* women in a variety of situations unusual in Western contexts.

The most impressive feature of these texts is the effort to work into each chapter ethnographic materials on women and on relationships between men and women, forcing the reader to recognize the role of women, as the Chinese proverb says, in "holding up half the sky." Women's activities in economics, politics, and religion as well as women's understandings of their world are no longer invisible in these texts.

Successful efforts to integrate ethnography on women into the body of most of the textbooks—the "add women and stir" method—still leaves untackled the question of thoroughgoing rethinking of the basic issues of the field from a feminist perspective, what di Leonardo has characterized as "the challenge of rewriting anthropology as if gender really mattered" (1991, 8). These efforts *have* been undertaken by feminist anthropology in all areas of the field and are continuing along the lines noted earlier, but they have yet to make their way into the introductory presentations of the discipline.

There remains therefore a wide gap between introductory representations of the field and the current state of the discipline. The difference is particularly evident in textbook chapters on theory or "schools of thought" in anthropology. Although certain perspectives are invariably discussed (such as evolutionism, structural-functionalism, structuralism, or symbolic anthropology) and others regularly represented (for example, cultural materialism, psychological anthropology, and political economy), discussion of feminist perspectives as a theoretical contribution in anthropology remain rare.

The scant theoretical treatment of feminist perspectives in introductory texts highlights the limitations of the additive approach to data on women, as equal attention to the cultural practices of both men and women is clearly not a sufficient catalyst for a more specifically feminist endeavor of gendering basic anthropological concepts.

Similar improvements and problems mark collections of supplementary readings. Old favorites and new collections alike are showing greater attention to gender issues and are placing articles on women and on gender throughout the topical sections of the volumes. Numerous ethnographic monographs on women and on gender, written for use at an introductory level, have appeared in recent years. Films and videos provide other avenues for portraying the gendered lives of others.

In summary, many teaching materials providing up-to-date and accessible representations of a feminist perspective in anthropology are now easily available. The claim that good material does not exist for entry-level students simply does not wash any longer.

To provide easier access to new works on women, on gender relations, and on gender issues, the American Anthropological Association's Gender and the Anthropology Curriculum project also included the production of a volume edited by Sandra Morgen (1989) analyzing feminist contributions in eighteen thematic and regional subfields. These essays relate feminist anthropological work to general anthropological developments, and provide extensive bibliographic references as well as teaching modules.[12] The American Anthropological Association, rather than another press, published the book to emphasize both the centrality of gender to the discipline and the association's support of the project. Those familiar with the volume responded to a 1992 survey with high praise for its usefulness in providing review essays on selected themes and specific world regions, for identifying bibliography, and for being a valuable resource in the preparation of lectures and course handouts.

Annual workshops with titles such as "Teaching about Race and Gender" have been held at the American Anthropology Association meetings since 1989, initiated by the late Sylvia Forman and her colleagues, as another avenue for curricular reforms. These sessions have provided numerous suggestions for teaching about diversity and difference and offer the opportunity for interested anthropologists to meet and exchange experiences, syllabi, bibliography, and other ideas. Review of the materials and experiences presented at the workshops suggests that feminist perspectives lend themselves to a more interactive, participatory type of teaching and learning.

In addition to changes in teaching materials and course content, feminism has influenced the institutional framework of anthropology in the United States. Judging by the self-descriptions printed in the American Anthropology Association Guide to Departments, most departments of anthropology have one or more faculty members specializing in gender issues. Courses specifically dealing with gender are offered at undergraduate and graduate levels. Some universities have begun to require a course in gender studies as part of their general education programs, and anthropology courses are often featured as options in these programs.

Where Do We Go from Here?

In her 1991 book, Micaela di Leonardo talks of anthropology as being at the crossroads of knowledge production and of gender being one of the most central and most interesting anthropological subjects. The essays in the volume provide an outlook on the many possible directions that feminist anthropology may take in the future, particularly as to how feminist ethnography can make links between the anthropological practices of the academic and the forging of a new agenda of feminist activism.

> The closer and more sympathetically feminists look at the world of women around them, the more we overhear the subtleties of submerged angry, world-reframing speech, the more challenged are the cultural, racial and class blinders of the dominant form of white feminism, and the more likely we are to see the political solutions already being formulated and promulgated by the women at the margins of published consciousness. (Lutz 1993, 394)

To make a greater impact on undergraduate students, however, three concrete steps might be taken: the writing of a (or several) feminist textbook(s) in introductory anthropology; perhaps more importantly (and more reflective of the anticanonical aspects of feminist viewpoints), the writing of a truly introductory textbook or collection in feminist anthropology, one that would not depend on prior familiarity with feminist classics (see, for example, Brettell and Sargent 1993); and finally, a continued pattern of cooperation such as was evident in the textbook project to thoroughly rework the basic concepts of anthropology so that gender is taken seriously.

But now really is not the time for conclusions. Feminist theory is not following a path of gradual linear or even multilinear evolution from which future forms might easily be extrapolated from current debates. We might more appropriately borrow from the new evolutionary models of punctuated equilibrium and envision ourselves situated within a moment of enormous, even explosive, change. The results may be transformations as yet unimagined.

The real measure of what impact feminist anthropology has had on the discipline of anthropology and its teaching lies less in my assessment than in the *other* articles in this volume and their attention to the concerns raised here. This article may reflect one aspect of feminist impact, but as Janet Wolff has written, alone it only represents more of the "'women and . . .' syndrome, whereby sympathetic and dutiful editors ensure that someone is invited to address the question of gender" (1990, 2). The 1963 volume had no such chapter; perhaps the volume thirty years hence will have no need for one either.

Notes

Acknowledgment: This paper rests on the work of many people, starting with Louise Lamphere, who, at Brown University in 1974, put together a course entitled "Anthropological Perspectives on Women" that shaped my first notions of what anthropology had been about and what it could be. Thanks also to Sandy Morgen and Mary Moran for providing the opportunity to write the first version of this paper. Members of the Association of Feminist Anthropology, my colleagues at the University of the Pacific, and all those who submitted syllabi and curricular materials to the Working Commission on Gender and the Anthropology Curriculum deserve note for their help, although the space available here precludes naming them individually.

1. Twenty years of critical feminist anthropology have produced a copious literature. Several excellent reviews of past trends and current issues may be found in Micaela di Leonardo's introductory essay in her edited collection *Gender at the Crossroads of Knowledge: Feminist Anthropology in the Postmodern Era* (1991), Sandra Morgen's introductory essay in her edited collection *Gender and Anthropology: Critical Reviews for Research and Teaching* (1989), and the review essays of Naomi Quinn (1977) and Carol Mukhopadhyay and Patricia Higgins (1988) in the relevant volumes of *Annual Review of Anthropology*.

2. See Morgen (1989, 7–9) for a discussion of how feminist anthropology has influenced or reshaped the work of several subdisciplines without recognition. Catherine Lutz (1990) does a fascinating quantitative study of citation rates of articles and of paper presentations at annual meetings dealing with feminist anthropology.

3. See, for more detailed treatment of the theoretical debates, di Leonardo (1991), Lamphere (1987), Moore (1988), Morgen (1989), and Sacks (1989), all of which include extensive bibliography.

4. The material presented in this section draws heavily on the works of Moore (1988), Morgen (1989), and di Leonardo (1991).

5. Margaret Andersen (1987) gives a helpful overview of the phases of curricular change.

6. See particularly Lamphere (1987), Mukhopadhyay and Higgins (1988), and Quinn (1977) for reviews of this stage of research.

7. I purposely note "any" rather than "either" sex as a nod toward the fascinating biological work of Anne Fausto-Sterling, which examines how the range of sexual characteristics are dichotomously categorized into two and only two sexes in American society. See "The Five Sexes," *The Sciences,* April/May 1993. See also the work by Collier and Yanagisako on the role of culture in defining the relationship between "sex" and "gender."

8. A simple dichotomous notion of gender can be biologically reductionist and heterosexist. Cultural anthropologists have made clear that other gendered notions of personhood categorize people in various overlapping ways—for example, in the literature on third/fourth gender categories such as the berdache (Blackwood 1984), hijra (Nanda 1990), and xanith (Wikan 1977). Anne Fausto-Sterling (1993) writes about how societal values force a range of biological conditions into rigid dichotomous categories in the United States.

9. A recent text makes the distinction in this way:
    Anthropologists use the term gender to refer to the cultural elaborations and meanings assigned to the biological differentiation between the sexes. The distinction between sex, which is biological, and gender, which is cultural, is an important one. (Haviland 1990, 32)

10. Note, for example, the following sentence: "The gender of the organizer(s) of each session was tabulated, as was the number of male and female paper givers" (Lutz 1990, 615).

11. Textbooks by Daniel Bates and Fred Plog, Carol and Melvin Ember, Marvin Harris, William Haviland, and Conrad Kottak were revised with the assistance of feminist anthropologists Lila Abu Lughod (Haviland), Louise Lamphere (Embers), Yolanda Moses (Kottak), Rayna Rapp and Ida Susser (Bates and Plog), and Nancy Scheper-Hughes (Harris). The AAA Project on Gender and the Curriculum, of which the textbook project is one part, is detailed in Sandra Morgen and Mary Moran (1990), "Transforming Introductory Anthropology: The American Anthropological Association Project on Gender and the Curriculum," *Women's Studies Quarterly*, 1 and 2:95–104.

12. The review articles cover the subfields of early hominid evolution, primate behavior, archaeology, and linguistics as well as major world areas including the Middle East, sub-Saharan Africa, southeast Asia, China, Latin America, the English-speaking Caribbean, several topics on the United States, and one on sexuality and gender variance.

References

Andersen, Margaret L. 1987. "Changing the Curriculum in Higher Education." In *Reconstructing the Academy*, edited by E. Minnich, Jean O'Barr, and Rachel Rosenfeld, 68. Chicago: University of Chicago Press.

Bates, David, and Fred Plog. 1990. *Cultural Anthropology*. 3rd ed. New York: McGraw-Hill.

Blackwood, Evelyn. 1984. "Sexuality and Gender in Certain Native American Tribes: The Case of Cross-Gender Females." *Signs: Journal of Women in Culture and Society* 10:27–42.

Brettell, Caroline B., and Carolyn F. Sargent. 1993. *Gender in Cross-Cultural Perspective*. Englewood Cliffs, N.J.: Prentice-Hall.

Butler, Judith. 1990. *Gender Trouble: Feminism and the Subversion of Identity*. New York: Routledge.

Collier, Jane Fishburne. 1974. "Women in Politics." In *Woman, Culture, and Society* edited by Michelle Rosaldo and Louise Lamphere, 89–96. Stanford, Calif.: Stanford University Press.

Collier, Jane, and Sylvia Yanagisako. 1987. *Gender and Kinship: Essays toward a Unified Analysis*. Stanford, Calif.: Stanford University Press.

Collins, Patricia Hill. 1991. *Black Feminist Thought: Knowledge, Consciousness, and the Politics of Empowerment*. New York: Routledge.

di Leonardo, Micaela. 1991. *Gender at the Crossroads of Knowledge: Feminist Anthropology in the Postmodern Era*. Berkeley: University of California Press.

Du Bois, Cora. 1963. "The Curriculum in Cultural Anthropology." In *The Teaching of Anthropology*, edited by David Mandelbaum, Gabriel Lasker, and Ethel Albert, 27–38. Berkeley: University of California Press.

Ember, Carol, and Melvin Ember. 1990. *Cultural Anthropology*. 6th ed. Englewood Cliffs, N.J.: Prentice-Hall.

Fausto-Sterling, Anne. 1993. "The Five Sexes." *The Sciences* 33(April–May):20–25.

Friedl, Ernestine. 1975. *Women and Men: An Anthropologist's View*. New York: Holt, Rinehart and Winston.

French, Marilyn. 1985. *Beyond Power: On Women, Men, and Morals*. New York: Summit Books (Simon & Schuster).

Harris, Marvin. 1991. *Cultural Anthropology*. 4th ed. New York: Harper and Row.

Haviland, William A. 1990. *Cultural Anthropology*. 6th ed. New York: Holt, Rinehart and Winston.

hooks, bell, Gloria Steinem, Urvashi Vaid, and Naomi Wolf. 1993. "Let's Get Real about Feminism: The Backlash, the Myths, the Movement." *Ms. Magazine* 4(2):34–43.

King, Deborah K. 1988. "Multiple Jeopardy, Multiple Consciousness: The Contest of a Black Feminist Ideology." In *Feminist Theory in Practice and Process*, edited by Micheline R. Malson, Jean F. O'Barr, Sarah Westphal-Wihl, and Mary Wyer, 75–105. Chicago: University of Chicago Press.

Kottak, Conrad Phillip. 1991. *Cultural Anthropology*. 5th ed. New York: McGraw-Hill.

Lamphere, Louise. 1974. "Strategies, Cooperation, and Conflict among Women in Domestic Groups." In *Woman, Culture, and Society*, edited by Michelle Rosaldo and Louise Lamphere, 97–112. Stanford, Calif.: Stanford University Press.

———. 1987. "Feminism and Anthropology: The Struggle to Reshape Our Thinking about Gender." In *The Impact of Feminist Research in the Academy*, edited by Christie Farnham. Bloomington: Indiana University Press.

———. 1991. "Foreword." In *Gender at the Crossroads of Knowledge: Feminist Anthropology in the Postmodern Era*, edited by Micaela di Leonardo, vii–ix. Berkeley: University of California Press.

Leacock, Eleanor. 1978. "Women's Status in an Egalitarian Society: Implications for Social Evolution." *Current Anthropology* 19:247–255, 268–275.

Lutz, Catherine. 1990. "The Erasure of Women's Writing in Sociocultural Anthropology." *American Ethnologist* 17(4):611–627.

———. 1993. Review of *Gender at the Crossroads of Knowledge*, edited by Micaela di Leonardo. *The Nation* 257(11):392–397.

Moore, Henrietta. 1988. *Feminism and Anthropology*. Minneapolis: University of Minnesota Press.

Morgen, Sandra, ed. 1989. *Gender and Anthropology: Critical Reviews for Research and Teaching*. Washington, D.C.: American Anthropological Association.

Morgen, Sandra, and Mary Moran. 1990. "Transforming Introductory Anthropology: The American Anthropological Association Project on Gender and the Curriculum." *Women's Studies Quarterly*, 1 and 2:95–104.

Mukhopadhyay, Carol C., and Patricia J. Higgins. 1988. "Anthropological Studies of Women's Status Revisited: 1977–1987." *Annual Review of Anthropology* 17:461–495.

Mullings, Leith. 1992. *Race, Class and Gender: Representations and Reality*. A publication of the Research Clearinghouse and Curriculum Integration Project. Memphis, Tenn.: Center for Research on Women.

Nanda, Serena. 1990. *Neither Man nor Woman: The Hijras of India*. Belmont, Calif.: Wadsworth.

Quinn, Naomi. 1977. "Anthropological Studies on Women's Status." *Annual Review of Anthropology* 6:181–225.

Reiter, Rayna Rapp, ed. 1975. *Toward an Anthropology of Women*. New York: Monthly Review Press.

Rosaldo, Michelle Z., and Louise Lamphere, eds. 1974. *Woman, Culture, and Society*. Stanford, Calif.: Stanford University Press.

Sacks, Karen. 1974. "Engels Revisited: Women, the Organization of Production and Private Property." In *Woman, Culture, and Society*, edited by Michelle Rosaldo and Louise Lamphere, 207–222. Stanford, Calif.: Stanford University Press.

———. 1989. "Toward a Unified Theory of Class, Race, and Gender." *American Ethnologist* 16(3):534–550.

Slocum, Sally (Linton). 1975. "Woman the Gatherer: Male Bias in Anthropology." In *Toward an Anthropology of Women*, edited by Rayna R. Reiter, 36–50. New York: Monthly Review Press.

Spelman, Elizabeth V. 1988. *Inessential Woman: Problems of Exclusion in Feminist Thought*. Boston: Beacon Press.

Strathern, Marilyn. 1981. "Culture in a Netbag: The Manufacture of a Subdiscipline in Anthropology." *Man* 16:665–688.

Ware, Vron. 1992. *Beyond the Pale: White Women, Racism, and History*. London: Verso.

Weiner, Annette. 1976. *Women of Value, Men of Renown*. Austin: University of Texas Press.

Wikan, Unni. 1977. "Man Becomes Woman: Transsexualism in Oman as a Key to Gender Roles." *Man* 12(2):304–319.

Wolff, Janet. 1990. *Feminine Sentences: Essays on Women and Culture*. Berkeley: University of California Press.

Yanagisako, Sylvia, and Jane Collier. 1990. "The Mode of Reproduction in Anthropology." In *Theoretical Perspectives on Sexual Difference*, edited by Deborah Rhode, 131–141. New Haven, Conn.: Yale University Press.

Teaching with Film—
Teaching with Video

Karl G. Heider

Teaching with film used to be pretty straightforward. You rented a film, arranged a projector, turned off the lights, ran the film, turned the lights back on.

There were some problems to solve: you could incorporate the film into the course to a greater or lesser degree. At the low incorporation end of the spectrum you could use the film as a baby-sitting device while you went off to the American Anthropological Association (AAA) meetings, moving quickly on to other topics on your return. Or you could choose a film with associated readings, set students up with study questions, and discuss it afterward. Another challenge was film selection. When I took my first introductory cultural anthropology course from Cora Du Bois in 1954, as I recall she showed some of the Bateson/Mead Balinese films, which had come out only two years earlier, and Robert Flaherty's *Nanook,* and also *WeeGee's New York.* There weren't many more she could have shown us that year. The proliferation of anthropological films since then has been astonishing. The seventh edition of *Films for Anthropological Teaching* (Heider 1983) listed over 1,575 titles, and the eighth edition (1995) doubled that.

From the standpoint of teaching with film, the greatest challenges were to find films that addressed the same sorts of subjects and theoretical issues on which we focused our courses or, even better, to find projects that had coordinated filming with writing such that the same cultures, the same events, or the same problems were treated on film and on the printed page.

There are now many admirable solutions to these problems, and we see more appearing constantly. I would just mention, as examples, two projects. Both are from the University of Southern California, both are on Bali: Stephen Lansing's book (1991) and film (*The Goddess and the Computer*), which deal with religion and irrigation and applications of anthropological insights, and the five Jero films and book (1986) on the spirit medium and ritual by Linda Conner, Patsy Asch, and Timothy Asch. Also, Indiana University Press has just published Margaret Thompson Drewal's book on Yoruba ritual (1992) with a thirty-minute companion video.

I do not mean that there is no more excitement in this direction. There will always be new and effective and innovative collaborations between filmmakers and anthropologists exploring new problems. And it is not just that filming will follow where anthropological thinking leads. Advances in film may feed back to anthropology. I suspect that the technical innovation of synch sound, which allowed people's own voices to be heard on film, thus displacing the omnipotent narrator's voice, helped to advance anthropological understandings of reality and reflexivity in postmodern thinking.

But the real excitement now, the real challenge, lies in the new technology of videotape. Five years ago, few of us used much video in our teaching; five years from now, few of us will be using much film. Our departments will hesitate to buy or rent films on celluloid when they can get the same film on videotape for a fraction of the cost. Money that used to be spent on 16mm projectors will now go into video equipment—to increasingly better and cheaper videocassette recorders (VCRs), monitors, and video projectors. We will continue to shoot and edit on celluloid, but what is used in classes will be on videotape. Thirty years ago, when Ray Birdwhistell contributed his chapter titled "The Use of Audio-Visual Teaching Aids" to the 1963 *Teaching of Anthropology* (Mandelbaum, Lasker, and Albert), he was primarily concerned with how to achieve close analysis of movie footage in the classroom. He used a PerceptoScope projector, which then cost $2000, an impossible expense for most departments.

Certainly, a decent 16mm print of a film gives a better image than even the best video screen or projector can. But few working departments of anthropology will buck the shift from film to video.

After a moment of silence to mourn the loss of visual quality——I want to shift the direction of this chapter from Teaching with Film to Teaching with Video. The fact is that I would add little on the film side to what I have already written in 1976:130–134, 1983, or 1997. But video is an entirely different matter, opening exciting new opportunities.

The great advantages that video does have over film are its low cost and its flexibility. This has tremendous implications for anthropological research of all sorts, but that is another story. Here, let us consider the opportunities for teaching.

An Audiovisual Anthropology Lab

It is now possible to set up, at reasonable cost, an audiovisual anthropology lab that can serve both teaching and research interests of a department. We assume basic equipment: viewing stations, each with a high quality VCR that allows variable speed forward and reverse, plus holding frames. These now cost about $500 (as opposed to a basic but dumb VCR at $200). We also need a monitor. Ideally a department would have several of these. There should be a minimum of two so that at times more than one team or individual could analyze material simultaneously. We are talking about constructing a sort of visual records reading room where students could work over video records the way they read difficult passages in print. One difference might be that instead of the silence of a library, there can be noise and shared, mutually stimulating discovery.

Different Videos for Different Purposes

Anthropological Films (Documentary Nonfiction on Ethnographic Archaeological and Other Subjects)

When anthropological films were available only on 16mm film, they generally would be shown to a class straight through. At best, there would be an opportunity for discussion before and afterward. The room had to be fairly dark, there was one scheduled screening, and it was not easy to stop the film in mid-path and review a scene. With the same films on videotape, they can be shown with enough room light to allow notetaking; they can be made available for students to study at the analysis stations, viewing and re-viewing crucial segments. Then students can be directed toward more penetrating questions. Standard films can be scrutinized; rare films can be revived. For example, the seven Bateson/Mead films on Bali and New Guinea, which demand intensive viewing, have just been released on video by Penn State. And Milestone has just released *Grass* (1925) and *In the Land of the War Canoes* (1914) on video.

Hollywood Feature Films of "The Other"

Video rental shops and specialist catalogues now make available a wide range of fiction films that demonstrate the construction of The Other. Ideas about Native Americans, African Americans, Africans, and Pacific Islanders can be traced through fiction films (as well as pseudo-documentary films) from the early 1930s through today, all easily available on video and most quite inaccessible just a few years ago. For example, Milestone has just released on video *Chang* (1927), *The Silent Enemy: An Epic of the American Indian* (1930), and *Tabu: A Story of the South Seas* (1931) for $39.95 each. To take up class time screening many feature-length films is wasteful, but with videotape it is possible to assign such films as outside viewing.

In the pre-Gutenberg Middle Ages, it was necessary for a professor to stand in front of a class and read out of a unique manuscript. Today we ask students to read published materials on their own and we use lecture time for other purposes. Likewise, 16mm films had to be screened in class. But now video allows us to move beyond this and use more films more flexibly.

Feature Films from Other Cultures

There have long been some feature films from other cultures available in 16mm, but they were few and expensive. (In the early 1970s, Eugene Hammel solved this problem for his introductory cultural anthropology course at the University of California-Berkeley by talking an off-campus theater into running *Shadows of Forgotten Ancestors* and *I Have Even Known Happy Gypsies,* and sending his students to see them. The video explosion has changed all this. There are the "foreign film" sections in local video rental shops, many specialized mail-order companies, and videotape selections at ethnic grocery stores (mainly Asian). The new South and Southeast Asia Video Archive at the

University of Wisconsin in Madison now has hundreds of films and television programs available through interlibrary loan. Indiana University Press has just issued a second edition of Chris Berry's book *Perspectives on Chinese Cinema* together with four important Chinese films on video.

These films are not meant to be ethnographic. They are cultural texts embodying culture, and can be so analyzed. I have used a dozen carefully selected Indonesian films as the core of a course on Indonesian film and culture (Heider 1991), and once tried a much more experimental short course on Chinese film and culture. The villages, tribes, and atolls of our traditional concerns did not offer us fictional fantasies on film. But as anthropology broadens its purview to include national cultures, we suddenly recognize these films as rich cultural resources.

These foreign films also provide a huge corpus of well-shot documentation of behavior. The action is all staged, of course, but the actors are performing for members of their own culture and however great the exaggeration, it is not random but culturally based. For a course in the anthropology of nonverbal communication, students have taken a single feature film and searched through it for hand gestures, proxemic behavior, use of public space, and the like. (Italian and Latin American films work best.) Also, students have located complex interaction in brief segments of these films for microanalysis, showing for example, Argyle's intimacy equilibrium model (1976, 64ff) in *Cinema Paradiso*, and complex respect behavior in *Tampopo* (see Ohnuki-Tierney 1990).

Specially Shot Interaction Footage

The same sorts of interaction can be usefully studied at various levels, micro to macro, in specially shot footage. A twenty-minute sequence of complex children's behavior on a Dani playground, shot in video, then transferred to film, and then back to video, maintains sufficient definition to be useful for a variety of such analysis projects (Heider 1977).

Home-Made Video Slide Tapes

Finally we circle back to the ethnographic film model, the documentation of cultural behavior and analysis, more or less theory driven. Making anthropological films (ethnographic, archaeological, and so on) is beyond the reach of most anthropologists, but now video allows us to rescue our images retrospectively and produce something approaching real film. We can turn our old still photographs, now languishing on the tops of our bookcases, into short, narrated, video slide tapes.

The low-tech approach uses two slide projectors and a video camera, equipment that most departments already have. The special equipment needed is a simple $50 box with mirror and opaque glass, and a device to allow one slide projector to dissolve to the other (costing a few hundred dollars). With this we can easily and cheaply produce video slide tapes to illustrate our articles and books. The high-tech solution, which should soon be within the reach of most departments, involves transferring slides or negatives onto compact disc (CD) imaging discs, then doing the editing on computer and printing out onto videotape.

For example, I have twice required students in an undergraduate Southeast Asia course to read the important new volume, *Power and Difference: Gender in Island Southeast Asia* (edited by Jane Monnig Atkinson and Shelly Errington, 1990). The book makes some important theoretical points through eleven well-written ethnographic chapters. However, students unfamiliar with Southeast Asia struggle through the jungle of similar but different ethnic groups. If the author of each chapter had also prepared a twenty-minute video slide tape, students could read and view, and they would come away with a much more profound understanding of both ethnography and theory. Robert Heizer did something like this with *Excavations at La Venta* (1963). That film is constructed almost entirely from still photographs. Unfortunately, it has been relatively ignored of late.

Conclusions

Videotape now allows great, even revolutionary, opportunities for teaching anthropology, and the equipment is within the means of most anthropology departments. I have two specific recommendations to further these ideas:

• Syllabi from courses making extensive innovative uses of films/videos can be collected and published through the AAA. (I have been using films and videos in teaching for a long time now and have found some things that work well. But I am still lifting great ideas from other people's syllabi.)

• We should approach video slide tapes in a systematic way, encouraging colleagues to use their old photographs and suggesting that those undertaking new research shoot photographs in anticipation of making video slide tapes (for example, always shoot horizontal, not vertical). We should develop a nonprofit distribution system through the AAA, comparable to the journal format, which makes short papers widely available. (Ethnographic films, like books, are a whole different matter, but our immediate teaching need is for these videotapes.)

References

Argyle, Michael, and Mark Cook. 1976. *Gaze and Mutual Gaze,* 64ff. Cambridge, England: Cambridge University Press.

Berry, Chris, ed. 1991. *Perspectives on Chinese Cinema.* 2d ed. Bloomington: Indiana University Press.

Birdwhistell, Ray L. 1963. "The Use of Audio-Visual Teaching Aids." In *Resources for the Teaching of Anthropology,* edited by David G. Mandelbaum, Gabriel W.

Lasker, and Ethel M. Albert, 49–61. Washington, D.C.: American Anthropological Association.

Conner, Linda, Patsy Asch, and Timothy Asch. 1986. *Jero Tapakan: Balinese Healer. An Ethnographic Film Monograph*. Cambridge, England: Cambridge University Press.

Drewal, Margaret Thompson. 1992. *Yoruba Ritual*. Performances, Play, Agency. Bloomington: Indiana University Press.

Heider, Karl G. 1977. "From Javanese to Dani: The Transformation of a Game." In *Studies in the Anthropology of Play: Papers in Memory of B. Allan Tindall,* edited by Phillips Stevens, Jr. Proceedings of the 2d Annual Meeting of the Association for the Anthropological Study of Play.

———. 1983. *Films for Anthropological Teaching*. 7th ed. Washington, D.C.: American Anthropological Association.

———. 1991. *Indonesian Cinema. National Culture on Screen*. Honolulu: University of Hawaii Press.

———. 1995. *Films for Anthropological Teaching*. 8th ed. Washington, D.C.: American Anthropological Association.

———. 1997. *Grand Valley Dani. Peaceful Warriors*. Fort Worth: Harcourt Brace.

Lansing, J. Stephen. 1991. *Priests and Programmers. Technologies of Power in the Engineered Landscape of Bali*. Princeton, N.J.: Princeton University Press.

Mandelbaum, D. G., G. W. Lasker, and E. M. Albert, eds. 1963. *The Teaching of Anthropology*. Berkeley: University of California Press.

Ohnuki-Tierney, Emiko. 1990. "The Ambivalent Self of the Contemporary Japanese." *Cultural Anthropology* 5(2):197–216.

Film Distributors

Milestone Film and Video, Inc. 275 West 96th Street, Suite 28C, New York, NY 10025. Phone: (212) 865-7449.

Audio-Visual Services, Pennsylvania State University Special Services Building, 1127 Fox Hill Road, University Park, PA 16803-1824. Phone: (814) 865-6314.

Festival Films, 2841 Irving Ave. S., Minneapolis, MN 55408. Phone: (612) 870-4744.

Facets Features, Facets Cinematheque, 1517 West Fullerton Ave., Chicago, IL 60614. Phone: (800) 331-6197; (312) 281-9095.

TEACHING
LINGUISTIC
ANTHROPOLOGY

"Humanizing" Language through
Its Anthropological Study

L. B. BREITBORDE

---

*The field of linguistics, the scientific study of human natural language . . .
is concerned with the nature of language and communication.*

Akmjian et al. 1990, 5

*Linguistics is about what we know as speakers (and hearers) of a language, about how to formalize that knowledge explicitly, and about
explaining how we acquire and use that knowledge.*

Smith 1989, 2

*Language is of primary interest to anthropologists for at least three reasons. First, fieldworkers need to be able to communicate with their informants. . . . Second . . . what is learned about the inner workings of
language can then be applied to other domains of culture. . . . Third . . .
by learning another society's language, we learn something about their
culture as well.*

Schultz and Lavenda 1995, 103

Linguistic anthropology, the fourth traditional subfield, is by most measures the smallest segment of the profession: it has the smallest number of practitioners, the fewest explicitly anthropological associations, the fewest journals. Not surprisingly, of all the subfields, linguistic anthropology is the one most easily blurred in our collective consciousness with an allied discipline—namely, linguistics. The centrality of language to the human condition has attracted so much interest that it would be surprising if its study had *not* gained a formidable level of sophistication and uniqueness of method, informed by research from many academic fields. Professional anthropologists today easily associate the study of language not only with autonomous linguistics departments, but with centers for the study of cognition, artificial language programs, and computer language institutes. Yet, even as this multidisciplinary attention seems to distance the focused study of language from the center of anthropological concerns, language remains an enduring and unique (although sometimes contested) marker of our humanity.

Perhaps because language is a domain that has been subjected to such formalized, exacting, and esoteric methods, general anthropology often remains puzzled by the relevance of formal notational systems and tree-diagrams. The result is that many anthropologists remain committed *in principle* but not in practice to linguistic anthropology. We breathlessly wait for others to tell us whether the latest information on chimps and porpoises has destroyed claims to the unique humanness of language; and having hung on to generative grammar but unable to really figure out linguistic pragmatics, we desperately hope no one will think to ask us to explain "government and binding theory."

There is no denying that the vitality of linguistics as an autonomous discipline, the attraction of psychologists and philosophers to its theoretical advances, and its methodological sophistication have distanced many anthropologists from the sense of comfort and "ownership" once much more common. But perhaps more unfortunate is the way in which the mystification of linguistics leads to an alienation of general anthropology from the study of language.

Perhaps an explanation for that "distancing" of anthropology from language study and the frequent surrender of language to the field of linguistics— as well as a promise for a revitalized subfield—lies in the special characteristics of our field. Education today (kindergarten through twelfth grade and university level) often emphasizes the necessity for interdisciplinary approaches to real-world issues. As an inherently interdisciplinary field, anthropology should be at the center of most such pursuits. But the emergence of a separate discipline—linguistics—confuses the division of labor in the interdisciplinary study of language. We might be better off if we remembered from time to time that anthropology's strength lies not simply in its broad scope but in its *integrative* character: we are the ones who seek connections; who look for relationships; who try, even in an increasingly collaborative and interdisciplinary enterprise, to function without blinders. This integrative character underscores the continuing and unique contribution anthropologists can make to language study; it also indicates how language-focused questions asked by anthropologists can reveal key features of social and cultural processes that "non-linguistic" anthropologists study.

Anthropology reminds us of the distinctive role of language in human behavior and human history. Anthropology considers language not simply an artifact, or human creation, but contextualizes its study in terms of wider questions we want to answer about human culture and social organization, their development over time, their diversity and variation, their power to shape behavior and our lives. These larger questions are not always systematically pursued by linguists; yet their study informs the tasks of contemporary linguistics in critical ways:

- Linguists study structural features of language systems, but anthropology provides the methodological and analytical tools for the systematic consideration of extralinguistic factors that shape linguistic structure and language use.

- Linguistic theory continues to recognize the importance of speaker intention, context of situation, and other culturally constructed factors; again, anthropology provides methodological tools and analytical frameworks that capture the patterns, regularities, contradictions, and creativity of the human use of language.

- Linguistics situates the exploration of language within the study of human cognition; anthropology asks, "When and how did this cognitive ability originate? How do its development and human prehistory intertwine?"

- Linguistics values language as a human ability; anthropology asks what the value of language is for human beings.

Linguistics and the *anthropological study of language* are not the same thing, yet the conflation of the two is evidenced by the common practice of anthropologists to list "linguistics" (not "linguistic anthropology") as a subfield. The following three chapters offer evidence of the difference, and remind us of the need to consider language from an *anthropological* viewpoint in any attempt to represent the human condition.

Nancy Hickerson suggests ways to integrate linguistic anthropology in the general anthropology curriculum, especially emphasizing how introductory anthropology is presented to students. Carol Eastman describes developments in the past several decades that have led to three major areas of current anthropological concern for language: (1) the focus on discourse—that is, language as a kind of behavior through which individuals negotiate social position, (2) a focus on the "cultural logic" reflected in the structures of particular languages, and (3) the relationship between language structure and the communicative uses to which it is put. And Jean DeBernardi demonstrates the potential for language-focused questions to illuminate broader cultural questions asked by anthropologists at all levels of their teaching.

All three chapters demonstrate again the centrality of language in what we do and think, how we behave as humans. And all three demonstrate that the central concern of teachers of anthropology should not be the number of linguistic anthropologists or the autonomy of the subfield in our departments of anthropology. Constraints of size and budget may limit the number of linguistic anthropologists, but they do not preclude giving ample consideration to language. Its absence diminishes our understanding of our own humanity—as well as teaching and learning about that humanity.

References

Akmajian, Adrian, Richard A. Demers, Ann K. Farmer, and Robert M. Harnish. 1990. *Linguistics: An Introduction to Language and Communication.* 3rd ed. Cambridge, Mass.: MIT Press.

Smith, Neil. 1989. *The Twitter Machine: Reflections on Language.* London: Basil Blackwell.

Schultz, Emily A., and Robert H. Lavenda. 1995. *Cultural Anthropology: A Perspective on the Human Condition.* 3rd ed. Mountain View, Calif.: Mayfield Publishing Company.

How to Save Linguistic Anthropology

NANCY P. HICKERSON

Language in the Undergraduate Curriculum

Is American anthropology, after almost a century of asserting a central role for language in our discipline, still uncertain about that role? Beginning with Boas's *General Anthropology* (1938), almost every introductory textbook has included a chapter on language and informed the student that linguistic anthropology ranks—along with ethnology, archaeology, and biological anthropology—as one of our primary fields of study. Today, however, linguistic anthropology appears to be in a decline: professionals openly predict its demise, linguistic courses are underenrolled, and linguistic positions are, in some departments, threatened or insecure. When linguistic specialists retire, will they be replaced? A recent Wenner-Gren Foundation conference found, among other problems affecting the future of anthropology, that "linguistic anthropology is not attracting enough graduate students to maintain itself" (*Anthropology Newsletter,* 1993).

Will linguistic anthropology endure? In some situations, the rise of linguistics as an autonomous, rather than interdepartmental, program has undoubtedly drawn a number of students away from anthropology. Within anthropology, new fields of specialization have arisen (educational anthropology, cognitive anthropology, and so on), and some professionals reject traditional rubrics entirely or advocate subdisciplinary autonomy. Subject matter proliferates and specialization increases, in linguistics as in other areas. As a countertendency, however, it seems increasingly difficult to isolate language and to maintain the traditional separation of "race, language, and culture." In today's anthropology, language cannot possibly be considered—as Franz Boas sometimes characterized it—an independent variable. A consideration of important recent research areas such as primate communication, linguistic and cultural origins, cognitive universals, and the ethnography of communication (to name a few) reveals the intense interrelatedness of biology and culture, of linguistic and nonlinguistic behavior. An anthropology stripped of linguistic content would be impoverished indeed! If we continue to teach a holistic anthropology, language must have a place; its relevance cannot be denied.

Linguistic anthropology, therefore, should not need a spokesperson to plead the case for its continued existence. However, it may be time for changes in the teaching of linguistic anthropology—changes that will make students more aware of its integral place in the field. Let me draw what may seem, at first, a far-fetched analogy. The women's studies movement began to influence

154

the social sciences roughly three decades ago. Through the 1960s and 1970s there was a drive to define and document the position of women in society and to introduce feminist courses into the curriculum. At this point, feminist anthropology was asserting its existence and sought a separate recognition, almost approaching the status of subdiscipline (and thus roughly comparable to the traditional status of linguistic anthropology). In the 1980s, however, the women's anthropology caucus began to move to integrate feminist content across the curriculum—an effort that paid off and is reflected in the best of the current textbooks. It is also reflected in the ideas and attitudes of today's students, who would be shocked by the sexist language and androcentric presentation of culture typical of the anthropology of an earlier generation.

A similar effort is long overdue to better integrate linguistic anthropology into the curriculum, especially at the introductory level. This is not to suggest that every department change its course offerings, and I surely cannot demand that every department hire a linguist. Further, I acknowledge that generalists cannot be expected to give technical instruction in linguistic methodology. What can be done, however, is to make sure that the findings of linguistic research are presented as significant, as part of the body of anthropological theory, and to stimulate student interest in that research. The problem, then, is the development of a strategy toward this end; this is especially pressing considering that many anthropology programs do not, at present, employ linguistic faculty or offer courses in this subdiscipline.

The Institutional Setting

American college and university students can pursue an anthropological education in a variety of settings. Universities with both doctoral and undergraduate programs in anthropology usually have specialist faculty, who teach required courses in all four subfields. This is not to deny that strength is uneven—students, especially at the graduate level, usually "shop around" for training in certain areas of specialization. There are, of course, highly respected linguistic anthropologists, mainly concentrated in graduate departments, who have a profound impact on anthropological theory and practice and who attract numbers of graduate students; but their numbers, overall, are evidently dwindling.

Institutions that offer the M.A. and B.A., and those that offer the undergraduate degree only, also reveal interesting variations in staff and curriculum;[1] there may be several courses in linguistic anthropology when a faculty member has expertise in that area.[2] With a few such exceptions, however, a typical pattern emerges: catalog statements usually point out the comprehensive or holistic character of anthropology and often name the four traditional subfields in describing the program. A minority lists only three subfields, however, and may omit any mention of linguistic anthropology (one of those sampled advises students who anticipate graduate study to take linguistics courses elsewhere).

Almost all the programs surveyed offer a one-semester introductory course in cultural anthropology, which usually includes some linguistic content; only one program was found to list an introduction to language and culture. A one-semester combined course in archaeology and physical anthropology may be paired with cultural anthropology as a two-semester sequence. (A comprehensive survey course—common a generation ago—is rarely offered.) In the cultural course, language is among several subordinate topics—including economics, religion, folklore, and others—that may be mentioned in the catalog description. Thus, in effect, *language* is not presented as being on par with *culture,* but in one among a number of subordinate rubrics; predictably, in such a course, only a small part of the term—perhaps a week—could be allotted to language.

In many smaller programs, introductory cultural anthropology appears to be the *only* course required of majors in which language is explicitly given any attention. Only a small minority require any upper-division course dealing with language (for example, language and culture). Most do permit one or more linguistic electives to count toward the undergraduate anthropology degree: descriptive linguistics, or language and culture, with sociolinguistics as the third most frequent offering. More often than not, these electives are double-listed courses taught in another department or program, usually the English or a foreign language department.

To summarize, my informal survey suggests that the majority of undergraduate anthropology programs either ignore linguistic anthropology completely or, at best, give it token coverage. They may acknowledge its relevance by giving interested students the opportunity to include linguistics courses in their degree plan; however, little is done to stimulate or encourage interest. There does not seem to be a consistent recognition of linguistics as essential to an anthropological education, and when one of the subfields is slighted, it is—more often than not—linguistic anthropology.

Introductory Cultural (cum Linguistic) Anthropology

If the tide is to be turned in favor of linguistic anthropology, efforts must begin at the introductory level. If student interest increases at this point, there will be increased demand for advanced courses and for graduate training. The first objective, then, is to increase the prominence of language in the cultural anthropology course. Rather than hearing about language in a pro forma lecture or two, accompanying an obligatory textbook chapter, students should encounter some focus on linguistic materials throughout the course, sufficient to raise their awareness of and stimulate their interest in this aspect of anthropology. Several strategies may be suggested toward that end: (1) Integrate linguistic information in general lectures on the anthropological perspective. (2) Focus on the findings of linguistic anthropology rather than on descriptive and analytic methods. (3) Include information on language throughout the course, when it is relevant. (4) Match changes in classroom presentation with a changed approach to language in future anthropology texts.

The Anthropological Perspective

It is in our introductory courses that anthropologists often make the greatest effort to convey, to majors and nonmajors alike, a broad general perspective on being and becoming human, or "human nature." It is judicious and important to include language in this perspective and to make clear that language counts for something in the total fabric of human nature.

Research always begins with the particular: ethnologists and linguists do fieldwork in particular communities, write descriptions of particular cultures, and record grammars of particular languages. From such particulars, generalizations of two kinds emerge. First, the commitment of the discipline to relativism rests on a knowledge of the range of variation, an understanding of what is actually possible in human language and culture. Applied as pedagogy, this type of anthropological perspective has served to promote tolerance of human diversity and to decry ethnocentrism. As counterpoint to this traditional anthropological theme, a second type of generalization has emerged as a recent focus in anthropology. This is the identification of common features that underlie diversity. The search for universals has contributed to a new interest in the basis of human nature and in the total process of becoming human. The counterpoint between these two themes is important. Exploration of variety alone invites curiosity but does not necessarily inspire empathy; on the other hand, a narrow emphasis on universals inspires empathy but may lead to complacency.

It is, first and foremost, in presenting these and other broad themes that the findings of anthropological linguistics should be brought into play. There is no better or more obvious illustration of human diversity than the several thousand existing and historically documented languages. Spending some time in exploring linguistic diversity, in terms of numbers of languages in various world areas, can be revealing, as can the contrast in numbers of speakers between the minority languages of tribes and ethnic groups and the expanding "worked languages." If the point is made that linguistic diversity is a correlate of social and cultural diversity, it should be clear that the changing linguistic map is a reflex of Western colonialism and today mirrors a tendency to cultural homogenization.

For insight into the workings of culture and the patterning of individual behavior, linguistic examples can be juxtaposed to those drawn from non-linguistic behavior. This is the point at which a simplified presentation of phonemic or morphophonemic alternation could actually be of some interest. One could point, for example, to the regular—though unconscious—nature of the choices that native speakers make in using the variants of the English plural morpheme (-s, -z, -iz); this could help to raise awareness of other types of culturally patterned behavior. The same sort of purpose, with more obvious relevance to overall cultural context, can be served by examples from areas such as kinesics, paralanguage, or pragmatics. A brief analysis of the use of terms of address in American English, as described by Brown and Ford (1949) or Ervin-Tripp (1969), can give students insight into an easily recognizable segment of their own experience. This can be an entree to cultural relativism, if followed by a contrastive example drawn from a more rigidly structured system such as Indonesian or Japanese, and/or a traditional society in which names are tabooed and the use of kin-terms is *de rigeur*. Hymes's *Language in Culture and Society* (1964) still provides the best orientation in such topics; another source that contains a wealth of examples of speech behavior, conveniently arranged for cross-cultural comparisons, is Wierzbicka's *Cross-Cultural Pragmatics* (1991).

For several decades, linguistic research has been at the forefront of a wave of interest in universals. One can point to the discovery of clearly defined universal structural and semantic patterns, beginning with Greenberg's typology of syntactic patterns (1968); such patterns can be related to the broader objective of defining basic human cognitive processes. I have used Donald Brown's *Human Universals* (1991) at the beginning of an upper-division seminar in which students went on to discuss and compare both linguistic and ethnological research on universals; I think that Brown's characterization of the "universal people" could well be presented in an introductory course.

The subject of universals can obviously be related to anthropological research on human origins and to the definition of broad tendencies in primate behavior and communication. Hockett's (1960) list of *design features* is often summarized, however briefly, in introductory textbooks. In addition, many students come into the class with some knowledge of the accomplishments of language-learning primates such as Washoe and Koko, and are interested in the implications of such experiments. My concern is that such primate studies—from the field or the laboratory—should be mainstreamed rather than being treated in a narrowly linguistic context. Lancaster's *Primate Behavior and the Emergence of Human Culture* (1975) can be useful for bringing language into a discussion of the hominization process. It is especially appropriate if used in connection with primate research films in which social behavior and communication can be observed.

As a third broad theme, anthropology promotes an interest in human creativity, seen in cultural change, innovation, and the emergence of new cultural forms out of old. Again, language is a rich source for examples that can both provide clues to cultural contacts and also, in themselves, give insight into the processes of changes. As a precedent, it might be noted that Sequoyah's Cherokee syllabary has appeared in several textbooks as a classic case of "stimulus diffusion" (Ember and Ember, 1996, 529). There are many other, similar examples—for one, the origin of the Roman alphabet, as a modification of the West Semitic syllabary, might be of interest as an example of the integration of a borrowed trait complex into a changed cultural setting. An examination of pidgin languages can highlight both creativity (in the reworking and syncretizing of vocabulary) and universality (in syntactic patterns). Language easily provides examples of cultural processes such as diffusion (loan words, for example, names of ethnic foods, clothing styles) or innovation (the coining of new words, such as *choca-holic* or *three-peat*). Lexical borrowing is a convenient topic, as students can usually come up with examples of loan words and can go on to speculate about the source and circumstance of their borrowing, along with the associated culture traits.

Language in Cultural Anthropology Textbooks

The most basic component of the introductory course, affecting both teacher and student, may be the textbook. It can be assumed that the prevailing text-book format reflects the usual organization of this type of course; conversely, however, the choice of textbook also influences both the content and the pacing of the course. I realize that most teachers review a number of texts to select one with which they feel comfortable; that they often supplement the text with readings and/or case studies; and that some—a minority—rely on such materials exclusively, without adopting a general text. However, for most, the textbook is important; and the format of introductory texts tends, in any era, to be fairly standardized.

We are all probably familiar with the current prevailing format: one or more initial chapters that introduce anthropology, its subfields and areas of study; and a unit on the culture concept, along with a discussion of field methods and ethics (a recent addition). The main body is a series of units in a sequence that seems to reflect a materialist theory of culture—subsistence and economics first, then several chapters on social and political organization, and, toward the end, religion and the arts. Language is always the subject of a separate unit; its placement is not totally standardized; it may be put toward the beginning (after the culture concept, before subsistence), or toward the end (along with religion and art). The language unit is, in any case, quite separate and self-contained; this conveys the impression that it is totally unrelated to anything else in the textbook. (It is, for this reason, the easiest chapter to omit if the class is behind schedule or if the teacher feels daunted at tackling "linguistics.")

The range of materials covered in the linguistic unit is often encyclopedic; even when well-presented, the range and variety of information seems overwhelming. In some texts, it amounts to a telescoped version of an entire linguistics curriculum. It may run the gamut, from a chart of the International Phonetics Alphabet; to a synopsis of analytic concepts, from allophones to syntax; to a summary of theories about the origin of language. It usually includes a segment on apes and sign language; a quick run-down on the Whorf hypothesis, illustrated by reference to a topic such as color terminology; and a smattering of examples drawn from sociolinguistic studies. Attention may be given to Grimm's Law, glottochronology, the history of the Indo-European language family; and finally, statistics on the number and variety of languages and language families of the world.

This is all excellent material, and the current textbooks incorporate examples of some of the latest and most interesting studies—in psycholinguistics, semiotics, sociolinguistics, and so forth. However, in the tight, condensed form in which it is presented, it is highly indigestible. It is daunting both for the linguistically naive student and for the instructor, who cannot do justice to more than a fraction of the material in the time allotted. Indeed, only a rare and unusually astute student might eventually deduce, after close study, that linguistic anthropology has something to contribute on *almost every topic* covered in the rest of the textbook! This is my point: why not present the material in such a way that its relevance becomes more obvious, and it is more useful?

In the 1963 volume on the teaching of anthropology, Dell Hymes listed a number of emphases for the linguistic anthropology curriculum (Hymes, 1963). He specified the nature of language; cultural focus and semantic field; worldview, perception and cognition; social structure and personality as functions of language; speech play as a verbal art; processes and results of change; systematic theory; fieldwork; and the history and delineation of the field. Although Hymes's interest was primarily in the overall education of future linguistic anthropologists, it would seem that his presentation has also served as a prototype for coverage of the linguistic field in the general textbooks.

One could hardly quibble with the inclusion of any of these topics. A few more could even be added to the list, which have become fashionable since Hymes's article appeared: the origin and evolution of language, primate communication, and proto-language; language classification and typology; linguistic paleontology. Others might suggest additional topics, and the list could grow indefinitely—surely too much for any introductory text. On a more general plane, however, any such list can be reduced to, perhaps, five major areas: (1) innate aspects of language; biology, evolution, language universals; (2) descriptive linguistics; field methods; structural theory; (3) ethnolinguistics; cultural focus; adaptive and expressive functions; (4) sociolinguistics; integrative, isolating, and socializing functions; and (5) historical linguistics; comparative method, language families, typology.

Inspection of these categories may suggest a variety of ways to position them within the larger framework of general anthropology. As a tentative strategy, I would suggest that materials from category (1) could be presented early, in conjunction with other discussions of human origins and cultural universals. A brief and simplified discussion of (2) might constitute a separate chapter, or a section of the chapter covering the culture concept and ethnographic field methods. Any in-depth treatment of discovery methods and analytic procedures should be held in abeyance, for introduction in a more intensive course (within or outside the anthropology department). In the 1963 volume, Kenneth Pike remarked that most students require a full semester to master the phoneme concept; it may be that three inches of text on this subject, as found in many introductory anthropology textbooks, does more harm than good in terms of the morale and motivation of the beginning student. What is important is the stimulation of interest and the realization that linguistic research produces exciting results; if this can be done, students will be eager to learn research methods (as they are in archaeology or physical anthropology).

There are many points at which information in area (3), the relationship between language and culture, can usefully be discussed, either set off as special inserts or integrated into the text. For example, the usual classification and description of subsistence strategies could be accompanied by a consideration of the impact of subsistence emphasis on lexicon, with examples (such as the botanical terminology of gathering peoples; pastoralists' vocabulary for important domesticated animals), any or all of which illustrate a general tendency to specialization of vocabulary in domains of cultural importance and demonstrate the usefulness of such research for cultural studies. Linguistic materials should also be included in any treatment of values or worldview; the Whorf hypothesis (by this or any other name) would come at this point. In addition, religious beliefs and supernatural concepts could be explored through a semantic field approach. Language development, another aspect of area (3), can be included in the discussion of the life cycle and socialization. Throughout, case studies in the ethnography of communication can supplement more traditional ethnographic examples.

Area (4), sociolinguistics, has become such a productive field that there is an abundance of material that can enrich textbook chapters on social organization. For example, gender, age, and class differences in speech; regional and occupational dialects; pidgin and creole languages; status vocabulary; terms of address; diglossia and bilingualism—any of these could be cited in relation to the study of political systems, class stratification and inequality, gender relations, and so on. When the subject is kinship, why not include an explication of a real set of kinship terms, along with—or instead of—schematic diagrams. Again, it is important to incorporate the linguistic material in a way that puts the emphasis not on language *qua* language, but on its contribution to the anthropological goal of understanding human culture and society.

Area (5), historical-comparative linguistics, could well supplement the presentation of prehistory and cultural change; in a two-semester sequence, there might be a place for this material in the course that includes archaeology and human evolution. Such topics as primate communication and the biology of language could also be included here.

Beyond the Introductory Course

A balanced introduction to the study of human culture and society should include linguistic materials in a judicious and realistic mix with other aspects of human behavior. Such an introduction would funnel students into more specialized linguistics courses, on a par with other topical and methodological courses in the curriculum. If they must take courses in linguistic methods and concepts outside the department (as is the case in many smaller programs), students will build a foundation that has at least shown them that language is integral to their major subject. If possible, an effort might be made to follow up such extra-departmental studies (phonology, morphosyntactics, and so on) with a junior/senior level seminar that is strongly anthropological in orientation—perhaps a seminar on language universals, or a field methods course that includes the recording of speech materials. We should not rely on English or Spanish department faculty to show our students how and why the study of language is important to anthropology. This is all the more important if these students are to become professional anthropologists.

As an anthropologist, I want to resist the pull toward fragmentation of the field. I feel that the integrity of anthropology—perhaps its survival—is supported by our tradition of holism. A curriculum that emphasizes the basic concepts, common objectives and the interrelatedness of the subdisciplines begins the socialization of students into that tradition.

As a linguistic anthropologist, I also want to be sure that my own subdiscipline remains a part of anthropology and continues to enrich it. As I have indicated, I think the way to this objective is through more, rather than less, integration of linguistic content. The need for this approach seems most critical in introductory level courses, though it should be pursued at all levels. I believe that this strategy has the potential to upgrade student awareness of linguistic studies, to motivate students to become proficient in linguistic methods, and to increase the demand for linguistic anthropology in the curriculum.

Notes

1. A survey was made of thirty-one non-Ph.D. programs, based on college and university catalogues in the microfiche collection in the Texas Teck University library. The sample included Maine, Macalester, Loyola, Ithaca, Indiana State, Hawaii-Hilo, Grinell, Lehman-City University, New Orleans, SUNY-Oswego, Pitzer, McMaster, Maryland, Louisville, Iowa State, Illinois-Chicago, Houston, Georgia State, George Washington, Nebraska, Oregon State, Wesleyan, Wake Forest, Vermont, Barnard, SUNY College-Buffalo, Montana, Howard, Indiana-Indianapolis DePauw, and Florida Atlantic. The American Anthropological Association's *Guide to Departments* was also consulted.

2. In the thirty programs surveyed, with 209 faculty (full-time, part-time, and adjunct), only eighteen faculty members indicate an interest in linguistics, as listed in the AAA *Guide*.

References

Anthropology Newsletter. 1990 (September), 68.

Boas, Franz. 1938. *General Anthropology*. Boston: Heath.

Brown, Donald E. 1991. *Human Universals*. New York: McGraw-Hill.

Brown, Roger, and Marguerite Ford. 1949. "Address in American English." *Journal of Abnormal and Social Psychology*, 454–462. Reprinted in Hymes, Dell H. 1964. *Language in Culture and Society*. New York: Harper and Row.

Ember, Carol R., and Melvin Ember. 1996. *Cultural Anthropology*. 8th ed. Upper Saddle River, N.J.: Prentice-Hall.

Ervin-Tripp, Susan. 1969. "Sociological Rules of Address." In *Advances in Experimental Social Psychology*, vol. 4, edited by Leonard Berkowitz. New York: Academic Press.

Greenberg, Joseph. 1968. *Anthropological Linguistics*. New York: Random House.

Hockett, Charles, F. 1960. "The Origin of Speech." *Scientific American*, 89–96.

Hymes, Dell H. 1964. *Language in Culture and Society*. New York: Harper and Row.

———. 1963. "Objectives and Concepts of Linguistic Anthropology." In *The Teaching of Anthropology*, edited by David G. Mandelbaum, Gabriel W. Lasker, and Ethel M. Albert, 275–302. Berkeley: University of California Press.

Lancaster, Jane B. 1975. *Primate Behavior and the Emergence of Human Culture*. New York: Holt, Rinehart and Winston.

Wierzbicka, Anna. 1991. *Cross-Cultural Pragmatics: The Semantics of Human Interaction*. Trends in Linguistics. Studies and Monographs 53. Berlin: Mouton De Gruyter.

How Culture Works
*Teaching Linguistic Anthropology as
the Study of Language in Culture*

CAROL M. EASTMAN

In this chapter, I focus on just two concerns: (1) what contemporary linguistics is and has become in theory and practice and how it affects what is taught in anthropology, and (2) what contemporary anthropologists can learn from the experience of linguists (and other scholars of language) as they seek to understand the nature of culture and the nature of language.

In 1963, Hymes wrote that linguistics is taught in anthropology because it is "relevant to questions which we, as anthropologists, ask" (277). These questions included the evolution and typology of language, the elaboration of vocabulary as evidence of cultural significance, the relationship of language to worldview and to social structure, the study of language change, and the manipulation of language for aesthetic effect. To some extent these concerns continue to prevail in anthropology, although they have ceased to be of interest to many linguists. Textbooks of introductory anthropology now regularly include sections on linguistic anthropology. One of the most popular texts today is the sixth edition of Conrad Kottak's *Anthropology: The Exploration of Human Diversity* (1994). In that text, "language" in Chapter 21 is specifically concerned with language structure (phonemes, phones), worldview (the Sapir-Whorf hypothesis), and language change (historical linguistics). Since *The Teaching of Anthropology* (Mandelbaum et al. 1963) appeared, only two new categories of interest in language have emerged in anthropology texts: transformational-generative grammar and sociolinguistics. As we see below, the inclusion of transformational-generative grammar is a cause of some wonderment, as linguists themselves have now begun to question transformational-generative grammar as a theory of language. Sociolinguistics, because it involves the study of language by anthropologists, is moving from the description of language use in context (performance) to a focus on understanding the way language use and context interact, are culturally constituted, and are interpreted. (See DeBernardi, this volume.) This shift is becoming increasingly important, not only with respect to the way linguistic anthropology is taught but also for the way anthropology as a whole is approached at many levels.

Just as sociolinguistics and the study of language and culture were becoming relatively autonomous enterprises, the first issue of the new *Journal of Linguistic Anthropology* appeared. One of its declared objectives is the "reintegration of linguistic anthropology into the broader field of anthropology"

(Blount 1991, 3). The "anthropological study of language" is being reconceptualized as a way to help answer

> questions about human origins, about the diversification and spread of human populations throughout the world, about the evolution of societal complexity, about the role of language and communication in the major cultural and technological revolutions that the human species has engineered, about the central role that language plays in the continual creation and recreation of human societies and cultures, and about issues in the modern world that affect the health, education, and welfare of its citizens.[1]

Current Linguistics and Anthropology

Since the 1960s in the United States, it has been common to find separate departments of linguistics and anthropology. This situation contrasts with early twentieth-century practice whereby anthropologists studied linguistics as a fieldwork tool. To go off to study the Azande, the Kwakiutl, or the Tiv, one was expected to learn how to do phonetic transcription and elicit data from native speakers sufficiently to learn a field language and, ideally, to use it in the field. Departments hired linguists to service fieldworkers in general.

As it became increasingly common for people to go to the field in order to describe languages never before analyzed, the hitherto accepted "tools" of transcription—hierarchically arranged levels of descriptive analysis and bottom-to-top progression from phoneme/morpheme to utterance—were called into question. Advocates of a top-down intuitive approach to understanding language as a cognitive structure turned their attention away from strict adherence to the *scientific method*. Angry battles ensued and practitioners of descriptive linguistics became the target of such epithets as *antediluvian structuralists* and *taxonomists*.

However, this very structuralist and taxonomic form of linguistics, eschewed by new Chomskyan theorists, came to be regarded by archaeologists, social and cultural anthropologists, and even physical anthropologists as a truly scientific endeavor worthy of emulation in theory and method. Only relatively recently has it been recognized in anthropology that the promise of rigor afforded by adhering strictly to structural methodology may not be realized. The linguistic evidence evinced by archaeologists to corroborate time-depth rests on the faulty assumption that certain vocabulary items are impervious to change. Recent examinations of the way languages in contact interact call into question most assumptions as well, regarding the way languages change over time. Tenets of historical linguistics having to do with the notion that languages go from one state to another on their own and that this process can be modeled once the influence of borrowing from other languages has been eliminated are falling by the wayside.

Linguistics departments, from the 1960s on, shifted their focus from taxonomy and structure toward modeling the phonological, syntactic, and semantic components of grammar as a theory of language. Theoretical linguists in these departments are proceeding to seek descriptively adequate grammars of specific languages. By accounting for all possible utterances in languages, they hope to arrive at a model of the knowledge people have that underlies the process of language acquisition.

Linguistics in Anthropology: The 1960s and 1970s

At the same time that linguistics was flexing its muscles as a separate discipline and Noam Chomsky had written *Syntactic Structures* (1957) and *Aspects of a Theory of Syntax* (1965), the mid-1960s saw ethnographers at full tilt, borrowing theory and method from linguistics to apply to the analysis of nonlinguistic material. Marvin Harris made much of the need for both *etic* and *emic* cultural analysis. Levi-Strauss modeled his approach to the structural analysis of myth and kinship after Jakobson and Troubetzkoy and the structuralist approach to phonological analysis. The idea of binary features of oppositional meaning that interrelate in cultural systems, be they religious, economic, political, social, or linguistic, derives from the work of the Prague School of linguists in the 1930s. Similarly, the idea of *marked* and *unmarked* forms, such as what is *marked* is somehow different or "other" while the usual is *unmarked*, derives from ideas in structuralist phonology as espoused by Troubetzkoy. Today this notion figures prominently in theories of social and cultural change, not insignificantly seen in the fact that *man* continues to be the *unmarked* lexical item for Homo sapiens while *woman* is the *marked* form. Cybernetic explanations of cultural behavior, likewise, had a linguistic foundation focusing on the meaning that emerges from structural entities interacting, rather than on meaning inherent in elements. Anthropologists became enamored of the idea that there is an underlying system of cultural behavior known as an *ideational code* akin to what linguists saw as the grammatical system underlying speech in particular communities—that is, the *langue* that underlies *parole*.

In order to examine systems of behavior underlying both language and culture, scholars developed a methodological approach known variously as *ethnoscience* or *cognitive anthropology*. Using techniques of formal semantic analysis, students in the 1970s were taught to analyze classificatory semantic domains such as plants, animals, or color terms. Discovering the basis on which people distinguish various named elements within a category allowed researchers to see how different people in different cultures segment their universe. It was thought that if different people labeled items differently—that is, if they carved up semantic domains in various ways—that would show that there are differing worldviews. Language constrains culture. Efforts to study worldview this way were not uniformly accepted. The discovery of features of meaning in a semantic domain was criticized as unearthing categories of meaning that represented no demonstrable psychological reality. As Burling (1964,

27) put it, it "sounds more exciting to say we are 'discovering the cognitive system of the people' than to admit that we are just fiddling with a set of rules which allow us to use the terms as others do." Cognitive anthropology as a way to show how language is used to label objects in the world has value, but claims that this approach reveals cognitive structures remain questionable.

Linguistics in Anthropology: The 1980s and 1990s

By 1980, anthropologists like the linguists of the late 1960s had begun to see that writing rules to account for cultural and linguistic behavior could be an exercise in futility. Again, anthropologists looked to linguistics in search of a new direction. But by then, linguistics had affiliated itself almost completely with cognitive psychology and philosophy. *Language*, the official journal of the Linguistic Society of America and considered to be relatively conservative, featured articles in the early 1980s with titles revealing concerns with "rules and schemas," "indeterminacy and social context in utterance interpretation" (June 1982), or with symbols and icons (September 1983). Such concerns, not surprisingly, mirror those of the postmodernists in anthropology today. To analyze "reality," postmodernists look at discourse and seek within it the many voices that hitherto may have been quiet in the analysis of culture. In such a view, language and culture are related in what can be seen as an extreme Whorfian way—that is, a view that language does structure reality. Terms of address and pronoun choice in different languages, for example, reveal a person's standing in society.

However, such postmodernist concerns (that is, with language in context and thought expressed in language) by nonanthropological linguists is the exception rather than the rule. By contrast, the teaching of linguistics in anthropology departments today has begun to look regularly toward models of linguistic interpretation in literary scholarship. The analysis of narrative, metaphor, and attention to voice and agency figure prominently. For anthropology, it is important to know what cultural actors say. In speaking, people reveal their social position. In conversation, we negotiate our position relative to one another. In today's anthropology classes, we make mention of the linguistics of Bakhtin (dialogue and heteroglossia), Peirce (semeiotics), and the linguistic philosophy of Wittgenstein (language games). Linguistics in anthropology in the 1990s has begun to take what Joel Sherzer (1987) refers to as a "discourse centered approach to the study of language and culture" (p. 296). Anthropologists have come to realize that it is "in discourse that the symbolic function of language is actualized" (Ricoeur 1979, 75). To understand that function, one must learn to read linguistic and cultural behavior together as *text*.

Anthropologists in the 1990s have embraced *discourse* as a unit of linguistic analysis, as "the pre-eminent expression of the way in which language and culture interrelate" (Ricoeur 1979, 75). Discourse consists of anything from spoken monologue or conversation to written text. By analyzing the way in which grammatical structures are symbolically manipulated in cultural contexts, we can understand the way language and culture interact. The study of discourse as the intersection of language and culture could be seen as rendering the question of any relativistic or deterministic relation of language and culture (as raised in the Sapir-Whorf hypothesis) beside the point. If language and culture are considered to be intertwined, efforts to determine the direction of influence (does language influence culture or culture influence language?) need no longer be pursued. Discourse analysis implies that language does not reflect culture but rather "creates, recreates and modifies" it (Sherzer 1987, 300), revealing the reigning interpretation of prevailing power relations. Discourse creates reality. This is a far more extreme stance than either the linguistic relativity or the linguistic determinist positions generated by the Sapir-Whorf hypothesis. From a discourse perspective, grammar provides potentials that are "actualized in discourse" (Sherzer 1987, 300) to realize a particular group's *cultural logic*. For example, an *ergative* language is one in which the objects of transitive verbs and the subject of intransitive verbs are the same form. This contrasts with English, in which we say "She is asleep" but "He hurt her" rather than "Her is asleep" and "He hurt her." In the cultural logic in the case of English, it might be agreed that *she* is responsible for being asleep: the subject has *agency*. In an ergative language the subject does not: sleep happens to *her* much as hurt does. Discourse analysts examine instances of language in use in the interest of discerning logical structure in culture. It remains to be demonstrated whether the logical structures found via discourse analysis are any more valid than were the cognitive structures found by ethnoscientists in the 1960s and 1970s.

Somewhat more modest a goal of linguistic anthropologists in the 1980s and 1990s is the analysis and description of human communication as grounded in thought, as contextually expressed. Language itself is the vehicle for adapting thought to context in an appropriate way. This idea is best embodied in what Dan Sperber and Dierdre Wilson refer to as the *principle of relevance*. This principle "is enough on its own to account for the interaction of linguistic meaning and contextual factors in utterance interpretation" (1986, vii). Sperber and Wilson, as well as the philosopher H. P. Grice before them, are interested in finding out what people intend to communicate as information and how they get their cultural intentions across in *speech acts* regardless of what they happen to be otherwise thinking or how their brains are structured. Speech acts consist of forms of verbal communication that, for example, demand, warn, suggest, or deny as well as others that have less easily identifiable understandings on the part of speakers and hearers. The teaching of speech acts theory in courses on linguistic anthropology provides students a *pragmatic* approach to the discipline. This approach provides for "the study of the meaning of linguistic signs relative to their communicative functions. The theory of speech acts is part of pragmatics and pragmatics itself is part of . . . performance" (Silverstein 1976, 20). Further, pragmatics "includes how language users apply knowledge of the world to interpret utterances (Fromkin and Rodman 1983, 189).

For a speech act to successfully communicate information, it must be an "act of ostensive communication" that "communicates the presumption of its own optimal relevance" (Sperber and Wilson 1986, 158). This means that an utterance has to attract an audience's attention and get the audience to focus on what the speaker intends. The speaker also has to want the audience to believe that what is being said is "worth listening to" (Sperber and Wilson 1986, 158) regardless of whether it is true, false, or even interesting—simply relevant. Sperber and Wilson provide the sample sentence: "Iris Murdoch's new book is in the book shops." Mary conveys this information to Peter knowing he is an Iris Murdoch freak. But, it turns out, Peter already knows, so the information is irrelevant to him. Nonetheless, Mary's utterance conforms to the principle of relevance as she at least had the right (and appropriate) intention to be relevant.

In a similar vein, philosopher H. P. Grice (1975) pays attention to conversational *maxims* that people use to communicate effectively. Speakers and hearers are assumed to want their conversations to work so they generally abide by what he calls the *cooperative principle* and an accompanying set of *maxims* to be informative, speak the truth, be relevant and clear. Another pragmatic model linguistic anthropologists use in examining language and culture may be seen in Penelope Brown and Stephen Levinson's (1986) work on *politeness theory*. They suggest that people seek to keep the possibility of "face-threatening acts" to a minimum when they talk to others. People seek to act *politely* in the interest of saving face. Politeness in language serves to create cultures in which face-saving behavior is maximized. What is interesting is that face-saving behavior differs cross-culturally and needs to be examined from such a perspective. An understanding of language, according to this view, can *only* be achieved via attention to cultural behavior.

Essentially in the mid-1990s, the teaching of linguistics in anthropology amounts to an explication of current approaches to the analysis of text. The study of language in literature and in conversation is leading toward a recognition that cultural behavior may best be understood by being read as a text. Concern with "culture writ large" and with "writing culture" represents one of the most dynamic approaches to the study of human behavior today. Anthropology's concern with *heteroglossia, text, semeiotics,* and *pragmatics* owes a great deal to the study of language, much as its concern earlier in the twentieth century with structure, function, levels of analysis, and systems of rules owed much to scientific and systematic linguists at that time. Anthropologists used linguistics to model their science then much as they now look to interpretivists to model their approach to a philosophy of human behavior.

In linguistics, various versions of Chomsky's linguistics are having to be revised in light of some recently discovered linguistic facts. The very idea of grammatical categories such as subject and object having cross-cultural validity has been put aside in light of evidence from other languages that have, for example, a topic/comment mode of organization. Such languages require an analysis of the context of language use in addition to a description of internal formative structure to be adequately described. Languages cannot be fully understood by attention to autonomous syntax, generative semantics, or systematic phonology. In a sense, new evidence, primarily from non-Western languages and from data described by anthropological field linguists, has posed a challenge to linguistic theorists.

Theoretical linguists are now paying some attention to anthropology as they encounter problems matching theory to fact. For example, they realize that suprasegmental phonology needs to be taken into account, that certain grammatical categories implicate the real world, and that it is unlikely that a finite set of universal features of semantic meaning will ever be found. Once the most "scientific" form of anthropological inquiry, the study of language has now had to take a new look at itself; linguistics has had to follow anthropology and turn reflexive. Language use as the interaction of one's linguistic cognitive ability with one's world is best examined interpretively. Linguistics and anthropology are coming back together again in a widening hermeneutic circle. Where the two disciplines were torn asunder by the attraction of scientism, recent examinations of language use in context see language in culture as just one form of behavior in society, where words become deeds.

To bring this point home, it is interesting to note that the June 1991 issue of *Language* features a review of George Lakoff and Mark Turner's (1989) book *More Than Cool Reason: A Field Guide to Poetic Metaphor* and heralds it as "an admirable attempt to bridge the gap between linguistics/cognitive science and literature" based on the "new and exciting" thesis that "much literary metaphor is based on the culturally conventional metaphors that pervade ordinary speech" (Jackendoff and Aaron 1991, 336).

The world of the anthropologist and the linguist have come full circle to find new energy in literary approaches taken to the study of the way language is used by writers to give characters life in literature. People who share a social world share a way of speaking as much as they share a way of worshipping, doing business, or electing public officials. Anthropologists seek to describe and understand human cultural systems. Linguists seek to describe and understand human linguistic systems. Both have as their main goal arriving at explanations that hold universally across cultures. Both agree, too, on the need to look at local context. To teach linguistics in anthropology today is to stress the importance of interpretation in the analysis of both verbal and cultural behavior as cultural text—that is, to take a discourse approach to the study of culture and to see language and culture as inextricably intertwined. Introductory texts that have moved beyond mentioning linguistics as a tool for doing good fieldwork to incorporating notions of sociolinguistics and worldview now need to relate modern theories of cultural interpretation to the literary study of language. It may even come to pass that theoretical linguistics will begin to see value in studying the *Dialogic Imagination* (Bakhtin 1981) as their interest in the study of language as a cognitive ability faces the inevitability that *linguistic performance* implicates both thought (intentional) and culture (attention) interactively.

The Future

As the study of linguistic anthropology has come to focus more on language use in context than on the description of languages, some concerns remain that need to be worked out in years to come. As the teaching of linguistic anthropology has become more a matter of teaching language in culture, certain gaps in what is known need to be filled for teaching to be effective. Hymes (1986), for example, finds speech act theory deficient for cross-cultural purposes. Indeed, none of the contemporary approaches to the study of language use (for example, the discourse-centered approach, speech act theory, pragmatics, notions of relevance, politeness, and appeals to Bakhtinian translinguistics) provides a comprehensive theory of language use. Aspects of these approaches are at times overlapping, yet some are mutually exclusive. Rarely is nomenclature compatible. The goal of linguistic anthropology is clear: to develop a comprehensive theory of language use and a model of language practice. This amounts to a radical shift from what the goal had been. Linguistic anthropology once focused on preserving dying languages, analyzing cultural texts (out of context), and equipping ethnographers with the requisite means to learn enough of a language to describe the culture of its users. Today, students of language and culture find themselves analyzing language as a most promising avenue for discovering how culture as a whole works. An understanding of how people use language leads to an understanding of culture. The pursuit of this understanding represents a most daunting future for the study and teaching of language in culture.

Note

1. Some notable exceptions to this general statement may be seen in Derek Bickerton's (1990) *Language and Species* and Philip Lieberman's (1991) *Uniquely Human: The Evolution of Speech, Thought, and Selfless Behavior*, both dealing with language and evolution. Bernard Comrie's (1989) *Language Universals and Linguistics Typology*, second edition, represents continuing interest in the comparison and classification of languages.

References

Bakhtin, M. M. 1981. *The Dialogic Imagination: Four Essays*, translated by M. Holquist. Austin: University of Texas Press.

Basso, Keith, and Henry A. Selby, eds. 1976. *Meaning in Anthropology*. Albuquerque: University of New Mexico Press.

Bickerton, Derek. 1990. *Language and Species*. Chicago: University of Chicago Press.

Blount, Benjamin G. 1991. *Editorial,* "Linguistic Anthropology." *Journal of Linguistic Anthropology* 1(1):3–4.

Brown, Penelope, and Stephen Levinson. 1986. *Politeness: Universals in Language Usage*. Cambridge, England: Cambridge University Press.

Burling, Robbins. 1964. "Cognition and Componential Analysis: God's Truth or Hocus-Pocus?" *American Anthropologist* 66:20–28.

Chomsky, Noam. 1957. *Syntactic Structures*. Boston: MIT Press.

———. 1965. *Aspects of a Theory of Syntax*. Boston: MIT Press.

Comrie, Bernard. 1989. *Language Universals and Linguistic Typology: Syntax and Morphology*. 2d ed. Oxford: Blackwell.

Fromkin, Victoria, and Robert Rodman. 1983. *An Introduction to Language*. 3rd ed. New York: CBS Publishing and Holt, Rinehart and Winston.

Grice, H. P. 1975. "Logic and Conversation." In *Syntax and Semantics*, vol. 3, edited by P. Cole and J. Morgan. New York: Academic Press.

Hymes, Dell H. (1963). "Objectives and Concepts of Linguistic Anthropology." In *The Teaching of Anthropology*, edited by D. G. Mandelbaum, G. W. Lasker, and E. M. Albert, 275–302. Berkeley: University of California Press.

———. 1986. "Discourse: Scope without Depth." *International Journal of the Sociology of Language* 57:49–89.

Jackendoff, Ray, and David Aaron. 1991. *Review*, "Lakoff and Turner: *More Than Cool Reason: A Field Guide to Poetic Metaphor*." *Language* 67(2):320–338.

Kottak, Conrad P. 1994. *Anthropology: The Exploration of Human Diversity*. 6th ed. New York: McGraw-Hill.

Lakoff, George, and Mark Turner. 1989. *More Than Cool Reason: A Field Guide to Poetic Metaphor*. Chicago: University of Chicago Press.

Levi-Strauss, Claude. 1967. *Structural Anthropology*, translated from the French by Claire Jacobsen and Brooke Grundfest-Schoept. New York: Basic Books.

Lieberman, Philip. 1991. *Uniquely Human: The Evolution of Speech, Thought, and Selfless Behavior*. Cambridge, Mass.: Harvard University Press.

Mandelbaum, David G., Gabriel W. Lasker, and Ethel M. Albert, eds. 1963. *The Teaching of Anthropology*. Berkeley: University of California Press.

Ricoeur, Paul. 1979. "The Model of the Text: Meaningful Action Considered as Text." In *Interpretive Social Science Reader*, edited by Paul Rabinow and William Sullivan, 73–100. Berkeley: University of California Press. (Originally published 1971 in *Social Research* 38(3):529–562.)

Silverstein, Michael. 1976. "Shifters, Linguistic Categories and Cultural Description." In *Meaning in Anthropology*, edited by Keith Basso and Henry A. Selby, 11–56. Albuquerque: University of New Mexico Press.

Sherzer, Joel. 1987. "A Discourse-Centered Approach to Language and Culture." *American Anthropologist* 89(1):295–309.

Sperber, Dan, and Deirdre Wilson. 1986. *Relevance, Communication and Cognition*. Oxford: Blackwell.

Troubetzkoy, N. S. 1937. *Grundzuge der Phonologie*. Travaux du Cercle Linguistique de Prague VII.

Language in Society

JEAN DEBERNARDI

Although linguistic anthropologists might be few in number, many cultural anthropologists like myself would argue that one must understand human communication systems to understand society. Many anthropologists who are not considered "linguistic anthropologists" have in fact made important contributions to the study of language in use. Radcliffe-Brown's study of "joking relationships" and respect behavior, for example, is a study of linguistic interaction, and is foundational for more recent work on politeness (Radcliffe-Brown [1952] 1965; Brown and Levinson 1987). Malinowski's linguistic functionalism (Malinowski [1935] 1978) inspired British linguists to a consideration of context (see, for example, Firth 1957), and Levi-Strauss based his exploration of human classification systems on linguistic models derived from DeSaussure and Jakobson (Levi-Strauss 1963; DeBernardi 1994).

More recently, cultural anthropologists have explored the performativity of ritual routines (Tambiah 1985) or the use of formulaic language as a means of exercising traditional authority (Bloch 1989). Ethnicity studies frequently assert the connection between language, identity, and power, and studies of bilingualism often examine this connection (Woolard 1989). As Haviland notes in his introductory textbook, "Language is so much a part of our lives that it permeates everything we do, and everything we do permeates language" (1994, 328).

Despite the potential breadth and interdisciplinarity of the field, linguistic anthropology has the reputation of being a narrowly focused and demanding subfield. This reputation is no doubt related to the fact that linguistic anthropologists explore issues derived from linguistics and philosophy as well as from anthropological debates. As a consequence, their theoretical contributions are sometimes relatively inaccessible to students of cultural anthropology.

There are dimensions of linguistic anthropology that are both accessible and relevant to undergraduate students of anthropology, however. I discuss here two possible ways a linguistic anthropology perspective can be fruitfully incorporated into the undergraduate curriculum: linguistic field methods, and the exploration of linguistic issues in ethnographic area courses.

Linguistic field methods were initially developed by Boasian fieldworkers, who also acquired the research methods necessary to explore the archaeology, physical anthropology, and culture of a single society or culture area. Although no one expects contemporary anthropologists to collect data in all these fields, certainly language and culture remain closely linked. Fieldwork requires communicative competence, and communicative competence requires a knowledge of society and culture. Now, as in Boas's time, a field researcher who seeks communicative competence will find the tools of descriptive linguistics (including most importantly the International Phonetic Alphabet) exceptionally useful.

At both graduate and undergraduate levels, I have taught a course in descriptive linguistics in which students devote the second half of the semester to learning a non-Western language through interviews with a native speaker. Undergraduates find enjoyable the intellectual challenge of analyzing a non-Western language, and their encounters with the "linguistic consultant" provide them with a convincing introduction to both the interconnections of language and culture and the limits of translation. For example, in one linguistic field methods course with a Swahili consultant, students were astonished when they discovered that the second person pronoun in Swahili is gender neutral. While they themselves expressed a preference for gender neutral language, they could hardly imagine a language that expresses "he," "she," and "it" with a single term.

In another linguistic field methods course, the Cree consultant's explanation of his translations of English sentences sometimes illuminated a very different worldview. One student noted, for instance, that the concept of relationship was far more important in Cree than in English. She observed that when we asked our Cree speaker to translate "The snow is melting," he responded with a Cree sentence that he glossed as meaning "The sun and snow are both living (animate), and they have entered into a relationship." The student also asked him to translate the English sentence "Now that it is cold, I can see the northern lights." He glossed the Cree sentence as "Now that it is cold, the northern lights are starting to show themselves." The student observed that while her English sentence had herself as the subject/actor, the Cree translation put the natural phenomenon as subject/actor.

Originally the four-field approach was developed as a method for the holistic study of culture areas, and it still has value as an approach to teaching area studies courses. A course on the peoples and cultures of a given world region appropriately includes content on the prehistory and history of the region as well as its linguistic and racial diversity. In a course on Southeast Asia, I discuss a range of topics, including kinship systems, religion, social hierarchy and the "theater state," ethnicity and the status of minority groups, nationalism and language planning. All these topics have linguistic dimensions.

Age and generation are important in many Asian cultures, and this emphasis is expressed in their kinship systems. Social hierarchy is also an important aspect of Asian society and is vividly illustrated with linguistic examples. Thus, in a lecture on Theravada Buddhist kingdoms in mainland Southeast Asia, I illustrate social hierarchy with a discussion of Thai palace language, a language derived from Sanskrit and Khmer that was used until quite recently in Thailand. The first-person pronoun used to address the King meant "I, the slave of the Lord Buddha"; the second-person pronoun meant "the dust beneath the sole of your august feet," and conveyed the sense that the speaker was so much lower in status than the King that he only dared address the dirt on the floor beneath the King's feet (Wales 1931, 40).

Similarly, in a course on Chinese society and culture, I discuss both the prestige of the Chinese written language and the development of the national language in the twentieth century (DeFrancis [1950] 1972; 1984). In examining recent Chinese history, students read about the use of language in "thought reform" campaigns (Chan, Madsen, and Unger 1992), as well as the Chinese communist reform of terms of address toward an egalitarian norm during the cultural revolution (Scotton and Zhu 1983). Students also learn about the Chinese use of poetry and allegorical theater in political critique. While language is not the sole focus of the discussion, these details of social interaction vividly illuminate the social revolutions that have taken place in Chinese society.

Published sources on these topics are rich in detail, and can be assigned to students and/or discussed in lecture. Instructors may convey the finer details of social interaction by having students read novels. For example, Gu Hua's *A Small Town Named Hibiscus* ([1981]1983) is an excellent complement to a qualitative sociological study of the Cultural Revolution (Chan, Madsen, and Unger 1992). The novelist conveys the discourse of the period, capturing in literary form the interactional realization of "revolution" in the village. The sociological study provides the history and context of thought reform campaigns and illustrates the experiences of a variety of participants.

The worldwide resurgence of nationalism is well addressed through a consideration of language. On the one hand, the pragmatic usefulness of shared national languages has led to their widespread development and adoption. On the other hand, the adoption of one linguistic variety as a national language may lead to linguistic stratification that socially disadvantages speakers of minority languages. In such contexts, minority languages may serve to mark off ethnic differences, and loyalty to such languages may express the political aspirations of their speakers (DeBernardi 1991; Edwards 1985; Smith 1986).

For minority group members, one consequence of the adoption of a national language is that they become bilingual and engage in frequent code switching (Heller 1988). A number of anthropological and sociolinguistic studies exist of bilingualism and code switching in a variety of world areas, including Africa (Breitborde 1983, Scotton 1988), Austria (Gal 1979), New York (Urciuoli 1991), Northern Europe (Gumperz [1972] 1986; Grillo 1989a), Spain (Woolard 1989), Mexico (Hill and Hill 1986), and Peru (Mannheim 1991). As well, there are recent studies of creole languages that situate them in a cultural matrix of plural societies (see, for example, LePage and Tabouret-Keller 1985).

Many anthropologists examine issues related to language and nationalism in the context of area studies courses. In Breitborde's course on Africa at Beloit College, for example, he explores Kiswahili as a historical creole, comparing its effectiveness as a national language and lingua franca in Tanzania to its more "contested" relationship to English in Kenya. He concludes a discussion of the origins of Kiswahili with a discussion of his own West African materials on Kru/English code switching as a way to consider how people construct complex systems of values (often competing) in their lives.

Breitborde also teaches a course titled "Language, Ethnicity, and Nationalism" in which he uses an original strategy to explore the issues involved in language planning. He creates a consulting company ("Lingua Associates"), and all students are hired as employees and divided into teams to do language assessments for various countries and states. A recent course included California, Finland, Russia, and South Africa. Each team member is a specialist in economic, cultural, or educational issues. In addition to the teams' working together, all the economics officers, cultural affairs officers, and educational officers also meet together to trade notes on useful resources. The projects culminate with a class presentation and a written team report, including an executive summary. These are collated and desktop "published" as the *Annual Report of Lingua Associates*.

Area courses also can make use of the growing literature on oral narratives. In her second-year survey course on the cultures of Native North America at the University of Alberta, Andie Palmer seeks to convey an understanding of how people of different cultures remember and interpret the significance of major events in their history. Transcribed and translated Tlingit oral narratives provide the Tlingit perspective on the history of a period of dramatic glaciation that crushed one of their villages. At the same time, these narratives provide insight into the Tlingit moiety system, funerary practices, and the rights and responsibilities of individuals in particular lineages to tell particular stories (Dauenhauer and Dauenhauer 1987). Ella DeLoria's translation of the Dakota text, *White Plume Boy*, offers a vision of the ideals of classic Plains Indian warriors (Rice 1992), and students confront Cibecue Apache satirical stereotypes of "the whiteman" in Basso's study of joking performances (1979). Works on oral narrative that would be appropriately assigned in an undergraduate course appear to be exceptionally rich for native North America (see, for example, Basso 1990; Cruikshank 1990; Tedlock 1983). In an undergraduate course, "American Indian Ethnolinguistics and Sociolinguistics," at the University of California, Los Angeles, Paul V. Kroskrity raises further issues regarding language, communication, and education in native communities for whom language retention is a critical issue (Kroskrity 1986).

Anthropological works on language in society are also didactically useful in revealing the interactional bases for social inequality in a wide range of societies. As Grillo notes, "Anthropology is especially helpful because it offers ways of handling the complex social data which constitute the evidence for linguistic inequality, providing means of analysing in processual terms how that inequality operates" (Grillo 1989b, viii). These complex data provide the scholar with insight into social organization but at the same time may provide the student with striking examples of the way social identities are transacted in other societies. An analysis of the Wolof greeting, for instance, illustrates how unequal status is expressed in a patterned interaction in which inevitably "one has glory, and the other shame" (Irvine 1974). Similarly, Javanese speech levels demonstrate that social groups may construct social inequality through the elaboration of linguistic style and form (Errington 1988; Geertz 1960). Such examples give life to a discussion of social hierarchy in a range of societies.

In conclusion, linguistic anthropology offers rich resources for teaching about human society. These resources include publications focused on topics that range from linguistic prehistory and the classification of language families to linguistic nationalism, bilingualism and code switching, oral narratives and poetics, linguistic etiquette, and kinship systems. Indeed, language would appear to be basic to any anthropological consideration of social structure and process in world cultures.

References

Basso, Keith. 1979. *Portraits of the "Whiteman": Linguistic Play and Cultural Symbols among the Western Apache*. Cambridge, England: Cambridge University Press.
——. 1990. *Western Apache Language and Culture: Essays in Linguistic Anthropology*. Tucson: University of Arizona Press.
Bloch, Maurice. 1989. "Symbols, Song, Dance and Features of Articulation: Is Religion an Extreme Form of Traditional Authority?" In *Ritual, History and Power: Selected Papers in Anthropology*, edited by M. Bloch. London: Athlone Press.
Breitborde, Lawrence B. 1983. "Levels of Analysis in Sociolinguistic Explanation: Bilingual Code Switching, Social Relations, and Domain Theory." *International Journal of the Sociology of Language* 39:5–43.
Brown, Penelope, and Stephen Levinson. 1987. *Politeness: Some Universals in Language Usage*. Cambridge, England: Cambridge University Press.
Chan, Anita, Richard Madsen, and Jonathan Unger. 1992. *Chen Village under Mao and Deng*. 2nd ed. Berkeley: University of California Press.
Cruikshank, Julie. 1990. *Life Lived like a Story: Life Stories of Three Yukon Native Elders*. Lincoln: University of Nebraska Press.
Dauenhauer, Nora Marks, and Richard Dauenhauer. 1987. *Haa Shuka, Our Ancestors: Tlingit Oral Narrative*. Seattle: University of Washington Press.
DeBernardi, Jean. 1991. "Linguistic Nationalism: The Case of Southern Min." *Sino-Platonic Papers* 25, edited by Victor Mair. Philadelphia: Department of Oriental Studies, University of Pennsylvania.
——. 1994. "Social Aspects of Language Use." *Companion Encyclopedia of Anthropology*, edited by Tim Ingold. London: Routledge.
DeFrancis, John. [1950] 1972. *Nationalism and Language Reform in China*. New York: Octagon Books.
——. 1984. *The Chinese Language: Fact and Fantasy*. Honolulu: University of Hawaii Press.
Edwards, John. 1985, *Language, Society, and Identity*. Oxford: Blackwell.
Errington, Joseph. 1988. *Structure and Style in Javanese: A Semiotic View of Linguistic Etiquette*. Philadelphia: University of Pennsylvania Press.
Firth, J. R. 1957. *Papers in Linguistics 1934–1951*. Oxford: Oxford University Press.
Gal, Susan. 1979. *Language Shift: Social Determinants of Linguistic Change in Bilingual Austria*. New York: Academic Press.
Geertz, Clifford. 1960. *The Religion of Java*. Chicago: University of Chicago Press.
Grillo, R. D. 1989a. *Social Anthropology and the Politics of Language*. London: Routledge.
——. 1989b. *Dominant Languages: Language and Hierarchy in Britain and France*. Cambridge, England: Cambridge University Press.

Gu Hua. [1981] 1983. *A Small Town Called Hibiscus.* Beijing, China: Panda Books.

Gumperz, John J. [1972] 1986. *Directions in Sociolinguistics: The Ethnography of Communication.* Oxford: Blackwell.

Haviland, William A. 1994. *Anthropology.* 7th ed. Fort Worth: Harcourt Brace.

Heller, Monica, ed. 1988. *Codeswitching: Anthropological and Sociolinguistic Perspectives.* Berlin: Mouton de Gruyter.

Hill, Jane H., and Kenneth C. Hill. 1986. *Speaking Mexicano: Dynamics of a Syncretic Language in Central Mexico.* Tucson: University of Arizona Press.

Irvine, Judith. 1974 "Strategies of Status Manipulation in the Wolof Greeting." In *Explorations in the Ethnography of Speaking,* edited by Richard Bauman and Joel Sherzer. Cambridge, England: Cambridge University Press.

Kroskrity, Paul V. 1986. "Ethnolinguistics and American Indian Education: Native American Language and Cultures as a Means of Teaching." In *American Indian Policy and Cultural Values: Conflict and Accommodation,* edited by J. Joe. Los Angeles: American Indian Study Center, University of California.

LePage, R., and A. Tabouret-Keller. 1985. *Acts of Identity: Creole-Based Approaches to Language and Identity.* Cambridge, England: Cambridge University Press.

Levi-Strauss, Claude. 1963. *Structural Anthropology.* New York: Basic Books.

Malinowski, Bronislaw. [1935] 1978. *Coral Gardens and their Magic.* Vol. 2: *The Language of Magic and Gardening.* New York: Dover Press.

Mannheim, Bruce. 1991. *The Language of the Inka since the European Invasion.* Austin: University of Texas Press.

Radcliffe-Brown, A. R. R. [1952] 1965. "On Joking Relationships." In *Structure and Function in Primitive Society: Essays and Addresses.* New York: Free Press.

Rice, Julian. 1992. "Narrative Styles in Dakota Texts." In *On the Translation of Native American Literatures,* edited by Brian Swann. Washington, D.C.: Smithsonian Institution Press.

Scotton, Carol M. 1988. "Code Switching as Indexical of Social Negotiations." In *Codeswitching: Anthropological and Sociolinguistic Perspectives,* edited by Monica Heller. Berlin: Mouton de Gruyter.

Scotton, Carol M., and Zhu Wanjin. 1983. "Tongzhi in China." *Language in Society* 12:477–494.

Smith, Anthony D. 1986. *The Ethnic Origin of Nations.* Oxford: Blackwell.

Tambiah, Stanley Jeyaraja. 1985. *Culture, Thought, and Social Action: An Anthropological Perspective.* Cambridge, Mass.: Harvard University Press.

Tedlock, Dennis. 1983. *The Spoken Word and the Work of Interpretation.* Philadelphia: University of Pennsylvania Press.

Urciuoli, Bonnie. 1991. "The Political Topography of Spanish and English: The View from a New York Puerto Rican Neighborhood." *American Ethnologist* 18(2):295–310.

Wales, H. G. Q. 1931. *Siamese State Ceremonies: Their History and Function.* London: Bernard Quaritch.

Woolard, Kathryn A. 1989. *Double Talk: Bilingualism and the Politics of Ethnicity in Catalonia.* Stanford, Calif.: Stanford University Press.

TEACHING
PALEOANTHROPOLOGY

Paleoanthropology in the 1990s

PATRICIA C. RICE

There is no single word or phrase that encompasses both archaeology and physical/biological anthropology, yet they often—as in the case in this volume—are combined into a seemingly single entity. Paleoanthropology might come closest to including both subdisciplines of anthropology in spirit, if not in technical accuracy; yet paleoanthropology literally means the science of past humans. If treated literally, it would include archaeology and human evolution but would leave out contemporary human variation. Because it comes closest to combining the two anthropological subdisciplines—archaeology and physical anthropology—under one generic term, the term *paleoanthropology* will be used here rather than the more cumbersome archaeology and physical anthropology.

Paleoanthropology is not a single subject because of *what* it studies, but because of *how* it studies humans. Archaeology studies our cultural past, and physical anthropology studies our biological past and present; one is the result of cultural invention and diffusion and the other the result of sexual reproduction. To refer to both as "evolutionary"—that is, cultural evolution and biological evolution—is stretching the concept of evolution. Instead of a linkage due to subject matter, it is *how* paleoanthropologists study humans that connects the specialties. The scientific method in its variability—inductive, deductive, quantitative, qualitative—is at the core of paleoanthropology; hypothesis generation and testing have always been at the forefront of paleoanthropological research and teaching. It would be rare to find a class session without using words such as *hypothesis, testing, evidence, data*.

As evidence of the methodological center of paleoanthropological specialties, in many curricula, students have a choice of where to "count" physical anthropology—that is, for either natural or social science distribution credits;

and in some programs, archaeology can be counted as a natural science. In both cases, it is the method of inquiry that sets them apart from their sister subdisciplines—sociocultural anthropology and linguistics—whereas the focus of the subject matter remains the same: the study of humans.

Paleoanthropology is often considered the "glamorous" part of anthropology because it has "bones and stones" as the visual glitz of teaching aids. What human evolutionist does not rely on a set of skulls to teach the relationships among the paleospecies in the human lineage? What archaeologist does not use a teaching collection of artifacts? What archaeologist does not figuratively, if not literally, do flintknapping in class to demonstrate the beauty and unique features of fluted blades? Although sociocultural anthropologists can keep student attention by telling stories of field experiences, the visual impact of "stones and bones" will always be an asset to archaeologists and physical anthropologists.

Although teaching paleoanthropologists have always used these teaching aids, students have changed over the years and so too must teaching strategies. The subject matter has changed so drastically over a single decade that a course outline in archaeology or physical anthropology from 1986 shows only shadowed resemblance to a course outline in 1996. Indeed, whole sections are substituted. Who talked of research on acquired immune deficiency syndrome (AIDS) in physical anthropology classes ten years ago? How large was a section on postdepositional effects in archaeology classes a decade ago?

Although there has always been a fascination about our human ancestry, both archaeologically and biologically, the interest in these two fields—too often being seen by nonprofessionals as interchangeable or the same thing—increased in the 1970s and 1980s by "spectacular" finds, beginning with the discovery of Lucy and the Laetoli footprints and continuing through the discovery of the Ice Man on the Austrian/Italian border. Newspaper headlines, videos, and more somber articles of a scientific nature have captured the imagination of the lay public, including students, and they often show up in our classes to find out more. We must be prepared to tell them more.

A comparison of the Mandelbaum et al. volume (1963) to the articles in this volume may be instructive in noting changes in subject matter, teaching techniques, or perceived student needs. Physical anthropology in the 1960s was apparently consistently and "traditionally" taught so that "what to teach" was not an issue. All authors agreed that human evolution and "race" were the two main subjects of teaching concentration. Many modern physical anthropologists would find Lasker's suggested sixteen-week syllabus in 1963 to resemble what they do in their classrooms in 1996, though most would not spend a week on the "question of racial differences in Upper Paleolithic man. Peopling of America" (103). It is interesting to note that in 1963 "there is disagreement about the use of the word 'race'" and that there was concern about "just what (or who) Oreopithecus was" (73). There is still disagreement on the former, but the status of Oreopithecus is no longer a controversy—at least not for now.

Archaeologists in the 1963 volume were at odds as to "what to teach" in the basic archaeology course, some favoring the "Big Problems" approach, and others favoring a combination of archaeological methods and prehistoric findings. Jennings (1963) appears to be somewhat ahead of his time with his "table top dig," suggesting that field and laboratory work was never seriously tried on the undergraduate level in archaeology. He noted that laboratory work was commonplace in other sciences (250).

By contrast, in this volume, physical anthropologists do not appear to agree on "what to teach" (see Poirier and Cohen) and do not agree on the concept of "race" (see Brues; Lieberman and Kirk); Alice Brues treats "race" as a real subject, yet Lieberman and Kirk provide the other side of the argument suggesting that although human variability is a "real" phenomenon, "race" is not, at least not in the biological sense.

The archaeologists in this volume also have some disagreement on "what to teach," with Plog arguing for the "Big Problems" approach and others preferring the archaeology-as-method approach. Michaels and Fagan, and Rice argue for new teaching techniques using computers and laboratory sessions, neither of which was more than speculation in 1963.

But some things have not changed over the thirty-year span. Both physical anthropologists and archaeologists continue to regard their specialties as science and insist that students learn the subject matter in a scientific way. And Frederich Hulse in 1963 (70) wrote that one important focus of physical anthropology was its ability to interpret biological variability in its contemporary cultural setting. Mark Cohen in this volume describes his success in teaching "race" and epidemiology, two subjects that interpret biological variability in contemporary cultural settings.

In 1990, *Anthropology and Education Quarterly* devoted an issue to "Strategies for Teaching Anthropology in the 1990s." In this issue, the issue editors cited ten themes found in the twelve articles in the issue (Erickson and Rice). Of these, critical reasoning, inductive learning, active learning, discovery, and open anthropology constitute themes that continue to be relevant in the 1996 volume. (The other themes are more appropriate to sociocultural anthropology, such as reflexivity and cross-cultural comparisons.)

In the following chapters, teaching anthropologists will explore their particular subfields with teaching as the focal point. What should we teach, how should we teach it, what can we expect of students? In different ways, each chapter will address these concerns. Several authors focus on the amount of new knowledge since 1960—epidemiology, AIDS, sociobiology (Poirier; Cohen); others focus on changing student needs and the need for change in teaching methods (Michaels and Fagan; Rice); most focus on the scientific nature of paleoanthropology (Stein; Lieberman and Kirk; Rice; Poirier); and others focus on the relevance of the subject matter to the everyday lives of students (Cohen; Poirier). Most chapters concentrate on strategies of teaching and specific methods of achieving our goals (Michaels and Fagan; Rice; Cohen; Poirier).

All the paleoanthropology chapters have a similar thread: all are successful ways archaeologists and physical anthropologists have "reached" their students. Some chapters can be used for semester-long mind-sets; others provide shorter exercises for inclusion during a semester. We all hope they provide sparks for our teaching colleagues because we are convinced that our common goal of superlative education is a group effort.

References

Erickson, Paul, and Patricia Rice. 1990. "Themes for the 1990s." *Anthropology and Education Quarterly* 21(2):101–105.

Hulse, Frederick S. 1963. "Objectives and Methods." In *The Teaching of Anthropology,* edited by David Mandelbaum, Gabriel Lasker, and Ethel Albert. Berkeley: University of California Press.

Jennings, Jesse D. 1963. "Educational Functions." In *The Teaching of Anthropology,* edited by David Mandelbaum, Gabriel Lasker, and Ethel Albert. Berkeley: University of California Press.

Lasker, Gabriel W. 1963. "The Introductory Course." In *The Teaching of Anthropology,* edited by David Mandelbaum, Gabriel Lasker, and Ethel Albert. Berkeley: University of California Press.

Mandelbaum, David G., Gabriel W. Lasker, and Ethel M. Albert. 1963. *The Teaching of Anthropology.* Berkeley: University of California Press.

The Teaching of Physical Anthropology

Philip L. Stein

Of the various disciplines encompassed within anthropology, physical anthropology stands somewhat apart because of its close relationship to the biological sciences. Several unique issues arise in a discussion of the role of physical anthropology in the college and university curriculum.

Physical Anthropology as General Education

The vast majority of our students enroll in physical anthropology to satisfy a general education requirement for their degree—and this is especially true in the community college. Therefore, it follows that the success of introductory physical anthropology is largely a function of its position in the general education package.

At colleges and universities where physical anthropology satisfies a natural science general education requirement, enrollments can be quite high. In this environment, introductory physical anthropology is often the anthropology course with the greatest enrollment.

Physical Anthropology as a Science

The popularity of physical anthropology as a natural science general education course may follow from nonscience-oriented students' viewing the subject as an easy way to meet the science requirement. There is usually no required laboratory though one may be optional. Many students have turned away from biology because of negative experiences in high school biology. And, let's face it, our subject matter is more romantic to the nonscience student than biology. Who would not rather study fossil hominids and primate behavior than the anatomy of the frog and the biochemistry of the citric acid cycle?

Students choose cultural anthropology from a list including such subjects as sociology, psychology, history, political science, and economics to meet a social science requirement. Cultural anthropology should therefore attract a fairly representative sample of the lower-division students. Those opting for physical anthropology, however, may include a disproportionate number of students who feel they are not capable of handling a "science course."

A modest survey of community college instructors in northern and central California showed agreement that physical anthropology students tend to be those who do poorly in science. Several instructors also noted that when physical anthropology does not fill a general education requirement, which is the case in many institutions, the students tend to be better students academically.

Topics Included in Introductory Physical Anthropology

Physical anthropology is a very broad discipline. In the design of an introductory course there are many topics from which to choose. Certain major themes, however, appear to dominate the introductory course. James Macdonald of Northeastern Illinois University, speaking at the 1987 meeting of the American Anthropological Association, identified two major headings (Newman and Macdonald, 1987). The first is evolution, both biological and cultural. Included under this heading are a variety of topics including genetics, population genetics, microevolutionary and macroevolutionary principles, and human evolution, emphasizing the integration of biological and cultural evolution. The second heading is race with three major themes: population variation, the adaptive value of variation, and the interplay of cultural and biological factors. I would add as a third heading the general topic of ecology.

Physical anthropology has evolution as a central theme. This is an important issue for college students and is, in some circles, controversial. Many biology classes, with their emphasis on biochemistry and physiology, do not give the introductory student a solid basis for the understanding of evolution and the tools for properly judging "creation science."

The degree to which many college students misunderstand the concept of evolution can be rather surprising. Alan J. Almquist and John E. Cronin (1988) discuss data based on questionnaires given to college students between 1974 and 1983. Although the responses to many questions showed an acceptance of scientific explanations, "Ten percent of responses . . . endorsed the assertion that evolution has a goal and is directed and 38% the assertion that the Garden of Eden is the point of origin for human life and that the origin itself was an act of creation performed by God as recorded in Genesis" (Almquist and Cronin, 1988, 520). Yet, it is interesting to note that 60 percent of the sample had completed one or more courses in biological science. The authors conclude:

> Our survey shows that college students' understanding of evolution, while greater than that of the general public, is in considerable need of improvement, especially in the areas of the origins of life, the geographical settings of human evolution, the fossil groups identified as links in the chain of human evolution, the concepts underlying carbon-14 and potassium-argon dating, and the theory of natural selection. (Almquist and Cronin, 1988, 522)

Kinds of Physical Anthropology Courses

Physical anthropology exists within an academic environment; that is, it occupies a particular "niche" in the academic "community." The kinds of students who tend to enroll and the central themes of the course will differ depending upon the characteristics of this niche.

Physical anthropology may theoretically fulfill one of three niches in the college curriculum: it may act as a biological science in fulfilling a natural science general education requirement; it may be an elective or, on occasion, act as a social science; or the course may be offered primarily for majors in the field—of course, this would be more likely in a research university.

We need to consider the emphasis and selection of specific subject matter when physical anthropology is "competing" within each of these niches. Where physical anthropology meets the science requirement there may need to be an emphasis on those topics that are more biology-oriented to keep our biology colleagues, who might like to change the scheme of things, happy. Biology instructors may show explicit concern over the anthropology subject matter and may attempt to monitor the course content.

Certainly an introduction to the history of science and the scientific method is vital to any course that is designed to serve as a window into the natural sciences. Central themes of such an anthropology course may emphasize genetics, cell biology, the chemical basis of genetics, growth and development, environmental physiology, taxonomy, comparative anatomy and physiology, while downplaying, but certainly not eliminating, paleoanthropology.

On the other hand, an anthropologist who is teaching a course for elective credit, or maybe for social science credit, may deemphasize the more "scientific" topics. Such a course may emphasize the more romantic topics in order to attract students: the fossil record, prehistoric archaeology, and primate behavior.

The Anthropology Major

What about the anthropology major? Anthropology majors in the community college represent a small proportion of our student body. At my college with an enrollment of approximately 18,500 students, only 0.3 percent are declared anthropology majors; in our anthropology classes less than 4 percent are majors. Relatively few students enter college with declared majors in anthropology because anthropology is infrequently taught in the high schools. The majority of college students learn about the subject by enrolling in an introductory college course, usually to fulfill a general education requirement, and later decide to change their major to anthropology.

Do our introductory courses adequately represent the research interests of professional physical anthropologists? Do our introductory courses provide a realistic background for the physical anthropology major? The answer to both questions is probably not.

In 1990–91, the members of the American Association of Physical Anthropologists were surveyed on various aspects of their training (Wienker and Bennett, 1992). The participants were asked to rank those academic areas they felt will be important to physical anthropology in the future. The areas fell into four groups. The first and most important group consists of anatomy, genetics, ecology, and paleontology, with the first two topics listed ranked highest. The second group contains physiology, zoology, demography, and archaeology. The third-ranking group consists of mathematics, cultural anthropology, geology, and chemistry, while the lowest-ranking group includes physics, psychology, and linguistics.

The data suggest that our lower-division courses do not necessarily reflect the direction in which physical anthropology is going. It would indeed be interesting to conduct a national survey to determine what topics are being taught in introductory courses and compare these with teaching and research specialties among physical anthropologists. In the 1990–91 survey, 13.9 percent of the physical anthropologists responding reported research and teaching specialties in growth, anatomy, morphology; 13.5 percent in evolutionary biology (including paleoanthropology); 12.8 percent in population studies; 12.2 percent in skeletal biology; 12.2 percent in biomedical anthropology and related areas; 11.1 percent in primatology; 8.8 percent in genetics; and 15.6 percent in other areas (Wienker and Bennett 1992, 390). To what degree is our introductory curriculum dealing with such topics as growth and development, molecular evolution, demography, dermatoglyphics, forensic anthropology, health and nutrition, and biochemical genetics?

Physical Anthropology in the Context of Anthropology

Of course, physical anthropology exists within the context of the broad discipline of anthropology, and on the introductory level it must be considered as part of the mainstream of anthropology. It is all too easy to see physical anthropology as biology and ignore its unique relationship to the social sciences and humanities. Stanley M. Newman (1990, 141) speaks of the introductory anthropology students at Northeastern Illinois University when he writes:

> Additional demographics indicate that for more than 90% of our students the introductory courses (Cultural Anthropology and Introduction to Anthropology) are their first encounters with anthropology and in all likelihood their last, given the inclination of most students to major in computer science and business.

We have an obligation to include in our courses an introduction to anthropology as a general discipline with reference to some of the basic themes of anthropology as a whole. Such an introduction may also bear later fruit when students are enticed to enroll in additional anthropology courses. Frederick S. Hulse wrote in 1963:

> Physical anthropology is recognized as including more than human biology, more than the study of evolution or genetics, more than designing equipment which will fit human beings, more than description and classification

of human variety. There seems to be agreement that we have as a unifying theme the concept of culture—just as do the other aspects of anthropology. In the words of one of my colleagues: "Physical anthropology's one claim to a place in the sun is its ability to interpret biological variability in its cultural setting." (70)

We can certainly bring cultural issues into discussions of the role of culture in natural selection, cultural stereotyping of human variation, and the role of culture in human evolution as seen in the archaeological record.

Yet the 1990–91 survey of physical anthropologists indicates that physical anthropologists may be moving away from an interest in the rest of anthropology. Wienker and Bennett (1992, 388) write:

> These results indicate without doubt that the traditional four-field or holistic anthropological approach toward training physical anthropology graduate students is no longer applicable. Cultural anthropology is thought to be of only marginal importance to our field. . . . It seems apparent that the great majority of physical anthropologists feel that graduate students in departments still demanding the holistic approach cannot be adequately prepared for a future professional career in physical anthropology unless these students further their education with postdoctoral research in more relevant areas.

Of course, these remarks address the education of students destined to become professional anthropologists. Yet these students will very likely find themselves teaching introductory physical anthropology at some point in their career, and their choice of topics will be influenced by their training and interests.

Contemporary Issues

There is another important area that we may explore on an introductory level. We, as teachers of introductory anthropology, must never forget the important role that anthropological theory can play in the understanding of many of the world's contemporary problems. Our students are constantly exposed to many scientific issues in the popular press and on television: use of DNA fingerprinting, gene splicing and genetic therapy, and racial issues. In addition, problems of overpopulation, human warfare, pollution, and so on gain new perspectives when viewed from the viewpoint of anthropology. Discussions of current ecological problems may be used to show relationships among environmental, biological, and cultural factors and how they relate to human evolution.

Indeed, we can view introductory physical anthropology as many possible separate courses. The traditional introductory course introduces Mendelian and population genetics, evolutionary theory, primatology, and paleoanthropology. A course at a research university with a large number of anthropology majors may reflect current research interests in physical anthropology: skeletal anatomy, morphology, molecular evolution, and so forth. Finally, it is possible to develop a more contemporary course stressing such issues as genetic engineering and ecology.

Conclusion

For those of us who are specialists in teaching introductory physical anthropology, there are no easy solutions. We are often faced with different academic situations in which we teach and different kinds of students in terms of background, ability, and goals. Each of us must seriously consider a number of variables to arrive at a course that is best for our students at our institution.

The goal of this article has been simply to provide some food for thought. I hope these ideas will lead to future discussion and debate, for it is only through such debate that physical anthropology will remain a strong and viable subject, both for majors and general education students.

References

Almquist, A. J., and J. E. Cronin. 1988. "Fact, Fancy, and Myth on Human Evolution." *Current Anthropology* 29:520–522.

Hulse, F. S. 1963. "Objectives and Methods." In *The Teaching of Anthropology*, edited by D. G. Mandelbaum, G. W. Lasker, and E. M. Albert, 70. Berkeley: University of California Press.

Newman, S. M. 1990. "Teaching Anthropology to 'Nonelite' Students: A Beginning Discussion." *Anthropology & Education Quarterly* 21:141.

Newman, S. M., and J. I. Macdonald. 1987. "Teaching Anthropology: Chicago Style." Presented as part of the symposium Strategies for Teaching Holistic Anthropology. Annual Meeting of the American Anthropological Association.

Wienker, C. W., and K. A. Bennett. 1992. "Trends and Developments in Physical Anthropology." *American Journal of Physical Anthropology* 87:383–393.

Teaching about Race

Alice M. Brues

The word *race* has acquired strong political connotations, but that should not deter us from talking about it. The more misconceptions there are about a subject, the more we can and should do to dispel the confusion. Dismissing the subject quickly will simply make our students fall back on folklore.

Race is one of those many words that has different meanings for different people. To the biological anthropologist, a race is a group of people usually living in a contiguous area, who resemble each other in hereditary characteristics more than they, as a group, resemble any other such group. The layman would say "They look more like each other than they look like other people." This means that they share ancestry with each other more than they do with other groups. Smaller groups that fit this definition may be combined with their neighbors into larger groups that also fit it; and by a reverse process, larger groups may be thought of as divided into subraces. Because all these races or subraces are part of the same species, all are capable of interbreeding in any combination; thus, their genetic differences blur where populations meet. This situation is shared by humans with other widespread species, so that biologists speak of *races* also. To keep from getting into meaningless detail, biologists require that 80 percent of individuals in a species are able to be assigned to one race or another to be considered a valid category. This decision immediately says that assignment of an individual to a race is not sufficiently precise to make legal distinctions, a lesson some people find hard to learn. The legal profession has difficulty dealing with definitions that are in any way fluid.

The greatest problem with the popular idea of race is a confusion between the transmission of physical traits from generation to generation and the transmission of culturally conditioned behavior. On the basis of simple observation, differences in physical appearance and social behavior may, at any given time, be correlated. People may look different from you; they may speak differently, dress differently, and have different norms of social behavior that may result in their doing, with the best of intentions, something that you consider rude. Then you begin to say "People who look like this are problems; let's avoid dealing with them."

With the perspective of history, we see clearly that the relation between appearance and behavior is brought about by historical accident. The genetic characters of a population stay much the same over long periods of time unless there are substantial population mixtures. But culture is far more volatile. Minor contacts between populations may initiate major changes in culture, beside which genetic changes are relatively slight.

There are good reasons that people so readily form connections in their minds between the visible characteristics of individuals or groups and expectations of how they will behave. An essential ability for social survival is being able to predict, by something seen or known now, such as outward appearance, how an individual will act in the future. We would say that people who could not make predictions of this kind were unable to learn by experience, or simply that they were not very intelligent. That is why folklore is full of predictive correlations, and why the function of science is to discredit misleading correlations as much as to establish valid ones.

One of the problems of defining terms in physical anthropology or other biological fields is the antiquated nature of the conceptual process, deeply rooted in the nature of language, which still controls much human thinking. The great principle of biology is variation, and our present view of the history of living things is based on biological variation and how external processes have operated on it to produce evolutionary changes. This has replaced the pre-Darwinian view that the biological world and its roster of species was constructed by a creator who thought grammatically—that is, in terms of classes of objects, denoted by specific nouns, which were uniform in essence even if they varied somewhat within the class. The varieties of the human species, which were observed to interbreed freely though they showed definite geographical differences in appearance, presented a puzzle. This led at one time to a short-lived theory that human races resulted from multiple creations in different parts of the world, of which the biblical creation of Adam and Eve was only one.

The misfit of the system of discrete classes of objects to the universal polymorphism of living things makes it necessary that students consider the range of meaning of words and statements. There are two kinds of declarative statements. "Men are taller than women" is one kind of statement; "Mary is taller than John" is another. It is because they are different kinds of statements that both can be true. The statement about classes is a statistical statement, whether or not it is phrased in statistical form. It is a statement about averages and is not complete unless we know the variation and overlap of the two classes. Students should be able to picture distribution curves and overlap of curves, and they should know that an average is not meaningful unless it is accompanied by a measure of variance. Next, the students must have some comprehension of what is meant by a "gene pool," as this is the permanent statistical basis of the species or the race and is what maintains its variation at a constant level.

Perhaps what I have said will disturb some readers. You may ask "Do we have to understand statistics and—good Lord—genetics???" Yes, you do, even if "math anxiety" steered you into cultural anthropology many years ago. Even if there is a biological anthropologist who will take over as guest lecturer for some of this material, the students will expect you to be able to field questions later about what the guest lecturer said. And students are often very good judges of whether you know what you are talking about.

A further important principle is that of Mendelian segregation, which follows on the concept of the gene pool. According to this principle, in any biological breeding group, characteristics that have a genetic basis will not, except in special cases, be inherited as a unit. Drawing the "makings" of different individuals from the same gene pool gives them only a *probability* of receiving identical genes from it. Thus, this principle represents the final blow to the belief that race is a mystical essence one inherits and which simultaneously affects all one's characteristics, including behavioral ones. One of the first American proponents of Mendelian genetics demonstrated that within a group of people having a homogenous mixture of "European" and "African" ancestry, there was no correlation between the color of the skin and the form of the hair. The results were published in 1913. It is not too soon to introduce your students to them.

Students must know early that populations differ because of different frequencies of genes in the gene pool. They must also know that individuals within a population differ because of different elements they drew from that gene pool. Then they can understand why populations maintain their visible differences from one another over long periods of time, even though many children do not even resemble their parents very much. They can also understand why the variation within a population also remains much the same. By this time they have the information to see clearly the contrast between biological inheritance and the transmission of culture. One was determined at the moment of conception, by purely biological factors; the other takes place after birth, with its greatest activity in childhood and adolescence, when by precept and example individuals acquire the behavioral norms of the community in which they live. Students will profit by knowing something of the history of race and its study. The earliest attempt to explain the phenomenon of race in the Western tradition is the account in Genesis of the three sons of Noah going out from the landfall at Mt. Ararat to repopulate the world. We do not know exactly when the idea originated that African blacks were the descendants of Ham, the Near Easterners the descendants of Shem, and people of Europe the descendants of Japheth. This idea, however, was firmly established in medieval legend, as we see in medieval paintings in which the three Wise Men of the Epiphany are shown as a rejoining of the three races that originated from the sons of Noah.

Serious consideration of the geographical variation of the human species began in the eighteenth century, when the people of Europe had acquired a fairly broad knowledge of other people all over the world. At this time it was possible to develop an inclusive classification by which human variation could be put in some kind of taxonomic order. (The idea of a hierarchical classification of life forms was being developed by the botanist Linnaeus during this same period.) It is interesting that the supposition, based on physical resemblance, that the New World was populated from Asia, had already been suggested at that time. There was speculation then as now about the causes of regional differences in physical traits. Then it was mostly in terms of Lamarck's inheritance of acquired traits; Darwin's insight into natural selection was yet to come.

Of all the eighteenth century classifications of race, the one that had the most lasting effect was that of Blumenbach, published in 1776. The system had five major categories that he termed Caucasian (from a belief that the Caucasus region was the original home of the archetypal Europeans), Mongolian, Ethiopian, American, and Malay. He gave as the first trait of these major races the color terms White, Yellow, Black, Copper (generally translated in English as Red), and Brown. This system is probably still the most influential on popular concepts of race and is responsible for the common emphasis on skin color as the primary criterion of race. The influence continues even though no human skin color is literally yellow or red; white skins are not really white or black skins literally black; and Blumenbach's "browns" grade imperceptibly into his "yellows" who live north of them. Many people seem to be so fixated on skin color that they are able to look at all kinds of faces innumerable times without ever noticing the many other features, especially in the face, by which races differ. Actually, these simplistic designations do not do justice to Blumenbach's careful descriptions of features other than color, but laypeople love an absurdly simple system because it does not strain their brains.

Conclusion

The real secret of teaching about race is to be able to do it in a one-semester, three-hour course. In this time, students must be given enough information that they will never again think of racial differences as so simple that any kind of practical or legal action can be based on them. Students must realize that there are equally dark-skinned people not only in Africa but in Australia, India, and the islands of Melanesia. They differ so much in other ways, however, that it is doubtful they are significantly related to each other. With a little practice, students can distinguish between an African black from Ethiopia and one from the lowlands of West Africa. They will understand that *black* is not a meaningful term unless it is qualified as "American black" or "African black," indicating historical origin and/or area of present residence. Our hope is that they will not use terms so vast as to lack meaning, like *non-white* or that latest verbal monstrosity, *persons of color*. My experience is that people who know their appearance is a little puzzling in the United States appreciate someone's taking the trouble to ask them *exactly* "what" they are. An Ethiopian does not want to be mistaken for a Nigerian or vice versa, and I suppose that is a form of racism. But to call them all "persons of color" signifies that you don't care what they are so long as they are different from you. That is the ultimate insult.

Last, consider that race does not have to be a dirty word because people have mistreated each other with it. Many more people have killed other people over the centuries because of religious differences than because of racial differences, and they are still doing it in the 1990s in Bosnia and India. Religion, race, or nationality are all concepts used to rationalize the ferocious territorialism we share with some of our primate relatives. The deadly emotions were there long before the words were attached to them. Let's not be afraid to use the words.

Teaching about Human Variation: An Anthropological Tradition for the Twenty-First Century

Leonard Lieberman and Rodney Kirk

Race is dying; long live human hereditary variation. One of the purposes of this chapter is to help explain to students how an increasing number of anthropologists have stopped gazing at the shadows called *race* on the walls of the cave. A second purpose is to suggest some strategies and answer some perplexing questions to help students see beyond the typologies of the tribe. If anthropologists do not teach about race at all, students are left with many erroneous and unexamined folk beliefs. Because psychologists, biologists, and sociologists say little or nothing about race as a biological concept, anthropologists must do so (see Lieberman, Hampton, Littlefield, and Hallead 1992; Yee, Fairchild, Weizmann, and Wyatt 1993); it is in fact essential to the anthropological tradition that we analyze human variation.

An early example of anthropological descriptions and classifications was Johann Friedrick Blumenbach's 1795 classification of five unequal races, although he did note they "graded without break from one region to another" (Blumenbach, as reported by Brace et al. 1993, 25). Since that time and through the nineteenth century, the lamentable anthropological tradition was one of supporting a hierarchy of discrete races. Beginning late in the nineteenth century and continuing with increased efforts as World War II and the Nazi Holocaust approached, Franz Boas and his students successfully challenged three parts of the race concept: the fixity of racial biology (Boas 1912), racial inferiority, and biological explanation of behavior.

After World War II, racism in the various sciences declined. While the modern synthesis of Darwinian and Mendelian genetics led to a more precise sounding definition of race, it was not one without faults. The middle decades of the twentieth century were the golden age of the scientific race concept; the concept would never get any better. In the mid-1960s, anthropological Armageddon erupted with a great debate over the very validity of the concept.

Within two decades, it would be clear that the race concept had lost its affirming consensus. As of 1985, only 50 percent of biological anthropologists at Ph.D.-granting departments agreed (and 41 percent disagreed) that "there are biological races in the species *Homo sapiens*." Among community college teachers of the subject, only 44 percent agreed and just over 41 percent disagreed. Among cultural anthropologists at both types of institutions, about 30 percent accepted the concept and 53 percent rejected it (Lieberman, Stevenson, and Reynolds 1989). A 1982 study (Littlefield, Lieberman, and Reynolds 1982), showed that the race concept was not supported in most college textbooks of physical anthropology; since then, the trend has continued, with only three textbooks explicitly supporting the concept from 1980 to 1995. The most significant measure of the concept's decline is the extremely low frequency of its use in research.

There is a danger in these figures. Anthropologists may conclude from them that they can ignore race and teach other topics. We strongly agree with Alice Brues (see this volume) that teachers of anthropology must teach about race. They should state that prior to the nineteenth century, it did not exist as a scientific concept; and before the time of Columbus, it was not a part of daily life and culture (Montagu 1942; Brace et al. 1993, 26). Race first emerged in the era of colonial expansion and was then taken up by scientists (Smedley 1993). If a concept can be constructed, it can also be deconstructed, and so it has been in the debate that began in the 1940s and intensified in the 1960s. Not to inform today's students of these developments is to allow tomorrow's teachers and researchers to be content with racial folk taxonomies and to allow these antiquated views to live on in future students.

The teaching of race should begin with the likelihood that students' *Weltanschauung* includes race as a reality. Students should be informed about the concepts and data used by the contending sides. For the side that rejects the concept of race, they should be told that there are five reasons for this rejection: empirical data, definitional problems, availability of alternative concepts, new fields of study, and humanitarian considerations (Lieberman and Reynolds, 1996).

In the first reason for rejection of race, empirical data now available indicate that biological characteristics affected by natural selection, gene flow, and/or drift are distributed in geographic gradations, or clines, such as those for sickling (Hb^s, ABO alleles, melanin, face form, and hair texture). These gradations cross putative racial boundaries and those of nation-states as if they did not exist. In the words of Frank B. Livingstone: "There are no races, there are only clines" (1958, 1962). The data on clines challenge the notion of races as populations that can be accurately represented by descriptive verbal portraits or mathematical averages within distinct boundary lines. Furthermore, any two or more of these gradations are likely to be distributed discordantly (Ehrlich and Holm 1964). For example, the gene for B type blood increases in frequency from West to East across Europe, reflecting migrations and gene flow out of Asia and, possibly, natural selection against A type blood with its susceptibility to smallpox; the genes for more melanin are distributed in a decreasing pattern from the upper Nile to Northern Europe (Brace 1964a, 1964b); and Hb^s is distributed in decreasing frequencies in a semicircle radiating out from West Africa. Given these discordant patterns, the description of any population as racially homogeneous is inherently incorrect, a product of selective perception.

Second, the definitional reasons for rejecting the race concept can be seen in the following mid-century statement: "We may define a human race as a population which differs significantly from other populations in regard to the frequency of one or more of the genes it possesses. It is an arbitrary matter which, and how many gene loci we choose to consider as a significant 'constellation'" (Boyd 1950, 207). The paramount weakness of this statement is that if a difference of one gene can identify races, then the number of races is as numerous as the number of human couples reproducing: every family is a different race. An improved definition is this: "A race is a division of a species which differs from other divisions by the frequency with which certain hereditary traits appear among its members" (Brues 1977, 2). Several traits are better than one, but the problem of discordant clines is not resolved by adding traits; more traits only add more discordance to the picture. The discordance of clines and their crossing of boundary lines leads to the wide variation in the number of races that have been identified (Molnar 1992). But, most importantly, the definition of race is neither useful nor necessary in order to design research. Nothing is gained by the use of race that the terms *population* or *biological population* cannot serve equally well.

The third reason for abandoning race is the availability of alternative concepts. The first of these, the idea of biological population, essential to genetic calculations, can substitute for race without carrying its problematic baggage because it does not refer to a biological unit (taxon) that requires a distinctive definition; rather, it refers to any breeding population, and these may have various degrees of fluidity over time. The second alternative concept is that of *cline*, referring to how the frequency of biological traits changes in a geographic gradient. The third concept is *ethnicity*, referring to the definition of any human social unit on the basis of "perceived cultural or physical differences" (Howard and Dunaif-Hattis 1992, 201; Gordon 1964). Montagu (1942) proposed "ethnic group" as a phrase that does not prejudge any group on "physical or other grounds" yet also recognizes that endogamous mating preferences will, over time, tend to produce some concentration of distinctive traits, although clinal in distribution. These tendencies are exaggerated in racial stereotypes. Ethnicity enables us to separate genetically based characteristics from learned characteristics and emphasizes that race is a social idea.

A fourth reason for the decline of interest in race is the availability of new research topics and specialties such as primate behavior and the biochemical analysis of DNA. With these influences, the core concept of race came to be peripheral in importance.

The fifth reason for abandoning race is humanitarian. Ashley Montagu was the first anthropologist in the United States to reject race by calling attention to scientific and humanitarian problems in the concept in his 1942 book *Man's Most Dangerous Myth: The Fallacy of Race*. In the United States, awareness had grown of the centuries-old use of race differences to justify colonialism, slavery, genocide, apartheid, and discrimination. That awareness expanded during the late 1960s and early 1970s when the civil rights movement captured the nation's attention, followed by the movement against the Vietnam War and by the women's movement.

In 1962–1964, just prior to the emergence of this milieu of protest, the debate over the existence of races erupted in the pages of *Current Anthropology,* with eminent specialists advocating both sides (Lieberman 1968; Smedley 1993, 272). The debate over race and the social movements coincided in time and intensified the concern over racial discrimination (see Hymes 1974). That concern made for wider involvement in the debate and much closer examination of the issues, the concept, and the clinal data.

A. R. Jensen (1982, 650) argued that the decline of race seems to have come about because anthropology allowed "one of its key concepts to be wafted about by the play of social and ideological forces that are not at all intrinsically related to the scientific elements of the argument." We believe this is a question that could best be asked of Jensen's own writing; but more concretely, Jensen looked at only one element and ignored the other four reasons for rejecting the concept.

For the various reasons sketched above, the concept of race has come to be reexamined and rejected by an increasing number of anthropologists. Informing students of this debate will breathe new life into their thinking about human variation and encourage them to understand science as a self-correcting process.

Strategies and Questions

In this section, several scenarios for teaching about human variation are proposed as well as questions for discussion. In an introductory course in physical or cultural anthropology, the press of time may permit use of only one or two; several can be used in a semester course on human variation.[1] Selection will depend on the instructor's purposes. In each case, it is necessary to explain the purpose carefully and to engage the imagination of the students whenever possible.

Focus on race and IQ.

According to Naftaly (1994), the "IQ controversy is highly relevant to beginning physical and cultural anthropology classes" precisely because it requires an integrated approach to the meaning of race, culture, and evolution. Naftaly's paper argues that this controversy is crucial because it deals with the relationship between biology and culture, it is an issue relevant to students' everyday lives, it is useful in developing critical holistic analyses, and it can be presented in a variety of ways such as using the dynamic CBS Reports film *The IQ Myth* (1975). Excellent readers on this controversy are *The Bell Curve Wars* (Fraser 1995) and *Race and IQ* (Montagu 1975, revised edition in press). Williams developed an African American IQ test called the BITCH 100 which can be taken by students from various ethnic groups to demonstrate the nature of test bias (1975). It should be preceded by some examples from the Stanford-Binet test (see Gould 1981). Scarr, Pakstis, Katz, and Barker (1977) took a sample of African Americans and tested them for IQ and degree of European ancestry. There was no relationship between ancestry and IQ. For a century, prominent IQ testers (Terman 1916; Jensen 1969; Herrnstein and Murray 1994) have claimed that environment has little influence on IQ. Very careful studies that refute that assertion are by Mercer (1972) and by Crane (1994). A summary of studies by Williams, Scarr, and Mercer are in Lieberman (1995).

Cross-cultural or multicultural perspectives underscore the important influence of environment on IQ. Kottak (1994a, 90) notes the above-average IQ reported for an Osage Indian population; he ties this finding to discovery of oil on the reservation, which contributed, among other things, to development of a high-quality school system. A study of children fathered by American soldiers and raised by their German mothers showed no difference in IQ performance of children of black versus white fathers (summarized in Brody 1992, reported by Nunley, n.d.).

Focusing on issues of test validity, Clara Rodriguez (1991) noted a general lack of predictive validity of standardized SAT tests for New York Hispanics. When SAT tests, adapted to the Spanish language context, were administered in Puerto Rico, they were found to be "better predictors of college success for Puerto Ricans in Puerto Rico than they are for non-Hispanic whites in the U.S."(1991, 126). Puerto Ricans, referred to by Rodriguez as the "Rainbow People," represent a rich blend of diverse global populations that defies simplistic racial classification.

Ask students what race means to them.

Considerable variation and misconception exist in the popular meaning of the term *race* and Fred E. Schneider (1989) developed an exercise to examine this. At least two meetings in advance of analysis in class, students are given an extra credit assignment; they ask one or two persons to write *their* definition of race as it applies to humans as well as to list a minimum of six races. Alternatively, the students in the class may provide their own answers to increase their involvement, and they complete the exercise in one class meeting. The instructor can summarize the results and present them to the class. If the class is small, the students can write the names of the races on the chalkboard and then group them by categories.[2] Either way, it will be apparent that a wide variety of meanings exist, including race as equivalent to skin color, language, nation, ethnicity, religion, or geographic region. It is necessary to clarify that only biological criteria were used by anthropologists to identify a race before the mid-twentieth century; but as a social concept, races are often defined on the basis of any available criteria. At this point, weakness in both approaches to race should be reviewed.

Introduce clines as an alternative to race.

Using clines rather than race has several purposes. You can demonstrate the idea of clines as geographic gradations in the frequency of hereditary characteristics by using a transparency[3] showing the distribution of the sickling hemoglobin. Most cline maps in physical anthropology texts lack the detail to convey clinal patterns fully. The most detailed cline map of Hb^s is found in Johnston (1982, 323). It demonstrates that the sickling trait is distributed at differing frequencies across populations around the Mediterranean, the Arabian peninsula, India, and southeast Asia. Instead of thinking about human variation as races—that is, as a homogeneous set of essential characteristics—students can think of one trait at a time and its distribution over a geographic range. Clinal maps are useful in demonstrating that members of a *race* are not homogeneous.

The word *cline* will baffle some students. Emphasizing geographic *gradations* will help them understand it. Show and analyze a transparency of the weather map in the daily newspaper with its isotherms. Also useful is a map showing variations in altitude: inclining and declining elevation. Cline is from the Greek *klinein*, to lean. Biologically, cline is a series of gradations in the frequency of a trait over a geographical range (Barnow 1971). Gradients in gene frequency are genoclines, and gradients in physical characteristics are phenoclines (Harrison, Weiner, Tanner, and Barnicot 1977, 1166). For a genocline map showing the frequency of the B allele in Europe and for a phenocline map of tawny hair in Western Australia, see Nelson and Jurmain (1991, 196–197). With clines, human variation can be studied one trait at a time and race is unnecessary.

Show how combining clines demonstrates that races are not distinct, and racial boundary lines do not exist.

The idea of discordance can be made more vivid in the classroom by taking cline maps of the Old World (four maps are in Brace 1964a) and making overhead transparencies of them. It may be necessary to enlarge or reduce a map to match up continental boundaries. Showing them one at a time and then showing all four together can illustrate how discordant patterns challenge the idea of distinct races and racial boundary lines. The four combined overhead transparencies of the Old World clines demonstrate that without boundary lines chaos emerges. Before this demonstration, it is useful to ask students to describe the genetic location of the three most often named races: Negroid, Mongoloid, Caucasoid. Then, on the overhead, show the map on page 23 of *People and Races* by Brues (1977 or 1990). Then, show the four overheads and the combination of the four. The combination can be copied in advance onto one overlay.

Demonstrate that clines are discordant, seldom concordant.

If clines were distributed with a high degree of concordant similarity, boundary lines between races would leap out of the combined cline maps. In fact, clines are almost always discordant; their geographic patterns do not coincide. An alternative to the transparencies involves reproducing all four cline maps on one sheet of 11" × 17" paper. Ask students to use three different colored pens to draw the clinal lines from three of the maps onto the fourth. This exercise takes about ten or fifteen minutes, but it focuses everyone's attention on the discordance of these gradations.

Felix Keesing used a different approach. He sorted "students according to one physical characteristic, such as stature, and then according to another, such as hair color" (Lasker 1963, 105). Sorting can be done by asking students to move literally from one group to another or to use their imaginations to accomplish the sorting. By sorting, Keesing demonstrated that "the physical characteristic in one trait does not determine how we will be classified in respect to another." It is necessary to explain that clinal patterns emerge from the operation of natural selection (see Livingstone, 1958, regarding malaria), gene flow, and random genetic drift (Molnar 1992).

Show that racial typologies are inaccurate because they ignore variations and discordance.

Racial typologies assume that members of a race are homogeneous in their characteristics. The exercise on clines demonstrates how much discordant variation exists. The characteristics used to describe races are stereotypes and do not correlate with one another.

> We can group all the black-skinned people together, but if we then examine [the members of] this group, we will find differences of hair form, nose shape, general body build, [and] distribution of hair—differences as great or greater than between Negroid and Caucasoid [averages]. If we decide to ignore skin color and group people according to hair form, or nose form, or shape of the eye, we find that we have groups containing all shadings of skin color. If we compare visible features with blood types, we find blood-group frequencies cutting directly across what appear to be absolute racial boundaries. (Downs and Bleibtreu 1972, 193–194)

Why are forensic anthropologists so good at identifying races?

Forensic anthropologists demonstrate a high degree of accuracy in identifying the "race" of a deceased person from skeletal material for police purposes. The National Crime Information Center provides a missing persons form that lists Asian (or Pacific Islander), Black, American Indian (or Alaskan Native), White, and Unknown. The forensic specialist must use one of these categories. But it is not race that is being identified; rather, it is the probable place of ancestry. According to Norman Sauer, a forensic anthropologist,

> to identify a person as having ancestors from, say, Northern Europe, does not identify a biological race of Northern Europeans. . . . Certainly we can teach the non-existence of race in the classroom and do our best to clarify

the use of races in forensic anthropology. At least, however, let us not fall into the trap of accepting races as valid biologically discrete categories because we use them so often. (1992, 110)

What is identified when a race label is assigned, is in fact the possible geographic origin of the ancestors and a clinal gradation that is more likely to be found in that locale.

Why do we say that race is a social construction?

The culture of the United States draws the world's sharpest distinctions between races; it is a black-and-white matter. If it were a matter of biological fact, then surely more societies would be in agreement. But the way we think about "our race" and the "others" is a product of history and embodies our cultural beliefs (see Smedley 1993; Horsman 1981). The comparative social construction of race can be illustrated by the Brazilian research of Marvin Harris. Seventy-two drawings combined various sets of three skin tones, three hair forms, two lip, two nose, and two gender types. These were shown to 100 male and female native-born Brazilians of all locales and classes. The 100 subjects reported 492 differing race names for the 72 drawings. Each drawing was identified by twenty or more categorical terms. There was no consensus that would suggest racial categories. Contrast this with the United States where the two major groups are labeled "whites" and "blacks" (Harris 1970; for a brief summary, see Bogin 1993, 40).

Consider another example of how racial identity, as commonly understood, is a social concept but not a sensible or scientific one. The issue is how to classify a child at birth when one parent is "white" and one is "Negro," or any other combination. The question is posed by Byrne (1993), citing the racial code matrix used until 1989 by the National Center for Health Statistics. The matrix is shown below. The same assumptions continue to be used in the culture of the United States.

In the matrix, the racial identity of the father is read vertically and the mother's is read horizontally. Thus, 1 is White, 2 is Negro, and so on (note that the nonparallel classifications are U.S. government issue). The race classification of the child is located at the point where the row of the father and the column of the mother meet. If the mother is Japanese (5) and the father is white (1) the child is classified as Japanese. The general principle expressed in the matrix is that the child receives the father's race code except when a white father has a nonwhite wife, in which case the child receives the nonwhite classification. This practice of *hypodescent* (Kottak 1994b, 52–53) leads to the placement of children of mixed unions into the less privileged, less powerful, and/or less ritually pure group. In this case, even patriarchy becomes subordinated to the color line. Byrne (1993, 99, 103) comments that "many American students have been taught that racial identification is a simple Mendelian dichotomy as if black genes dominated white genes and . . . male genes dominated 'weaker' female genes."

Matrix Showing Code for Classifying Race of Newborn
(U.S. Public Health Service—to 1989*)

CODE FOR RACE OF FATHER	CODE FOR RACE OF MOTHER									
	1	2	3	4	5	6	7	8	0	9
	CODE FOR RACE OF CHILD									
1 White	1	2	3	4	5	6	7	8	0	1
2 Negro	2	2	2	2	2	6	2	2	2	2
3 Indian	3	3	3	3	3	6	3	3	3	3
4 Chinese	4	4	4	4	4	6	4	4	4	4
5 Japanese	5	5	5	5	5	6	5	5	5	5
6 Hawaiian	6	6	6	6	6	6	6	6	6	6
7 Other nonwhite	7	7	7	7	7	6	7	7	7	7
8 Filipino	8	8	8	8	8	6	8	8	8	8
0 Chamorro Guamanian	0	0	0	0	0	6	0	0	0	0
9 Unknown	1	2	3	4	5	6	7	8	0	a/

*Code "was changed to be the same for all races: the infant's race is that of the mother" (Hahn and Stroup 1994, 9).

a/ Where both races are unknown or not stated, the race of the child to be assigned is that of last known race.

Hahn and Stroup (1994, 9) note that in 1989 this "complex algorithm was changed to be the same for all races: the infant's race is that of the mother." They also note that applying this algorithm to 1987 births would "'increase' white births by 1.7 percent while 'decreasing' black births by 4.7 percent, American Indian births by 19.2 percent, and Hawaiian births by 29.7 percent."

Indeed, there is a story, perhaps apocryphal, that Papa Doc Duvalier responded to a U.S. journalist's question by stating that over 95 percent of the Haitian population was "white." The journalist was incredulous but the old dictator explained that a person with "any white blood" is classified as white. It also makes no social sense in terms of accuracy to ignore one-half of a person's origins. Many persons with complex ancestry feel there is a need for mixed categories in birth classifications and census identifiers. In everyday social relations, individuals should be free to define their own ethnic identities (see Root 1992).

How do race and racism originate?

Races can be arbitrarily created by those with power and authority in a society, even if there are not groups with physical differences. Once created, this social order must be defended by defining one group as inferior to another. Stereotypes that make up racist ideology emerge. This creation of inferiors is well demonstrated in the twenty-nine-minute film *Eye of the Storm* (1971). The film shows Miss Jane Elliot, a teacher in Riceville, Iowa, arbitrarily dividing her third-grade class, all of Northwest European origin, into "blue-eye" and "brown-eye" groups. On alternate days in 1968, one group is treated by Miss Elliot as superior and has more privileges, and the other is described as inferior and has fewer privileges with accompanying pejorative labeling. *A Class Divided* (1985) is a fifty-four-minute film examining the long-term positive effects of the 1968 experiment by Miss Elliot. Years later, Miss Elliot met with her former students. As adults, they testified to the power of the experience in making them aware of the unfairness of discrimination. Ask students whether they wish to do the same experiment. Discuss why and why not. Did Miss Elliot succeed? What is the role of social structure and authority in creating discrimination and prejudice? What social function did the racist stereotypes perform? What benefits were gained by the "superior" group, and what were the losses for the "inferior" group? (See Shanklin 1994, 106–108; Peters 1971.)

If races don't exist, what happens to black racial pride and the right to redress under civil rights legislation?

As a scientific concept, race is useless. African Americans who have worked to build black pride are of course entitled to speak of their race; to many it means social race, a form of ethnicity. As to civil rights legislation, the U.S. Supreme Court has recognized that anthropologists reject the concept, but the Court has ruled in favor of a plaintiff claiming discrimination on the basis of race. The Court's decision stated that the laws were predicated on the older meaning of discrimination because of "ancestry or ethnic characteristics. Such discrimination is racial discrimination that Congress intended . . . to forbid, whether or not it would be classified as racial in terms of modern scientific theory" (U.S. Supreme Court 1989, 18).

Race does not determine behavior of its members, but culture does strongly influence behavior. Is there no relationship between biology and culture?

Biology does influence culture. For example, populations of small stature, such as the Mbuti of the Ituri forest, build smaller shelters than do the tall Nilotic peoples. Biology is especially relevant to anthropology because only the human species has complex culture and spoken language. But the differences between the cultures and languages of different societies are not the product of a particular gene or set of genes (Washburn 1980). Culture influences gene frequencies in several ways. Cultural rules affect preferential mating and gene flow between populations as well as patterning the deviation from those rules. Culture and biology also interact, each affecting the other, as in the case of sickle cell anemia (see Livingstone 1958; Jackson 1992; Durham 1991).

Conclusion

Limitations of space prohibit consideration of other dimensions of human variation. Useful analyses are found in Marks (1995), Molnar (1992), and in several introductory texts (see Kottak 1994a; Stein and Rowe 1993; Weiss and Mann 1993). A comprehensive and insightful history and analysis of the race concept in North America is found in Smedley (1993). Numerous useful examples and emphases on the need to teach about race and racism are identified in Shanklin (1994); new analyses and the concept of clines and clusters are discussed in Brace et al. (1993).

We suggest that even when instructors adhere to the mid-century concept of race, it is their scientific responsibility to present both views on the race concept. First, they should report that among physical anthropologists, the specialists on this concept, there is no longer consensus on the scientific accuracy and utility of race. Second, they should emphasize that scientific consensus does exist on the principle that 85 percent of human variation is found *within* human populations and that there is more variation within than between so-called races (Lewontin 1973). Third, they should point out that discordant gradations make most racial boundary lines impossible to identify, and that continued human migration and interbreeding will accentuate these conditions. Fourth, they should stress that in the past the use of the race concept has had harmful consequences and that such uses have no scientific justification.

In her statement on race, Brues (this volume) concludes by stating that "Religion, race, or nationality are all concepts used to rationalize the ferocious territorialism we share with some of our primate relatives." The implication is that territorialism is part of our primate heritage. Did we inherit and/or learn territorialism? Students should be informed about the endless debate on this topic, too. Religion, nationality, ethnicity, race, and territorialism are all learned concepts that can be used to define "us" so that we may justify controlling the resources of "them," the others. We agree with Brues that teachers of anthropology can and should create awareness of all these destructive processes.

Notes

Author's Note: Portions of this chapter have appeared in Lieberman and Byrne (1993).

1. Syllabi for several courses in human variation are available on the Human Biology Interest Group Discussion List through e-mail: MAILSERV@ACC.FAU.EDU (Bitnet users send to MAILSERV@FAUVAX) with the request in the message body: *SUBSCRIBE HUMBIO-L your-full-name.* To unsubscribe, send: *UNSUBSCRIBE HUMBIO-L.* Send questions to List Manager: R. P. Carpenter (RALPH@ACC. FAU.EDU, RALPH@FAUVAX) or to List Owner: M.Y. Iscan (ISCAN@ACC. FAU.EDU, ISCAN@FAUVAX).

2. If the class is large, an alternative is to use a transparency of question items 4 and 7 from a decade U.S. Census form as an authoritative source of named races. Comparison of census questionnaires from past decades provides a particularly vivid frame for discussion of race as a sociopolitical construct. Of particular note is the changing conceptualization of question 4 from "4. Color or Race" (1970) to "4. Is this person . . ." (1980), to the more recent and more blunt "4. Race" (1990). As in Schneider's exercise, labels are varied and inconsistent in apparent criteria used and, therefore, no claim can be made that race is a scientific concept as employed by the U.S. government. U.S. Latinos, a spectacularly diverse segment of the population, were omitted altogether from the 1970 census. Subsequently this group was added, albeit not as a race but as identified in a separate question: "7. Is this person of Spanish/Hispanic origin or descent?" Using the census questions and categories, ask students to classify themselves, General Colin Powell, and Secretary of Housing and Urban Development Henry Cisneros. Discussion should focus on difficulties posed by the terms used and difficulties that arise in their application.

3. According to the copyright committee for the Author-Publisher Group, Authors League of America, and the Association of American Publishers, Inc. (March 19, 1976), minimum standards of fair use in section 107 of H. R. 2223, the Copyright Revision Bill, permits single copying by teachers for scholarly research or use in teaching of a chapter from a book, an article from a periodical or newspaper, and a chart, graph, diagram, drawing, cartoon or picture from a book, periodical, or newspaper.

References

A Class Divided. 1985. Pubtel, color, 16mm, 54 min., #50839.16. Penn State Audio-Visual Services, University Park, PA 16802.

Barnow, Victor. 1971. *Physical Anthropology and Archaeology*. Homewood, Ill.: Dorsey Press.

Boas, Franz. 1912. "Change in the Bodily Form of Descendants of Immigrants." *American Anthropologist* 14:530–562.

Bogin, Barry. 1993. "Biocultural Studies of Ethnic Groups." In *Research Strategies in Human Biology*, edited by Gabriel W. Lasker and C. G. N. Mascie-Taylor, 33–61. New York: Cambridge University Press.

Boyd, W. C. 1950. *Genetics and the Races of Man*. Boston: Little, Brown.

Brace, C. Loring. 1964a. "A Nonracial Approach towards the Understanding of Human Diversity." In *The Concept of Race*, edited by Ashley Montagu, 103–152. New York: Free Press.

———. 1964b. "On the race concept." *Current Anthropology* 5:313–320. Brace, C. Loring, Shelley L. Smith, and Kevin D. Hunt.

Brace, C. Loring, David P. Tracer, Lucia Allen Yaroch, John Robb, Kari Brandt, and A. Russell Nelson. 1993. "Clines and Clusters versus 'Race': A Test in Ancient Egypt and the Case of a Death on the Nile." *Yearbook of Physical Anthropology* 36:1–31.

Brody, Nathan. 1992. *Intelligence*. San Diego: Academic Press.

Brues, Alice. 1977. *Peoples and Races*. New York: Macmillan. Reprint 1990. Prospect Heights, Ill.: Waveland Press.

Byrne, William G. 1993. "Teaching the Social Nature of the 'Race' Concept." In *Anthropological Perspectives: Resources in Teaching Anthropology*, edited by Mario Zamora. New York: Reliance Publishing.

CBS Reports. 1975. *IQ Myth* (a CBS film). Penn State Audio-Visual Services, University Park, PA. (51 min., Cat. #50321, Video Rental $25.50. Tel.: 1-814-865-6314).

Crane, Jonathan. 1994. "Exploding the Myth of Scientific Support for the Theory of Black Intellectual Inferiority." *Journal of Black Psychology* 20:189–209.

Downs, James F., and Hermann K. Bleibtreu. 1972. *Human Variation: An Introduction to Physical Anthropology.* Beverly Hills, Calif.: Glencoe Press.

Durham, William H. 1991. *Coevolution: Genes, Culture and Human Diversity.* Stanford, Calif.: Stanford University Press.

Ehrlich, Paul R., and Richard W. Holm. 1964. "A Biological View of Race." In *The Concept of Race,* edited by Ashley Montagu, 153–179. New York: Free Press.

Eye of the Storm. 1971. Chuman, color, 16mm, 29 min., #31685.16. Penn State Audio-Visual Services, University Park, PA 16802.

Fraser, Steven. 1995. *The Bell Curve Wars: Race, Intelligence, and the Future of America.* New York: Basic Books.

Gordon, Milton M. 1964. *Assimilation in American Life: The Role of Race, Religion, and National Origins.* New York: Oxford University Press.

Gould, Stephen J. 1981. *The Mismeasure of Man.* New York: W. W. Norton.

Hahn, Robert A., and Donna F. Stroup. 1994. "Race and Ethnicity in Public Health Surveillance: Criteria for the Scientific Use of Social Categories." *Public Health Reports* 109 (1):7–15.

Harris, Marvin. 1970. "Referential Ambiguity in the Calculus of Brazilian Racial Identity." *Southwestern Journal of Anthropology* 26:1–14.

Harrison, G. A., J. S. Weiner, J. M. Tanner, and N. A. Barnicot. 1977. *Human Biology.* New York: Oxford University Press.

Herrnstein, Richard J., and Charles Murray. 1994. *The Bell Curve: Intelligence and Class Structure in American Life.* New York: Free Press.

Horsman, Reginald. 1981. *Race and Manifest Destiny: The Origins of American Racial Anglo-Saxonism.* Cambridge, Mass.: Harvard University Press.

Howard, Michael C., and Janet Dunaif-Hattis. 1992. *Anthropology, Understanding Human Variation.* New York: HarperCollins.

Hymes, Dell, ed. 1974. *Reinventing Anthropology.* New York: Vintage.

Jackson, Fatimah L. C. 1992. "Race and Ethnicity as Biological Constructs." *Ethnicity and Disease* 2:120–125.

Jensen, Arthur R. 1969. "How Much Can We Boost IQ and Scholastic Achievement?" *Harvard Educational Review* 39:1–123.

———. 1982. "Comment." *Current Anthropology* 22:649–650.

Johnston, Francis E. 1982. *Physical Anthropology.* Dubuque, Iowa: Wm. C. Brown.

Kottak, Conrad Phillip. 1994a. *Anthropology.* New York: McGraw–Hill.

———. 1994b. *Cultural Anthropology.* New York: McGraw-Hill.

Lasker, Gabriel W. 1963. "The Introductory Course." In *The Teaching of Anthropology,* edited by David G. Mandelbaum, Gabriel W. Lasker, and Ethel M. Albert. Berkeley: University of California Press.

Lewontin, Richard D. 1973. "The Apportionment of Human Diversity." *Evolutionary Biology* 6:381–397.

Lieberman, Leonard. 1968. "The Debate over Race: A Study in the Sociology of Knowledge." *Phylon* 39:127–141.

———. 1995. "Herrnstein and Murray: IQs Are Us." Unpublished manuscript, Department of Sociology and Anthropology, Central Michigan University, Mt. Pleasant, MI 48859.

Lieberman, Leonard, and William Byrne. 1993. "Race and How to Teach It." *SACC Notes* (American Anthropological Association.) Spring–Summer:2–3.

Lieberman, Leonard, Raymond E. Hampton, Alice L. Littlefield, and Glen Hallead. 1992. "Race in Biology and Anthropology: A Study of College Texts and Professors." *Journal of Research in Science Teaching* 29:301–321.

Lieberman, Leonard, and Larry T. Reynolds. 1996. "Race: The Deconstruction of a Scientific Concept." In *Race and Other Misadventures: Essays in Honor of Ashley Montagu*, edited by Larry Reynolds and Leonard Lieberman. Dix Hills, N.Y.: General Hall.

Lieberman, Leonard, Blaine W. Stevenson, and Larry T. Reynolds. 1989. "Race and Anthropology: A Core Concept without Consensus." *Anthropology and Education Quarterly* 20(2):67–73.

Littlefield, Alice, Leonard Lieberman, and Larry T. Reynolds. 1982. "Redefining Race: The Potential Demise of a Concept." *Current Anthropology* 23:641–647.

Livingstone, Frank B. 1958. "Anthropological Implications of Sickle Cell Gene Distributions in West Africa." *American Anthropologist* 30:533–562.

———. 1962. "On the Non-existence of Human Races." *Current Anthropology* 3:279–281,470.

Marks, Jonathan. 1995. *Human Biodiversity: Genes, Race and History*. New York: Aldine De Gruyter.

Mercer, Jane R. 1972. "IQ: The Lethal Label." *Psychology Today* 44: 46–47, 95–97.

Molnar, Stephen. 1992. *Human Variation: Races, Types and Ethnic Groups*. 2d ed. Englewood Cliffs, N.J.: Prentice-Hall.

Montagu, Ashley. 1942. *Man's Most Dangerous Myth: The Fallacy of Race*. New York: Columbia University Press.

———. 1952. *Man's Most Dangerous Myth*. 3rd ed. New York: Harper & Bros.

———. 1975. *Race and IQ*. New York: Oxford University Press.

Naftaly, Phillip. 1994. "Teaching Culture and Biology: The Use and Abuse of IQ Testing." *Society for Anthropology in the Community College Notes* 4–6,17–18.

Nelson, Harry, and Robert Jurmain. 1991. *Introduction to Physical Anthropology*. St. Paul, Minn.: West.

Nunley, Michael. n.d. Oral report of a panel discussion, "The Bell Curve: Too Smooth to Be True," held at Central Michigan University, March 1, 1995.

Peters, William. 1971. *A Class Divided*. Garden City, N.Y.: Doubleday.

Rodriguez, Clara. 1991. *Puerto Ricans: Born in the USA*. Boulder, Colo.: Westview Press.

Root, Maria P. P., ed. 1992. *Racially Mixed People in America*. Newbury Park, Calif.: Sage.

Sauer, Norman J. 1992. "Forensic Anthropology and the Concept of Race: If Races Don't Exist, Why Are Forensic Anthropologists So Good at Identifying Them?" *Social Science and Medicine* 34:107–111.

Scarr, Sandra, Andrew J. Pakstis, Solomon H. Katz, and William B. Barker. 1977. "Absence of a Relationship between Degree of White Ancestry and Intellectual Skills within a Black Population." *Human Genetics* 39:69–86.

Schneider, Fred B. 1989. "Towards Student Self-Discovery of the Race Concept." Presentation to the Annual Meeting of the American Anthropological Association, Washington, D.C.

Shanklin, Eugenia. 1994. *Anthropology and Race*. Belmont, Calif.: Wadsworth.

Smedley, Audrey. 1993. *Race in North America: Origin and Evolution of a World View*. Boulder, Colo.: Westview Press.

Stein, Philip L., and Bruce M. Rowe. 1993. *Physical Anthropology*. 5th ed. New York: McGraw-Hill.

Terman, L. M. 1916. *The Measurement of Intelligence*. Boston: Houghton Mifflin.

Supreme Court. 1989. *Saint Francis College Petitioners et al. vs. Majid Ghaidan Al Khazravi*, No. 85-2169, May 18.

Washburn, Sherwood L. 1980. "Human Behavior and the Behavior of Other Animals." In *Sociobiology Examined*, edited by Ashley Montagu, 254–282. New York: Oxford.

———. 1993. *Human Biology and Behavior*. 5th ed. Glenview, Ill.: Scott, Foresman.

Weiss, Mark L., and Alan E. Mann. 1975. *Human Biology and Behavior*. Boston: Little, Brown.

Williams, R. 1975. "The BITCH 100: A Culture-specific Test." *Journal of Afro-American Issues* 3:103–116.

Yee, Albert H., Halford H. Fairchild, Fredric Weizmann, and Gail E. Wyatt. 1993. "Addressing Psychology's Problems with Race." *American Psychologist*, November: 1132–1140.

Paleoanthropology
The "Exotic" and "Esoteric" Become Relevant

FRANK E. POIRIER

In 1963, Gabriel Lasker noted that of the approximately 330 members of the American Association of Physical Anthropologists, perhaps sixty physical anthropologists taught undergraduate classes. However, only about thirty of these had responsibility for an introductory physical anthropology course. Things have certainly changed and an amazing educational opportunity has been presented to physical anthropologists. Physical anthropologists now reach thousands of students per year, especially if the introductory course fulfills a natural or biological science component of the curriculum. Our teaching aids and our "cheerleaders"—TV, movies, popular books, and even the tabloids—put our discipline front and center and force us to be relevant. We will sink or swim in the limelight, and our personal tragedies and our collegial and rancorous disagreements have become news. We need to turn this attention to our advantage. We also need to be wary of the motives of some of the attention-givers.

For most practicing physical anthropologists, the discipline is biologically and quantitatively oriented (Wienker and Bennett 1992). Thus, the antimath and antiscience proclivities of many American students are problems. This obstacle not withstanding, we must continue to stress the scientific roots and basic lessons of physical anthropology: for example, lessons of evolutionary survival, adaptation, and the survival value of social living. Humans are consistently bipedal, cultural animals that have language. These and other human traits can easily be presented to students in challenging and interesting ways. Given the fascinating nature of our data and the current favorable press coverage of subjects of anthropological research, even the most uninspired teacher can make paleoanthropology and primatology interesting and relevant.

Human evolution has long been a mainstay in the teaching agenda of physical anthropology, and rightfully so. Primatology is a rather recent addition to the curriculum, being taught in its current format since the mid-1960s. Fortunately, both human evolution and primate behavior fascinate most students—perhaps because they have seen so much of the work portrayed on TV and in the *Indiana Jones* and *Gorillas in the Mist* movies, among others. I think both topics are central to the teaching of physical anthropology at the introductory and upper-division levels, where aspects of one or the other are the focus. Teachers of physical anthropology can use what others might see as the exotic and esoteric nature of our subject to our advantage. Some examples of how this can be done are presented in the rest of this chapter.

The future funding and growth of our discipline lies with reaching the educated layperson. An undergraduate in introductory and upper-level classes may be the person to fund the next important anthropological study or to vote on important conservation issues. Reaching these people should be a priority. Michael Crichton, author of *Jurassic Park,* was quoted as saying, "Biotechnology and genetic engineering are very powerful." Referring to the movie based on his book, Crichton said, "The film suggests that [science's] control of nature is elusive. And just as war is too important to leave to the generals, science is too important to leave to scientists. Everyone needs to be attentive" (*Newsweek*, p. 61, June 14, 1993). Writing in *Science,* Nicholas Hackerman (1992, 157) notes that for scientists generally it is "in our best interest, as well as for the society as a whole, . . . [to] put our best creative efforts into solving the problem of how to fan the interest of non-science majors in nature's phenomena." A major failure of American higher education has been a reluctance to broadcast the relevance of what is being taught. Anthropology has been no more successful in advertising its relevance to modern life than have many other disciplines.

It is hard to argue with a medium, TV, that has focused so much interest on paleoanthropology and primatology. This concentrated attention has made it especially challenging to teach these subjects. Faculty are expected to be as exciting as the researchers featured in the films. We are left to explain the understated controversies, to clarify theoretical differences, to "clean up" after these films, and to fill in the details. For example, I have had to explain that the monkeys I study eat, sleep, and do many other mundane things that are seldom depicted in the movies. On balance, however, anthropological films (and films with an anthropological backdrop) have been a boon to our subject and are an important teaching tool.

The wide press coverage given such ideas as the unfortunately dubbed "African Eve" hypothesis has probably resulted in increased course enrollments, increased awareness of anthropology, and, in this specific case, a more diverse student body. Paleoanthropology can redress the Eurocentric bias present in much of the science taught in American universities. There is a correlation between the discussion of evolution in Africa and increased enrollment in my classes of African American and African students. Some of these students realize that paleoanthropology addresses their concerns, and this awareness creates exciting possibilities for broadening participation in our research endeavor. (Unfortunately, students from East and South Africa, where many important fossils have been found, are often unaware of the primate fossil riches in their countries. That they learn about discoveries in their own countries at foreign universities is rather sad. Because of social and religious strictures, many of these students do not accept the fossil evidence for human evolution. Rather than gain pride from the fact that Africa is central to human evolution, some of these students may reject the fossil record!)

The subject of human evolution catches the student's fancy. In our courses students learn about themselves. As Philip Stein (this volume) suggests, "Our subject matter is more romantic to the nonscience student than biology. Who would not rather study fossil hominids and primate behavior than the anatomy of the frog and the biochemistry of the citric acid cycle?" Some biologists have fought the inclusion of physical anthropology courses in the biology or natural sciences curriculum. On the other hand, because they recognize the interest in and the exciting nature of our data, more biologists may be "speaking anthropology" in their classes. It is entirely possible that two major aspects of physical anthropological research, primatology and paleoanthropology, might be usurped by biologists.

Newspapers and magazines regularly feature articles dealing with human evolution. New fossil finds, primate studies, discoveries of long-lost life forms, genetic engineering, and medical breakthroughs are common knowledge to an educated audience. A *Newsweek* (May 10, 1993) article entitled "The Flintstone Diagnosis" discussed how scientists are looking at prehistoric evidence to understand and treat modern ailments. James McKenna, one of the anthropologists mentioned, is providing new insights into research on acquired immune deficiency syndrome (AIDS) based on primatological data. Anthropologists are popping up all over the place with relevant insights from our discipline! I am inundated with reading materials that students in my large introductory classes bring to me. Each of these bits of information starts a new lesson. I use Gary Larson's "Far Side" cartoons to begin many lectures because the jokes carry a message. The educational technique can be labeled "learning with a laugh."

Research using the polymerase chain reaction (PCR) process fascinates my students. Many of our students have read or seen M. Crichton's *Jurassic Park*, based on Hendrik Poinar's and Raul Cano's work of extracting samples of mosquitoes, biting flies, and other insects from seventy- to eighty-million-year-old amber (De Salle, Gatesy, Wheeler, and Grimaldi 1992; Grimaldi 1993; Morrell 1992). As Sharon Begley (1993) notes in *Newsweek*, "All great science fiction must be science first and fiction second. Even more, it must tap into the reigning scientific paradigm of its era" (57). The paradigm for *Jurassic Park* is biotechnology, and biotechnology is rapidly changing the face of physical anthropology.

The push to extract deoxyribonucleic acid (DNA) has produced amazing results. First, it was DNA from a seventeen-million-year-old magnolia leaf. Then there was DNA from a thirty-million-year-old termite and a forty-million-year-old bee. But this is a mere tease compared to the extraction of DNA (two fragments of a single gene) from a weevil preserved in amber 120–135 million years ago and preliminary results in extracting DNA from scales of a 200-million-year-old fish. (So rapid is the development of the PCR process that these figures will probably be outdated before this manuscript appears in press. There are currently unconfirmed reports of DNA being amplified from a 400-million-year-old mollusk.) The suggestion that insects encased in amber may contain dinosaur red blood cells (although at this time, researchers have not found amber-encased insects containing dinosaur blood) should lead to a discussion of why, even with possible dinosaur DNA, we will not clone a dinosaur. (One figure estimates that scientists will do that in about 1,000 years. However, given the rate of research, 1,000 years is surely too long—if it can be accomplished at all [Morell, 1993].) Cloning a dinosaur may be out of the question, but since DNA can survive for millions of years under the right conditions, a technique that we might call *molecular paleontology* will yield fascinating discoveries. Ancient DNA is sure to be useful in understanding evolutionary relationships. For example, the paleontologist Jack Horner hopes to use DNA extracted from dinosaur bones to assess the relationship between dinosaurs and modern birds. If successful, this will open the door for clarifying evolutionary relationships based on the primate fossil record. We may very soon be close to answering our central question of where did we come from and who were our closest fossil ancestors?

A discipline that might be called *molecular medical paleontology* may be on the horizon. DNA has been sequenced from a 2,500 year-old Egyptian mummy. Direct comparisons of the health status between ancient and modern populations are now available. Thomas Loy, an archaeologist at Australian National University, found human blood stains on stone tools from Iraq dated to 100,000 years ago. If this blood came from a Neandertal, it will provide interesting new insights. There are other fascinations, such as DNA from 7,000-year-old human brain tissue preserved in a Florida bog, the recovery of a glacier-entombed Neolithic inhabitant of Europe (Seidler and others 1992; Sjøvold 1992, 1993; and letters to the editor in *Science* 260, 146–147), and bacteria from the stomach of an 11,000-year-old mastodon buried in Ohio. Using new analytical techniques, the past becomes the present. The fossil record is brought back to life! Stones and bones as well as blood, hair, and other organic material can now "talk" to us from the past (Cherfas 1991).

Much emphasis in the undergraduate curriculum is on multicultural education. Because physical anthropology is not species exclusive, paleoanthropology and primatology provide an even wider perspective, a multispecies education. Furthermore, an understanding of biological competition and co-existence are important for human survival. We must help our students understand how humans compete with and coexist with other living creatures. That understanding, even if not on the conscious level, was as important for the first six million years of human survival as it is for the future survival of humanity.

Primate evolutionary biology introduces students to some of the complexity of variation and diversity in life. Understanding inter- and intraspecies variation is our forte. Once students accept the importance of genetic variation in the context of human and nonhuman primate evolution, it may be easier for them to handle diversity within their own social/cultural context. Primatologists can impart the idea of species relativism—a concept akin to the cultural relativism of our cultural anthropology colleagues.

Interpreting Data

Students are often poorly prepared to handle intellectual disagreement. For example, many students in paleoanthropology courses are unable to understand disagreement over taxonomic issues. The ubiquitous theoretical disagreements (for example, concerning *Australopithecus afarensis*, *Homo habilis*, *Homo erectus*, and the origins of *Homo sapiens sapiens* [Poirier 1993]) among paleoanthropologists provide an opportunity to explain how science works. Often students are amazed that scientists disagree, that there can be more than one way to interpret the same evidence, and that a scientist can be wrong and must correct an earlier interpretation. Some students experience difficulty handling conflicting viewpoints and the intellectual chaos that often accompany scientific debates. The spate of popular books that supposedly informs the outside world about the latest dirt between scientific parties (the scientific equivalent of "Inside Edition") can do more harm than good. Scientific arguments that are reduced to personality conflicts may help to sell books. However, by encouraging such publications, by repeating stories of personal conflicts in our classrooms, and by trivializing important scientific debates, perhaps we are our own worst enemies. What messages do we send? Personalities may become more important than theoretical differences for some, and some scientific debates are venues to belittle opponents and reduce the argument to a personal level. Instead of attacking people, the effort needs to focus on attacking/understanding the interpretive processes (see Harraway 1989; Landau 1991).

Scientific disagreements reaching the popular press allow us not only to talk about the scientific method—and here is a good place to distance the scientific method from a resort to authority, as is true of creationists—but also let us discuss the reality that, like the general populace, scientists carry cultural and intellectual baggage. The April 16, 1993, issue of *Science* (420–429) discusses how research by female primatologists and a shift of emphasis from watching male nonhuman primates to watching female nonhuman primates has altered our view of monkey and ape behavior. Primatologists must be careful not to impart their hopes/values and their likes/dislikes (their cultural baggage) on our monkey and ape relatives. As an example, please recall the charged reactions of Jane Goodall's audiences to her first reports of chimpanzee warfare and cannibalism (Goodall 1986). There was nervous panic and near despair in some audiences. Some were horrified to learn that chimpanzees are not the "noble savages" that so many want them to be.

The treatment/mistreatment of the Neandertals is an example of how cultural baggage probably affected interpretations of the fossil record. Whatever is the final resolution concerning Neandertal linguistic abilities, cultural abilities, and survivability, cultural biases affect the interpretations (Trinkaus and Shipman 1993). The acceptance of the Piltdown finds and the long rejection of the australopithecines as early hominids are further examples of cultural biases affecting the interpretation of the fossil record (Lewin 1985).

Because some people incorrectly ascribe infallibility to the scientific method, some students come to idolize science and scientists. This can become harmful. Unfortunately, some scientific disagreements have been exploited for political, social, or religious gain by individuals with a questionable agenda. For example, creationists and a relatively recent U.S. president misunderstand or misrepresent the word *theory* as used in the scientific context. Others misrepresent the disagreement between gradualism and punctuated equilibrium as a rejection of Darwin and of evolution. Some castigate paleoanthropologists because of the Piltdown hoax, the original rejection of the Taung baby as a hominid, and the taxonomic misplacement of "Ramapithecus," among other issues. Primatologists have been cast disparagingly because of an earlier failure to emphasize female roles, friendships, the importance of matrilineal kin, and the existence of nonhuman primate cultures. Baboons have not changed since anthropologists began watching them in the 1950s, but our interpretations about baboons have changed. Baboons have not recently developed friendships and other relatively newly described behaviors (Smuts 1985; Strum 1987). What is recent and new is the investigator's willingness to look for these behaviors. Incorrect or incomplete views are important venues for discussing how new data demand changes in theory—the scientific method requires change when necessary. We should turn theoretical mistakes to our advantage because students can learn from our mistakes.

Paleoanthropology and primatology have important lessons to teach on how to interpret data. For example, deductions drawn from archaeological and fossil samples can lead to a discussion of forensics. Perhaps because of a high crime rate in the United States, many students are interested in forensic anthropology. The use of DNA analyses in forensics, such as the recent breakthrough of obtaining mtDNA from teeth, addresses issues that students read about daily.

Like philosophy and the humanities generally, paleoanthropology and primatology must challenge the student's concepts of our humanity. Our evolutionary concept of what it means to be human (including the hallmark of bipedalism) will probably contrast markedly with the student's concept (which will probably include traits like a large brain, language, and perhaps some idea of culture). You can engage students intellectually by having them generate a list of what they consider to be important human evolutionary traits. The biological definition of what it means to be human is largely based on what we know of chimpanzee behavior. Because of chimpanzee meat eating, predatory behavior, and tool use and manufacture, we have had to recast our definitions of humanity. Students can be motivated on learning that we know who and what we are because we have learned who and what chimpanzees are (Gibbons 1992b). This allows one to talk about evolutionary relationships between humans and the other primates. Primate models for diseases like AIDS and liver transplants from baboons to humans attract the student's interest and are springboards to other topics.

Centripetal Role of Paleoanthropology

Understanding our evolutionary roots should be a central focus of the liberal arts undergraduate curriculum. Physical anthropology is the spoke around which the study of human evolution revolves. We need to discuss the place humans occupy in nature. The biological relatedness of all humans, of human and nonhuman primates, and of humans to other mammals is a key to understanding our survival. The question is not only Who are we? but What are we? Why are we? and Where are we?

In paleoanthropology and primatology classes we can make a case for the study of one of the world's threatened species—ourselves. Humans are the only threatened species able to speak for itself, to plead its own case. Data from paleoanthropology and primatology can be used to make a case to monitor the environment and to recognize the integrity and future of the human species. The relationship between the appearance of the genus *Homo* and environmental changes (Howell 1991), Elizabeth Vrba's turnover-pulse hypothesis (Shell 1993; Vrba 1993), and examples of how nonhuman primates adapt or fail to do so in the face of environmental challenges (Poirier 1977) are vehicles for understanding the consequences to modern humans resulting from environmental change.

We (humans) are in charge of our own evolution; therefore, we need information to make the correct choices. Advances in medicine and dentistry have drastically affected human survival. For example, the health and longevity outcomes of a visit to the dentist to correct tooth decay can be compared to baboon deaths resulting from dental abscesses and resultant infection. The affects of modern medicine and dentistry are seen in a different light when contrasted to early health standards and longevity as these are documented in the human fossil record or compared with the disease and mortality records of nonhuman primates.

My students are fascinated that nonhuman primates use medicinal plants (Gibbons 1992a; Strier 1993) and that female howler monkeys may affect the sex of their infants and their own fertility by food choices (Glander 1992). The use of botanical contraceptives and abortifacients by humans dates back thousands of years. Although the history is long, much of it seems lost because it was rooted in women's lore, an aspect of knowledge not always appreciated (Riddle and Estes 1992). Most students have thought about birth control and many know practitioners of herbal medicine. Increasing evidence suggests that humans have seasonal birth and fertility patterns, not unlike the nonhuman primates (May 1993). This information can be used to stress the fact that humans are also members of the animal kingdom and are affected by some of the same factors as others in the kingdom. A modern scourge, stress, can be elucidated by discussing the affects of stress in baboons (for example, Sapolsky 1989). The fact that animals in Amboseli and Maasai Mara, both in Kenya, are contracting human diseases from scavenging in tourist-generated garbage dumps, or that tourist-habituated gorillas may have contracted human diseases, allows one to discuss the evolutionary relationship between human and nonhuman primates.

Teaching human evolution is teaching a philosophy of life. Students need to see the relationship between humans and the rest of the natural world. Because this orientation is often outside the pale of Western philosophies, it allows the teacher to introduce concepts from non-Western philosophies and to acquaint students with systems of scientific thought developed in Asia, Africa, and the Middle East. Teaching human evolution, by virtue of the international nature of the evidence and of the research and the researchers, provides a venue to expand the student's intellectual universe.

Even supermarket tabloids can be used to discuss evolutionary relationships. A 1992 article with the emblazoned headline "Ape Gives Birth to Human Baby!" provides an opportunity to discuss such possibilities and to introduce not only scientific concerns but the interplay between science and ethics. Such discussions can stimulate students intellectually. Tabloid publications with their misuse or ignorance of scientific facts often make good springboards. Students asked to critique these articles do so with a flourish not seen when they evaluate scientific publications.

Paleoanthropological and primatological data allow one to address gender differences in behavior. The frequent inability to identify male and female skeletons in the fossil record reveals something about early hominid sex roles. If "Lucy's" pelvis more closely resembles the pelvis of modern males than that of modern females (Lovejoy 1988; Lovejoy, Heiple, and Burstein 1973), students ask how we know that "Lucy" was a female. Sexing fossil remains on the basis of modern sexual dimorphism prompts astute students to suggest that we are tainting our interpretations of the fossil record. Sex roles in nonhuman primates provide an entry into a discussion of gender differences in human behavior. Different sex roles in different nonhuman primate species (like the migration patterns of the sexes in different species or different mating strategies) show that a variety of behaviors is possible. This allows us to talk about learning gender roles and cultural differences in practicing gender roles. Tool use among female chimpanzees; personality differences in leadership styles among Japanese macaques; the role of kinship and possibly nepotism among vervets, macaques, hamadryas, and gorillas—all provide very important lessons for understanding human evolution and cultural diversity. The possibility that the protective baboon male, the one who befriends mothers and infants, may father more offspring than the baboon bully (Smuts 1985, 1987; Strum 1987) strikes a resonant chord with many students.

Conclusion

When teaching physical anthropology we need to employ more linking concepts, those ideas such as evolution, culture, and diversity, that are actually or potentially useful in two or more disciplines. Anthropology may be a student's major, or only, contact with the comparative method and with field research. Physical anthropology's eclecticism allows it to be a model for generalizations drawn from many related fields. Therefore, perhaps unfortunately, we too have joined the march to specialization. We might one day reach the absurd stage where the generalized undergraduate physical anthropology introductory course is beyond the teaching ability of the specialized Ph.D. instructor!

We need to be cognizant of the political and social messages of our research. Some people see us as inflammatory because we teach about the unity of humanity, our close relationship to chimpanzees, the learning of sex roles, and the biological bases of certain behaviors. Our data elicit many parallels to modern social problems or concerns. Some people perceive us and our discipline as dangerous to their political and social agendas.

Our greater visibility is a double-edged sword. As more people learn about physical anthropology, we must be more careful how we use words and concepts. The popularization of physical anthropology may dilute our data and further emphasize personality and not scientific disagreements. Despite the pitfalls, we cannot miss. We deal with all the "hot issues," the impact of new medical technologies, sex and society, sex and survival, and family matters.

References

Begley, Sharon. 1993. "Here Come the DNAsaurs." *Newsweek*, June 14, 56–61.

Cherfas, Jerem. 1991. "Ancient DNA: Still Busy after Death." *Science* 253:1354–1356.

De Salle, Richard, J. Gatesy, W. Wheeler, and D. Grimaldi. 1992. "DNA Sequences from a Fossil Termite in Oligo-Miocene Amber and Their Phylogenetic Implications." *Science* 257:1933–1936.

Gibbons, Ann. 1992a. "Plants of the Apes." *Science* 255:82.

———. 1992b. "Chimpanzees: More Diverse than a Barrel of Monkeys." *Science* 255:287–288.

Glander, Kenneth. 1992. "Are Female Mantled Howling Monkeys Able to Choose the Sex of Their Offspring?" *American Journal of Physical Anthropology Supplement* 14:82.

Goodall, Jane. 1986. *The Chimpanzees of Gombe: Patterns of Behavior.* Cambridge, Mass.: Belknap.

Grimaldi, David. 1993. "Forever in Amber." *Natural History* 6:59–61.

Hackerman, Nicholas. 1992. "Science Education: Who Needs It?" *Science* 256:157.

Harraway, Dana. 1989. *Primate Visions: Gender, Race and Nature in the World of Modern Science.* New York: Routledge.

Howell, F. Clark. 1991. "*Homo Habilis* in Detail." *Science* 253:1294–1297.

Hrdy, Sarah Blaffer. 1988. "Daughters or Sons?" *Natural History* April:63–83.

Landau, Misia. 1991. *Narratives of Human Evolution.* New Haven, Conn.: Yale University Press.

Lasker, Gabriel. 1963. "The Introductory Class." In *The Teaching of Anthropology,* edited by David Mandelbaum, Gabriel Lasker, and Ethel Albert, 99–110. Washington, D.C.: American Anthropological Association.

Lewin, Roger. 1985. "The Taung Baby Reaches Sixty. *Science* 233:720–721.

Lovejoy, C. Owen. 1988. "Evolution of Human Walking." *Scientific American* November:118–125.

Lovejoy, C. Owen, Kingsbury Heiple, and Albert Burstein. 1973. "The gait of *Australopithecus.*" *American Journal of Physical Anthropology* 38:757–780.

May, Mike. 1993. "Cycles of Sex Examined for Environmental Influences." *Science* 260:1592–1593.

Morell, Virginia. 1992. "30 Million-Year-Old DNA Boosts an Emerging Field." *Science* 257:1860–1862.

———. 1993. "Dino DNA: The Hunt and the Hype." *Science* 261:160–162.

Poirier, Frank Eugene. 1977. "The Human Influence on Subspeciation and Behavioral Differentiation among Three Nonhuman Primate Populations." *Yearbook of Physical Anthropology* 21:234–241.

———. 1993. *Understanding Human Evolution*. 3rd ed. Englewood Cliffs, N.J.: Prentice-Hall.

Riddle, John, and J. Worth Estes. 1992. "Oral Contraceptives in Ancient and Medieval Times." *American Scientist* 80:226–233.

Sapolsky, Richard. 1989. "Stress in the Wild." *Scientific American* January:116–123.

Seidler, Horst, and others. 1992. "Some Anthropological Aspects of the Prehistoric Tyrolean Ice Man." *Science* 258:455–457.

Shell, Ellen. 1993. "Waves of Creation." *Discover* May:54–61.

Sjøvold, Torstein. 1992. "The Stone Age Iceman from the Alps: The Find and the Current Status of Investigation." *Evolutionary Anthropology* 4:117–124.

———. 1993. "Frost and Found." *Natural History* 102:60–63.

Smuts, Barbara. 1985. *Sex and Friendship in Baboons*. New York: Aldine.

———. 1987. "What Are Friends For?" *Natural History* February:26–44.

Stein, Philip. 1990. "The Teaching of Physical Anthropology." Paper delivered to the 89th Annual Meeting of the American Anthropological Association, New Orleans.

Strier, Karen. 1993. "Menu for a Monkey." *Natural History* 3:34–42.

Strum, Shirley. 1987. *Almost Human*. New York: Random House.

Trinkaus, Erik, and Pat Shipman. 1993. "Neandertals: Images of Ourselves." *Evolutionary Biology* 1:194-201.

Vrba, Elizabeth. 1993. "The Pulse that Produced Us." *Natural History* 104:47–51.

Wienker, Curts, and Kenneth Bennett. 1992. "Trends and Developments in Physical Anthropology, 1990–1991." *American Journal of Physical Anthropology* 87:383–394.

Central Themes in Archaeology

FRED PLOG AND STEPHEN PLOG

Our message is a simple one. As anthropologists, we must always remember that we, better than any other discipline, can explain to students and to the public the diversity of cultural patterns and behavior. As archaeologists, we have information on thousands, and in some cases, millions of years of cultural evolution to help us illustrate that diversity and reveal patterns of change over time. Although it is undoubtedly important for us to convey some sense of the research process that helps us answer such questions—the nature of fieldwork and the methods, assumptions, and theoretical perspectives we bring to bear on our data—we must not allow those discussions to overshadow our attempts to address these central issues that guide our research and that spark the interest of the student and the general public.

Cultural Diversity

In the United States, archaeology is anthropology. We should strive to be viewed—as a colleague once referred to the senior author—as cultural anthropologists masquerading as archaeologists. The issues we learn to explore reflect the training that we ourselves received in anthropology departments. Foremost of those lessons is the knowledge that there are a thousand ways to bake a cake. Humans breed, marry, cook, dwell, build, and bury in a diversity of ways and this variation exists not only among but within societies. Given that archaeologists study the products of human behavior, not the behavior itself, it is more difficult to monitor this diversity. But monitoring behavioral diversity is the essence of what we must do.

To achieve that goal, we must teach each other theories and methodologies for understanding the past. The importance of understanding dating methods or transformation processes is undeniable. The record of the past will be incorrectly understood if we do not attend to knowledge of how that record was formed or to the strengths and weaknesses of various dating methods. But although such issues are critical to our research, we will succeed with the public and with our students when we teach them the diverse ways in which humans behave and how we came to do so.

We also will fail as communicators when we overly attend to those times and places where the patterning of the record we study is substantial, where "normative patterns" were quite strong. The Magdalenian period, the Xian burials, and the Chacoan system did happen and are important. The focus they receive, however, more directly reflects museum interests in artifacts than it does either the duration or evolutionary importance of the materials used to identify the manifestations. Such periods were rare in relation to the vast periods of time during which humans behaved in eclectic, nomadic, or less strongly normative patterns. We must ensure that we address the full range of cultural diversity and not just the periods when particular materials or settlements attract our attention.

Central Topics

As Robert Adams, mentor of the senior author, once said to him, it is hard to understand why a person would come to the discipline of anthropology without a principal interest in the "big questions." Most archaeologists would probably agree that the following big questions are worth investigating, and we believe that this list represents the questions about which Adams speaks:

1. After millions of years of adaptation as generalists, hunters, and gatherers, why did humans choose to specialize by relying on farming?

2. After millions of years of living in small settlements, why did humans come to live in large ones?

3. After millions of years of considerable mobility throughout the yearly cycle, why did humans begin to reside permanently in villages?

4. After millions of years of consensual leadership, why have humans come to submit to authoritarian patterns?

5. After millions of years of living in simple societies, why did humans come to live in complex ones?

These five queries can be rendered as dozens of more specific questions, however. The most basic of these is the manner in which we departed from our primate ancestors in respect to sharing. Nonhuman primates do not routinely share food whereas humans do. How this sharing pattern evolved warrants major attention.

The relationship of biology to culture is another area of importance. Perhaps the most basic consideration is how the mental capacities we possess developed. Our ability to concentrate, plan, and organize exceeds that of other primates. There are also other important issues. How and why estrous was replaced by menstruation has profound implications for how we came to be the species we are. How we came to develop the ability of verbal communication is of equal import: did Neandertals speak or did they not? What is the import of nonverbal communication as reflected in cave art and other forms of ritual behavior?

One final issue is the increasing energetic component of our pattern of food production; we invest more and more to produce less and less with a far more destructive impact on our environment. A variety of studies now shows that the "natural" environment in which we live is something less than natural. Human modifications of the environment in most areas are substantial ones. When did such major transformations begin and on what scale?

Problems

We do not believe there are new issues in archaeology. The questions we attempt to answer pertain to those fundamental changes that occurred as humans came to be as they are. We do believe that there are problems in the manner in which these issues have sometimes been addressed, problems that result less from clarity in respect to theme and more from a lack of clarity in respect to definition and conceptualization. Some of our own basic concepts are confusing. For example, in most cases we use the concept of complexity in a completely Victorian sense. Recent societies are complex. Those of the prehistoric past were not. States are complex; bands are not. Yet states and bands share many characteristics that are not shared by tribes and chiefdoms. Complexity is a characteristic of those societies in which behavior is not limited in regard to diversity or in which behavioral diversity is promoted. Simplicity is a characteristic of tribes and chiefdoms in which norms are highly valued and behavioral diversity low.

Similarly, we also fail to distinguish effectively between resilient and stable societies. In some times and some places, societies survived because of their abilities to buffer against or to manage the environment. These societies were based on the principle of stability. In most times and places, societies were based on the principle of resiliency; they changed with change in their social and/or natural environment. Inattention to these fundamentally different principles is a major source of our problems in understanding the prehistoric record. Stable societies leave tablets and books; with the exception of the *Bible*, resilient ones do not.

In addition, there are problems in the ways we attempt to convey our messages. Although it is terribly important to have journals or textbooks in which we document the empirical details of our field studies, it is equally important to recognize that this detail may appear as trivia to others. Although it is terribly important to have journals or textbooks in which methodological and theoretical issues, the bases of our practice, are explored, it is equally important to recognize that such issues may be of little importance to those who wish only to know what we have learned. *Natural History, Smithsonian, Scientific American, Innovation and Technology,* and the *Biblical Archeology Review* are excellent examples of how disciplines publish their central themes in a manner appealing to the public. Anthropological archaeology does not lack central themes, but we often fail to tell the public and our students what those themes are.

Conclusion

Sedentism and nomadism, hunting-gathering and agriculture, cities and camps: these are the oppositions around which discussions of the prehistoric record revolve. Complexity and simplicity and resiliency and stability are terminologies imposed by us on that record. We err when we fail to see the ebb and flow of prehistory, history, and process in relation to these themes and terminologies and this is an important message to be conveyed to students. When the senior author had the chance to sit in the E. E. Evans-Pritchard room in Moosegard, he could not help wondering how our perception of both the present and the past might have been changed had Evans-Pritchard chosen to discuss the interaction between Nuer and Dinka rather than writing *The Nuer* (1940). In only a single sentence of that book does one learn of the major Dinka component of Nuer villages. Similarly, the conflict among Hutu, Tutsi, and Twa is a major incident at present. Yet Jacque Macquet's elegant analysis of interaction among the three groups is rarely cited in the literature. We like simple stories. Perhaps we should prefer complex ones.

I believe that we also should attend more to the cyclical nature of the archaeological record with which we deal. Patterns come and go; generally they are short-lived. The theory of chaos as described by Glieck (1987) and others provides a new and more powerful basis for interpreting change over time that contrasts with our current tendency to see change as linear. Glieck and others who have followed him are correct in seeing the ebb and flow of change. Households go through domestic cycles. Agriculture comes, goes, and changes in form. Environment is impacted by both human and natural factors, affecting what humans are able to do. Order and disorder are not necessarily different. Students who have used the computer programs based on chaos theory quickly understand that the opposition of order and chaos, of stochastic and deterministic processes, of heterogeneity and homogeneity are considerably overdrawn in our literature. As use of such programs in the classrooms increases, not only our students' understanding but our own comprehension of the archaeological record will improve.

If there is a single theme to be addressed in prehistory, it is why in a very few times and places large and highly normative populations developed and why some persisted for only a few hundred years while others lasted for thousands. Only by addressing this basic theme will we confront the fragility of the societies and institutions that we see around us and take to be enduring.

Note

Author's Note: After the presentation of this paper at the American Anthropological Association symposium, Fred Plog died on June 18, 1992. Stephen Plog has attempted to change the informal style of the original into one more appropriate for publication while maintaining the content and structure.

References

Evans-Pritchard, E. E. 1940. *The Nuer.* Oxford: Oxford University Press.
Glieck, James. 1987. *Chaos: Making a New Science.* New York: Viking.

Teaching Biocultural Anthropology

MARK NATHAN COHEN

Research at the intersection of cultural and physical anthropology has expanded in a number of new directions since 1963 and it would be impossible to do justice to them all. There has been a large increase in our knowledge of the energetic efficiency of different types of foraging and other food-getting behaviors (Winterhalder and Smith 1981). There has been an expansion of analysis of human skeletal remains to assess directly the health of prehistoric and modern populations and, indirectly, to measure the relative success of different cultural strategies in promoting the health, nutrition, and longevity of human groups (Cohen and Armelagos 1984; Cohen 1989). One could also cite a major expansion of interest in the interaction of culture change and human genetic evolution and an expansion in the application of Darwinian theory to human culture (popularly known as "sociobiology") so that we now commonly talk of the genetic components of behavior and the contributions that culture and behavioral variables make to an organism's reproductive fitness (Durham 1991; Smith and Winterhalder 1992). There has been an increase in anthropologists' knowledge of nutrition (Stinson 1992), of human growth (Garn 1980; Frayer and Wolpoff 1985; Dettwyler and Fishman 1992) of fertility (Wood 1990; Ellison 1991), of epidemiology, and the role that human behaviors play in encouraging or discouraging disease transmission (Cohen 1989; Inhorn and Brown 1990), of adaptation to the stresses of modern living (Huss-Ashmore and Johnston 1985; Weiss et al. 1993), and of adaptations to variations in the earth's climate and physical geography (Loomis 1967; Post, Daniels, and Binford, 1975; So 1980; Hanna and Brown 1983; Greska 1991). In addition, there has been steady increase in our knowledge of fossil primates and fossil hominids (Trinkaus 1986; Fedigan 1986; Rightmire 1988).

What is new in anthropology should not be confused with what we ought to teach, however—at least at the introductory or precollege level. It is a mistake to allow our research goals to dictate the contents of our introductory courses. Our goals as teachers should be to interest students and then to empower them by providing first the skills and then the necessary data for them to answer their own questions. The curiosity, empowerment, and skills we transmit are more important than the informational content of the lesson. The means to this end is engaging students as active participants in the classroom process. Course content should be built from viable *problems* designed at a level that students can grasp—problems that affect student lives, that stimulate their reactions and their minds, and not the least, that demonstrate the relevance of anthropology and anthropological thinking for their lives. Good teaching at introductory levels depends more on good models for thinking than on presenting the newest data. (In fact, good teaching will often involve simplifying the data or purposely withholding some of the newest findings in an attempt to keep problems manageable.) As examples, consider teaching strategies in two areas—human geographical variation and epidemiology—that lend themselves particularly well to the style of teaching we should be trying to employ.

The following two examples are teaching strategies that have been tried and found to hold student interest, to permit young students to manipulate ideas, and to seduce young students into active problem solving both inside and outside the classroom. They are also examples that need not become dated because the essential problems remain even when new data are generated.

Geographical Variation

The first example involves getting students to evaluate the adaptive value of regional variations in human biological design ("race") in relationship to health. This has the extra value of demystifying "race" and making differences between human beings something that can be openly discussed in the classroom. (See Lieberman and Kirk, this volume, for more discussion of human variation.)

It is important first to distinguish between "races" (that is, distinct and sharply bounded groups of human beings distinguished from one another by marked differences in several traits)—which do not exist despite all the efforts of early classifiers to find them—and "variations" or individual variables like color, size, length of limb, or shape of nose that not only exist but that may have important predictive value in public health, disease diagnosis, and preventive and corrective medicine that we cannot safely ignore. There are two important points of distinction between races and variation, both easily illustrated with slides. First, many variations are graded in their expression or their frequency: they do not show abrupt boundaries as racial classifications imply but display geographical *clines*—gradual quantitative transitions across space. To take the most obvious example, people come in a range of colors, not just in black or white (and most people of color between the extremes do not result from recent intermarriage, as racial classifiers have suggested). The great majority of people are somewhere between. The gradual transition can be seen by anyone who travels over land from Europe to Africa via the Middle East as well as other parts of the world.

The second point, which may be more important, is that human variations are largely independent of one another. They are largely independent variables that are not bound to one another and that do not correlate with one another in the manner or degree that "race" classifications predict. For example, despite our racial stereotypes, the color of human skin and the shape of human noses have independent distributions. Dark skin occurs throughout the tropics but populations in the tropics vary in nose shape from broad to narrow according to the altitude and humidity of the area they inhabit historically.

Having made this distinction between race and variations, it is possible to discuss the adaptive value and medical importance of particular variations. Skin color provides the best starting point because it is on people's minds but also because the pattern is clearest, our knowledge of it richest and most accessible intuitively (Loomis 1967; Post et al. 1975).

The discussion begins with the teacher describing the world distribution of human skin colors (and the probable distribution before A.D. 1500) and asking students why they think color shows this distribution. For each guess or hypothesis advanced, reasoning is discussed and additional information solicited that might help support the hypothesis. With the teacher's help, a model of reasoning is gradually built that can be described in both specific and general application. That is, the teacher records both the general *kinds* of question asked as well as the specific answers obtained.

Following are the general questions and the specific answers regarding skin color that should be generated. Most of these points will come up in discussion and need only minor rephrasing by the teacher.

Is there a pattern to the distribution of the variation? In the case of skin color, of course, prior to 1492 darker skin clustered markedly near the equator and lighter skin occurred at higher latitudes. The pattern is the key to subsequent discussions.

Does the pattern correlate with something in the natural environment? Both temperature and ultra violet radiation correlate crudely with the distribution of skin color. Relative cold and relatively low exposure to ultra violet both characterize regions in which lighter skin is common; intense heat and high ultraviolet light characterize areas where darker skin is common. There are exceptions to both generalizations that will be addressed.

Can coincidence be ruled out by replication? How do we know that the distribution of skin colors by latitude did not simply occur by chance? The repetition of a pattern rules out coincidence much as it does in everyday common sense. *Does the skin color co-occur with these environmental features independently in more than one place?* In this case, the distinction in skin color and the association of skin color with latitude occurs repeatedly in various regions of the globe among otherwise diverse groups of people. Not only do Europeans and Africans range from dark to light as one moves away from the equator; so to varying degrees do central and East Asians and even Native Americans. The repetition of the pattern suggests that more than coincidence is involved.

Can we find a plausible causal link between the environmental variables and the human variations? Correlation by itself does not mean that one thing causes another. For example, there is a correlation between the size of a person's feet and the size of the person's vocabulary, but foot size does not affect vocabulary nor the other way around. The link however is that both are dependent on the individual's age. In the same way, ultraviolet light and skin color might be connected by an unknown third variable. In order to infer a causal relationship between the two, we then have to find a plausible causal mechanism linking color to latitude and determine whether the mechanism works. Heat, cold, ultraviolet light, and other factors are considered for their known effects on the body. Ultraviolet light has been linked to suntanning or darkening of skin, suggesting that there is some direct relationship between the two; it is known to stimulate the production of vitamin D in the body. Ultraviolet light is also related to sunburn and skin cancer and to potentially harmful excess production of vitamin D, which can lead to vitamin D intoxication and excessive calcification of soft tissues. Lack of exposure to the ultraviolet light is known to produce rickets or osteomalacia, the softening or loss of bone caused by vitamin D deficiency. Extreme cold can produce frostbite. Melanin, the pigment that makes skin dark in varying degrees, blocks the effects of ultraviolet light (both bad and good) and is susceptible to damage by frostbite.

Is the variation between people of real significance to health? Dark-skinned people are in fact more susceptible to frostbite and to rickets than light-skinned people in the same environments, but they are more resistant to sunburn, skin cancer, and vitamin D poisoning, which may be an advantage of increasing importance as the earth's ozone layer is depleted.

If the intent is to focus on evolutionary change, as is often the case, two other questions can be asked:

Is the variation important enough—and the health effects timed early enough in the human life span—so that Darwinian fitness or reproductive success is affected? Skin cancer, although important, occurs relatively late in life, reducing its impact on fitness and raising a question of whether it alone could have affected human evolution. But rickets occurs early and can interfere directly with reproduction and fitness if a woman's pelvis is deformed. Sunburn can occur any time in life and leads to the failure of sweat glands, which affect the body's ability to cool itself, with potentially lethal consequences. Frostbite can have serious consequences for people forced to work outside and can lead to fatal infection.

Is the trait inherited genetically? Skin color clearly is inherited. The critical test is that adopted children or children moved to new environments retain, on average, the traits of their biological parents. However, some human variations, particularly those linked to growth (stature and limb length) and adaptations to high altitude, may not be inherited.

If the hypothesis is supported that dark skin has adapted to (and evolved for) warm, high UV radiation climates and whiter skin has adapted to (and evolved for) colder, low UV environments, it ought to be possible to make *accurate predictions*. According to the hypothesis, for example, rickets should be most common among dark-skinned people living indoors in smog bound cities in northern latitudes. It should also be common among people like women in *purdah*, who are kept indoors for social reasons. Skin cancer, on the contrary, should and does occur most commonly on the body parts that light-skinned people expose to the sun, especially in the tropics. These predictions generally hold true.

If the hypothesis is supported that skin colors are adapted to ultraviolet light and cold, it ought to be possible to *explain apparent exceptions.* (In a correct translation from the Latin, exceptions don't "prove" the rule they "test" the rule.) For example, we ought to be able to explain why Inuit (Eskimos) are not exceptionally light as our hypothesis predicts. The answer seems to be that fish are a rich dietary source of vitamin D that can render the manufacture of vitamin D in the body less necessary. Eskimos rely heavily on fishing and did not enter their recent environment until after fishing technology had developed. Moreover, they have only been in their present location for a relatively short time span in terms of evolutionary change. But, if frostbite accounts for light skin, why are the world's lightest people from Europe, which is kept relatively warm for its high latitude because of the effects of winds and ocean currents and where in consequence, frostbite is less of a risk than in northern Asia?

The available information for these discussions may be changed by new discoveries. And it should be stressed that new discoveries are constantly modifying our understanding. Students should understand that the data are not—are never—complete, and they should be encouraged to do more research on the topic. The style of argument can be repeated for any human variation (such as hair shape and color, chest and heart size, eye color and shape, blood type, nose form, length of limbs, lactase deficiency, the sickle cell trait). Many of these traits can be found to satisfy one or more of the criteria presented but not all. The method can even be applied to imaginary examples.

One of the important advantages of this exercise is its demonstration that knowledge comes on a sliding scale of certainty. Rarely can the examples be shown unequivocally to be "adaptive" or "not adaptive." Instead, some are convincing, some are less satisfactory, and all are subject to reinterpretation in the face of new information. The solution is not truth but only the closest we have come, so far.

Epidemiology

The second example involves teaching about the logic of individual diseases and the use of "uniformitarian" thinking to understand how we can learn to predict and avoid certain diseases. "Uniformitarianism" refers to the idea that nature obeys uniform laws and did so also in the past—that is, that the workings of forces like gravity and disease can be analyzed and then predicted given reasonable knowledge. This is a concept that in my experience most college students have to be taught and that may be the most important thing we have to teach them. Many have little sense of the distinction between science and pseudoscience. At least they need to be taught to think about the issue consciously. The concept can be illustrated by the following exercise.

Ask students how many have ever had diarrhea. They will all (grudgingly, when pushed) hold up their hands. Explain that most diarrhea is a "fecal-oral" disease. This leaves some students looking extremely disgusted and some looking puzzled. The teacher can then bring classroom barriers tumbling down by using the word *shit* in a scientific context while explaining in detail how a fecal-oral infection moves from one person to another. Emphasize that *specific actions* rather than vague "dirtiness" or "primitiveness" are responsible for disease transmission. Why restaurants have to have signs in their restrooms warning employees to wash their hands can be discussed at this point. Introduce the idea of parasite life cycles, noting that disease can occur only if the specific worm or "germ" in question can live and reproduce and disseminate its offspring. Ask the students to discuss the mechanisms an individual or a community might use to break the cycle and avoid infection, including handwashing, toilet flushing (if sewage is kept separate from water wells, which has not always been the case), ritual bathing, restricted community size, and community mobility. (Small, mobile bands of hunter-gatherers commonly suffer much less from diarrhea than sedentary villagers.) We then discuss behaviors that are not explicitly directed at disease but nonetheless affect it, both trivial things like which hand one eats with and major economic strategies such as the use of irrigation or the use of human excrement as fertilizer.

A wonderful, very readable essay by Alan Desowitz called "New Guinea Tapeworms and Jewish Grandmothers," in his book by the same name, provides a good second step. The title alone is usually enough to generate fair interest. The article introduces tapeworms and the pattern of tapeworm life cycles and some of the ways that specific human behaviors either facilitate or discourage their transmission. This leads to a discussion of how many different ways there are to stop and/or avoid tapeworm infection. The article also conveys the idea that (irrational) cultural constraints may force a population that could otherwise avoid a disease to suffer it. It has the additional value of showing that mainstream Americans face the same disease logic as New Guinea natives and display the same irrationality in their response. Desowitz closes by finding a parallel between the irrationality of New Guinea natives and his own smoking habit.

Hookworm provides a third example of an infectious disease cycle that is affected by human behavior. Many other infectious diseases could be discussed. The same style can be used to discuss nutritional and other illness as well. For example, the known behavior of iron both inside and outside the body can be used to explain the distribution of iron deficiency anemia and to predict its occurrence.

After this discussion, students can be assigned to research particular infectious diseases, determining each organism's life cycle and predicting how various human behaviors might affect the occurrence of the disease. Standard medical references such as Hubbert, McCulloch, and Schnurrenberger (1975), which are regularly updated, provide the data. (In keeping with the theme of this article, however, it is not really very important whether the newest sources are available.) Similar exercises can be directed beyond infectious diseases to analyze the natural distribution and flow of essential nutrients and show how human behavior affects the availability of specific nutrients not just in the diet but to the body.

Once students have practiced working from a known parasite or nutrient to predict its interaction with human behavior, it is possible to turn the problem around and work from a pattern of disease to try to determine unknown causes. Reference can made and readings or films assigned about John Snow, the nineteenth-century Englishman, who, before germ theory was fully understood, deduced the mode of transmission of cholera by observing patterns in its occurrence. His experience provides a very vivid demonstration of the power of patterns to suggest causes. Students can then be asked to deal with unknowns. Although not believed to be an infectious disease, multiple sclerosis provides an outstanding "unknown" for the class to work on; there are lots of clues and partial patterns but no definitive solution. Various cancers, especially breast cancer, also provide interesting cases for analysis. Students can get to "data" by asking good, focused questions of the instructor, or, time permitting, by outside research. The data are available in standard medical reference books. The emphasis in discussion is on good questions and deductions rather than on facts.

Fossil Hominids

There is also a negative example of teaching strategies. In the last thirty years, there has been an expansion both in the known sample of fossil hominids and in the range of scientific tools for their analysis (Fedigan 1986; Trinkaus 1986; Rightmire 1988 and others). The most recently discovered fossils are often slavishly taught in introductory anthropology courses and fossils may be the one aspect of physical anthropology most widely taught and most likely to appear in curricula and texts. This should not be the case, however, for two reasons: first, such courses tend to reinforce stereotypes about anthropology and college itself, as studying dry bones and other data of marginal relevance. At the same time, far more important work that anthropologists are doing in human growth, nutrition, fertility, epidemiology, and the like is displaced. Second, the fragmentary nature of the fossil record, the esoteric nature of the related sciences, and the degree to which we need to build rickety scaffolds of knowledge to interpret the data do not readily lend themselves to teaching young students to practice scientific reasoning. They have to take too much on faith and they see too many bad examples.

If the fossil material is to be taught, however, problem-oriented teaching is still possible if one presents competing hypothesis and asks students to evaluate them based on the fragmentary evidence. For example, the classic "hunting" hypothesis and the Tanner-Zihlman "gathering" hypothesis (Tanner and Zihlman 1976; Zihlman 1978) can be compared. Each hypothesis makes some "predictions" about where fossils might be found and about the probable sequence of emergence of modern human traits that can be compared to the sequence displayed in the fossil record. The exercise tends to emphasize just how frail the fossil record is and to undermine rather than enhance students' faith in anthropology. Fossils should not be at the core of physical anthropology 101 and they do not belong in high school classes except on bulletin boards.

References

Cohen, M. N. 1989. *Health and the Rise of Civilization*. New Haven, Conn.: Yale University Press.

Cohen, M. N., and G. J. Armelagos, eds. 1984. *Paleopathology at the Origins of Agriculture*. New York: Academic Press.

Crews, D. E., and G. D. James. 1991. "Human Evolution and the Genetic Epidemiology of Chronic Degenerative Diseases." In *Applications of Biological Anthropology to Human Affairs*, edited by N. Mascie-Taylor and G. Lasker, 185–206. Cambridge, England: Cambridge University Press.

Desowitz, R. S. 1981. *New Guinea Tapeworms and Jewish Grandmothers*. New York: W. W. Norton.

Dettwyler, K. A., and C. Fishman. 1992. "Infant Feeding Practices and Growth." *Annual Review of Anthropology* 21:171–204.

Durham, William. 1991. *Coevolution*. Stanford, Calif.: Stanford University Press.

Ellison, Peter. 1991. "Reproductive Ecology and Human Fertility." In *Applications of Biological Anthropology to Human Affairs*, edited by N. Mascie-Taylor and G. Lasker, 14–54. Cambridge, England: Cambridge University Press.

Fedigan, L. M. 1986. "The Changing Role of Women in Models of Human Evolution." *Annual Review of Anthropology* 15:25–66.

Frayer, D. W., and M. Wolpoff. 1985. "Sexual Dimorphism." *Annual Review of Anthropology* 14:429–473.

Garn, S. M. 1980. "Human Growth." *Annual Review of Anthropology* 9:275–292.

Greska, L. P. 1991. "Human Physiological Adaptation to High Altitude Environments." In *Applications of Biological Anthropology to Human Affairs*, edited by N. Mascie-Taylor and G. Lasker, 117–142. Cambridge, England: Cambridge University Press.

Hanna, J. M., and D. E. Brown. 1983. "Human Heat Tolerance: An Anthropological Perspective." *Annual Review of Anthropology* 12:259–284.

Howell, Nancy. 1986. "Demographic Anthropology." *Annual Review of Anthropology* 15:219–246.

Hubbert, W. T., W. F. McCulloch, and P. Schnurrenberger. 1975. *Diseases Transmitted from Animals to Man*. Springfield: C. C. Thomas.

Huss-Ashmore, R., and F. E. Johnston. 1985. "Bioanthropology Research in Developing Countries." *Annual Review of Anthropology* 14:475–528.

Inhorn, M. C., and P. J. Brown. 1990. "The Anthropology of Infectious Disease." *Annual Review of Anthropology* 19:89–117.

Loomis, W. D. 1967. "Skin Pigment Regulation of Vitamin D Biosynthesis in Man." *Science* 157:501–506.

Mascie-Taylor, N., and G. Lasker. 1991. *Applications of Biological Anthropology to Human Affairs.* Cambridge, England: Cambridge University Press.

Moore, L. G., and J. G. Regensteiner. 1983. "Adaptation to High Altitude." *Annual Review of Anthropology* 12:285–304.

Post, P. W., F. Daniels, Jr., and R. T. Binford, Jr. 1975. "Cold Injury and the Evolution of 'White' Skin." *Human Biology* 47:65–80.

Rightmire, G. P. 1988. "Homo Erectus and Later Middle Pleistocene Humans." *Annual Review of Anthropology* 17:239–260.

Smith, E. A., and B. Winterhalder. 1992. *Evolutionary Ecology and Human Behavior.* Chicago: Aldine.

So, J. K. 1980. "Human Biological Adaptation to Arctic and Subarctic Zones." *Annual Review of Anthropology* 9:63–82.

Stinson, S. 1992. "Nutritional Adaptation." *Annual Review of Anthropology* 21:143–170.

Tanner, N., and A. Zihlman. 1976. "Women in Evolution" (pt. 1). *Signs* 1:585–608.

Trinkaus, Eric. 1986. "The Neanderthals and Modern Human Origins." *Annual Review of Anthropology* 15:193–218.

Winterhalder, B., and E. A. Smith. 1981. *Hunter-Gatherer Foraging Strategies.* Chicago: University of Chicago Press.

Weiss, Kenneth et al. 1993. "Amerindians and the Price of Modernization." In *Urban Ecology and Health in the Third World,* edited by L. M. Schell, M. T. Smith, and A. Bilsborough, 221–243. Cambridge, England: Cambridge University Press.

Wood, James. 1990. "Fertility in Anthropological Populations." *Annual Review of Anthropology* 19:211–242.

Zihlman, A. 1976. "Women in Evolution" (pt. 2). *Signs* 4:4–20.

Introductory Archaeology
An Identity Crisis in the Temple of Doom

JAMES DEETZ

An archaeologist working in the Ozarks was approached by a couple of good ol' boys, who asked him what he was doing. He patiently explained that he was excavating a prehistoric site, and that the deeper occupational levels in the earth were the older. One of the locals thought for a minute and then said, "Oh, yeah, just like they do over in egg wiped." Now while he had never heard the word *Egypt* pronounced, he certainly connected Egypt with archaeology. In this, he was not alone, for to most laypeople who have not been exposed to archaeology in any systematic, serious way, it is synonymous with pyramids, temples, buried treasure, and even aliens from outer space. This popular image of archaeology was strongly reinforced by the Indiana Jones movies, which added snake pits and bullwhips to the picture, and due to their immense popularity, reinforced the image in millions of people's minds. But this is only the beginning, for the biggest problem confronting anyone teaching an introductory course is that of multiple expectations and how to accommodate them. Indiana Jones is the easiest to deal with as it is not all that difficult to explain what archaeology is not; quite another thing is explaining what it is. This uncertainty actually stems from one in the mind of the instructor. What should I deal with in an introductory course? Should I give priority to a consideration of human prehistory on a global scale, or should I treat the complexities of archaeological method, archaeological thought? Or is there some way to accommodate both? Personal experience in teaching such a course on many occasions at Harvard, Brown, the University of California at Berkeley and Santa Barbara, and the University of Virginia forms the basis for the following considerations.

An introductory archaeology course is just that: an introduction.
We have all shared in that heady experience of entering the classroom on the first day and looking out at as many as 500 bright eager faces. And all too often, we experience an urgent need to communicate to them everything we learned in graduate school. After all, isn't that one of the reasons we learned all that stuff in the first place? So they too are going to learn all about optimal foraging strategy, seriation, central place theory, the Mousterian, obsidian hydration, the hypothetico-deductive-nomothetic paradigm, Folsom bison hunters, La Tene fibulae, Lewis Binford, the Anasazi, post-processual archaeology, critical theory, phytoliths, Ian Hodder, and everything in between from archaeometry to zooarchaeology. Now this is not to say that these are not important things to consider, for they are. But without some unifying framework, one

runs the risk of teaching a course that resembles dim sum, where one nibbles on a great variety of delicious items but is left wondering later what it was all about. The best remedy for this problem is to be very stringent about what will be included and what will not. Some of this information is better suited to upper-division courses on more specialized topics; indeed, there are instructors who load so much into their introductory courses that they run the risk of some repetition in more advanced ones. The purpose of an introductory course is to expose students to a discipline in such a way that they can see it as a coherent whole, and one important way to do this is to introduce relatively fewer topics, treated in some detail and connected by some unifying theme. We often forget that although we know what we are omitting, the student does not, and as long as what the student does receive is a part of an integrated whole, no one is the poorer for it. Incidentally, the same can be said for the occasional missing slide that we feel is needed for a presentation. We know it is not included, but our audience will never miss it for they have no way of knowing it was not shown. Properly chosen readings can free the instructor from concerns over comprehensive inclusion of subject matter. Although there are mixed feelings in the teaching profession about the utility of textbooks, they can be used critically in guiding students to subjects that particularly engage their interest and as backup to some of the material covered in class presentation. Used this way, the text becomes a reference volume rather than a set of assigned readings, although certain parts of it will doubtless be required. It seems reasonable to assume that unless a course is modeled on a given textbook, an unwise procedure at best, not all the text will be equally relevant to class discussions. Furthermore, lectures and readings should complement each other for the most part rather than lectures repeating what can as easily be read.

In sum, an introductory course in archaeology should attempt to convey a certain number of understandings about the field, with a strong unifying theme, but it should not attempt a comprehensive treatment of the field. For those students who opt to major in anthropology, there will be ample opportunity to take other courses, which, when combined, will provide such a comprehensive coverage. But at the introductory level, the most important goal is to present material that will engage students' interest so they will want to take additional courses to amplify their knowledge.

An introductory course must deal with two rather different bodies of subject matter: prehistory and archaeological thought—what we know about the past and how we think and find out about it.

Most introductory courses are given in a single semester or quarter, so there are genuine time constraints on what is covered. Add to this the dual nature of the field of archaeology, and some careful decisions must be taken in designing such a course, with a need to balance the empirical with the theoretical components. Of course, one could easily decide from the outset to teach a course on world prehistory, and many instructors do just that, usually prefacing it with some brief statement of archaeological method. Also, the entire course could be a treatment of the various methods used by archaeologists in their work, along the lines of David Hurst Thomas's text *Archaeology* (1989). But neither alternative seems ideal. Courses in prehistory run a real risk of becoming overly descriptive even when due consideration is given to the processes of culture change. Conversely, courses that focus on archaeological thought can become so abstract that the student is left wondering what is being thought about. Somehow, we must find a way to combine these two aspects of archaeology in a way that engages the student's interest and also serves as a proper introduction to the field, keeping in mind what has been said earlier in this chapter. One way this can be accomplished stems from an explicit acknowledgment of archaeology's position in the broader discipline of anthropology and the way in which the two are articulated. As the Old Timer said in Kent Flannery's classic Golden Marshalltown, "I don't believe there's any such thing as 'archaeological theory.' For me there's only anthropological theory" (Flannery 1982, 269).

Because with few exceptions, archaeology is taught in the United States in departments of anthropology, an introductory course should make clear the way in which archaeological thinking is largely the product of more general ethnological thought.

Many of us still subscribe to a four-field approach to anthropology and still use the concept of culture as the organizing theme of the material we present. What follows is predicated on these two points, even though in this so-called postmodern era, there will be those who would not agree. Taught as a required prerequisite in an anthropology major, introductory archaeology should ideally show students how the subject matter relates to what they will learn in other introductory courses, particularly in social-cultural anthropology. It is the establishment of these connections that is just as important, if not more so, than conveying a basic understanding of archaeology per se. There are many ways in which such a course might be designed, but personal experience has shown that a most effective way of presenting the material is from a historical perspective in a course that might well be called A History of Anthropological Thought as it Relates to Archaeology, or something to that effect. I have taught this course for the last seven years, and it has consistently received very high student evaluations and produced written work by students that shows they have a genuine understanding of all the basic issues dealt with. It works well with both large classes (over 200) and small (less than thirty). The following summary outline is of necessity brief and will not detail every part of the course; rather, it is intended to convey the basic approach and manner in which certain connections can be made.

Initially, three or four lectures are offered, treating certain basics of archaeology, largely through providing definitions of everything from archaeology itself and its place in anthropology to sites, stratigraphy, dating methods, and basic field procedures. After that, the approach is historical. The beginning could be any number of points in the past, but the seventeenth century is a reasonable place to start. After a brief discussion of early explanations of creation, artifacts (thunderstones, fairy darts), and chronology (the obligatory reference to Archbishop Ussher, although he was anticipated by some sixteen years by John Lightfoot), we examine the emergence of both antiquarians and dilettanti in the seventeenth and eighteenth centuries. Thomas Jefferson's place in the history of American archaeology is touched on; we also note that over two hundred years ago he anticipated the lexicostaticians in suggesting the validity of what we know as glottalchronology.

The concepts of catastrophism and uniformitarianism are introduced, for they have had an effect on the way certain explanations have been framed up to the present day: witness the differing views of the relationship between Neandertal and modern forms of humankind and the archaeological evidence that supports them.

A section on the development in northern Europe of the three-age system naturally leads to the whole subject of Lewis Henry Morgan, unilineal evolution, and our cultural propensity to divide everything into three parts. Lower, Middle, and Upper (or Early, Middle, and Late) are constructions that are just as artificial as the three races of humankind perceived by the fourth. This tripartite mind-set is also discussed in the context of Alan Dundes's "The Number Three in American Culture" (1968). Also at this point, you can demonstrate that in Europe, a deductive framework was in place before much excavation took place, while in the United States, it did not make its appearance until the 1950s. This difference shaped the development of archaeology in this country in significant ways. A brief gloss of early diffusionist thought is necessary to provide a context for a somewhat longer treatment of Boasian anthropology, as it was in part a reaction to extreme and opposing views of culture history. The Boasian position of historical particularism lies at the base of various American archaeological classifications current in the 1940s and 1950s. This section of the course also accommodates discussion of the age-area hypothesis and the culture area concept, as both derive from trait distribution studies.

Somewhere in this part of the course (it varies a bit from year to year), a case study is presented based on C. Loring Brace's article "The Fate of the 'Classic' Neanderthals: A Consideration of Hominoid Catastrophism" (1964). This study serves as an example of how constructions of the past depend greatly on those who are making them and how the same data can lead to very different explanations. It also permits, as contextual background, a brief treatment of Old World paleolithic culture history, thus accommodating the need for some treatment of prehistory.

Returning to North America, the roles played by both Julian Steward (1949) and Gordon Willey and Philip Phillips (1958) are discussed and shown as the reemergence of evolutionary thinking. In treating this matter, it is quite easy and natural to summarize, in a lecture or two, the salient aspects of New World culture history (Willey and Phillips) as well as later prehistory in the Old World (Steward). This sets the stage in a natural way for a discussion of the culture process school, cultural ecology, and deductive and inductive research strategies and their relationship to each other, which brings us into the seventies. I purposely end the historical survey with examples of structural analysis as exemplified by the work of Henry Glassie in folk housing in Middle Virginia (1975). Because this work is concerned with typology and classification, among many other things, it forms a good context for a discussion of typology in general. Furthermore, it provides a very natural point of departure for a discussion of historical archaeology, which as David Hurst Thomas has said, is now a part of the mainstream of American archaeology.

This brief summary of course content only touches on some of the material covered and is offered simply to suggest ways in which a course can establish, in a natural and logical way, the relationships between archaeology and the larger discipline of which it is a part. The work of other scholars—J. J. Bachofen, John McLennan, G. P. Murdock, Elman Service, Leslie White—is also considered to a lesser degree. These have in common with each other and the rest of the course a shared concern with what happened in the past and the way thinking about the past has changed over time. Not all this material is archaeological per se, but archaeology has played a central role in our construction of the past and has been influenced in turn by the work of others who were not archaeologists themselves.

In keeping with the earlier caveat that one should be very selective about what is included in an introductory archaeology course, it is obvious that a course structured in this fashion does indeed leave out certain things. But it is integrated by a historical perspective, and the textbook used, David Hurst Thomas's *Archaeology*, makes an excellent complement to the lectures. When the course is taught with discussion sections, the Thomas book forms the basis for these; when it is not, care is taken to refer students to those parts of the book that relate to the lecture material. Students are also encouraged to read as much of the book as is of interest to them. Experience has shown that most of them read almost all of it, if not the entire volume.

A course structured like this one may not be to everybody's taste. It does, however, provide a format in which you can present an overview of world prehistory, not in isolation, but as it relates to certain intellectual issues in archaeology and anthropology. It can also demonstrate the way in which archaeology forms an integral part of general anthropology. As such, it allows the student to perceive more clearly the relationships between what otherwise might be seen as unrelated and disparate parts.

Some comments on teaching style: a personal view.

We all have our own ways of teaching, and if we are at all sensitive to what is going on in the classroom, we learn what works and what does not and take steps to remedy any problems. For the past thirty-four years, I have had the very great pleasure of teaching what by now must be tens of thousands of undergraduates, and they have taught me as much as I have them. I prefer undergraduate teaching. I find that classes come to have a corporate personality. One year it is flippant; the next, slightly shy; and the next, very intense.

Once that quality is sensed, and I find that it takes surprisingly little time for it to emerge, I can relate to the class as if they were a single individual and thus tailor our relationship accordingly. Mystical as this may sound, it is nonetheless true.

When there is a choice, I prefer to use material with which I have had at least some firsthand involvement. Obviously, this cannot be done all the time, but surprisingly, it is possible more than one might expect. Of course, the older we get, the more experience we have had, and we can discuss more things from a firsthand perspective. It is a sobering thought to realize that I took my first introductory cultural anthropology course from Leslie Spier. But there is no substitute for experience, and if more senior faculty can be convinced of the great value and importance of teaching introductory courses, the field will be much the better for it. It has been suggested that in academia we do things backward, and that the more senior a faculty person becomes, the greater value that person has in teaching beginning students. Conversely, who are better suited to give courses on specialized subjects that represent the latest thinking than brand new Ph.D.s?

I don't hesitate to be outrageous when teaching, sometimes bordering on the absurd. But one effective tactic to guarantee class attention is to create a situation in which students never know what is coming next. "Weird" is an adjective that pops up from time to time in my class evaluations, and I find that a positive thing. Students should know that God invented time so that everything would not happen at once. Also, because each of us is the product of two people, it is quite obvious that the further back in time one goes, the more people there would have been. Curiously, this latter fact forms the basis of a linear regression that shows that in 4004 B.C., there was exactly one person for each square foot of the earth's surface, lending support to the older view of the date of the creation. A good supply of such important "facts" is of immense use in keeping the class on their toes, and it works. I try always to avoid jargon, and indeed, poke fun at some of our favorite expressions and phrases. Why on earth say "lithic resource utilization" when "using rocks" conveys exactly the same information? Simple, straightforward declarative English is particularly needed in the context of the spoken word, which is what lectures are made of.

I have never found team teaching to be the wonderful thing that many people think it might be. It is one of those ideas that sound great in theory but more often than not fail in practice. The problem might be that with two or more people involved, both must be somewhat compromised in their style and teaching philosophy or the course falls into dissimilar parts from a pedagogical point of view. This is not to say that occasional guest lecturers should not present their research to an introductory class. Quite the contrary; such guests, one's archaeological colleagues in the department, can convey to the students the variety of archaeological research and at the same time give them a better idea of what areas of research various department members are involved in. This variety can serve as a kind of "preview" of more specialized advanced courses that are available.

Last, I suspect that the most important component of an introductory course is the amount of enthusiasm the instructor has for the material. If you get excited over it, that comes across to the students, and the better the course becomes, the more the students take from it. So although each of us might present our material in different ways, this does not mean that these are not all good ways. There is no one good way with all others of lesser quality. But I hope that the remarks made in this chapter might at least provoke some thought about our teaching mission, which in my opinion is the most important part of our job. We can do no less than excel.

References

Brace, C. Loring. 1964. "The Fate of the 'Classic' Neanderthals: A Consideration of Hominoid Catastrophism." *Current Anthropology* 5:3–43.

Dundes, Alan. 1968. "The Number Three in American Culture." In *Every Man His Way: Readings in Cultural Anthropology*, edited by Alan Dundes, 401–424. Englewood Cliffs, N.J.: Prentice-Hall.

Flannery, Kent V. 1982. "The Golden Marshalltown: A Parable for the Archaeology of the 1980s." *American Anthropologist* 84:265–278.

Glassie, Henry. 1975. *Folk Housing in Middle Virginia: A Structural Analysis of Historic Artifacts*. Knoxville: University of Tennessee Press.

Steward, Julian H. 1949. "Cultural Causality and Law: A Trial Formulation of the Development of Early Civilizations." *American Anthropologist* 51:1–27.

Thomas, David Hurst. 1989. *Archaeology*. 2d ed. Fort Worth: Holt, Rinehart and Winston.

Willey, Gordon R., and Philip Phillips. 1958. *Method and Theory in American Archaeology*. Chicago: University of Chicago Press.

The Past Meets the Future
New Approaches to Teaching Archaeology

GEORGE H. MICHAELS AND BRIAN M. FAGAN

These are very dynamic times to be teaching anthropology. The diversity of theoretical perspectives, new methodological developments, and the ethical and political imperatives and implications of what we do as a profession are in a constant state of flux. Improvements in information technology serve to quicken the pace of information exchange and squeeze us into an ever smaller, more accessible, world. Given this scenario, it is understandable that we have difficulty in deciding what elements of our professional universe should be conveyed to our students. What elements of this information will have a lasting utility to our students, most of whom will not become professional anthropologists? How can we provide them with a sense of what anthropology is, how it works, and most important, what its value is to them personally? As the other chapters in this volume indicate, these are not easily answered questions, nor will our chapter provide complete answers to those questions. Rather, we hope to stimulate thought on a related and equally important question: how can we improve the *way* we teach anthropology?

Anthropology has, and always has had, a blind side. That blind side has been a lack of attention paid to the ways in which we communicate to the rest of the world what we do, how we do it, and why it is important. In particular, we have been remiss in assessing our effectiveness in communicating those things to the single largest audience we as a profession have—our undergraduate classes. Whether we are teaching archaeology, physical anthropology, or cultural anthropology, we have always had the luxury of teaching an inherently interesting subject with a wealth of attention-getting textual and visual material to draw on. Although that might have been enough to get our students' attention in the past, it is much less effective today. The world is constantly with them thanks to modern information technologies. As a result, our traditional attention getters are much less exotic and much less effective than they once were. That simple fact, combined with the serious reading, writing, and analytical deficiencies with which our students come to us, after years of being taught that learning is ingesting and regurgitating on command, makes our task as teachers much more difficult.

Educational reform will be one of the single most important national agendas in the 1990s. As that reform progresses in the kindergarten through twelfth grade arena, we will reap some benefit in the form of students who are truly prepared for the university or college learning experience. We are confronted with a double-edged problem. How, on the one hand, can we best serve our students of the moment by motivating them and providing them with the necessary analytical skills to be successful while also inculcating in them an appreciation for what we do as a profession. On the other hand, are we ready to serve the students yet to come who will probably be better prepared and who will also arrive in our classrooms expecting much more from us personally and professionally? This chapter discusses these emerging realities in the light of major changes we have introduced in our introductory course in archaeology at the University of California at Santa Barbara over the past five years. While our efforts have achieved some level of national notoriety as an example of innovative applications of information technology in teaching, there is much more to the equation than teachers + technology + students = higher cognitive skills. For this reason, our paper deemphasizes technology and deals with broader issues.

Pedagogical Philosophy

We know from development anthropology and other fields that in most cases, when people adopt new technology, they start by applying the innovations to the same old tasks. Thus, in archaeology, when we first started using computers, we used them for sorting catalogs and automating the categorization process. In teaching, the new microcomputer technologies of word processing and database management were applied to grade keeping, test production, and the creation and maintenance of handouts. Early efforts at computer-aided instruction throughout the world were adaptations of traditional rote learning drills. In all these cases, and hundreds more, the technology was adapted to an existing set of processes—sometimes to good advantage, sometimes catastrophically. It is usually only in the second or third generation of both users and the technology that people begin thinking of completely new processes that are enabled by the new technology and start rethinking the old processes to take maximum advantage of the new tools. Teaching and the new information technologies are just coming into that second stage. What we do here is briefly describe the traditional teaching process and then illustrate how we have modified that process in our course. The fundamental elements are not the technologies employed but the pedagogical philosophy behind the processes. By way of example, we contrast the way we formerly taught introductory archaeology with the way we teach it today.

Traditional Teaching: The Factory Model of Education

The traditional version of Anthropology 3 was designed on the familiar lecture course format to serve 300 students per quarter and was offered once a year. It was organized around four basic elements common to almost all college courses and suffered from all the general deficiencies inherent in what we call the factory model of education. The four elements are briefly summarized here.

The first element was, of course, the lecture. In the original version of Anthropology 3, lecture sessions met for three hours a week. Although the lecture in this format did not ignore the entertainment and motivational elements that all good oral presentations must have, its emphasis was on the verbal conveyance of substantive information. In this format, the emphasis was on the instructor as the authority, and the course was instructor oriented. For the students, it provided, at best, a passive learning experience. In addition, they felt isolated from the professor, the teaching assistants, and each other.

The second element was a discussion section led by a teaching assistant. Each discussion section of twenty to thirty students met for one hour a week. The teaching assistants often spent much of their time lecturing, trying to tie together the disparate pieces of information from lectures, readings, films, and so on for the students. Again, students generally were put in the position of passive learners. Teaching assistants' efforts to generate discussion usually failed because the students were often not prepared for discussion. As a result, the sections often devolved into a series of test preparation sessions. Because of the smaller size of the group, it provided an experience that was somewhat less passive, but often not much less.

The third component of the traditional course was assigned readings. The reading component often fell short of its intended goals. Sometimes this was because of a lack of specificity (for example, "read Chapter XX by Monday and extract the pertinent information," or worse, "it's ALL important"). For the students, the readings were often seen as disembodied information that held no interest for them because they did not have a cognitive framework with which to associate the information. As a result, they often treated the readings as such—the highlighter method of learning. And while print is still one of the most effective forms of conveying certain types of substantive information, it again relies on mostly passive learning by students.

The final component was evaluation of student performance. It has long been obvious that multiple choice/true-false/short answer tests are not effective tools for assessing students' comprehension of a body of material. It continues students' perception of the information they receive as disembodied bits and pieces rather than as parts of a larger epistemological whole. This form of evaluation also results in the simple regurgitation of particularistic information. These methods have little benefit for students because once the test is over, their requirement to retain that information ends also. Students are seldom engaged in self-assessment, and therefore are not motivated to try to improve their performance. For this reason, we abandoned such tests many years ago, even in the traditional class.

Written assignments in the class often fell short of the mark, also. They were frequently not really problem oriented but were just exercises in accumulating and presenting particularistic information. Problems with writing style often took away from the instructor's ability or time to comment on the analytical aspects of the papers. Students received no reinforcement for trying to improve, especially if the paper was an end-of-term paper.

Finally, traditional grading structures (such as curves) encouraged student competition more than cooperation and enhanced students' feeling of isolation from the instructors and their fellow students.

This model of education is almost completely passive rather than interactive. Students are treated like empty vessels waiting for information instead of individuals who already have established knowledge bases that should be built on. Student evaluation is still contingent on some form of testing and is external to the student—that is, self-assessment is not encouraged. This traditional model did not really draw the students into the subject matter, and although entertaining and informative, it probably did not affect the students' higher-order cognitive skills nor their long-term appreciation of archaeology as a science.

Principles of the New Approach

The principal goal of our revised course is effective learning, not only for students, but also for instructional staff. The course is structured so that the prime responsibility for learning is on the students' shoulders. This goal presupposes that effective learning is dynamic and interactive—not a static passive process. To this end, we strive to improve basic knowledge skills and analytical skills by engaging the students with the subject matter. In short, we use the subject matter to help them learn how to digest information critically, how to form opinions, and how to defend a position once taken. We believe that the course should provide a lasting intellectual legacy for our students. We are not trying to train professional archaeologists in this course but to provide our students with the opportunity to learn firsthand about the rigor and complexity of modern archaeology, to give them entrée to important sources of information about the discipline, and—we hope—to instill a lifelong interest in the past and their heritage as human beings. Our new course design, first implemented in 1990, was based on these principles.

The first and perhaps most critical element of the new course design was that the student should be the center of a highly integrated resource network including the following elements: teaching assistants and instructors as resources and managers of learning, readings, experiential learning using computer-based simulations and visualization tools, combinations of individual and small group problem-solving exercises, and a study guide to provide the overall framework for the course. The course study guide is a desktop-published document that serves as a guide to the material, providing signposts to information destinations and problems to be solved. The student version of the study guide is printed on punched paper so it can be inserted in a binder. Students are expected to interleave their written work with the pages of the study guide so that the combined document serves as a journal of their progress through the course. The study guide tells them what will be covered in a given week and what work is expected in that week; it highlights the major points that will be emphasized in lecture and discussion sections, directs them to reading assignments and computer exercises, and sets them off on various kinds of synthetic writing assignments. It is the backbone of the course. Because the study guide is desktop published, it can be easily modified from quarter to quarter to keep it fresh and up to date. The costs of production are small and the cost to the students is the cost of reproduction at the local copy shop.

At the same time, we reduced lecture time from three hours to one hour a week. We wanted to deemphasize the instructor as the primary conduit of information and provide other resources that could accomplish that task more efficiently and effectively. In addition, because the primary structure of the course was provided by the study guide, that traditional function of the lecture was also superseded. We use the weekly lecture not for information transfer but to foster a sense of community among the students and instructors, reinforcing the notion that we are all in this together. We use slides and other visuals and the lecture itself as a device for motivation and entertainment, both important ingredients in a large introductory course. Finally, the lecture is the one place where the intellectual glue that holds the course content and structure together can best be provided.

The one-hour weekly discussion section was retained in the new version of the course as well. The role of teaching assistants in the new version has changed radically, however. Because students tend to be more deeply involved in the subject matter, they come to the section prepared with questions, and these can be very challenging. As a result, a true dialogue develops between the students and teaching assistants as the quarter goes on. Another difference from the traditional course is that teaching assistants spend more of their time involved in coaching students in their work and evaluating the thinking skills and writing of the members of their sections. The reduced emphasis on grades and the elimination of a grading curve also reduces the feeling of competition between students and allows them to interact more freely in discussion without feeling that they may be giving up some advantage they have over their neighbors. Grading is by mastery, not artificial criteria.

Much of the information transmission is still accomplished through reading assignments. The reading assignments come from two standard archaeology textbooks and a selection of readings that are incorporated in the body of the study guide. Few mechanisms will replace books as efficient, convenient, reasonably inexpensive conduits for information at any time in the foreseeable future. The study guide, however, points the students to very specific reading assignments that only cover material essential to the particular topic at hand. The specification is to the page, even the paragraph, so there is no irrelevant reading. The study guide also usually follows one of these reading assignments with either a synthetic writing assignment, in which the students have to think about what they have just read, or a computer exercise. Here the students will get either additional or reinforcing information that complements the reading or a simulation exercise in which they have to apply the information from the reading to solve one or more problems.

We also incorporated microcomputer-based visualization and simulation tools into the course. Although this feature of the course often receives the most scrutiny, it is not the most important. As part of our effort to use the most effective vehicle for conveying information, the use of multimedia exercises to accomplish specific goals was obvious to us from the start. Just as lectures and readings are good for some kinds of learning and not very useful for others, so too are computer-based instructional materials. Computer software can do a number of things better than any traditional medium. To begin with, credible visualization tools are only possible with microcomputer-based software. The explanation of complex or very small- or large-scale phenomena is much more effective with various interactive animated approaches than with traditional media. It is much easier, for example, for a student to grasp the global consequences of the advance and retreat of the major ice sheets during the Pleistocene through a global animation than through a series of static maps.

Furthermore, microcomputers and the new generation of development tools for them allow us, as content experts, to create simulations of archaeological and ethnographic situations that force the students to apply what they have learned to solving a problem. For example, through computer simulation, members of Anthropology 3 spend seven years in Central Africa's Middle Zambezi Valley learning the realities of subsistence farming among the Gwembe Tonga. Although a simulation can be set up without the use of computers, the degree of realism and the immediacy of feedback available in a computer simulation cannot be matched with pencil-and-paper techniques.

In addition, well-designed simulations and visualization tools promote self-evaluation, serve to integrate learning and testing, and demonstrate that in science there are no nice, neat, *right* answers. These types of exercises actively engage the students with the subject matter, putting them in the position of having to use information rather than just absorbing it. Simulations in particular provide students with a context within which new information makes sense and can be tied into their existing knowledge structure—promoting retention. More important, the exercises emphasize critical thinking, problem solving, the thoughtful construction of arguments based on data, and the critical evaluation of those arguments. All these strategies offer a much longer lasting legacy to our students than being able to recite the progression of fossil hominids and their sites of first discovery, all of which they forget within hours of a multiple-choice test.

The final element in the web of learning resources is, of course, the other students in the course. At all stages of Anthropology 3, we actively promote cooperation in the class rather than competition for grades. We have gone to great pains to deemphasize the importance of grades as a gauge of student performance. The grading structure of the course allows all students an equal opportunity of getting a high grade if they do the work. There are clear-cut rewards for improvement during the course. On the other hand, we are absolutely ruthless about no negotiation of grades. We maintain very high standards for the work expected of the students and do not back down from them. In fact, the course has been compared by some students to their introductory calculus classes in terms of challenge and the work expected of them. In our experience, although initially intimidated, the students enjoy the personal responsibility and rise to the level of expectation. In addition, a number of the exercises are designed as small group projects, again promoting cooperative effort and a team spirit within the groups, the sections, and the class as a whole. The students feel connected to each other and to the teaching assistants and ourselves in a way that is really not possible in a large, traditional, lecture-driven, lower-division course.

Anthropology 3 does not revolve around an anonymous lecture hall, but an informal learning center. This is an informal study lounge where all course activities occur, with the exception of the lecture. The learning center houses the computer workstations as well as large tables for group study and meetings with faculty and teaching assistants. We and the teaching assistants hold our office hours in the learning center; we also pass through the center periodically to answer questions, chat, and observe how the students are interacting with each other and the learning materials. We have gone to some trouble to make it a comfortable, workable environment, and the students have responded very favorably. Above all, 90 percent of the students' interaction with the instructors is on a one-to-one basis, to the point that we meet over 95 percent of the students enrolled each time we teach Anthropology 3, a remarkable statistic for a large, lower-division course.

Finally, just as the students are in a constant state of self-evaluation and peer evaluation, so, too, is the course itself undergoing constant formal evaluation. Because of the increased contact with individual students, specific problems with exercises, the study guide, and writing assignments can be detected early and corrected quickly. The course has undergone formal evaluation twice in its early stages through questionnaires and focus groups. At the end of each quarter, we have a formal review of all elements of the course by a group that includes ourselves, the teaching assistants, and interested students. We are constantly asking the students for feedback on all aspects of the course to keep it effective. In short, the course itself is in a constant state of evolution as we learn from our students. Anthropology 3 is driven by its participants, not by the arbitrary whim of an instructor.

Conclusion

The results of our new course structure and philosophy are many and varied. One of the most important from our standpoint has been improved personal interaction between students and instructors (97 percent compared to less than 10 percent). There is clearly an enhanced student appreciation for the process of archaeology and its value to society. We and the students have recognized improved basic learning skills and enhanced self-confidence in their own problem-solving abilities. The course has enjoyed increased enrollment. Revision and modification of course materials is much faster and easier than was possible in the traditional course. And perhaps most telling, all the upper-division method and theory courses in our department are being converted to similar formats. This last, somewhat unexpected, result is based on the perception of our colleagues that the students they are receiving in their courses are much better prepared than they have been in the past. After having seen the benefit of this approach for the large enrollment, lower-division course, they have rightly concluded that the benefit would be even greater when applied in their smaller, more focused, upper-division courses.

The new version of the course is an unqualified success. Elements of the course were made possible by dramatic improvements in the software authoring tools available today compared to even a few years ago. The costs of developing and maintaining this type of course are not dramatically higher than for a standard course, as most costs are faculty salary, which is paid anyhow. The work of developing a course along similar lines is about the same as for a traditional course, but most of it is up front, rather than as you go along.

As we enter a period in which enrollments are rapidly increasing, are consisting of higher percentages of returning students, and are marked by dramatically increased cultural, economic, and ethnic diversity at the same time that financial support for anthropology departments is declining, we are faced with some very tough choices. *What* we choose to teach is one of those tough choices. Our contention here is that *how* we choose to teach is another tough choice that must be made. We can no longer assume that the traditional teaching methods we have employed are the best ways to serve our students. There are effective ways to break down the anonymity of the large introductory class. There are better ways to present complex concepts and processes. There are ways to raise academic standards and make the students like it. There are ways to keep learning interesting and even fun—for the teachers as well as for the students. Some of the self-same information technologies that serve to complicate our lives can also be made to serve us as very powerful tools for learning and communication.

As we hope our case has illustrated, technology can help to offload tasks better done by a machine, and technology can serve as a powerful amplifier and multiplier of our own teaching abilities. The ultimate solution, however, lies not with technology but with people—that is, the instructors. What is wanted is creativity, imagination, and a willingness to experiment, to rebel—even just a little bit—against an outdated and barely adequate educational philosophy. Finally, the question each of us must ask ourselves, individually and collectively, is not whether we should put ourselves on the cutting edge of teaching innovation, but rather can we afford not to?

Participant Archaeology

PATRICIA C. RICE

The days of the three-credit, lecture, "sit-and-absorb and then regurgitate-back-on-exams" introductory archaeology class is or should be over. Instead, even introductory-level students should be active participants in their own learning experience. If the 1960s ushered in the New Archaeology, the 1990s should be the decade that seriously begins the New Teaching Archaeology, a strategy that requires active participation by the student, not just the instructor. I call this Participant Archaeology.

Professional educators insist (with good reason) that students in elementary, junior, and high school learn best "by doing." Then, why do we shut off the valve of hands-on learning once those same students enter a college or university setting? The process of learning has not changed, and although the students have matured, they are still students; if learning by doing is the best way to learn in high school, then it is the best way to learn in college as well.

The following two anonymous proverbs are self-explanatory:

Tell me, I'll listen.	I hear and I forget.
Show me, I'll believe.	I see and I remember.
Involve me, I'll learn.	I do and I understand.
(Native American proverb)	(Chinese proverb)

Archaeology has always been one of the more "active" disciplines, since both its data collection and data analysis involve physical as well as mental activities. It should, theoretically, take no huge leap of faith for teachers to be convinced that archaeology is a natural hands-on adventure for their students. Then why is it that so many archaeology courses are driven basically by the lecture format?

It may be that many professional archaeologists, who also teach, are justifiably dismayed by reports in newspapers about simulated "digs" sponsored by museums or done as part of a class project for precollegiate age students, that appear to be nothing more than "treasure hunts." Such "digs" often teach what we do not want students to learn, that is, that archaeologists come upon a pile of dirt and start tossing it aside to get at some artifact (treasure). Instead, we want students of any age to accurately note the provenience of artifacts while learning proper excavation techniques. Granted, measuring the exact location of an artifact is not as much fun as throwing dirt around, but there is room for both fun and learning in any excavation experience. Since this kind of "treasure-hunt-dig" is such a turnoff to professional archaeologists, perhaps this is the reason why many collegiate-level teachers cling to the passive lecture method of teaching.

Simulated excavations, however, need not be "treasure hunts." Indeed, as teaching tools, simulations are often better than the real thing for the obvious reason that they can be controlled: no road construction is being held up while an instructor explains an unusual element of stratigraphy, and excavators do not need to be told to excavate faster than they are comfortably able to, just because "the pipe has arrived." Beyond data collection, data analysis in archaeology is also a participant activity: artifacts must be washed, labeled, categorized, and counted; bones, seeds, and nuts have to be identified as to species; tools have to be analyzed for microwear; soils have to be screened and color matched. One begins to wonder why all archaeology courses are not active participant courses, complete with excavation learned by excavating and data analysis learned by analyzing data. By analogy, this would be similar to teaching computer science to students who have no access to computers.

I suggest that some of the following "excuses" are at the root of the "absorb-by-listening-to-me" approach that is so common in teaching the introductory course:

- Excavation is too expensive to permit students to be taken into the field.
- Excavation destroys sites.
- Excavation is time costly.
- Equipment for analysis of any kind is expensive.
- Laboratory sessions are too structured by two-hour segments for real archaeological understanding.

In this chapter, I suggest that these obstacles, which can become excuses, can be overcome by creative imagination, a relatively small budget, and some elbow grease. The benefits to students are tremendous relative to the work required. To overcome the excuses that "excavation is too expensive, it destroys sites, and is time costly," I suggest building a full-scale simulated site and having students excavate it, not as a "treasure hunt" but as if it were a real excavation. To overcome the argument that "equipment for analysis is expensive," I can show that a "revolving" type of laboratory can be quite inexpensive. And, to overcome the excuse that "laboratory sessions, by definition in two-hour blocks of time are too structured for archaeology," I propose the creation of laboratory hands-on experiences that can be done in this amount of time. The result is a full laboratory course that contains a segment devoted to learning field techniques by excavating a simulated site and doing a number of other exercises; the result is participant archaeology.

Although it is possible to make a three-credit introductory-level archaeology course a hands-on experience, given the amount of material necessary to adequately introduce students to the field of archaeology, a four-credit, full laboratory course seems more appropriate. First, it will provide thirty to forty-five additional hours of participation in the archaeological adventure—that is, the laboratory segment; second, it releases class time that was once spent doing quasi-laboratory exercises that can now be spent on other important topics; and third, it will parallel the laboratories that are mandatory in biology, physics, chemistry, and geology, giving students the important reinforcement that archaeology *is* science, just as other science courses with laboratories are science.

Relative to this last point, it can be stated in class that archaeology is science because it uses the scientific method when going about its investigation, and that science is a way of thinking about particular problems and not bubbling retorts. In class, archaeology can be compared to other historical sciences like geology, astronomy, and evolutionary biology, and the instructor can claim that like other historical sciences, archaeology cannot—without a time machine—verify its knowledge. Historical sciences can be contrasted to ecological biology, physics, or chemistry, pointing out that archaeology cannot replicate the past the way that nonhistorical sciences can replicate the present through experiments, but that this does not mean that archaeology is not a science. Astronomy and geology cannot replicate the past through experiments either.

The perception that laboratory equals science even pervades the professional arena. When I first pursued the idea of changing my three-credit, primarily lecture course to a four-credit course with a full lab, I was asked by a fellow faculty member if I intended to change the course from social science to natural science credit, as if adding a laboratory segment would change the nature of the discipline. This was particularly interesting because over half the laboratory sessions were in the original course in one form or another. (See Rice 1990 for a description of short versions of several laboratory exercises.)

Once teaching archaeologists are convinced of the value of participant archaeology, which includes a laboratory component at the introductory course level, the important question is: what should be learned in the laboratory segment? This is, of course, not the same as asking what should be taught in the laboratory segment. For the former—what should be learned—the following is suggested: students should learn how to think and write, how to do critical reasoning, and how to do certain technical jobs in archaeology. The specifics of what should be learned and what should be taught will depend to a great extent on the instructor's biases and training. A prehistoric archaeologist trained in England and researching French prehistoric art will probably not have exactly the same laboratory sessions as an historic archaeologist trained in the U.S. and researching the interface between Native Americans and early Anglo-American colonists. Nor should they.

At a minimum, the following *types* of participant activities are suggested because they will allow students to learn to reason critically, think and write independently, and learn certain technical skills; they also do not depend on instructor bias or training:

- Using the principles of dating techniques
- Doing experimental archaeology
- Excavating

- Reconstructing environmental contexts
- Analyzing artifacts
- Analyzing material culture
- Reconstructing cultures

The Inexpensive Archaeology Laboratory: A Personal Recommendation

Although I have required a number of laboratory segments in my introductory-level archaeology course for a decade, only recently have I turned this into a four-credit, full laboratory course. Using many of the excuses referred to previously, I had convinced myself that laboratories were too expensive and students were learning just as much under the present, basically lecture, teaching mode. Tucked away in the back of my brain were a dozen or so hands-on exercises that students "could" do if I suddenly had a financial windfall. What happened to trigger the full laboratory was not a windfall, but a realization of *how* to equip a laboratory very inexpensively. This quickly blew away the excuse that students were learning as much in the old format.

Most laboratory segments of science courses purposely minimize the instructor-to-student ratio so a good deal of personal attention can be paid to each student. To have twelve students in a laboratory is typical, and I made the decision to divide the seventy-two-student class into six twelve-student laboratories. The overall number can and probably will be increased in the future. Since the lecture portion can grow to almost any size, the limiting factor is the number of laboratory personnel who can be hired or enticed into being laboratory assistants through teaching-practicum credit. Twelve-person laboratories would normally mean twelve sets of equipment; in a science-based archaeology laboratory, that would mean twelve artifact microscopes, twelve slide microscopes, twelve sets of sieve/screens, et cetera. But, a twelve-student laboratory can be made quite inexpensively by borrowing or making as much equipment as possible and by making the laboratory a "revolving" laboratory. A revolving laboratory puts the twelve students into four sets of three students each. Each of the four sets will be doing a different laboratory exercise in each lab; thus, only three microscopes of each type are needed, and in some cases, three—but not twelve—can be borrowed from biology or anatomy departments. And, for example, only one set of sieves is needed if there are three parts to the paleosediment exercise, since each of the three students in the set will be doing the screening portion of the exercise at a different time.

A simulated site can be built at a reasonable cost as well, and miniaturized sites on card tables can be built for even less. With some creative scrounging and some imagination, cost need not be the excuse for not having a laboratory.[1] (Discounting the cost of the simulated site—which was built eleven years ago and has been used every year since then—the full cost of my laboratory, in 1992–93, was less than $600; add a miniaturized excavation segment and the total might be $700; add a professionally built, full-sized simulated site and the total would be about $1,200, but much less if students build it. Most of this is a one-time-only cost; yearly expenses run about $100. Students purchase the *Archaeology Laboratory Textbook* (Rice 1994) as their text; it contains the readings and the exercises for the laboratory segment of the course, including the writing up of various parts of each exercise.

What can you get for $600? Let me briefly describe the twelve hands-on exercises in my laboratory. In a fifteen-week term, the first session is devoted to mechanics of the course and there are two quizzes, leaving twelve two-hour sessions for exercises. They are discussed here in order of appearance in the *Archaeology Laboratory Textbook* (Rice 1996), but since the laboratory is revolving and students are randomly doing the twelve exercises, only the three exercise-sessions of the excavation unit and the last two exercises are of necessity done consecutively.

Exercise 1. Paleopollen Analysis: Using the slide microscope, students learn how to recognize five "popular" pollen grains, one species per slide; they spend forty-five minutes counting pollen on a "mixed pollen slide," noting each on a master count list. They calculate simple proportions of each pollen. Using information provided on "indicator" species of plants, they decide the relative gradients of warmer/colder and wetter/dryer as well as ground cover, as inferred through their analysis. A layered chronological gradient chart showing four strata with a purposely missing segment (representing one archaeological layer/strata) is provided in the laboratory text and students draw the gradients inferred from their analysis onto the chart, supporting their decisions with evidence.

Exercise 2. Paleofaunal Analysis: Students pull apart a barn owl pellet, identify the prey species items, and calculate simple proportions of prey species. Using information on micro "indicator" animals, they infer the relative gradients of temperature, moisture, and ground cover, and note gradients on charts, as in the first exercise.

Exercise 3. Paleosediment Analysis: Students do simple tests with the three sediment groups: clay, sand, silt (PSA, color matching, "squeeze and sludge" tests, edge rounding via microscope observation). Using information provided by sediment clues, they infer the relative gradients of temperature, moisture, and ground cover, and note gradients on charts, as in the first exercise.

At the end of the three exercises, students must come to a general conclusion about the three gradients they have noted on the individual charts, as evidenced by three different kinds of environmental evidence—pollen, fauna, sediment—since the missing layer on each chart represents the same layer/strata. Students must support their decisions with proper evidence, and account for discrepancies in their inferences, if there are any to explain.

Exercise 4. Microwear Analysis: Using artifact microscopes, students become familiar with a small reference collection of use-wear tools (the edge damage, striations, and/or polish caused by cutting antler, boring bone, cutting grass, scraping wood, cutting wood). They then spend fifteen to twenty minutes using a previously unused flint tool that was made from a prepared blank;

knowing how they used the tool, the students observe the microwear results under the microscope. Finally, they attempt to identify the "mystery function" of an already prepared and used tool by matching its microwear signature with the reference collection pieces and their own experimentally used tool. They must justify their conclusions with proper evidence.

Exercise 5. Ethnoarchaeology and Spatial Analysis: Students in their set of three, sit around a simulated camp site and eat lunch, tossing their lunch debris. After lunch, each carefully maps the toss/drop zones. As if they were archaeologists with no knowledge of the actual behavior of the debris tossers, students then make inferences on how many people were responsible for leaving the debris and inferences on the concentrations of weight/size of the debris. Then, they reanalyze the debris, using the knowledge they have from being an observer/participant, comparing the results of their two analyses.

Exercise 6. Rubbish, Trash, and Garbage: As if they were volunteers at William Rathje's Garbage Project, students sort through a "pre-sorted" sack of garbage (no slops), and make inferences on the socio-economic "class" of the debris tossers by comparing their observations with data from other classes, as inferred from their garbage. In a second part of the exercise, the students reconstruct the culture of the debris tossers as if the students were twenty-first century archaeologists with no knowledge of the culture. They gain insights on the restrictions of reconstructing culture based on only materials remains.

Exercise 7. Dendrochronology: Students begin with a tree boring from bark to core, mount it, shave it down, read the ring patterns under the microscope, and graph the findings as is standard practice. They compare their resultant skeleton plot with others to make a composite plot, and then graph a growth curve. Finally, they match their graphs with the modern master chronology to date the hypothetical artifact.

Exercises 8, 9, and 10. Field Experience: Students learn field techniques of prehistoric archaeology on the full-scale, indoor, simulated site that represents a four-layer/stratum French Upper Paleolithic site, fictionally located halfway between the Dordogne and the Pyrenees. The "site" is stocked with appropriate flint and bone tools, debitage, hearths, art objects, a full human burial complete with grave goods, adornment, shells, and other ecologically related materials. (See Rice 1982 for a discussion on the pros and cons of building and stocking a simulated site.) In three two-hour sessions, students learn the rudiments of any field excavation: mapping, measuring, locating artifacts, identifying artifacts, sieving.

Exercise 11. Differential Recovery Techniques: Using each of the four major techniques of recovering archaeological materials (manual sieving, dry sieving, wet sieving, and flotation), students learn the recovery rates of each method, tracking recovery variability via poppy seeds as well as identical amounts of carbonized and uncarbonized plant materials, flint chips, and pottery shards placed in each "sample."

Exercise 12. Reconstructing Paleodiets: Using the carbonized and uncarbonized plant materials from the previous exercise, students separate plant materials into species, identify them by morphology, weigh the samples, and attempt to reconstruct paleodiets based on these recovered materials.

The exercises described above are examples of the kinds of hands-on exercises that can be developed for a full laboratory in participant archaeology. Teacher-archaeologists can use their own experiences to develop different exercises for their students. As long as the exercises teach archaeology as science, allow students to make critical decisions, and do independent thinking and writing, the exact content of the exercises is of lesser importance. Although my twelve exercises also attempt to cover the timely and important foci of archaeology (excavation, Middle-Range Theory in experimental archaeology and ethnoarchaeology, spatio-temporal analysis, and environmental reconstruction), it is perhaps more important to make the laboratories part of participant archaeology than to cover the field evenly.

The success of the introductory level archaeology course is measured by how students apply it in their future lives (Rice 1992). If students get jobs, even in the summer, because they have had laboratory experience in archaeology, the course is successful. If excavations and analyses are more accurate because the workers have experience in participant archaeology, the course is successful. If students can be made more aware that archaeology is science, the course is successful. And if students enjoy their initial formal exposure to archaeology more, it is a bonus to the success of the laboratory format. None of this is possible in the lecture-only format.

Note

1. As an example of how to make a laboratory inexpensive, instead of purchasing an expensive Munsell Color Chart, I went to three local paint stores and asked for paint chips. From the local variety store, I purchased plastic notebook "sleeves" and a notebook, which I cut in half vertically. The chips were ordered by color, given generic names by categories, and a binomial designation (Y-1, R-5, and so on); they were then placed on double-sticky tape on the paper that came with the plastic sleeves. This Munsell Color chart simulation cost less than $5 and is as useful for color matching (in-house only) as any expensive chart.

References

Rice, Patricia. 1982. "Site Simulation in Teaching Archaeology: A Hands-on Approach." Paper given at the 81st American Anthropological Association annual meeting, Washington, DC. On ERIC Microfiche.

Rice, Patricia. 1990. "Introductory Archaeology: The Inexpensive Laboratory." *Anthropology and Education Quarterly* 21(2):167–172.

Rice, Patricia. 1992. "Teaching Archaeology: Do We Preach What We Practice?" *Practicing Anthropology* 14(1):31–32.

Rice, Patricia. 1996. *Archaeology Laboratory Textbook*. (Unpublished) Morgantown: Department of Sociology and Anthropology, West Virginia University.

TEACHING APPLIED ANTHROPOLOGY

Training in Applied Anthropology
Uniting Theory and Practice

Conrad Phillip Kottak

Applied anthropology, recognized by the American Anthropological Association (AAA) as our fifth subdiscipline, focuses on anthropology's role with respect to contemporary human problems. I see applied anthropology (also called practicing anthropology) as the use of anthropological data, perspectives, theory, and methods to identify, assess, and solve social problems. All the applications considered in this section involve sociocultural anthropology, but there are varied applications of the other subdisciplines as well.

Building on a typology originally proposed by Ralph Piddington (1970), I have suggested elsewhere (Kottak 1994, 468) that anthropologists hold three different positions about professional practice. In the "ivory-tower" view, we should avoid practical matters and concentrate on research, publication, and teaching. According to the "schizoid view," anthropologists can help carry out but should not make or criticize policy; personal "value judgments" should be kept separate from scientific investigation. The third view is advocacy. Its proponents assert that precisely because anthropologists are experts on human problems and social change and because we study, understand, and respect cultural values, we should make policy affecting people. In this view, proper roles for applied anthropologists include (1) identifying needs for change that local people perceive, (2) working with those people to design socially appropriate intervention strategies, and (3) protecting local people from harmful policies and development schemes.

The teaching of (applied) anthropology proceeds not just in the classroom but in many other contexts. Anthropologists serve as social commentators, problem solvers, and policy makers, advisers, and evaluators. We express our policy views in books and journals, through participation in social and political movements, and through professional associations, such as the Society for Applied Anthropology and the National Association of Practicing Anthropologists (NAPA). Part of the AAA, NAPA is designed to help applied anthropologists refine their skills and market their services. NAPA fosters information sharing among practitioners, publishes materials useful to them, helps train them, and works to support their interests in and outside academic settings.

An increasing number of anthropologists work for groups that promote, manage, and assess programs aimed at influencing human social conditions. The scope of applied anthropology includes change and development abroad and social problems and policies in North America. Practicing anthropologists work (regularly or occasionally) for nonacademic clients: governments, nongovernmental organizations (NGOs), tribal and ethnic associations, interest groups, businesses, social service and educational agencies.

In their contributions to this section, John van Willigen and Karin Tice note the centrality of application to early anthropology in Great Britain (in the context of colonialism) and the United States (in the context of Native American policy). Also, during World War II and its aftermath, many or most American anthropologists focused on application. Applied anthropology did not disappear during the 1950s and 1960s, although academic anthropology did most of the growing as a result of the baby boom, which fueled the expansion of teaching and academic institutions.

In their early applied work, as many critics (such as Escobar 1991) of applied anthropology have noted, anthropologists supported colonialism by working on projects aimed at economic and cultural change. Colonial anthropologists, like many of their modern counterparts, faced problems posed by their inability to set or influence policy and the difficulty of criticizing programs in which they had participated. Anthropology's professional organizations have addressed some of these problems by establishing codes of ethics and ethics committees. And, as Tice notes, attention to such ethical issues are paramount in the teaching of applied anthropology today.

As I note in my introduction to this volume, even by 1963 a trend toward the increasing prominence of applied anthropology was perceptible. As the papers by Chambers, van Willigen, and Tice make evident, that trend has intensified, as the arenas in which anthropology is routinely practiced have expanded (see Tice especially). Courses and programs, including graduate programs, in applied anthropology have proliferated. Van Willigen gives us the perspective of a scholar, teacher (of graduates and undergraduates), and applied anthropologist who routinely combines theory with practice. Tice describes one of the major programs (Columbia University Teachers College) offering a doctorate in applied anthropology. Chambers notes the spread of applied anthropology into undergraduate curricula, despite lingering hostility and uncertainty about its proper place in the academy.

Special training is needed for those who would apply anthropology. Van Willigen summarizes the research methods that should be taught: qualitative research based on observation and interviewing, sometimes followed by a survey; simple statistical analysis; multidisciplinary team research; and "group process research methods" such as reconnaissance surveys, rapid assessment procedures, and focus groups. Applied anthropologists are especially aware of the time constraints of their profession. Research techniques are designed to gather as much relevant information in as short a time as possible. This is not the "at least a year in the field" model that typifies recent cultural anthropology. (The Boasians often spent just a few months in the field.)

Change is intrinsic to applied anthropology—as the objective, or the object of study. Policies involving socioeconomic change often affect whole regions, so that applied anthropologists must gather multisite data. However, besides rapid and multisite appraisals, applied anthropology might also better connect to academia by incorporating opportunities for more leisurely and detailed studies of change. Academics should encourage graduate students to do dissertation research on development projects and other policy products. Such in-depth understanding can supplement the quick and broad approaches typically used by applied anthropologists.

As more and more graduate students will become practicing anthropologists, we need to strengthen the academic-applied interface. Tice suggests several ways of doing this. Graduate students need not only brief internships, but they should also be encouraged to do their dissertations on application scenarios. International development organizations and agencies could help with this by offering funding and research locales. On the other side, academics should more systematically invite their practicing colleagues to collaborate through cooperative teaching and training, and universities could make it easier for faculty to enrich their teaching and research through work in applied settings. Faculty, students, practicing anthropologists, and community members can all collaborate in "hands-on" community projects of the sort van Willigen describes.

Chambers's chapter explores ways of making applied anthropology more central to the college curriculum, where it now exists mainly as an elective, if taught at all. Viewing applied anthropology as a full-fledged fifth subdiscipline—with subject matter and methods comparable to those of the other four fields—would, in Chambers's view, lead to its most effective incorporation. Most texts, he notes, do not accord applied anthropology this centrality. Either they ignore it altogether, or they confine it to a single chapter at the end. Practice, he suggests, should be incorporated throughout our texts, as an intrinsic part of anthropology.

We also teach and learn applied anthropology outside academia. As Tice observes, practicing anthropologists have to teach their field constantly, because they work in so many contexts in which sociocultural anthropology is unfamiliar. But *we also learn in such settings*. Many of us, myself included, never imagined as graduate students or young academics that we would eventually do applied anthropology. But the world has changed, more rapidly and radically than we imagined, and most of our field sites have been affected by global forces. Academic anthropologists find ourselves invited to consult about the direction of change in nations, regions, even communities where we originally did "academic" research focusing on "theoretical" issues. And we accept consultancies for varied reasons: (1) They allow us to return to "the field" without the paperwork and uncertainty of the research grant application process. (2) They let us play a role in advocating, designing, implementing, and evaluating policies involving people we know and care about. (3) Practice enriches theory: applied anthropology offers research opportunities; the linkages and transformations in the modern world system are intrinsically interesting.

Many scholars have trained themselves in applied anthropology by reading and through personal experience with projects and the agencies and individuals that design and implement them. As consultants, we benefit from our own informal internships. In this role, we use our eyes and ears, as ethnographers, to study people, organizations, and institutions involved in social change. Sometimes, especially working full time for such agencies, we feel frustrated. Often we have to argue perspectives and positions unfamiliar to, or challenged by, associates. (This, of course, also happens in academia.) We have to fit into "results-driven" deadline-oriented organizations and sometimes confront goals we regard as unwise. As advocates, we argue for our views, but they do not always prevail. Tice's article describes some of the frustrations faced by full-time practicing anthropologists.

There is feedback between academic and applied anthropology, as my own experience illustrates. My applied anthropology career began in 1981 with a short-term consulting assignment in Madagascar, where I had previously done (nonapplied) research on the social, political, and economic correlates of the expansion of wet rice cultivation. My 1981 assignment was to find out why an irrigation project was failing. That brief fieldwork acquainted me with a development project that did not fit its social, cultural, and demographic setting, and it led to an invitation by the World Bank to do a comparative study of sixty-eight economic development projects from all over the world. The goal was to determine the extent to which social and cultural factors had been considered during planning, whether the project was culturally appropriate or inappropriate, and the effects of such factors on the project's economic success. That comparative study, in which development projects became my research focus, enabled me to explore, and eventually contribute to, theories of development, innovation, and social change (Kottak 1990, 1991).

I concluded that to maximize social and economic benefits, projects must (1) be culturally compatible, (2) respond to locally perceived needs, (3) involve people in planning and carrying out the changes that affect them, (4) harness traditional organizations, and (5) be flexible. In my comparative study, I found that the compatible and successful projects avoided the fallacy of overinnovation (too much change). Instead, they (intuitively) applied "Romer's rule," named for the paleontologist A. S. Romer (1960), who formulated it to explain the evolution of land-dwelling vertebrates from fish. The ancestors of land animals lived in pools of water that dried up seasonally. Fins evolved into legs to enable those animals to get back to water when particular pools dried up. Thus an innovation (legs) that later proved essential to land life originated to maintain life in the water.

Romer's lesson is that an innovation that evolves to *maintain* a system can play a major role in *changing* that system. Evolution occurs in increments. Systems take a series of small steps to maintain themselves, and they gradually change. Romer's rule can be applied to economic development, which, after all, is a process of (planned) socioeconomic transformation. Thus, we would expect people to resist projects that require major changes in their daily lives, especially ones that interfere with subsistence pursuits. People usually want to change just enough to keep what they have. Motives for modifying behavior come from the traditional culture and the small concerns of ordinary life. Peasants' values are not such abstract ones as "learning a better way," "progressing," "increasing technical know-how," "improving efficiency," or "adopting modern techniques." Instead, their objectives are down-to-earth and specific ones. People want to improve yields in a rice field, amass resources for a ceremony, get a child through school, or pay taxes. The goals and values of subsistence producers differ from those of people who produce for cash, just as they differ from the intervention philosophies of development planners. Different value systems must be considered during planning.

My comparative study also exposed me to what I came to call the fallacy of underdifferentiation—the tendency to view "the less-developed countries" as more alike than they are. Development agencies have often ignored cultural diversity (for example, between Brazil and Burundi) and adopted a uniform approach to deal with very different sets of people. Neglecting cultural diversity, many projects also have tried to impose incompatible property notions and social units. Most often, the faulty social design assumes either (1) individualistic productive units that are privately owned by an individual or couple and worked by a nuclear family or (2) cooperatives that are at least partially based on models from the former Eastern bloc and socialist countries.

The fieldwork and comparison I have done in applied anthropology have consistently fed back on my academic work, providing opportunities, practice, classroom material, and research topics for me and my students—graduate and undergraduate. I like applied anthropology because it offers me—an academic anthropologist—new and varied opportunities to do research on change. For me, a key role of the *applied* anthropologist is to facilitate "bottom up" social change. Doing so entails going to local people to discover their wants and perceived needs at the very beginning of project planning. "Participatory development" is currently a buzz phrase among international planners and NGOs, but participatory development runs the risk of being more an externally imposed requirement than an emanation of a local setting. That is, many donors seem to be taking the attitude, "Participation is a good thing; let's get people to do it"; or even, "We'll force participation on them if they want our money." Paradoxically, "participation," perceived as end rather than means, seems to have joined or supplanted "progress" as an external value being pursued for its own sake in a new variant on modernization theory.

Mandelbaum (1963, 10) believed that studies in applied anthropology "show how theoretical concepts are deployed empirically and how the empirical data feed back into the development of theory." My own experience leaves me with no doubt that theory and practice are intertwined.

References

Escobar, A. 1991. "Anthropology and the Development Encounter: The Making and Marketing of Development Anthropology." *American Ethnologist* 18:658–682.

Kottak, C. P. 1990. "Culture and Economic Development." *American Anthropologist* 92(3):723–731.

———. 1991. "When People Don't Come First: Some Lessons from Completed Projects." In *Putting People First: Sociological Variables in Rural Development*, 2d. ed., edited by Michael Cernea, 429–464. New York: Oxford University Press.

———. 1994. *Anthropology: The Exploration of Human Diversity*. 6th ed. New York: McGraw-Hill.

Mandelbaum, D. G. 1963. "The Transmission of Anthropological Culture." In *The Teaching of Anthropology*, edited by D. G. Mandelbaum, G. W. Lasker, and E. M. Albert, 1–21. Berkeley: University of California Press.

Piddington, Ralph. 1970. "Action Anthropology." In *Applied Anthropology: Readings in the Uses of the Science of Man*, edited by James Clifton, 127–143. Boston: Houghton Mifflin.

Romer, A. S. 1960. *Man and the Vertebrates*. 3rd ed., vol. 1. Harmondsworth, England: Penguin, 1960.

Contested Territories
Teaching the Uses of Anthropology

Erve Chambers

Two factors have proven significant in determining how applied anthropology is introduced into the undergraduate curricula of particular academic institutions. The first is the attitude of other anthropologists toward the work done by their applied colleagues. In this regard, considerable progress has been made during the past two decades. The rapid growth of applied anthropology, particularly in the employment of anthropologists outside academic settings, has contributed to increased interest and support at the departmental level. However, this support is not consistent across departments. Some faculty continue to resist introducing applied anthropology into their curricula, and there is considerable variation in the manner in which the subject is offered in other departments.

The second factor, of equal importance, relates to how applied anthropologists view their contribution to anthropology and thereby the way they feel their specialty should be taught. There remain striking differences in this regard. The greatest of these is between those who see applied anthropology solely as the production of research that has the potential to be useful, leaving the determination of actual utility to others, and those who argue that special knowledge and new professional roles are required to ensure and to monitor the uses of anthropological knowledge.

In considering these issues, it is useful to start by making a distinction between anthropology as a *profession* and anthropology as a *discipline*. The professional aspect of anthropology relates primarily to how we perceive ourselves vis-à-vis other fields of endeavor. Here we are concerned with matters of employment opportunity, training and education, ethics, and the representation of anthropology to the rest of the world. The disciplinary aspect of anthropology relates, on the other hand, to the development of that body of knowledge with which we most commonly identify—the subject areas, methods, and perspectives that inform our work. Here we are most often interested in the independent and critical advancement of our inquiries.

This distinction is offered to point out that most of the recent progress that has been made in representing and advocating applied anthropology falls within the realm of professional concerns. We have, over the past decade or so, made great strides in identifying a broad range of employment opportunities for anthropologists, in establishing a realm of practice that is independent of academic employment, in developing graduate training programs devoted to application, and in addressing some of the ethical concerns that arise in applied work. In these areas, applied anthropology has become institutionalized to an extent never before realized by our profession.

We have made less progress in terms of realizing the relationship between this burgeoning interest in application and the rest of our discipline. This lack of progress is partly reflected in the rather limited and sometimes misguided ways in which applied anthropology continues to be represented in many undergraduate programs. For the most part, applied anthropology is given little attention as a distinct subject for undergraduate instruction. Whatever attention it does receive is more often than not related to matters of profession rather than of discipline. Examples of application might be used, for example, to demonstrate that a background in anthropology can lead to interesting employment opportunities, or to show how anthropological insights might help us better understand particular human problems. But only rarely have undergraduates been encouraged to think of applied anthropology as an increasingly specialized body of knowledge, reflecting a distinct sense of inquiry and discipline.

When considering ways applied anthropology might be better incorporated into undergraduate education, any suggested approach will convey additional ideas and assumptions about how application fits within our discipline—how important it is, how it is to be represented, and how much attention should be allotted to this aspect of our work. Approaching the topic in this manner, there appear to be three major modes for integrating applied anthropology within the undergraduate curriculum. Each of these approaches assumes some degree of sympathy with the task, and they are thereby distinguished from views still held by some nonapplied colleagues, that there is no place at all for applied anthropology in the undergraduate curriculum.

The first approach can be characterized as the *"wait and see" approach*. Here, the utility of anthropology and its place in contemporary human problem solving is acknowledged, but little attention is actually devoted to the subject of applied anthropology. The sense of application that underlies this approach is that practice is entirely incidental to basic inquiry. The applied problem, whatever it might be, derives from outside the discipline. If the insights garnered from basic anthropological research prove useful in better understanding human problems, that is well and good, but there is no need to emphasize or dwell on these practical but tangential concerns. The idea that anthropology can be made more useful through the exploration of those factors that lead to effective application is absent. This approach has its roots in an early approach to applied anthropology that limited the role of the anthropologist to the production of knowledge about others and proscribed direct involvement in decision making or human intervention (Malinowski 1929).

With this approach, it is assumed that no special knowledge or preparation is required of the anthropologist who becomes involved in applied work. The criterion of success or failure is simply good anthropological research. It follows that there is no need to pay much attention to applied anthropology as a part of the undergraduate curriculum; there is, in effect, no special avenue of inquiry that informs application. There are no particular skills to be acquired, and there is no subject matter to be learned apart from that of general anthropology. This remains a fairly common view in our discipline. Unfortunately, it is the view of applied anthropology that most often informs introductory anthropology texts.

The second approach can be thought of as the *"on the other hand" view.* Here, applied anthropology is accorded some recognition and some importance within the undergraduate curriculum but nearly always as a separate subject. This recognition might be manifested as a chapter in an introductory text, as an undergraduate elective devoted to applied anthropology, or even in the development of applied modules, certificate programs, or practical internship opportunities for undergraduate anthropology majors. There has, over the past decade or so, been considerable movement in this regard. Part of the development appears to be a direct result of student demand, and much of the rest can be attributed to a growing number of younger faculty with an interest in applied anthropology.

What is of concern about this approach is the lack of integration of applied coursework with the rest of the anthropology curriculum. While it is a major step in the right direction to acknowledge that there is a particular body of experience and knowledge that can be identified and taught as "applied," the fairly routine treatment of this realm as separate from general anthropology leads us down the same path as the "wait and see" approach. Applied anthropology is still an option, more highly valued in this instance, but it is not generally deemed a necessary subject for the instruction of undergraduates. It has become an elective and is not yet viewed as a part of that core of instruction that describes and informs the discipline as a whole.

The "on the other hand" approach is becoming a fairly common way to represent applied anthropology in the undergraduate curriculum. It is often regarded as an option to be offered to those students who are struggling to justify an interest in anthropology but who seem to have no interest in academic careers. Importantly, both the "wait and see" and the "on the other hand" approaches derive from the temptation to regard applied work as being somehow relevant to our professional concerns, but also as having little relation to those core themes and inquiries that constitute the discipline.

A third approach can be called the *"fifth field" view.* This approach suggests that our teaching of applied anthropology might be better informed, and certainly more thorough, if application were regarded as a major subfield of our discipline, equal in bearing and potential to those four subfields that have traditionally described anthropology. In this view, applied anthropology becomes that part of our discipline that is concerned in fundamental ways with the relationships between anthropological knowledge and its uses (Chambers 1987). These relationships are no longer taken for granted or closeted away (as they normally are in the "on the other hand" approach), and they are no longer easily dismissed (as they tend to be in the "wait and see" approach). Rather, the correspondence between knowledge and utility becomes the subject of inquiry that describes this subfield and serves to inform the discipline as a whole. This approach maintains that it is as important to anthropology for us to understand how decisions concerning human well-being are made in the "real world" as it is for us to understand how anthropological knowledge is attained within the parameters of the academic discipline. When this view is integrated into the undergraduate curriculum, students have the opportunity to consider that knowledge needs to be judged in terms of both its validity and usefulness, and that these two criteria are not always the same.

This approach is nowhere fully realized. It is, however, implied in any number of professional decisions made in recent times. The fact that applied anthropology is offered in this volume as a subject matter that should be considered along with our four traditional subfields is representative of one such decision. This decision is replicated in the institutional development of some leading professional associations and in the editorial bodies of some professional publications; to some extent it is beginning to be represented in departments of anthropology. In other ways too, although much less apparently, this approach is also beginning to influence decisions about what we teach our students. This is almost inevitable, considering the large numbers of younger colleagues in academia who are now bringing significant applied interest and experience to their teaching jobs.

How might a view of applied anthropology as a fifth major subfield help reshape undergraduate education in our discipline? First, with such a view, there would be no more introductory text material that either ignored application altogether or relegated the subject to a chapter near the end of the text. The aim would no longer be simply to acknowledge the possibility of applied work; rather, the goal would be to describe its potential in relation to the discipline as a whole. In this vein, relevant applied work could be integrated into each chapter of a text. Such a text might begin by pointing out that applied anthropology is not a recent phenomenon at all but is a presence that has informed the field, tested mettle, and helped shape inquiries from the start of the discipline. The tendency to dismiss this connection is actually a fairly recent phenomenon, based in part on attempts to reinvent American anthropology during the 1960s.

The "fifth field" approach is consistent with a recent trend in anthropology, represented by a shift from a focus on the uniqueness and durability of cultures to an interest in the processes by which cultures interrelate and are transformed. Applied anthropology anticipates this interest in that its subject is almost invariably cultural interaction and process rather than cultural stasis. The focal points of application are those areas where meaning systems intersect and where such issues as cultural conflict, breakdown, and authenticity become paramount (Agar 1983).

Any curriculum that has as its aim the integration, rather than simply the inclusion, of applied anthropology will incorporate consideration of such problems as the correspondence between practice and theory, and more particularly, the relationships between the generation of knowledge and its uses. In the past, anthropologists have most generally posited a direct and uncomplicated relationship between research and utility, assuming that valid research should lead to good decisions (and consequently blaming the rest of the world when anthropological insight is ignored or misused). The recent, and often more critical, experience of applied anthropology has begun to challenge this view in informative ways. There is a growing appreciation of the idea that an empirical understanding of a human problem is not necessarily a sufficient means for arriving at solutions, or that understanding *what is* seldom provides the full means for determining what *might be* or *should be*. In some respects, a number of applied anthropologists have found common cause with recent, more introspective trends in the discipline, such as critical and interpretive theory. Applied anthropology provides the opportunity to explore ideas of usefulness not only with the aim of identifying the criteria of effective uses but also with a more critical eye on the fragility of all human science as well as on the role "neutral" anthropological inquiries have sometimes played in the domination of others.

Applied anthropology has already contributed substantially to helping reshape the way anthropological work is done as well as where it is done. More systematic inclusion of applied endeavors in our undergraduate curriculum should greatly expand student appreciation of the variety of settings in which anthropologists have worked. This will challenge the view, still apparent in many introductions to the field, of anthropology as a field of study devoted almost exclusively to long-term, often solitary field research in relatively small and isolated communities. It will also help expand student awareness of the range of methods and research techniques currently available to anthropologists. An understanding of the different models that have been offered for applied research and practice will provide students with an increased appreciation of the ethical and moral dilemmas that are inherent in all human inquiries.

Finally, applied anthropology offers, and in a few departments has already begun to demonstrate, the potential for experiencing the value and practicality of anthropology at firsthand. Whether this is developed in brief classroom exercises, in field courses, or in practica and internships, the opportunity for students actually to participate in the discovery process that is central to anthropological understanding is greatly expanded whenever applied anthropology becomes central to the undergraduate curriculum.

Declaring applied anthropology as a fifth field remains controversial. Perhaps there is another way to make the argument and achieve the aims described above. Regardless, consideration of the unique potential of applied anthropology leads us to two important points. First, it is to the benefit of the discipline as a whole to move ahead in fully *integrating* the work of applied anthropology into the undergraduate curriculum. Second, there is much for all of us, students and professionals alike, to explore in the extent to which applied work (applied *theory,* if you will) can challenge and help shape our view of the relationships between knowledge and its uses. This final potential seems of considerable importance in a time when the value of anthropology, and indeed of all the social sciences, is being questioned both from within and without.

The recent popularity of applied anthropology and its increased institutionalization within the profession has begun to affect the way we teach and what we choose to teach. The next decades are likely to see many of these issues brought to the fore, resulting in an increased *intellectualization* of applied anthropology within the discipline. Those who remain skeptical and persist in viewing applied anthropology as a current fad from which we will hopefully recover are almost sure to be disappointed. It seems much more likely that applied anthropology will continue to shape professional concerns and, as a result, will also begin to have a more profound influence on our sense of the discipline. It follows that this influence will contribute in many ways to the view of anthropology that is conveyed to students.

References

Agar, Michael H. 1983. "Inference and Schema: An Ethnographic View." *Human Studies* 6:53–66.

Chambers, Erve. 1987. "Applied Anthropology in the Post-Vietnam Era: Anticipations and Ironies." *Annual Review of Anthropology* 16:309–337.

Malinowski, Bronislaw. 1929. "Practical Anthropology." *Africa* 2:23–38.

Innovative Applied Anthropology Research Practices Should Be Used in the Precollegiate and Undergraduate Classroom

JOHN VAN WILLIGEN

Since the emergence of the discipline, the practitioners of applied anthropology[1] have served as important sources for new theory and practice that has been incorporated into teaching anthropology in higher education. There are also influences in precollegiate education but this appears limited when compared to collegiate education. In this chapter, I discuss this topic from two perspectives. First I consider the potential contribution of applied anthropology to precollegiate and undergraduate education. I conclude with a discussion of the incorporation of new theory and practice of applied anthropology into the discipline itself in historic and contemporary perspectives.

Applied and practicing anthropology is an important source for materials for precollegiate and undergraduate training. There are three major areas of potential contribution. These are (1) collaborative models of action for dealing with societal problems at the local level (Stull and Schensul 1987; Paine 1985); (2) comprehensive knowledge of the "ethnography of social issues"; and (3) a workable, accessible, and comprehensive research methodology. It is possible to think of these as three separate areas or as an integrated problem-solving method. I do not want to create the impression that there is a single, unified applied anthropology research and action method or that applied anthropologists would be well served by such a thing. Nevertheless, it might be useful to identify some of the attributes of such a unified research and action method as we discuss the incorporation of new theory and practice into education.

I think there are special circumstances operating right now that increase the utility of what practicing applied anthropologists know and do and therefore increase the potential for incorporation into undergraduate and precollegiate education. These circumstances relate to the nature of the educational reform process in the United States. Kentucky, for example, is currently involved in a comprehensive educational reform effort. I have seen certain themes in the reform movement that create needs that applied anthropologists can meet by contributing to curriculum.

Educational change may entail increased emphasis on (1) "learning-by-doing," (2) cooperative learning or group process learning, (3) production of real products rather than test scores, and (4) articulation with the community and its problems. Reformers hope that students will be much less passive and will learn more by doing. Increasingly they will have to show an actual portfolio of work rather than a simple list of test scores. More class work may involve cooperative group learning experiences to emulate work situations. There may also be increased commitment to multidisciplinary perspectives on community problems. I think this will increase demand or potential for use by undergraduate and precollegiate educators for instruction in applied anthropology practice.

What are some of the characteristics of the research methodologies used by applied anthropologists? Applied anthropological research appears to have the following properties: (1) It makes extensive use of qualitative data collected through direct research observation and interviewing. (2) These data are often augmented by quantitative data collected from a random sample of people through the use of standardized survey instruments that include questions that are ethnographically grounded. (3) Quantitative data analysis makes use of simple and widely known descriptive and inferential statistics including frequencies, measures of central tendency, t-tests, and chi-square.[2] (4) Research is almost always done in teams that contain persons other than anthropologists, for "audiences" other than other anthropologists, and may involve collaboration with community or agency people. (5) The concepts that underlie the research are often meaningful to the people being researched (that is, emic) and they may be relevant to policy makers and the general public. (6) Extensive use is made of the new group process research methods[3] such as reconnaissance surveys (Chambers 1990; Molnar 1991; van Willigen and DeWalt 1985), rapid assessment procedures (Scrimshaw and Hurtado 1987), and focus groups (Merton 1987; Merton, Fiske, and Kendall 1990; Krueger 1988). This discussion concentrates on the last category, using reconnaissance surveys to illustrate how this might work.

The group process research methods are well suited to use in precollegiate and undergraduate settings where one wants "learning-by-doing," cooperative learning, real-life products, and empowered educational activities. I refer to them as group process research methods because they all require skill in facilitating communication in small groups for various purposes. These purposes always include group interviewing and may frequently require group goal setting and research design, and data analysis through group discussion. In addition to their shared group process features, these techniques often place an emphasis on the use of secondary data.

These techniques are useful in precollegiate and undergraduate education because they are accessible and can be completed quickly. Accessibility is based on their relatively natural and nontechnical nature. One can, with very simple instruction or a trained group leader, just do it. At the same time, because of the clarity of their focus and emphasis on teamwork, one can design, collect data, analyze, and write up a worthwhile project quickly. Meaningful enquiry can be completed in a week or less. The write-up and documentation may take longer, but informed conclusions will be formed very quickly by the group.

These techniques were developed to save time and money, to facilitate multidisciplinary understanding, and to root research in the realities of real life

(Hildebrand 1981). This can be seen in the following definitions. What is termed *rapid rural appraisal* is described as "a study used as the starting point for understanding a local situation; carried out by a multidisciplinary team; lasting at least four days but not more than three weeks, and based on information collected in advance, direct observation and interviews where it is assumed that all relevant questions cannot be identified in advance" (Beebe 1985, 2). The box below lists the key features of the reconnaissance survey.

Transposing this research method to the precollegiate and undergraduate classroom is highly feasible and would serve many useful purposes. My proposal is that the students enrolled in a class can be redefined as a rapid reconnaissance research team and, with training, carry out enquiry into school and community problems. In this way they could contribute to an "ethnography of social issues" mentioned earlier. This work could be carried out in collaboration with school administrators and community members, thus expressing another dominant theme in contemporary applied anthropology research work. It would seem that work of this type has the potential to contribute to individual problem-solving ability as well as the students' capacity to work in teams. These practices can be inexpensive and have the advantage of being easy to rehearse.

The incorporation of these kinds of practices in education would be facilitated by various activities. It would be very useful for an anthropologist to prepare a short, inexpensive, concrete methods guide for the nonfiction market for the appropriate school level. This should be targeted at social science methods in general. I am not aware of any high school-level social science methods texts at present. Such a book could include chapters on ethnographic process, field notes, survey, interviewing, preparing interview schedules, sampling, and analysis including some discussion of statistics. As most teachers will not have experience in these areas, it may also be useful to prepare a video that can help the teacher model the activity. The methods handbook could be focused on community issues, perhaps even a single issue. There may be a potential for a number of methods publications for the high school student that anthropolo-

---

Reconnaissance Survey
Key Practice Features

- Topical outline guides data collection.
- Secondary data are used extensively.
- Purposive sampling procedures are used.
- On-site observation is important.
- Data are processed as experience.
- Data needs are redefined daily by team.
- Analysis is based on group discussion process.

Franzel 1984

gists could provide. One place to gain perspective on this is to consult *School Library Journal, the Magazine of Children's, Young Adult and School Librarians.* This journal publishes reviews of instructional material for precollegiate settings. A publisher of nonfiction materials of this type is Franklin Watt.

The research methods material that is the core of this idea can be expanded to include the other dimensions discussed earlier. In the last ten years there has been a tremendous improvement in documentation of applied anthropology that would serve well as a foundation for the full development of comprehensive curriculum in the applied anthropology research and action method for undergraduate and precollegiate education.

Publications that would support the inclusion of applied and practicing anthropology into both precollegiate and undergraduate education are enumerated here. The fall 1991 issue of *Practicing Anthropology* has a section entitled "Undergraduates in Applied Research," edited by Cynthia A. Cone, that contains several articles describing useful examples of the incorporation of applied research into undergraduate education (Cone 1991; Stoffle, Jensen, and Halmo 1991; Trotter 1991; Garcia 1991; O'Connell 1991). Also of use are the recently published case books. These include *Anthropological Praxis, Translating Knowledge into Action* (Wulff and Fiske 1987), *Collaborative Research and Social Change* (Stull and Schensul 1987), *Advocacy and Anthropology: First Encounters* (Paine 1985); *Anthropology and Development in North Africa and the Middle East*, (Salem-Murdock, Horowitz, and Sella 1990), *Practicing Development Anthropology* (Green 1986), *Applied Anthropology in America: Past Contributions and Future Directions* (Eddy and Partridge 1987) and *Making Our Research Useful: Case Studies in the Utilization of Anthropological Knowledge* (van Willigen, Rylko-Bauer, and McElroy 1989). Also useful are the Training Manuals in Applied Anthropology published by the American Anthropological Association; the Bulletin Series of the National Association for the Practice of Anthropology (NAPA); and *Practicing Anthropology.*

In addition to the potential contribution of applied anthropology to precollegiate and undergraduate education, the relationship between applied anthropology and the rest of the discipline should receive attention. Application has always been an important source for theory and practice in the discipline; yet, there are times when this relationship is not clear. There is no reason that the techniques discussed here cannot be applied to graduate education in the discipline. Often, it seems that the historic linkages between basic and applied anthropology are forgotten as we attempt to understand the discipline historically and from the perspective of contemporary cohorts of graduate students.

Applied anthropology was important in the establishment of the original academic institutions of the discipline, as evidenced in the early history of academic anthropology in Britain and the United States. The first British departments were justified on the basis of the practical contribution of anthropology to British colonial administration.[4] The founding departments of the discipline were "applied training programs" preparing practitioners for work in colonial administration. In fact, the term *applied anthropology* appears to have been used first to describe the program at Cambridge. Early faculty consisted of practitioners turned academics. The earliest professional anthropologists were engaged in research or instruction motivated by policy questions. In the United States, the facts are somewhat different but the meanings are the same: the first organizations to hire anthropologists were policy research operations. The Bureau of American Ethnology was intended as a policy research operation in the name of *applied ethnology*—so termed in an early report of that bureau.[5] It is my view that theoretical anthropology grew out of applied anthropology. Historical accounts of the development of the discipline do not make this point (Voget 1975; Harris 1968).

Further topical growth of the discipline is largely based on application. Anthropologists seeking data that addressed policy problems often led the way into new areas of inquiry. Early research into political life, land tenure, labor, legal anthropology, medical anthropology, urban life, nutrition, and other topics were supported as applied research efforts. This pattern of adaptive radiation continues to the present. One would expect that this will accelerate because of the radical increase in the numbers of anthropologists involved in applied work and that applied anthropologists will continue to make a mark on teaching at various levels. I think the methods that have been learned through the application process can benefit and improve the outcome of contemporary basic anthropology training and should be incorporated into the training process at all levels.

Notes

1. When I use the term *applied anthropology*, I mean cultural or social anthropology. Clearly the applications of archaeology, biological anthropology, and linguistic anthropology are very important and socially useful and could be discussed in this context. Further throughout this chapter I use *applied anthropology* and *practicing anthropology* interchangeably. There may be contexts in which it is useful to make a distinction between these terms and their related concepts.

2. Although reports frequently contain numeric data, the analysis is often limited to frequencies presented in numeric or graphical form.

3. Various group process approaches are reviewed in *Soundings: Rapid and Reliable Research Methods for Practicing Anthropologists* (van Willigen and Finan 1991).

4. Early development of academic anthropology in Great Britain was based on the justification of potential application. Many early faculty were in fact ex-colonial administrators. At Cambridge, what Fortes calls the "first inaugural lecture" on anthropology was given by Sir Richard Temple who was formerly of the Indian Civil Service. Other early faculty were T. C. Hodson and J. H. Hutton, both former civil servants. E. B. Tylor received the first academic appointment in anthropology. Tylor was appointed Reader in Anthropology at Oxford. Justification of this position included the training needs of the colonial regime; that is, the first anthropology department was an applied anthropology training program. What may be the first use of the term *applied anthropology* appears in an article that describes the Oxford

program. C. H. Read wrote, "The great importance to an imperial nation of what may be called 'Applied Anthropology' has been pointed out so often that it is unnecessary to insist upon it further here" (1906, 56).

5. The Bureau of American Ethnology (BAE) was founded "to produce results that would be of practical value in the administration of Indian affairs" (Powell 1881). Thus, the first organization to hire anthropologists in the United States was an applied research organization, not an academic program. Later annual reports of the bureau spoke of "applied ethnology." Their contribution to theory was significant. The term *acculturation* was first used in a BAE document.

References

Beebe, James. 1985. "Rapid Rural Appraisal: The Critical First Step in a Farming Systems Approach to Research." Networking Paper No. 5. Gainesville: University of Florida, Farming Systems Support Project.

Chambers, Robert. 1990. "Rapid and Participatory Rural Appraisal." *Appropriate Technology* 16:14–16.

Cone, Cynthia A. 1991. "Teaching Applied Anthropology as Humanistic Social Science." *Practicing Anthropology* 13(4):17–20.

Eddy, Elizabeth M., and William L. Partridge, eds. 1987. *Applied Anthropology in America: Past Contributions and Future Directions*. 2nd ed. New York: Columbia University Press.

Fortes, Meyer. 1953. *Social Anthropology at Cambridge Since 1900*. Cambridge, England: Cambridge University Press.

Franzel, Steven. 1984. "Comparing the Results of an Informal Survey with Those of a Formal Survey: A Case Study of Farming Systems Research/Extension (FSR/E) in Middle Kerinyage, Kenya." Unpublished paper presented at FSR/E Symposium, Manhattan, Kansas.

Garcia, Mikel Hogan. 1991. "Teaching Theory and Practice: A Constructivist Approach." *Practicing Anthropology* 13(4):11–14.

Green, Edward, ed. 1986. *Practicing Development Anthropology*. Boulder, Colo.: Westview.

Harris, Marvin. 1968. *The Rise of Anthropological Theory: A History of Theories of Culture*. New York: Crowell.

Hildebrand, Peter. 1981. "Combining Disciplines in Rapid Rural Appraisal: The Sondeo Approach." *Agricultural Administration* 8:423–432.

Krueger, Richard A. 1988. *Focus Groups: A Practical Guide for Applied Research*. Newbury Park, Calif: Sage.

Merton, Robert K. 1987. "The Focused Interview and Focus Groups: Continuities and Discontinuities." *Public Opinion Quarterly* 51:550–566.

Merton, Robert K., Marjorie Fiske, and Patricia L. Kendall. 1990. *The Focused Interview, a Manual of Problems and Procedures*. New York: Free Press.

Molnar, Augusta. 1991. "Rapid Rural Appraisal Methodology Applied to Project Planning and Implementation in Natural Resource Management." In *Soundings: Rapid and Reliable Research Methods for Practicing Anthropologists*. NAPA Bulletin 10, edited by John van Willigen and Timothy Finan.

O'Connell, Barbara H. 1991. "Becoming an Anthropologist through an Applied Program." *Practicing Anthropology* 13(4):14–16.

Paine, Robert. 1985. *Advocacy and Anthropology: First Encounters*. St. John's, Newfoundland: Institute of Social and Economic Research, Memorial University.

Powell, John Wesley. 1881. *First Annual Report of the Bureau of American Ethnology* (1879–80). Washington, D.C.: Government Printing Office.

Read, C. H. 1906. "Anthropology at the Universities." *Man* 38:56–59.

Salem-Murdock, Muneera, Michael M. Horowitz, and Monica Sella, eds. 1990. *Anthropology and Development in North Africa and the Middle East*. Boulder, Colo.: Westview.

Scrimshaw, Susan C. M., and Elena Hurtado. 1987. *Rapid Assessment Procedures: For Nutrition and Primary Health Care*. Tokyo: United Nations University.

Stoffle, Richard W., Florence V. Jensen, and David B. Halmo. 1991. "The Reciprocal Development Model for Field Schools." *Practicing Anthropology* 13(4):3–6.

Stull, Donald D., and Jean J. Schensul, eds. 1987. *Collaborative Research and Social Change*. Boulder, Colo.: Westview.

Trotter, Robert T. II. 1991. "Ethnographic Research Training at a National Park." *Practicing Anthropology* 13(4):7–10.

van Willigen, John, and Billie R. DeWalt. 1985. *Training Manual in Policy Ethnography*. Washington, D.C.: American Anthropological Association.

———, and Timothy Finan. 1991. "Soundings: Rapid and Reliable Research Methods for Practicing Anthropologists." *NAPA Bulletin 10*.

———, Barbara Rylko-Bauer, and Ann McElroy, eds. 1989. *Making Our Research Useful: Case Studies in the Utilization of Anthropological Knowledge*. Boulder, Colo.: Westview.

Voget, Fred W. 1975. *A History of Ethnology*. New York: Holt, Rinehart and Winston.

Wulff, Robert M., and Shirley J. Fiske, eds. 1987. *Anthropological Praxis: Translating Knowledge into Action*. Boulder, Colo.: Westview.

Reflections on Teaching Anthropology for Use in the Public and Private Sector

KARIN E. TICE

Flint, Michigan — It is before 8:00 A.M. on a snowy cold morning in January. I am "hanging out" at the building where youth participating in the Michigan Neighborhood Youth Corps must sign in before going to their work sites. I spend the rest of the morning visiting work sites and talking with youth and their site supervisors about their work and their experiences in the Corps. We walk through the abandoned buildings they are renovating as we talk. Then I meet the program supervisors for lunch at a run-down inner-city Chinese restaurant, conduct an instrumented interview, and discuss the programs strengths and weaknesses. One person asks for my business card. He announces loudly, "She has a Ph.D. and lives in Ann Arbor." There is complete silence. I start to feel like someone just announced I have leprosy when the supervisors begin to comment . . ." You don't dress like someone with a Ph.D. and you certainly don't act it." "Ph.D.s from Ann Arbor are snobs." I explained that I was a social anthropologist, talked about what that meant to me, and told them about my work in Latin America. They seemed to be quite interested and said they had never heard about anthropology. They invited me back to Flint any time.

Battle Creek, Michigan — Dressed in a suit and wearing high heels, I join a room full of community foundation executive directors and trustees at a session being held on community foundation growth at the new W. K. Kellogg Foundation headquarters. As part of evaluating a five-year, thirty-five-million dollar, grant from the W. K. Kellogg Foundation to the Council of Michigan Foundations, I am attending one of the sessions at the Council's annual conference. The room is filled with professionals. Some have Ph.D.s; others have law or medical degrees; all have passed through the halls of academe in some form or another. During the two days I am at the conference, people often ask me about my professional background. Saying that I have a Ph.D. in social anthropology brings either confused looks and follow-up questions about what digging up bones has to do with my work as a program evaluator, or looks of awe as if I were something rare and exotic.

Whatever their reactions, neighborhood program supervisors in inner-city Flint and executive directors of foundations have something in common. No one really knows much, if anything, about what an anthropologist is or does. Images of digging up bones, measuring skulls, and doing ethnography in far-away places do not accurately reflect the wide range of work that anthropologists do, especially anthropologists who work outside academia. Examples of the types of positions held by professional anthropologists include social science adviser for the Agency for International Development; program director for the U.S. Department of Commerce; legislative secretary for the Friends Committee on National Legislation; director of research for Public Sector Consultants Inc.; project director for the Micronesian Endowment for Historic Preservation; senior vice president of Development Alternatives Inc.; acting director for the Center for Organizational Risk Reduction; ethnomusicologist at the American Folklife Center at the Library of Congress; senior anthropologist for the National Park Service; consultant for the Rockefeller Foundation; administrator of research for the New York City Public Schools Division of Strategic Planning, Research and Development; senior research scientist at the General Motors Research Laboratories; researcher for the Navajo Nation Historic Preservation Department; and refugee services coordinator for a State Department of Social and Rehabilitational Services. These are only a few of the titles held by professional anthropologists and do not include work done by applied archaeologists, forensic anthropologists, educational anthropologists, and medical anthropologists with cities, police departments, hospitals, community health services, and schools.

This chapter combines personal reflections about the usefulness of my doctoral training in an applied anthropology program to my current work with information that will offer a broader view of professional anthropologists in the United States—who they are, the training they have received, and the work they do. The last third of the chapter is based on the perspective and information I gained while serving for two years as the secretary/editor for the National Association for the Practice of Anthropology (NAPA). I identify training and professional development needs, review what is already in place to meet some of those needs, and identify areas that need to be strengthened and improved. Finally, I offer some thoughts about teaching applied anthropology.

Professional Anthropologists in the Workplace

Professional anthropologists work in both academic and nonacademic settings. Over 50 percent of the individuals listed in the NAPA directory work in nonacademic settings (25 percent in the private sector, 14 percent in the public sector, 11 percent for nonprofit organizations, and 8 percent in other settings).[1] Most practitioners working outside academia in the United States are based in large urban areas including Washington, D.C., New York City, San Francisco, Chicago, the Los Angeles metropolitan area, and the Detroit-Ann Arbor area. The remaining NAPA members (44 percent) listed in the directory are academically based. Primary areas of expertise for professional anthropologists, whether based inside or outside academia, are evaluation (31 percent), public health and health services (29 percent), social impact assessment (24 percent), private sector organizations (23 percent), agricultural development (14 percent), natural resources (13 percent), education (12 percent), and legal (4 percent). The American Anthropological Association (AAA) 1990 survey of anthropologists with Ph.D.s shows that 30 percent of anthropologists with doctorates surveyed (166) work in nonacademic settings.

Professional anthropologists holding advanced degrees serve in a wide range of capacities including those listed here:

- Owning and managing their own consulting firms
- Serving as advisers to public policy makers
- Working as program officers in foundations
- Working in the corporate sector doing research or organizational development
- Teaching in anthropology departments, medical schools, and schools of education, among others
- Serving as administrators or staff in academic, corporate, governmental, and nonprofit institutions
- Consulting with, or serving as staff members of, international development agencies
- Working as program evaluators

Training Professional Anthropologists

Out of the 531 practicing anthropologists listed in the NAPA directory, 80 percent have Ph.D.s or have completed all the requirements for the doctorate except the dissertation. Only 11 percent indicated that a master's degree was their highest degree. Even fewer (4 percent) have B.A.s or nonanthropology degrees. Although the NAPA directory does not list every individual who is applying anthropology, it is a good indicator that most professional anthropologists do have Ph.D.s. Slightly over half the individuals listed in the NAPA directory are female (58 percent). A 1990 AAA survey of anthropologists shows that in both academia (85 percent) and applied settings (90 percent), most Ph.D.s are European Americans. The rest are Hispanics (7 percent academic and 4 percent nonacademic), African Americans (0 percent academic and 3 percent nonacademic), and Asian/Pacific Islanders (8 percent academic and 4 percent nonacademic).

The Society for Applied Anthropology's Guide to Training Programs in the Applications of Anthropology (published in 1989) lists fifteen doctoral programs or concentrations in applied anthropology. All but one coexist with a master's-level program in applied anthropology, and seven also include

B.A.-level programs.[2] Four programs offer only a master's degree, and six offer both a B.A. and master's.[3] Two programs offer only a B.A.[4]

Ph.D. programs that emphasize the application of anthropology focus on international development, cultural resource management, medical anthropology, development anthropology and food policy, public archaeology, cross-cultural family interactions, bioanthropology, agricultural research, and anthropology and public administration. Most programs that focus on a particular area also emphasize providing students with a solid background in anthropology; some require expertise in a second field. Most also offer students internship or practicum opportunities. Several programs do not have a specific focus and train students as anthropologists who are also taught to apply anthropology.

The Joint Program in Applied Anthropology at Teachers College/Columbia University is one such program. Key components of this program are described here to provide an example of what an applied program might involve and to serve as background for the next section, where I reflect on what was most useful about the training I received. Students with bachelor's or master's degrees are admitted to the Ph.D. program in applied anthropology. Alternatively, students may focus on anthropology and education and receive an M.Ed. or an Ed.D. A central focus of the program is a colloquium that is attended by both professors and students. During the first year in the program, students learn anthropological theory and develop a proposal for summer fieldwork to be submitted for funding. Each first-year student presents and defends his or her proposal at the colloquium, which is attended by professors, students, and program alumni. The first-year students spend the summer conducting fieldwork, then write up their research and present it to the colloquium. By the end of their second year, students have gone through the entire process of developing a research proposal; applying for funding; conducting research; and writing, presenting, and defending the results. The colloquium provides an opportunity for students to discuss ethics and the politics of research and funding as they relate to specific situations. Students also receive core training in anthropological methods and the history of applied anthropology, including a critical look at its role in colonialism and national and international development. Students are required to take course work in at least three of anthropology's four subfields. The rest of the program is tailored to individuals' interests and needs. Because of its location in New York City, opportunities for internships and additional field research are abundant.

Useful Aspects of Training

Currently, I work as a senior associate at FERA (Formative Evaluation Research Associates) evaluating innovative social programs in the nonprofit sector. I was hired by FERA as an anthropologist to join their multidisciplinary team of researchers. My job responsibilities include developing evaluation designs and proposals, directing projects, conducting research, managing client relationships, negotiating contracts for service, marketing FERA's services, conducting workshops, making oral and written presentations to clients, teaching qualitative research methods to FERA staff members, and assisting with the overall development and administration of the company. FERA's expectation is that senior staff members will remain active in their discipline and will bring that intellectual growth and expertise to their work at FERA.

Most of the clients I work with are in the process of developing innovative programs to address social needs. I work with foundations, state and federally funded programs, and social agencies. Anthropological methods are especially useful in evaluating pilot programs, whose administrators are interested in utilizing evaluation findings, to improve and refine the project and to assist in dissemination efforts. A case study approach is also highly effective when programs are multisite, and local-level staff are encouraged to develop the program in a way that meets the specific needs of their local community or region. One concern, expressed by many clients, is that an evaluator understand and respect the diversity of local sites while at the same time analyzing programs in all the sites collectively as a whole program. Ethnographic vignettes combined with the presentation of other quantitative and qualitative data are highly valued by many clients. These vignettes make reports more interesting and help to capture success stories and program variability as well as the depth of the problems, contradictions, and complicated logistics that program administrators encounter when trying to effect social change, provide services in new ways, or change existing paradigms.

Specifically, I have valued the following about my training in anthropology and its applications:

- Learning the history of anthropology and the roles (positive and negative) it has played in colonialism and the development of policies and the implementation of national and international programs
- Developing critical thinking skills
- Understanding the complexities of class, ethnicity, and gender
- Gaining a solid background in the history of anthropological theory and methods
- Developing highly refined listening, recording, and observation skills
- Learning about the interrelationships between politics, economics, social organization, kinship, and social change
- Learning enough about sociology to understand and explain its main theoretical and methodological approaches
- Developing proposals, conducting fieldwork, writing up the findings, and presenting them to colleagues
- Learning about the logistics and the politics of acquiring funding for research

- Learning how to receive, use, and give constructive criticism
- Gaining an appreciation for, and understanding of, anthropology's four fields
- Learning about some of the pitfalls and ethical dilemmas encountered when one engages in the process of social change

Training, Informational, and Professional Development Needs

Students have perhaps the most obvious needs for training. However, a closer look reveals four groups with training, informational, and professional development needs related to the practice of anthropology.

1. *Nonacademically and academically based individuals (not in anthropology departments) who are already working as professional anthropologists:* These individuals have different professional development needs based on their years in the work force, employment sector, and job responsibilities. People who were hired as "anthropologists" and those whose employers may not know or even care that they are trained anthropologists may have somewhat different needs.

2. *Individuals with anthropological training who have little or no background in applied anthropology:* This group is quite diverse and includes (a) students who are seeking graduate training in the practice of anthropology, (b) students graduating with Ph.D.s in anthropology who have not received any special training in the application of anthropology, (c) anthropologists teaching in anthropology departments who want to, or are forced to, make a career change, and (d) individuals teaching in anthropology departments who want to start consulting in addition to their teaching responsibilities.

3. *Professionals who have been trained in other disciplines with an interest and background in anthropology who want to use this knowledge in an applied setting:* Some of these people have a B.A. or a master's degree in anthropology, in addition to a Ph.D. or professional degree in another field. Others have taken course work in anthropology at the undergraduate or graduate levels but do not hold degrees in anthropology. (Some of these people already have a solid background in applying anthropology. This group's needs are similar to those of individuals already working as professional anthropologists.)

4. *The public:* This group includes those who employ or might employ anthropologists.

Individuals with little or no background in applied anthropology, professionals trained in other disciplines, and the public at large all need basic information about what professional anthropologists do, what they have or could contribute, how they have been trained, what skills they have to offer, how these skills are translated and used in different arenas, what employment/ career opportunities and paths exist, and how to find a professional anthropologist when needed.

Professional anthropologists' needs are related more to professional development opportunities, although many people who are practicing anthropology are also unaware of the depth and breadth of what their colleagues do. Throughout the life span of their careers, professional anthropologists need opportunities

- for engaged teaching, reflection, and writing
- to think critically about the implications of new theories, methodological approaches, and data collection techniques for the practice of anthropology
- to discuss ethical issues with colleagues

Specifically, they need to learn (1) consulting and business skills (such as contracting, compensation, insurance); (2) applied research skills; (3) new data collection and analysis techniques; (4) the latest developments and debates in anthropological theory and method; (5) how to write for nonacademic audiences; (6) how to design and implement program evaluations; and (7) how to contract with, and effectively use, a program evaluator.

Meeting Training and Professional Development Needs

Doctoral and master's-level training programs exist that provide students with a solid background in anthropological theory and methods and that train them to apply their skills as professional anthropologists. In a less systematic way, individuals teaching in departments without an applied program or concentration may also provide their students with some of these same perspectives and skills. Although there are many fine professional anthropologists who have not been trained in applied anthropology programs, many of these individuals have struggled hard to find niches for themselves outside academia and to learn how to translate their skills and knowledge to nonanthropology audiences. In addition to training programs, other vehicles already exist to meet some of the needs identified in the previous section. A number of these are described below.

- *Local practitioner organizations (LPOs)*. LPOs are city- or region-specific groups of practicing anthropologists who meet to network, share information, provide mutual support, conduct professional development activities, and lessen the feeling of isolation experienced by many professional anthropologists. (A list of LPOs can be found at the end of this chapter.)
- *NAPA-sponsored workshops at the AAA meetings*. Past workshops have focused on resumé writing, program evaluation, advertising and promotional tools for the anthropreneur, developing a consulting business, and using simulations for intercultural training and multicultural education.
- *NAPA regional advanced methods workshops*. NAPA has held two regional advanced methods workshops and plans to continue this professional development opportunity.

- *Publications.* Relevant publications include NAPA bulletins on specific topics relevant to the practice of anthropology (available from the AAA), *Human Organization* and *Practicing Anthropology* both published by the Society for Applied Anthropology (SfAA).

- *Newsletters.* The NAPA column in the *AAA Newsletter,* the SfAA newsletter, Cultural Anthropological Methods (CAM) newsletter, LPO newsletters, and *Global Business: The Newsletter of Corporate Anthropology.*

- *ANTHAP.* ANTHAP is an electronic communications network of professional anthropologists. It provides users with information about jobs and other opportunities and an opportunity for dialogue with colleagues. Special by-invitation-only discussion channels are also available for individuals who want to confer about a specific issue or topic. ANTHAP is accessible to any NAPA or SfAA member. For more information, contact James Dow at the Department of Sociology and Anthropology, Oakland University, Rochester MI 48309. His e-mail addresses are dow@argo. acs.oakland.edu or dow@oakland (Bitnet).

- *Special NAPA events at the AAA meetings.* NAPA regularly sponsors special events at the AAA meetings. These events have included a NAPA careers forum, opportunities for current and potential NAPA mentors and mentees to meet, networking for business anthropologists, discussions of ethical dilemmas in the field, roundtable discussions for students, information about new initiatives in support of indigenous ethnodevelopment in Latin America, and agenda-setting sessions for the practice of anthropology.

- *The NAPA video titled* Anthropologists at Work: Careers Making a Difference. This forty-minute (VHS color) video captures anthropologists working at home and abroad in diverse settings—from government and human services to manufacturing and retail industries: conducting research; implementing policy; teaching and providing expertise in the areas of health, development, education, and the corporate world. It is available for purchase ($30 for a nonmember of NAPA) through the AAA (703) 528-1902. The video may also be rented.

- *The Society for Applied Anthropology annual meetings.* SfAA holds annual professional meetings. Meeting locations alternate between the United States and other countries. These meetings are a wonderful opportunity to learn about the practice of anthropology around the world.

- *The NAPA Mentor Program.* The NAPA Mentor Program provides anthropology students and recent graduates with a direct link to the world of practicing anthropology. Through a relationship with a specially selected mentor, each preprofessional has the opportunity to benefit from the experiences, knowledge, and background of a practicing anthropologist. For more information, call (312) 503-3087 or FAX (312) 503-5868.

- *Directories of Professional Anthropologists.* NAPA and SfAA both publish membership directories. There is also a Directory of Anthropological

Consultants published by the Anthropology Consultant's Network for the AAA and NAPA. Call (816) 543-8707 to obtain a consultant's directory.

- *The Archive Collection of Applied Anthropology Materials.* This collection was started as the Applied Anthropology Documentation Project at the University of Kentucky. It collects the so-called fugitive literature produced by anthropologists during their problem-solving work. The collection has a wide range of different types of materials: technical reports, research monographs, conference papers, practicum and internship reports, legal briefs, proposals, and other materials. Materials submitted are catalogued according to Library of Congress subject headings and are available through interlibrary loan. For more information, contact John van Willigen at the University of Kentucky (606) 257-6920.

- *The International Commission on Anthropology in Policy and Practice.* Sponsored by the International Union of Anthropological and Ethnological Sciences (IUAES), this recently formed commission has two primary objectives. The first objective is to build a worldwide network of applied and practicing anthropologists that would enable the formation of a Commission Council of Representatives at the 1998 IUAES Congress. The council would consist of delegates from organizations of applied and practicing anthropologists in all nations and regions of the world. A second objective is to establish the basis for a *global community of practitioners* who can share knowledge, engage in collaborative research and teaching, and address issues of mutual concern. For more information, contact Meta Baba, Department of Anthropology, Wayne State University, Detroit, MI.

Three areas related to the teaching of practicing anthropology need to be strengthened. These are (1) relationships between academic institutions and nonacademic based-anthropologists; (2) opportunities and resources for individuals who know little if anything about applied anthropology to learn more; and (3) strategies for teaching the general public about what anthropologists, especially professional or practicing anthropologists, can offer.

In Denmark, social scientists are required to move back and forth between academia and the public and private sector. Currently, in the United States this is not a viable option. Although a few tenure-track appointments exist that require a percentage of the faculty's time to be spent consulting, most anthropologists must choose between academic and nonacademic jobs. Creating an environment that allows movement between academia and nonacademic sectors would require effort and changes in academic and nonacademic institutions alike. For example, directors of an organization in the private sector might need to provide their professional anthropologist with a leave or sabbatical to teach. A task force could be organized to study the logistics of how this might occur, to learn from Denmark's experiences, and to study how other disciplines have addressed this issue.

There are other ways to strengthen relationships between anthropologists working in the academic and nonacademic sectors that require less dramatic changes. Local practitioner organizations (LPOs) can provide a vehicle for developing mutually beneficial collaborative relationships. Listed below are some of the potential benefits.

Benefits for professional anthropologists working outside academia:
- Opportunities for teaching courses
- Inclusion in departmental activities (such as colloquiums, social events)
- Access to information (receiving departmental newsletters, library materials, and other university publications)
- Access to resources (libraries, computer accounts, e-mail, sports facilities)
- Breakdown of stereotypes of academics as "not interested in applied anthropology"
- Availability of students as interns, research assistants, potential employees
- Availability of faculty as part-time consultants
- Institutional affiliation for funding purposes
- Lessening of professional isolation
- Renewed involvement in anthropological professional associations

Benefits for anthropology departments:
- Access to a network of practicing anthropologists who could teach a variety of courses as adjuncts, visiting lecturers, or postdoctoral lecturers
- Job and internship networking for students
- Opportunities for faculty and students to learn more about applied anthropology
- Breakdown of stereotypes about applied/practicing anthropologists
- New opportunities for faculty to do part-time consulting
- Professional support and lessening of isolation for faculty in small departments (smaller colleges may have only one anthropologist on staff)
- Access to information (reports, public policy-related documents, issue-specific newsletters)
- Consulting opportunities for faculty
- New resources for funding research
- Access to new methodologies

Readily accessible resource materials for individuals who know little, if anything, about the practice of anthropology would be very useful. For example, a great need exists for an updated guide to training programs in applied anthropology. A resource book with course syllabi, bibliographies, and other resources would be useful to individuals who are teaching in academic settings. Other materials are also needed.

Teaching the public about the uses of anthropology is a task that, as demonstrated by the vignettes at the beginning of this article, professional anthropologists attend to every day. Resource materials such as the NAPA careers video would greatly assist this effort. Additionally, an opportunity or a series of opportunities for professional anthropologists to share information with each other about their successes and failures in this area would be useful, especially if the findings were published and disseminated.

Some Reflections

Teaching individuals how to apply their anthropological training to solving real-world problems does not, and indeed should not, occur only within the walls of academic institutions, nor is it unidirectional. While opportunities for reflection and skill building must be made available for professional anthropologists throughout the life span of their careers, practicing anthropologists have a great deal to teach other anthropologists, colleagues from other fields, and the public at large. This could occur in several ways:

- Creating mutually beneficial linkages between professional anthropologists based outside academia and anthropology departments. Other disciplines with more experience integrating their professional colleagues could provide us with lessons about the benefits and logistical challenges of developing exchange opportunities.
- Developing workshops, miniseminars, and resource materials for the public at large. This would not only be a potentially lucrative opportunity for professional anthropologists but it would also serve to further the public's education about what anthropology has to offer.
- Developing resource materials for teachers and students who are not in applied training programs.

A note of caution: Although academically based anthropologists are expected to attend and present at professional meetings, participate in the AAA, and in general contribute to the growth of the discipline, there is usually no such expectation on the part of employers outside academia. Professional anthropologists based outside anthropology departments must usually divide their energies between contributing to anthropology and to another field or area such as medicine, evaluation, or international development—each with its own set of meetings, journals, newsletters, and professional expectations. Most of us must choose very carefully how we spend our time. Creating opportunities for professional anthropologists to share their expertise with colleagues and the public must be carefully crafted so that everyone benefits. These opportunities should lead to professional rejuvenation and not to burnout.

Local Practitioner Organizations

Washington Association of Professional Anthropologists (WAPA)
Philadelphia Association of Practicing Anthropologists (PAPA)
Professional Association of Anthropologists (in New York City)
New Jersey Association of Anthropologists
Chicago Association for Practicing Anthropologists (CAPA)
Detroit Association of Practicing Anthropologists (DAPA)

Great Lakes Association of Professional Anthropologists (GLAPA—based in Michigan and formerly the Ann Arbor Association of Applied Anthropologists)

Mid-South Association of Professional Anthropology (MSAPA)

High Plains Society for Applied Anthropology, Practicing Anthropologists of Washington, Idaho, and Oregon (PAWIO)

Association of Professional Anthropologists (APA—in the Bay area)

Southern California Applied Anthropology Network (SCANN)

North Florida Network of Practicing Anthropologists (NFNPA)

Sun Coast Organization of Practicing Anthropologists (SOPA)

Real World Anthropologists (in Tempe, Arizona)

An LPO for the Southeast is being or has recently been organized (Atlanta, Georgia)

For more information or names of contact people for LPOs, call Art Campa (NAPA LPO Committee Chair) at (303) 492-5419 or the SfAA offices (405) 843-5113.

Notes

1. Multiple responses were possible so percentages do not add to 100 percent. Other areas were listed but received 1 percent or less of the responses.

2. American University, Boston University, University of California–San Francisco, Catholic University, Columbia University Teachers College, University of Connecticut, University of Florida, Indiana University, University of Kentucky, McGill University, State University of New York at Binghamton, State University of New York at Buffalo, Rensselaer Polytechnic Institute, University of South Florida, Syracuse University, and Wayne State University.

3. City College, University of Colorado–Denver, Georgia State University, Iowa State University, University of Maryland, University of Massachusetts–Boston, Memphis State University, Montclair State College, Northern Arizona University, Oregon State University, and University of South Carolina.

4. California State University–Chico and Southern California College.

Intrusive Anthropology

CORINNE SHEAR WOOD

There is an area of anthropology that seems virtually to have been ignored for the past twenty years. I call this area "intrusive anthropology." Using a case study approach, I consider here two personal experiences with anthropological studies that constituted direct intrusion into the lives of people in two contrasting cultures: Native Americans of Southern California and Maori populations of New Zealand. Because I assume the past has some relevance for the present and the future, after this review based on personal experiences, I make some general suggestions relative to "intrusive anthropology."

The classical anthropology most of us imbibed in graduate school had us witnessing "our" people, recording the areas that opened up to us, and carrying our data back home, in the hope of developing relevant theories of human behavior based on our keen, insightful, noninvasive observations. The aim is epitomized in the familiar "collective stance" instantly associated with Boas and his students. To intrude, much less to introduce change, was a grievous anthropological sin.

At what point do we plead mea culpa? When do we acknowledge the contradictions in the reality of the anthropological experience?

Throughout graduate and undergraduate training, students have learned that the only acceptable orientation in this regard was to become "invisible," noncorporeal. Perhaps this was epitomized by Jane Goodall's initial approach with chimpanzees—to barricade herself behind a heavy bamboo screen. Eventually, she had to shed her covers, and as everyone who has worked in the field soon learns, there is no cover. Our very presence, never mind the proffered bananas, augurs change.

My own field experiences were ostensibly of an investigative nature. In the two I discuss, which are sharply contrasting cultures, I went rapidly from observer to "agent of change." In the process, I was scarcely cognizant of my own gradual, almost unconscious transition. It was only from the perspective of many years away from some of the sites and the people, indeed from the entire transfixing milieu, that the transformation became apparent.

In retrospect, what is even more striking is how little, if at all, I was prepared, much less trained, to act as an agent of change. Unfortunately, this is at least partially true for our students today. I remain uncomfortably aware of how little I prepare my own students for their approaching roles.

What preparation should we be offering our students? What are some of the crucial, ethical, political, moral, and legal problems for which they should be armed? These are questions that deserve thoughtful attention from each of us. My own experiences, which follow, point unmistakenly to the incredible naivete that borders on stupidity with which I entered my first field experience.

Some twenty years ago, I participated in a physical-medical anthropological study on three reservations in Southern California, home for several hundred Cahuilla, Luiseno, and Cupeno Native Americans (Bean and Wood 1969; Wood 1970). Employed as a clinical laboratory technician, I performed extensive blood, urine, and nutrition studies.

These Native American reservations, on the edge of ultra-wealthy, deluxe Palm Springs, had been "terminated" by the government. In other words, California had separated itself from a relationship, somewhat protective, somewhat nurturing, ostensibly adopted by most states in their guilt-ridden interactions with indigenous populations.

As one government official suggested later, the residents of the Southern California reservations had the same rights and privileges as had any other poverty-ridden population in California, never mind that their land had been parched, their water table lowered to nonavailability, when real estate developers of Palm Springs drained the reservation's water.

My findings indicated a plethora of medical problems in need of attention. The California political scene ruled out any meaningful medical intervention for the reservation residents. Most of the conditions disclosed by my test results—diabetes, liver damage, obesity, intestinal parasites—would require ongoing, long-term medical commitments. Local doctors almost unanimously accepted only patients who could pay up front or who provided evidence of private insurance. My Native American contacts fulfilled neither of these conditions; their only recourse was to drive, or be driven, some thirty to thirty-five miles to a county hospital, where lines were long, treatment was cursory, and the entire experience totally demeaning.

Here was an ethical, moral dilemma, for which I and my professors were completely unprepared. What are the responsibilities of the uncoverer of bad tidings? None of our anthropological training or reading had even hinted at the presence of these seemingly insoluble problems, which in a strange sense had become manifest as a result of our own anthropological *intrusion*. Virtually all the conditions disclosed by our testing were amenable to medical care; in all probability, without medical intervention, all would deteriorate, resulting eventually for the affected individuals in severe illness, even premature death.

Despite frantic, impassioned, occasionally hysterical attempts on our part, no reservation was able to obtain the services of a physician for even the few hours per month for which we pleaded. Weeks went by as we pursued one government official after another. Each office smoothly referred us to another, equally impotent and/or disinterested.

Demoralized and guilt ridden because of the Pandora's Box we had opened and could not satisfactorily close, we edged out, loaded with data we were unable conscientiously to resolve. Maintaining some degree of contact with friends on the reservations, we learned that more than a year later, a mission-oriented church established a clinic on the largest reservation.

From my perspective, it was a far from satisfactory conclusion. The "rescuing" sect advocated total elimination of dietary meat, questionable in a milieu already marked by its heavy reliance on starchy carbohydrates. Many aspects of the sect's ideology gave little honor to the fundamental beliefs and history of the Native Americans.

On the other hand, we in academia had been able to offer little other than bad tidings. How could our academic training have prepared us for the onslaught of this medical and political reality? I submit that we have not addressed problems of this nature yet. I vigorously advocate a strong, realistic preparation to avoid such impotent encounters in the future.

Many years later, I was given an opportunity to conduct a medical-physical anthropological study among a sizable Maori population in New Zealand. Again, initial studies of my own as well as those of many indigenous scientists (Beaglehole, Prior, Salmond, and Eyles 1978; Murchie 1984; Pomare 1980), revealed problems of blood pressure, obesity, heart disease, and the now familiar panoply of "Western diseases." Here too, the indigenous population of Maoris experienced discomfort and cultural turnoff in the medical facilities of the majority population (Wood and Maipi 1989; Wood 1982, 1990).

But here the resemblance to the U.S. Indian Reservation experience ended. Coinciding with, perhaps even prompted by, our studies, the National Health Department of New Zealand declared Maori health its number one priority for the year. I was invited to make recommendations and had gained enough anthropological background by then to know that the beliefs, customs, and particular practices that distinguished the Maori cultures could not readily be met by the medical facilities of the European-oriented medical population.

Through the years, I had learned from field experience, not from classrooms or seminar study, and had internalized the belief that basic health improvements related to such illnesses as high blood pressure, obesity, and adult diabetes could be achieved only through culturally acceptable lifestyle changes—from within the culture, not imposed from outside.

With the willing financial cooperation of national and local governments, a Maori Health Center had emerged. It became the initial founder of a Maori-based, Maori-oriented, largely Maori-staffed health movement. The government's role was primarily one of financial assistance and staff training. The anthropologist was actively involved at every step, recording observations as part of the overall frantic activities.

The Maori community selected from its own members the people who would lead the project. In time, these would define the health problems on which to focus. Aping the anthropological stance, they began to ask many crucial questions: What does the community believe? What do they consider important? What are the primary cultural and health interactions?

Within a few years, the initiating role of the anthropologist was over. Given the right moment and adequate backing, the movement had developed its own life. The anthropologist could revert to the traditional role of observer and recorder. Further interference was entirely inappropriate and probably unacceptable.

The health concerns of the Marae-based Maori people now have begun to change into a system of government-financed universal health care rooted in the Maori culture and oriented toward consciousness-raising, education, and disease prevention.

If this brief summary implies a smooth transition as well as a totally unerring path for the anthropologist, I must add that there were innumerable bumps along the road. It is time for additional anthropological evaluation and review of where the movement in New Zealand stands. Further, one hopes that one day a Maori anthropologist in some Pacific university will do a doctoral dissertation on how several Maori communities have been impacted by an anthropologically initiated cultural intrusion.

I propose that we consider ways of measurement to gauge the effects of our presence on the field setting. Primarily, I urge that we develop a fuller understanding of some of the dynamics of our interactions, aiming for an acceptable degree of predictability of our impact on our focal society. In so doing, we would encompass considerations of some of our most difficult areas: the ethics of intrusion, the effects of our presence, the requisite degree of preparation before entering a culture different from our own. I believe these are problems that can be dealt with, and that to the extent we do so, we will achieve a new maturity and responsibility within our discipline.

References

Beaglehole, R., I. Prior, C. Salmond, and E. Eyles. 1978. "Coronary Heart Disease in Maoris: Incidence and Case Mortality." *New Zealand Medical Journal* 88:138–141.

Bean, L. J., and Corinne Wood. 1969. "Crisis in Indian Health: A California Example." *Indian Historian* 3(2).

Murchie, E. 1984. *Rapuora: Health and Maori Women.* Wellington, N.Z.: Maori Women's Welfare League.

Pomare, Eru W. 1980. *Maori Standards of Health: A Study of the 20-Year Period 1955–1975.* Medical Research Council of New Zealand and Special Report Series No. 7. Wellington, N.Z.: Medical Research Council of New Zealand.

Wood, Corinne. 1970. "A Multiphasic Screening Survey of Three California Indian Reservations." *Social Science and Medicine* 4:579–587.

———. 1982. *Blood Pressure and Related Factors among the Maori and Pakeha Communities of Huntly.* Occasional paper #17. Hamilton, N.Z.: Centre for Maori Studies and Research, University of Waikato.

———. 1990. "Maori Community Health Workers: A Mixed Reception in New Zealand." In *Anthropology and Primary Health Care,* edited by Jeannine Coreil and J. Dennis Mull, 123–136. Boulder, Colo.: Westview.

Wood, Corinne, and Raitimu Maipi. 1989. "Maoris Take Up the Fight against Ill Health." *World Health Forum* 10:58–61.

TEACHING ANTHROPOLOGY TO PRECOLLEGIATE TEACHERS AND STUDENTS

Problems, Issues, and Solutions in the Teaching of Anthropology K–12

Jane J. White

The Need for Anthropology

In *The Teaching of Anthropology,* Mandelbaum (1963, 5) argued for the teaching of anthropology to inform "the student, [who] . . . must move in an alien culture from time to time, even if it is only the unfamiliar environment of a new job or neighborhood." Thirty years later, elementary and secondary students and their teachers and parents live in a world that, in contrast, must seem overwhelmingly filled with alien peoples, cultures, and objects. From the clothes students wear to the cars their parents buy, the material goods Americans use are assembled all over the globe. The nightly TV news brings worldwide reports of devastating ethnic wars to which American forces are sometimes assigned.

U.S. workplaces and schools show dramatic demographic changes. The 8.7 million immigrants that settled in the United States during the 1980s rival in number the immigrants at the turn of the century. However, recent immigrants are far more diverse: they come from Central America, the Caribbean, Eastern Europe, and Asia speaking languages as disparate as Kurdish, Arabic, Hmong, Spanish, and Korean (Rand Study 1993). School systems that served 14 percent and then 30 percent minority students now project 47 percent minority students by the year 2002 (Fairfax County Public Schools 1993 *Update*).

Elementary and secondary students and their teachers need the perspective and accumulated wisdom of anthropology every bit as much if not more than undergraduate students. Anthropology is useful because of its ability to frame the big picture and ask significant questions that cut across economics, geography, history, literature, biology, geology, and math. Using the anthropological perspective, students and teachers can be engaged as field researchers, "looking closely, clearly and dispassionately at what people actually are doing as well as listening to what they say they are doing as well as what others say about them" (Mandelbaum 1963, 5). Anthropology has enormous potential for powerful explanations and for being able to help students and teachers bridge the gap between vital knowledge of the real world and dry, distant, and disengaging brands of school knowledge.

In the United States, an increasingly monocultural population of teachers does not know how to teach about diverse cultural, ethnic, and racial groups. Traditionally, primary teachers cheerfully teach units about children around the world who wear different clothing, eat different foods, and celebrate different holidays. However, young children learn that they are to look past their exotic coverings and customs to find that others are basically just like you and me (White 1980). Intermediate and middle school teachers teach about the European immigrants who came to the United States a century ago. Materials and activities are used that illustrate important values: our nation is a place where different peoples come, dream the American Dream, work hard, get ahead, and become just like you and me. Cultures far away and long ago are selected and taught in terms of ideas and inventions they have "contributed" that have shaped our Western way of life today—for example, Egypt "contributed" papyrus for paper and Greece "contributed" democracy (White 1980).

However, it is becoming obvious that there are enduring and perhaps permanent differences among groups of people both external to and within this country, and precollegiate teachers often do not know what to do about it. Themselves products of schools that were generally silent on the issue of cultural differences, teachers feel unprepared. Lacking guidance in sorting though the shifting interpretations (such as current stances on black/white relationships and ethnic differences) that have troubled and obsessed our country, teachers often choose to remain silent. They feel that sins of omission are preferable to the risk they run of offending an ethnic or minority group or (even more important) making specific students in their classroom feel uncomfortable.

This continuing silence does not allow teachers and students to encounter and resolve multicultural issues. In *White Teacher* (1979), Paley describes her struggle to face the truth that lay behind her own polite and well-meaning facade as a teacher in a multiracial classroom. She came to feel that when she intended to spare feelings, she was in fact ignoring feelings. Her "silence communicated the impression that there might be something wrong with being black" (1979, 131). If teachers and students do not talk about racial and ethnic issues in classrooms, students learn that these issues are in some way unmentionable.

Too many taboo topics can result in "school knowledge" and school itself becoming meaningless and irrelevant to students. The Carnegie Council for Adolescent Development found students from ages ten to fourteen disengaging from school (1989). McNeil (1989) found both high school students and teachers "deskilling" and "dumbing down," ignoring their own personal, more sophisticated, and complex knowledge of the real world as they engaged in mock discussions of "school knowledge"—that is, efficient and easy-to-grade fragments of fact.

If students are to acquire knowledge needed to function effectively within culturally diverse classrooms, communities, nations, and a global economy, teachers must know how to assist them to move beyond stereotypes and ethnocentrism to acquire understanding of cultures other than their own. Haviland (in this volume) argues that such provinciality and ignorance is "downright dangerous in a world that has become a sort of global community in which all of its people are interdependent upon one another, yet in which we North Americans constitute a small minority." If students and teachers are to construct "school knowledge" that is connected to and useful in functioning in the real world, teachers must solve problems of being able to talk about taboo topics in ways that do not make them and their students uncomfortable.

Six Problems in the Practices and Beliefs Involved in Teaching Anthropology in K–12 Schools

Getting anthropology to teachers and students, or teachers and students to anthropology as the case may be, is by no means a simple task. There are at least six problems that must be overcome if the perspectives, knowledge, and wisdom of anthropology are to be used in the schools.

Problem 1

Information presented in social studies is constrained by the demand to present only what is good about our society and our country. Even more important than transmitting public scholarly knowledge, elementary and secondary schools serve as institutions that enculturate the young of our nation with the core values, beliefs, and practices of the contemporary mainstream American culture. Training students to become good citizens is a goal that transcends all others in social studies education. Curriculum materials are chosen to elicit a sense of unquestioning pride as young students learn about their country's place in the world. Therefore, historical, geographic, economic, or political events that do not reflect the United States and its inhabitants at their finest hour, embodying the ideals for which we stand, tend to be ruthlessly edited out when "what is or was" meets the filter of "what should be."

In a review of American history textbooks, FitzGerald (1979, 77) found the United States portrayed as

> a kind of a Salvation Army to the rest of the world; throughout history it had done little but dispense benefits to poor, ignorant and diseased countries. In the nineteenth century and the beginning of the twentieth, it had opened doors for the Chinese, saved Cuba from the Spanish, protected Puerto Rico,

separated Panama from Colombia in order to wipe out yellow fever, and taken on the Philippines in order to "educate" and "civilize" the Filipinos. . . . In the twentieth century, the United States had spent most of its time . . . saving Europe and Asia from militarism, Fascism, and Communism.

FitzGerald uses the delightful metaphor of "crabgrass theory" (1979, 75) to describe the way many textbooks handle our internal problems. They rarely mention the suffering caused by slavery, the plight of the working class during early industrialization, or the Vietnam war. Rather, these events are introduced as sudden troubles that inexplicably sprang up, rather like crabgrass, and as soon as they were noticed, the United States did something about them. Today Ladson-Billings (1991) still finds that although schools put up posters and bulletin boards to celebrate the many obvious inequities the United States has overcome—for example, the treatment of African Americans (Abraham Lincoln freed the slaves, Rosa Parks refused to move to the back of the bus)— overt discussions of race, cultural conflict, social inequities, and oppression are lacking.

In my doctoral dissertation (White 1980), a four-year ethnographic study of how teachers and students in a working-class neighborhood made meaning about different cultures, I found teachers to be unaware that they inaccurately taught aspects of different cultures so as to reinforce middle-class American ideals, values, and practices. For example, when a kindergarten teacher introduced the Iroquois, she followed the county curriculum guide in which Native American families were erroneously presented as identical to an idealized American middle-class family:

Each student will draw four pictures—Indian father, Indian mother, Indian sister and Indian brother that will show or portray what each member of the family does. (White 1980, 133)

This activity ignored the organization of Native American families, which is based on an extended family network. An opportunity was lost for elementary students to learn about a different form of social organization—that the Iroquois are matrilocal and matrifocal.

Even more alarming, though, are times when cultural differences are represented as negative examples of American ideals (thus, of course, justifying American actions). In a sixth-grade curriculum guide on the settlement of Texas, the chart shown below contrasted the U.S. and Mexican ways of life (White 1980, 124):

Americans	*Mexicans*
1. Spoke English	1. Spoke Spanish
2. Accustomed to electing leaders	2. Not accumstomed to electing leaders

Thus, in addition to not exploring cultural differences from the "insider" perspective of the people studied, curricular texts and materials may sometimes actually create stereotypes that intensify cultural insularity. Anthropological content and processes challenge and contradict inaccuracies and ethnocentrism that currently exist in many social studies textbooks and curriculum guides.

Problem 2

Students initially react negatively, both emotionally and intellectually, to examples of cultural differences. Precollegiate teachers prefer to avoid lessons that make them or their students feel uncomfortable.

When fifth-grade students in Newton, Massachusetts, were shown films of the Netsilik Eskimo from *Man, a Course of Study* (a curriculum based in part on the anthropological research of Asen Balikci), Jones (1968) found that the films evoked powerful negative emotions in the children as they saw animals killed and an old grandmother left behind on the ice. Martin (1975) found that sixth-grade students in Mill Valley, California, initially reacted to the Netsilik films with ridicule, condescension, and disgust.

In my doctoral research, I saw first-grade students who initially reacted to culturally different artifacts such as a dhoti (worn by Pakistani boys) with expressions of derision and "put-downs": "Diapers!" and "He looks like a baby! Ha Ha" (White 1980, 367). Fourth-grade students reacted to a description of a different cultural practice—the eating of seaweed and raw fish by the Japanese—with sudden in-drawn breath and expressions of disgust: "Yuck," "Ooh," "Gross," and "That's sick!" (White 1980, 172).

But curiously, I came to value these outbursts of student outrage and culture shock. I found that only after initially negative emotions had been elicited were students able to consider the alien practices in a more cognitive fashion. Only then were they able to find them reasonable given the context in which they occurred. For example, during the Japanese fourth-grade unit, students later raised their hands and volunteered comments such as "You know, given the population density of the Japanese on those little islands, the Japanese are pretty smart to use the fish. After all they are surrounded by the ocean and they are using the fish to supply the protein needs of their people." Martin also found that there was a significant decrease in ethnocentrism toward a foreign culture and that this reduction does not require any systematic downgrading of one's own culture (1975, 386). Martin notes, "The teacher's expressed acceptance of pupils' initial ethnocentrism had an observed positive relationship to reduced ethnocentrism at the end of the treatment period" (1975, 384).

Problem 3

Teachers use "politeness rules of speech" to smooth over cultural differences; but too glib an acceptance of cultural differences can mistakenly lead to a view that any system of practices and beliefs is just as good as any other. Elementary teachers are not comfortable with student expressions of negative emotion. They believe students should learn to be "polite" when talking about others who are different (White 1989). *How* teachers talk about potentially trouble-some or taboo topics serves as unarticulated but cautionary models for their students. For example, a kindergarten teacher introduced photographs of culturally different Native Americans with nonverbal cues indicating that increased interest and approval were appropriate (and that negative comments were not):

> As she begins to lift up the first picture (of Native Americans), Mrs. Bedford dramatically lowers her voice to a stage whisper and says in tones of exaggerated enthusiasm:
>
> Mrs. Bedford: Now *(whispering)* I have brought in some very special pictures for you all to see.
>
> *(Dramatically raises picture).*
>
> Students *(in unison)*: OOOOOOOoooooooooh.
>
> Mrs. Bedford: I want you to look at the picture. Don't say anything for a minute.

Later in the lesson, a student asks whether one of the artifacts is a tomahawk. This left Mrs. Bedford in the ludicrous position of responding (as she had about every artifact), "Yes, isn't it lovely?" (White 1980, 308–314.) Strategies of being cheerful, polite, and positive, initially growing out of legitimate concerns for not making derogatory statements about "others," if not checked, end by constraining student engagement and the ability to ask questions and explore ideas.

Thus, if teachers do not encourage students to examine cultural differences actively, they deny their students the opportunity of seeing a different culture realistically. Gearing (1970) argues against teachers and students adopting the seemingly nonjudgmental view that "they have their ways and we have ours." Gearing finds this view troubling because teachers and students are denying any connection between "them" and "us." Gearing characterizes this attitude as "cultural estrangement," and maintains, instead, that we do not necessarily have to like a people to understand their way of life. He insists that the goal of education is to "know enough to find a people believable."

By teaching students to respect cultural differences, teachers can also teach children that they have a right to and should respect their own culture. Breitborde eloquently argues:

> So we must not understand cultural relativism as a way to *rationalize* differences or *abandon* values, but we must use it in our classrooms to a) understand differences, b) strengthen values and c) help students search for accommodations between their values, practices and beliefs and those of other groups in our society. In these terms we must use cultural relativism to help students learn to *cross* cultural boundaries. (1991, 9)

Teachers of elementary and secondary students must be willing to engage them in the study of cultural variability. Their initial confrontations with cultural differences must be planned so that students are allowed to express their own emotions honestly. Intensive inquiry may then be needed to help students ground the object, practice, or belief within its cultural context as seen by its practitioners. The confrontation with alien "others" can also be used to initiate grass-roots study of the students and their culture. Both are necessary before students will be able to cross cultural borders.

Problem 4

Elementary and secondary teachers often lack background content knowledge of anthropology. Thus, they cannot call on relevant case studies and practices for comparison at "teachable moments." In *Making Sense of Social Studies,* Jenness (1990, 245) found that "teachers continue to have very little background in the field, the number of university degrees in the field has been declining since the 1970s and anthropology is far down in publishers' rating of likely textbook markets." In the first chapter in this section, Selig gives a historical overview of how the discipline of anthropology has been excluded from the precollegiate curriculum as well from the background knowledge necessary to become a teacher. Selig, at the Smithsonian and herself a major player in keeping the flame of anthropology alive for several decades in the schools through *AnthroNotes,* includes a case study that describes how anthropologists at the Smithsonian and George Washington University developed a teacher training program that worked.

Cheek, coordinator of mathematics, science and technology and social studies for the state of Rhode Island, confirms the "marginal position" and "superficial" level of understanding of anthropology within K–12 education. Cheek describes the struggles for control of the curriculum at the national, state, and local levels and presents possibilities that are available during the current climate for national educational reform.

Problem 5

Elementary and secondary teachers lack processual knowledge of how to conduct the field research that is needed if they are to help students inquire into the real world outside the classroom. Moloney, Institute of Archaeology, University College London, describes how she translates her expert archaeological knowledge into teaching materials for children. Although she is influenced by the National Curriculum in England, her main goals are to pass on her "own enthusiasm for archaeology," "to show the range in topic and period covered by archaeology," "to present archaeological methods and techniques in detail," and "to stimulate a problem-solving approach." One of the best ways for teachers who would like to use core anthropological concepts, processes, and perspectives is to seek out high-quality nonfiction literature for children and adolescents. Like the Spindlers, Moloney organizes the information in a series of case studies. Exciting teaching units that actively involve students can be developed, for example, from descriptions of how archaeologists study the earlier African hominid evidence to recent garbage projects that students can undertake to understand their own society.

At the local level, Cheek encourages anthropologists to volunteer to work within a school. Frankowski, University of Maryland–Baltimore County, describes how she assisted a fifth-grade class and their teacher conduct a year-long anthropological inquiry. Much as McCurdy has described how undergraduates can be successful ethnographers, so Frankowski illustrates how fifth-grade students can successfully conduct their own anthropological research. Along the way, she shows how the students use primary source documents, collect data, develop problem-solving skills, find and use patterns in the data, and develop ownership of their work.

Given the selection of culture as the first theme in the national standards of the U. S. National Council for the Social Studies, my chapter explores the strengths and the problems involved in using this powerful concept as a framework by which students can organize their notions of how things work in the world. I briefly describe several cases in which an elementary and a middle school teacher successfully teach about other people using the construct of culture.

Problem 6

An increasingly monocultural teaching force needs to conduct anthropological inquiries to find out about the multicultural students and communities in which they teach. As the teaching force becomes more monocultural while students become increasingly more culturally diverse, teachers are finding it more and more difficult to know how to start where the student is or to know "where a student is coming from." In "Shut My Mouth Wide Open," Ladson-Billings serves as a model for how educators can learn from teachers who are successful in working with a specific cultural group. In contrast to all the reports of low test scores and difficulties that minority students have in schools, it is important to note that Ladson-Billings gathers data and documents how a group of successful teachers have enabled African American students to succeed. Based on teacher reflections on videos of their teaching, Ladson-Billings directs us toward features and interactions of the school day that are often ignored in current teacher training: how to develop and maintain positive identification with the African American community; how to listen to the structure of stories told by some African American students, how not to hassle children but help them solve their own problems, how to build a sense of community.

In a final chapter, Gonzalez and Amanti, an anthropologist and a teacher, show how anthropological knowledge, both the process and the content, "itself becomes a pedagogical tool" as teachers enter their students' homes as field-workers:

> Outfitted with an anthropological perspective, teachers went to the homes of their students, not with an agenda to "teach" the parents or to inform

them about classroom concerns but as "learners," as anthropologists seeking to construct a template for understanding the quotidian lives of their students.

Because they did not base their work on a "deficit" model of supposedly needy and dysfunctional students, teachers were welcomed into the homes in a position of honor and respect. They developed warm and affective ties as they gathered oral histories about families. The teachers began to see the students and their families as "valuable sources of knowledge." The teachers began building on their students' prior knowledge as they began using information about household activities in their math, science, literature, and social studies lessons. They also found that their concept of culture was greatly expanded from the minimal notion of food, clothing, and shelter to include information about labor, residential history, and literacy.

These seven chapters describe how elementary and secondary students, elementary and secondary teachers, curriculum writers, and teacher educators are beginning to use both the process and content of anthropological knowledge to bridge the gap between "real" experiential knowledge of the world, the local community, the students, and the frequently dry and irrelevant body of school knowledge that is all too often transmitted in the precollegiate grades. Teacher education needs to prepare teachers to overcome some of the problems of discussing culturally different people so that rather than "being 'conned' by their own culture into believing a lot of things about themselves and other people that are not necessarily true" (Haviland, this volume), students will learn to function more effectively as citizens in our complex, problematic, multicultural classrooms, communities, and society.

References

Breitborde, Larry. 1991. "Multiculturalism, Cultural Relativism and Competing Perspectives on the 'Encounter.'" Presentation made in the symposium Anthropology, Columbus and the Commemoration: A Workshop for Teachers, chaired by L. B. Breitborde and C. Ellenbaum. November 20, 90th Annual Meeting of the American Anthropological Association, Chicago.

Carnegie Council for Adolescent Development. 1989. *Turning Points: Preparing American Youth for the 21st Century.* Report of the Task Force on the Education of Young Adolescents. New York: Carnegie Corporation of New York.

Fairfax County Public Schools. 1993. *Update: Framing the Future for the 21st Century.* Fairfax (Virginia) County School Board.

FitzGerald, Frances. 1979. "Onward and Upward with the Arts" (History Textbooks—Part II.) *The New Yorker.* March 5:40–91.

Gearing, Frederick. 1970. *The Face of the Fox.* Salem, Wis.: Sheffield.

Jenness, David. 1990. *Making Sense of Social Studies.* A Publication of the National Commission on Social Studies in the Schools. A Joint Project of the American Historical Association, Carnegie Foundation for the Advancement of Teaching, National Council for the Social Studies, and Organization of American Historians. New York: Macmillan.

Jones, Richard M. 1968. *Fantasy and Feeling in Education.* New York: Harper Colophon Books.

Ladson-Billings, Gloria. 1991. "Coping with Multicultural Illiteracy: A Teacher Education Response." *Social Education* 55:186–187, 194.

McNeil, Linda. 1989. "Empowering Students: Beyond Defensive Teaching in Social Studies." In *Locating Learning: Ethnographic Perspectives on Classroom Research,* edited by C. Emihovich, 117–139. Norwood, N.J.: Ablex.

Mandelbaum, David. 1963. "The Transmission of Anthropological Culture." In *The Teaching of Anthropology,* edited by David G. Mandelbaum, Gabriel W. Lasker, and Ethel M. Albert. Berkeley: University of California Press.

Martin, David. 1975. "Ethnocentrism toward Foreign Culture in Elementary Social Studies." *Elementary School Journal* March:380–388.

Paley, Vivian. 1979. *White Teacher.* Cambridge, Mass.: Harvard University Press.

Rand Study. 1993. As reported by Mary Jordan in "Newcomers Remake Schools: Study Finds Severe Adjustment Problems." *Washington Post,* 28 July, A1, A12.

White, Jane. 1980. "An Ethnographic Study of the Construction of Knowledge about Different Cultures in an Elementary School." Doctoral dissertation, University of Pennsylvania, Philadelphia.

———. 1989. "The Power of Politeness in the Classroom: Cultural Codes That Create and Constrain Knowledge Construction." *Journal of Curriculum and Supervision* 4(4):298–321.

The Challenge of Exclusion:
Anthropology, Teachers, and Schools

RUTH SELIG

In an increasingly multicultural and diverse society, anthropology has much to offer precollege teachers and students, yet it is rarely offered as a separate course in the precollege curriculum. Anthropology is relevant to a wide variety of subjects and grade levels, and it can impact deeply teachers' perspectives and the subjects they teach. An integrative or infusion approach to anthropology and the precollege curriculum is one response to the challenge of exclusion, but such a strategy depends heavily on successful anthropology teacher training. Fortunately, new opportunities and imperatives within the American educational system make this an opportune time for the dissemination of anthropology into American schools and should encourage the anthropology profession to take a more proactive role in advancing anthropology in precollege curriculum and teacher training. This chapter explores these themes as well as ways anthropologists successfully have reached out to teachers, through teacher training programs and publications, including *AnthroNotes,* the only U.S. publication specifically designed for anthropologists and teachers.

We live in a rapidly changing society, in a time of global transformation, clashing cultures, and multicultural diversity. Teachers face different classrooms from those of twenty years ago. Approximately 30 percent of our students are from racial and ethnic minorities; many speak English as a second language, and in some schools most children come from immigrant or minority backgrounds. Students need to understand and value the strength of the pluralism and diversity that make up our national heritage.

Anthropological concepts, perspectives, and resources provide teachers and students with powerful tools for understanding themselves and others in our changing world today, a world that is increasingly called the "global village." Anthropology provides a framework for teachers to help their students prepare for living in the twenty-first century.

Anthropology looks at peoples and cultures from the broadest possible perspective, seeking to understand the essential nature of human beings and their varied cultures—through all human history and in all societies around the earth. Unlike other social scientists such as geographers or historians, psychologists or economists, sociologists or political scientists, anthropologists use an all-encompassing framework within which to study human physical and cultural development and variation. Regardless of whether they are cultural anthropologists, physical anthropologists, archaeologists, anthropological linguists, or applied anthropologists, all anthropologists share training and interest in three fundamental questions:

- How can we best understand our fellow human beings?
- How did the human species in all its variation develop over time and space?
- How can we best explain and understand the diverse cultures and subcultures that share our globe?

Most teachers find such questions fascinating and a challenge to teach in a variety of curriculum subjects. Anthropology, and particularly the concept of culture, enriches almost any school subject. Geography teachers can add cultural studies to their curricula, demonstrating how people have adapted to climates and environments around the world. U.S. history teachers can add authenticity by including cultural materials to lessons on Native Americans, immigration, and ethnic diversity. World history teachers can add information on health practices, beliefs, and literature of peoples from Africa, South America, and Asia. Science teachers can detail the story of early hominids and the beginnings of human culture, or the relationship of disease to population density. In language arts, any reading can be discussed as a reflection of cultural beliefs and practices. Dance, music, and art provide marvelous avenues into other cultures' beliefs, practices, and cultural expressions. Even in mathematics, students can do research reports on mathematics in other lands and times.

Though some anthropologists may argue otherwise, many would probably agree that anthropology belongs in our nation's schools, integrated into both curriculum and teacher education. Because anthropology provides a broad cross-cultural perspective and a framework within which to teach many other precollege science and social science subjects, some would even argue that it should be the basic building block for elementary education and a required subject for secondary school science and social studies teachers. When teachers are taught anthropology, they are offered a perspective and a framework within which they can better understand the many seemingly diverse fragments of their curricula, enabling them to approach their subjects—geography, social studies, world cultures, history, biology, earth science, language, literature, and the arts—in a more coherent and less ethnocentric fashion.

Exclusion of Anthropology from the Precollege Curriculum

As psychology and economics continue to increase their visibility in the secondary school classroom, anthropologists might ask why anthropology has not become more a part of the precollege curriculum. Psychology, economics, and sociology all have familiar career paths, each with a practical application that high school students can grasp. Anthropology cannot compete with traditional subjects like history, which students are required to take, or social sciences like psychology, which students want to study. Over the last twenty-five years, moreover, the other social sciences have made concerted efforts to produce textbooks and teacher training opportunities as well as to offer national association support services for precollege teachers.

Part of the answer for anthropology's exclusion from schools also may lie in the history and nature of the anthropology profession's involvement with teaching (Selig 1982). From its beginnings, anthropology has been primarily a research profession. It has been a teaching profession as well, but almost exclusively in colleges and universities. Showing little interest in precollege education, anthropologists have placed virtually no effort into their discipline's expansion into schools. Unfortunately for the future of the discipline, most of its early pioneers were unable to see the value of "popular anthropology," or the value of anthropology for school students. Whereas other social sciences had a more "applied" aspect and reached out for public understanding, anthropologists remained aloof, suspicious of those like Edgar Lee Hewett and Margaret Mead who believed passionately that the public should benefit from their field (Selig 1982). The majority of anthropologists stood firmly for rigorous scholarship, which they felt was threatened by overt popularization.

Given this orientation, it is not surprising that until the 1950s little anthropology was taught in schools, as almost no anthropologists were interested in writing for younger students. The 1960s and 1970s, with their upheavals in American society, brought some change. As during the 1930s and 1940s, the notion that anthropology might have a practical use in helping to combat a host of societal ills (racism, the aftermath of colonialism, the threat of war) appeared in print. Anthropology grew as a discipline at the university level through increased numbers of departments, undergraduate majors, and graduate degrees. For the first time in the profession's history, professional anthropologists became involved with formal programs aimed at precollege teachers—through federally funded curriculum projects and teacher training institutes (Higgins 1993; Rice 1993).

The social and intellectual ferment of the times left a clear impact, particularly seen in textbook writing. In social studies and history classes, the traditional text, once a chronology of political and economic events and elites, now began to include treatment of the everyday lives of ordinary people, women's experiences, contributions of ethnic and minority groups, and cultures previously ignored, such as pre-Columbian Native American societies or West African cultures ravaged by the slave trade. Many of the data and concepts came, of course, from anthropology, and teachers with anthropology backgrounds found themselves better equipped than many others to deal with the new topics and concerns. It is not surprising that the evidence shows some slow but marked improvement in the presence of anthropology in the precollege curriculum (Dynneson and Coleman 1986).

Anthropology's Increased Presence

This more recent history of anthropology in schools has been described and documented in detail elsewhere (Dynneson 1975; Selig 1982; Higgins 1993; Rice 1993) and need not be repeated here. In summary, the first major effort to expand anthropology in precollege education occurred in the 1960s when the aftermath of Sputnik brought new levels of federal funding into curriculum development and teacher training for many of the sciences and social sciences. Several national projects in anthropology produced well-received materials, but few achieved widespread or long-term use. According to Marion Rice, the demanding nature of the materials, teachers' generally weak background in anthropology, and the lack of funds for dissemination and teacher training accounted for the failure of these early attempts to have anthropology adopted into the precollege curriculum (Rice 1986). In addition, some projects such as the elementary curriculum project *Man, a Course of Study* (MACOS) became the focus of local and even national controversy.

Thomas Dynneson conducted three surveys of the status of precollegiate anthropology—in 1971, 1978, and 1985. These studies revealed a small but increasing presence of anthropology in schools (Dynneson and Coleman 1986). The curriculum projects of the 1960s apparently had left a mark, reflected both in textbook adoption of many of the ideas of the curriculum projects and in the increased presence of anthropology in the curriculum (Higgins 1993). According to Dynneson and Coleman, anthropology "had emerged as a distinct discipline in contrast to its earlier more limited role as a supportive or hidden aspect of the school curriculum" (4–5). For example, "in 1985 anthropology was included in the education and training of secondary school teachers in 19 states" (Dynneson and Coleman 1986).

During the 1970s and 1980s, the National Science Foundation supported the Pre-College Teacher Development Program that funded several anthropology teacher training programs. Written materials as well as films useful for teaching precollege anthropology increased, and in 1988 a Task Force for the Teaching of Anthropology formed within the American Anthropological Association, with a particular emphasis on precollege anthropology. In 1990, on behalf of this task force, Paul Erickson at St. Mary's University in Canada and Patricia Rice at West Virginia University undertook a survey to assess the presence of anthropology in the precollege curriculum, in teacher training, and in teacher certification (results of this survey are reported in Higgins 1993). Thirty of the forty-three state social studies specialists responding to the survey indicated that anthropology could be taught as an elective in high schools in their state. The 1990 survey also revealed that nineteen of the fifty U.S. schools of education responding offered a required course for teachers in training, although seven of these required it only for those training to teach anthropology. In twenty schools of education, anthropology could be taken as an elective. Five schools trained some teachers explicitly to teach anthropology. Of the thirty U.S. state certification agencies responding to the survey, thirteen said anthropology was required for some types of teacher certification. It would appear that there had been some progress in the inclusion of anthropology in the curriculum, in teacher education, and in certification.

Case Study: Smithsonian Programs in Anthropology Teacher Training

In the late 1970s and 1980s, the Smithsonian Institution's Department of Anthropology undertook a major initiative in teacher training in cooperation with the Department of Anthropology at the George Washington University. The Smithsonian Institution/George Washington University Anthropology for Teachers Program was funded from 1978 to 1982 with an annual grant of $50,000 from the National Science Foundation (NSF). In 1983, a similar teacher training program was developed by the Smithsonian with the departments of anthropology, history, and American studies at the University of Wyoming in Laramie, Wyoming, with funding from the National Endowment for the Humanities (NEH) and the Wyoming Council for the Humanities (WCH). These two teacher training programs illustrate ways in which anthropologists can become involved with teachers, schools, and teacher training.

The Anthropology for Teachers programs in Washington and Wyoming had four major objectives, illustrating what its organizers believed teachers wanted and needed from a successful teacher training effort: (1) a solid foundation in anthropology; (2) ways to integrate anthropology into the precollege curriculum; (3) approaches to using community resources; and (4) a network of teachers, anthropologists, and museum educators interested in encouraging precollege anthropology.

The programs were structured to include a tuition-free, semester- or year-long graduate credit course specifically designed for teachers. The programs also included the creation of Anthropology Teaching Resource Centers; a publication for teachers, *AnthroNotes;* and additional evening lectures by distinguished visiting anthropologists. In Washington, the full-year course involved seventy-five junior and senior high school teachers in three sections each year; in Wyoming the semester-long course was a single section of twenty-five teachers who represented every school in Laramie (six elementary, one junior high, and one high school) as well as two rural schools and a high school fifty miles away in Cheyenne, the state capital. In both Washington and Wyoming, the Anthropology for Teachers course was structured around monthly topics of particular relevance to teachers.

The monthly topic approach emerged during the planning stage as a way to meet the needs of both teachers who had had no anthropology courses and those who already had studied anthropology. In addition, this approach offered teachers an in-depth introduction to a few topics they could learn well and then teach in their own classes rather than a more traditional, college survey approach. The topics changed each year but included at various times human evolution, archaeology and ecology, civilizations of the past, Native American cultures, anthropological fieldwork, socialization in non-Western societies, and the anthropology of American life.

Each monthly topic involved an introductory lecture reviewing recent research, a workshop with at least four experiential teaching activities, a seminar session with museum and university scholars discussing their research related to the monthly topic, and a workshop at which teachers viewed teaching materials and films and shared curriculum units they had developed related to the topic. In Washington, for three weeks each month, on a different day each week, the three sections of the course met at three different school locations from 4:00 to 6:00 P.M. During the fourth week, teachers from all three sections met together with anthropologists on a Saturday morning at a resource location—for example, at the National Museum of Natural History, the Alexandria Archaeology Laboratory, or the National Zoo.

In Washington, a team of four staff members worked together to develop the course, write and edit *AnthroNotes,* organize the resource center, and organize the evening lectures. Two team members taught most of the classes, with museum and university anthropologists participating as Saturday morning seminar leaders. In Laramie, with only one Smithsonian team member present, four university professors served as monthly consulting scholars, usually teaching two of the four classes each month and helping to develop the classroom materials. In both Washington and Wyoming, program participants received tuition-free graduate credit and stipends to cover travel and books.

What Makes a Successful Teacher Training Program?

Why did these university-based teacher training programs work? Probably because they included several key ingredients:

1. Initial background research conducted to determine teacher needs so that programs would be relevant and useful to teachers. Background research included studying the precollege curriculum in the communities, interviewing teachers and administrators, and systematically surveying teacher interests and needs.

2. Core classes specifically designed for precollege teachers, not just college courses slightly modified for a new audience, and not just survey courses. Focusing on specific topics for intense periods appeared to be a critical strategy.

3. Hands-on, practical teaching activities and/or strategies that had been tested and shown to work with precollege students, combined with in-depth exposure to the topic. This combination made the core classes both intellectually sound and practical. Each pretested activity presented had both intellectual merit and utility in the classroom.

4. Programs built on the basic premise that both teachers and anthropologists were professionals working together in a joint project as equals. Teachers appreciated working with anthropologists as colleagues and vice versa.

5. Ways to continue interaction between the two groups of professionals once the formal programs ended.

Both students and their teachers responded strongly to professionals with real-life experiences. Through these two teacher training programs, anthropologists demonstrated they have an important contribution to make by communicating and working with precollege teachers and their students. Teachers in both programs were surprised at how much of relevance to their classes they could learn from anthropologists, and anthropologists, in turn, were surprised at how much they learned from interacting with teachers.

For several reasons, anthropologists are particularly well suited to working in American schools. Because they have been trained to build bridges and to work as sensitive outsiders participating in other cultures, anthropologists possess essential skills for working in and promoting innovations within the subculture of schools. As anthropologists, they share with teachers the role of interpreter, for just as anthropologists try to understand and then interpret their subject matter to the outside world, so teachers interpret their subject matter to their students. In addition, anthropology often entails a strong personal commitment with which teachers can identify.

If anthropologists are serious about wanting greater public understanding of their discipline, they must become more heavily involved with precollege anthropology by working more intensively with teachers and schools. Through every teacher who believes in the importance of anthropology and converts her or his students to this view, 120 students can be reached each year.

Someone who teaches for thirty years can impact 3,600 students. If an anthropologist effectively teaches anthropology to a class of thirty teachers, potentially 108,000 high school students can be influenced. The Smithsonian Institution's two anthropology teacher training programs reached over 350 teachers who were involved in an in-depth, year-long experience; through these teachers, anthropologists potentially impacted 560,000 students—such is the multiplier effect of teacher training!

AnthroNotes

The success of *AnthroNotes* reflects the increasing interest among teachers and other educational professionals in anthropology. *AnthroNotes,* celebrating its fifteenth year of publication, originated in 1979 as a six-page newsletter for participants in the National Science Foundation–funded George Washington University/Smithsonian Institution Anthropology for Teachers Program. Like the teacher training program out of which it grew, *AnthroNotes* is a team effort, based on the belief that teachers want (1) updated, relevant, research-based information; (2) practical strategies for classroom application; (3) new resources and field opportunities.

The editorial team for *AnthroNotes* is the same team that created the "Anthropology for Teachers" programs in Washington and Wyoming. The team consists of four editors: Ann Kaupp who is head of the Smithsonian's Anthropology Outreach and Public Information Office; Ruth O. Selig, executive officer for Programs, Office of the Provost, Smithsonian Institution; Alison S. Brooks, chair, Department of Anthropology, George Washington University; and JoAnne Lanouette, chair, Department of English, Sidwell Friends School. Altogether the editors represent over fifty years of teaching experience, from elementary school through graduate school, including extensive experience teaching teachers.

New Opportunities

If anthropology were an important part of teacher training as well as the high school curriculum—as psychology has been for decades—students would automatically go to college knowing about the subject. As a matter of course, public understanding of anthropology would increase, as would awareness of anthropology's potential role in the world today and tomorrow.

The 1990s present some fairly unique opportunities for disseminating anthropology into the American educational system. These opportunities grow from new directions within education and within society as well as from changes within anthropology itself (Selig 1989). Within the field of education, national studies and reform movements, increased anthropology-related subject matter in the curriculum, and the growing ethnic diversity in American classrooms provide a strong context and imperative for the infusion of anthropological concepts and subject matter into the precollege curriculum. Within the discipline of anthropology, a growing acceptance of applied anthropology and a willingness to work within mainstream cultures afford opportunities for anthropologists to become more involved with precollege anthropology. As anthropologist Lawrence Breitborde from Knox College has argued, if more anthropologists were to conceive of precollege education as one special form of applied anthropology, perhaps more would be willing to become involved in this important arena critical to the public understanding of the discipline (Selig 1989). Most important, the American Anthropological Association appears to be increasingly cognizant of the potential impact that greater awareness of anthropology might have on the overall health and future of the discipline. This awareness is reflected in the association's new division overseeing outreach efforts, including initiatives involving public education.

Conclusion

It is time for the national association as well as for individual anthropologists to become involved with precollege anthropology, through working with teachers, students, and schools. If anthropology belongs in our nation's schools, if teachers function better when trained in our discipline, then anthropologists must bear a major responsibility to work with school administrators, train teachers, and write and evaluate textbooks and curriculum materials. Fortunately, such work is not only important but also personally satisfying, intellectually stimulating, and professionally productive.

Notes

AnthroNotes, a National Museum of Natural History Bulletin for Teachers, edited by Ann Kaupp, Ruth O. Selig, Alison S. Brooks, and JoAnne Lanouette, contains articles on current research in the field of anthropology, on teaching activities and resources, and on fieldwork opportunities. Write Anthropology Outreach and Public Information Office, NHB MRC 112, Smithsonian Institution, Washington, D.C. 20560; or call (202) 357-1592. *Teachers Resource Packet in Anthropology* is available from the Anthropology Outreach and Public Information Office (Department of Anthropology, Smithsonian Institution, Washington, D.C. 20560). This packet, updated on a regular basis, includes listings of anthropology teaching resources for all levels of the curriculum, bibliographies of books and articles as well as numerous teaching activities and practical strategies for incorporating anthropology into a wide variety of curriculum units and courses.

References

Dynneson, Thomas L. 1975. *Pre-Collegiate Anthropology: Trends and Materials.* Athens: University of Georgia, Anthropology Curriculum Project.

Dynneson, Thomas L., and Fred Coleman. 1986. "Precollegiate Anthropology in the U.S." In "Anthropology in Pre-College Education," edited by Ruth O. Selig and Patricia J. Higgins. *Practicing Anthropology,* 8(3–4), special double issue.

Higgins, Patricia J. 1993. "Anthropological Programs in Education." *International Encyclopedia of Education.* 2d ed. London: Pergamon.

Rice, Marion. 1986. "Curriculum Artifacts: The Remains of Three Anthropology Projects." *Practicing Anthropology* 8(3–4):6, 19. Special double issue of *Practicing Anthropology in Pre-College Anthropology,* edited by Ruth Selig and Patricia Higgins.

Rice, Marion J. 1993. "Precollege Anthropology/Archaeology." In Virginia S. Wilson, James A. Litle and Gerald Lee Wison, eds., *Teaching Social Studies: Handbook of Trends, Issues, and Implications for the Future* 201–226. Westport, Conn.: Greenwood Press.

Selig, Ruth O. 1982. "Anthropology in the Classroom: Perspectives and Prospects. In "Anthropology in Pre-college Education," edited by Ruth O. Selig and Patricia J. Higgins. *Practicing Anthropology,* 8(3–4), special double issue.

Selig, Ruth O. 1989. "Anthropology in Public Schools: Why Should We Care?" *Anthropology Newsletter* 30(2):28, 3.

Anthropology in the Science
and Social Studies Curriculum

Dennis W. Cheek

Foreign visitors to the United States are frequently perplexed by the size and diversity of our K–12 educational system. A total of 15,577 public school districts (down from 17,995 in 1970–71), comprising over 82,000 buildings, educate over 43.4 million K–12 students. Ten percent of these districts contain more than 61 percent of the total K–12 student population. Another 5.5 million students attend private schools throughout the nation. A total of over 2.8 million teachers in private and public schools attempt to prepare these students to successfully face the twenty-first century. Total expenditure for public K–12 education was estimated at over 279 billion dollars in 1992–93 (National Center for Education Statistics 1994).

Anthropology as a course of study, or anthropological concepts and principles within various school subject areas, presently holds a marginal position within K–12 education. Although schools introduce students to other cultures under the guise of history, geography, and the social studies, a professional anthropologist would register shock at the superficial understandings evidenced by large numbers of teachers and students. Only recently have large-scale, coordinated efforts begun to increase attention to anthropology as a legitimate focus of school learning (Erickson 1994). This venture must clearly be recognized as a sociopolitical struggle in which significant allies must be recruited, "propaganda" must be created and disseminated, and pressure brought to bear locally, statewide, and nationally by the anthropological community (cf. DeBoer 1991). This chapter provides a context for these efforts and suggests specific strategies that anthropologists may employ as they seek to expand attention to anthropological ideas and concepts within the K–12 school systems of this country, especially through disciplines associated with the sciences and the social studies.

Locus of Control

Recent years have witnessed an increasing state presence in education with a focus on increased graduation requirements, statewide learning goals, subject matter frameworks, and expanded means and modes of statewide assessment. One result of these efforts is that 17.3 percent of all 1990 high school graduates had completed four years of English and three years of studies in social studies, science, and mathematics. This result compares favorably with the 1.9

percent of 1982 graduates who had similar course-taking patterns (National Center for Education Statistics 1994). The trend suggests that there is more opportunity than ever before to expose a wider array of students to anthropological concepts and principles through science and social studies education.

The current federal focus on coordinated (systemic) changes throughout the entire K–12 education system from teacher preparation and certification to high school graduation and teacher professional development is the newest educational reform wave (Fuhrman 1993; Jacobson and Berne 1993; Conley 1993). The two major policy documents that will drive federal efforts in education are the Goals 2000 legislation and the reauthorization of the Elementary and Secondary Education Act (ESEA). Although these pieces of legislation increase coordination, overall policy and standards setting, and monitoring of system quality at the state level, they also involve an increase in local autonomy for school districts to choose the modes and means by which they are to achieve state benchmarks for student achievement, equity, and access.

The current reform climate reinforces the importance of the local school district in regard to resource allocation, instructional materials choices, and the organization of schooling. Current reforms, however, diminish local control over broad, overarching instructional goals and standards for student and teacher performance. This means that anthropologists must simultaneously work at both state and local levels to effect changes in the school curriculum.

Activities at the State Level

A large number of states are either creating for the first time or substantially revising their science and social studies curriculum frameworks in response to the Goals 2000 legislation, U.S. Department of Education frameworks development funding, or National Science Foundation–funded Statewide Systemic Initiatives (SSI) in Mathematics, Science, and Technology (Briggs, Cheek, and Yager 1992; Cheek and Kohut 1992).

These frameworks development efforts involve large numbers of representatives from diverse levels of the K–collegiate educational system, business and industry, public and private organizations and associations, and scholars in varied disciplines. Anthropologists should contact their respective state education departments to obtain information on work contemplated, in progress, or completed. For the former two stages, significant input can be directly fed into the process to ensure that anthropological principles and concepts are addressed in a comprehensive manner within the K–12 school curriculum. Documents that have already been completed should be studied to identify points of access within the K–12 curriculum where anthropologists and anthropological materials might find a ready fit.

Many states are currently creating statewide assessment systems to monitor student progress toward subject matter benchmarks and common core learning; all students will be required to demonstrate command of these at some level to graduate from high school. In this climate, there is ample room for input from the anthropological community. Professionals can volunteer their services to help develop banks of test items and to read and score essays or other extended response submissions by students.

Anthropologists can also collaborate with state science and social studies supervisors in seeking funds to develop state-specific curriculum materials that relate curriculum frameworks to anthropological materials and investigations (cf. the "Respecting Ethnic and Cultural Heritage" and "Religion in Human Culture" materials available from the National Diffusion Network in Leutheuser 1994).

Activities at the Local Level

Classroom teachers generally welcome anthropologists and other professionals into their classrooms as long as school district protocols are followed. Generally, those wishing to enter a school to talk about their work or to offer their services start with a call to the principal's office. The principal, as the chief building administrator, can best determine where the volunteer's services might be employed most effectively. Sometimes volunteers are asked to make a short presentation about their plans or ideas to a mixed group of administrators within the central district office or to a group of teachers within a local school building. The professional should place a few ideas for collaboration and assistance on the table and then be prepared to entertain additional ideas offered by the educational community. Such partnerships, where communication and insights are two-way, have become an established part of the educational landscape across the United States (Grobe 1993).

Anthropologists can bring to the school many benefits for both teachers and students. Teachers can benefit from an anthropologist's views of their classroom teaching strategies, the culture and subcultures evident within the school and the classroom, perceptions of the set curriculum and the materials within which it is embodied, and interpersonal relations among the school staff. Students can benefit from exposure to the day-to-day work of an anthropologist, the forms of inquiry and problem solving used by professionals, and a sense of how the anthropologist both chose and prepared for a field of specialty. With some assistance, students can conduct their own limited anthropological investigations within their local communities or even the school itself.

Finding a Subject Matter Niche

The social studies and the sciences are the most natural arenas within which the study of anthropology can reside within the K–12 curriculum. Because these curricula in the United States change frequently, it is unwise to devote too much time here to discussion of a particular one. Instead, some general trends will be noted and the reader is referred to other sources for more extended, time-sensitive information.

Social studies education in the United States has a long and checkered history in K–12 schools. A twentieth-century creation of the educational community, social studies was defined by the National Council for the Social Studies Board of Directors in November 1994 as

> the integrated study of the social sciences and humanities to promote civic competence. Within the school program, social studies provides coordinated, systematic study drawing upon such disciplines as anthropology, archaeology, economics, geography, history, law, philosophy, political science, psychology, religion, and sociology, as well as appropriate content from the humanities, mathematics, and natural sciences. The primary purpose of the social studies is to help young people develop the ability to make informed and reasoned decisions for the public good as citizens of a culturally diverse, democratic society in an interdependent world.

The National Governors Association and the U.S. Department of Education did not recognize social studies as an entity within the K–12 school curriculum that was worthy of special attention in the form of either national educational goals or funding for the development of national subject matter standards. Instead, funding was provided for separate subject matter curriculum standards for (1) U.S. and world history, (2) civics and government, (3) geography, and (4) economics. Large groups of individuals and associations have been working on consensus standards for these four subject matter areas for the past several years. The National Council for the Social Studies, the largest professional association of K–12 educators in the social sciences and humanities, devoted some of its own funds to the creation of curriculum standards for the social studies. These standards were released in April of 1994 and subsequently approved by the Board of Directors (National Council for the Social Studies 1994). Ten thematic strands are used to tie together concepts and principles within the social studies:

- Culture
- Time, Continuity, and Change
- People, Places, and Environment
- Individual Development and Identity
- Individuals, Groups, and Institutions
- Production, Distribution, and Consumption
- Power, Authority, and Governance
- Science, Technology, and Society
- Global Connection
- Civic Ideals

The document specifies for each strand appropriate content understandings on the part of students at elementary, middle, and high school levels. This important national document is a valuable point of access to promote anthropology in the schools among state and local boards of education, state, district, and local administrators, classroom teachers of the social studies, and university and college faculty who prepare social studies teachers. The Civitas framework for civic education (Quigley and Bahmueller 1991) is also a potentially useful document for promoting the study of anthropological concepts and principles as lived in the arena of public decision making and politics.

Social studies instruction within schools has tended to follow an Expanding Environments Model which begins in grade 1 with a look at oneself, one's home, and one's school. Grades 2 and 3 broaden out to the community, grade 4 is the usual point for state and local history, grade 5 introduces U.S. history, and grade 6 generally focuses on the world. Grades 7–9 usually involve more U.S. history, geography, and civics. High school social studies for most students consists of further study of world history, geography, U.S. government, and U.S. history (Cheek and Kohut 1992; Marker and Mehlinger 1992). Many high schools also offer elective courses in subjects like philosophy, economics, anthropology, sociology, psychology, and archaeology. The latter two courses are probably the most pervasive and popular for both teachers and students.

Education in the sciences within K–12 schools is being markedly influenced by a number of national projects as well as multiyear and heavily funded federal initiatives in mathematics, science, and technology education emanating in particular from the National Science Foundation under the general rubric of "systematic change." The National Committee on Science Education Standards and Assessment of the National Research Council (1994) is coordinating the development of national science standards. A first full draft will be released in the fall of 1994 for national distribution and comment. The standards are organized under seven general themes:

- Science as Inquiry
- Physical Science
- Life Science
- Earth and Space Science
- Science and Technology
- Science and Societal Challenges
- History and Nature of Science

Anthropology, by its very nature, consists of science as inquiry. Many of its concepts and principles are part of the arena of the life sciences, and some of the techniques of archaeology, in particular, significantly intersect the physical, earth, and space sciences. The study of early tool making, the industrial revolution, and other forms of ancient and modern technology are science and technology connections familiar to every practicing anthropologist. Similarly, the societal impact of science and technology is an arena of scholarship and investigation to which anthropologists have contributed a great deal. The philosophical debate over the nature of science and the degree to which it is culturally sensitive or culturally biased is an important arena where anthropologists and anthropology should have a voice.

A second project of national significance in science education and to anthropology is the multiphase initiative of the American Association for the Advancement of Science Project 2061. The name of the project is an acknowledgment that the present generation of students will be alive to witness the return of Halley's comet in 2061. A group of over 300 individuals assisted the Project 2061 staff in developing a book-length exposition of the science literacy that its proponents believed should be in the possession of every senior graduating from high school (Rutherford and Ahlgren 1990). The "Science for All Americans" which was advocated was a much more integrated, conceptually focused, and interdisciplinary science education than most present teachers or adults experienced in their own K–12 education. Themes and concepts from varied fields of human endeavor such as the arts, history, economics, and yes, anthropology, were woven into the fabric of science education for all students.

Teams of teachers in six regional sites across the United States took on the next phase of the project, which was to create a set of curriculum benchmarks that would specify what each student should know, appreciate, or be able to do at particular points on the K–12 continuum (American Association for the Advancement of Science 1993). These curriculum benchmarks were organized around twelve chapters that correspond to those in the earlier book, *Science for All Americans:*

- The Nature of Science
- The Nature of Mathematics
- The Nature of Technology
- The Physical Setting
- The Living Environment
- The Human Organism
- Human Society
- The Designed World
- The Mathematical World
- Historical Perspectives
- Common Themes (systems, models, constancy and change, scale)
- Habits of Mind

Only a few selected examples from the Benchmarks document related to anthropology can be cited here:

- Early in human history, there was an agricultural revolution in which people changed from hunting to gathering to farming. This allowed changes in the division of labor between men and women and between children and adults, and the development of new patterns of government. (end of grade 8)

- Mass media, migrations, and conquest affect social change by exposing one culture to another. Extensive borrowing among cultures has led to the virtual disappearance of some cultures but only modest change in others. (end of grade 12)

- Although rules at home, school, church, and in the community stay mostly the same, sometimes they change. Changes in social arrangements happen because some rules do not work or new people are involved or outside circumstances change. (end of grade 5)

Science is typically not emphasized in lower elementary grades but becomes increasingly more prominent as one ascends the K–12 continuum, tapering off again around grade 11. (Further information on contemporary trends and curricula are not mentioned here [Briggs, Cheek, and Yager 1992; Fensham 1992]). As anthropologists become more familiar with these national documents of importance and enter dialogues with K–12 educators at national, state, and local levels, there are clearly many points of entry into the K–12 education arena for practicing professionals. Remaining attuned to the local political climate while knowing the central features of influential national documents will aid anthropologists in effectively arguing the case for and promoting implementation of anthropological ideas and principles within K–12 school settings.

References

American Association for the Advancement of Science. 1993. *Benchmarks for Science Literacy. Project 2061.* New York: Oxford University Press.

Briggs, Robert, Dennis W. Cheek, and Robert Yager, eds. 1992. *Science: A Practical Guide for K–12 Science Curriculum.* Millwood, N.Y.: Kraus International Publications.

Cheek, Dennis W., and Sylvester Kohut, Jr. eds. 1992. *Social Studies: A Practical Guide for K–12 Social Studies Curriculum.* Millwood, N.Y.: Kraus International Publications.

Conley, David T. 1993. "Roadmap to Restructuring: Policies, Practices and the Emerging Visions of Schooling." Eugene, Ore.: ERIC Clearinghouse on Educational Management.

DeBoer, George. 1991. *A History of Ideas in Science Education: Implications for Practice.* New York: Teachers College Press.

Erickson, P. A. 1994. "Anthropology Teaching at the Precollege Level." In *The International Encyclopedia of Education,* vol. 1, edited by Torsten Husen and T. Neville Postlethwaite, 2d ed., 297–300. New York: Pergamon Press.

Fensham, Peter J. 1992. "Science and Technology." In *Handbook of Research on Curriculum,* edited by Philip W. Jackson, 789–829. New York: Macmillan.

Fuhrman, Susan H., ed. 1993. *Designing Coherent Education Policy: Improving the System.* San Francisco: Jossey-Bass.

Grobe, Terry. 1993. *Synthesis of Existing Knowledge and Practice in the Field of Educational Partnerships.* Washington, D.C.: U.S. Department of Education, Office of Educational Research and Improvement (PIP 93-1102).

Jacobson, Stephen L., and Robert Berne, eds. 1993. *Reforming Education: The Emerging Systemic Approach.* Thousand Oaks, Calif.: Corwin Press.

Leutheuser, Jami, ed. 1994. *Educational Programs That Work: Catalogue of the National Diffusion Network.* 20th ed. Longmont, Colo.: Sopris West.

Marker, Gerald, and Howard Mehlinger. 1992. "Social Studies." In *Handbook of Research on Curriculum,* edited by Philip W. Jackson, 830–851. New York: Macmillan.

National Center for Education Statistics. 1994. *Mini-Digest of Education Statistics 1993.* Washington, D.C.: Office of Educational Research and Improvement, U.S. Department of Education (NCES 94-289).

National Council for the Social Studies. 1994. *Curriculum Standards for the Social Studies.* April 1994 Draft. Washington, D.C.: National Council for the Social Studies.

National Research Council. 1994. *National Science Education Standards.* Discussion Summary of May 1, 1994. Washington, D.C.: National Research Council.

Quigley, C. N., and Bahmueller, C. F., eds. 1991. *Civitas: A Framework for Civic Education.* Calabasas, Calif.: Center for Civic Education.

Rutherford, James, and Andrew Ahlgren. 1990. *Science for All Americans.* New York: Oxford University Press.

Archaeology for the Young Reader

NORAH MOLONEY

I have recently written a children's book on archaeology. It is one of a new reference series published by Oxford University Press; the first will appeared in the fall of 1994. Other topics in the series are ecology, astronomy, the prehistoric world, medicine, architecture, and literature. Oxford University Press's approach to these volumes is that they be "*real* books about *real* subjects": in other words, they should be of a length (160 pages or about 50,000 words) that will permit an in-depth introduction to the subject matter. The books themselves are large format (276 × 219 mm) and are well illustrated with commissioned artwork, photographs, maps, diagrams, and time lines. The authors have been chosen not only because they are specialists in a particular field but also because of an ability to communicate their enthusiasm and knowledge to a young audience. Although the target age range is ten- to fourteen-year-olds, the books will appeal to the general public, regardless of age.

My brief from Oxford University Press was simply presented: to provide an introduction to the wide-ranging scope of archaeology for children. Deciding on the content was not quite so simple; the needs of the prospective audience had to be considered. These and my own particular background played a role in my approach to the book.

I had originally trained as an elementary school teacher and worked in a variety of teaching roles in England, Canada, Australia, and the United States. Between positions I traveled in Asia, Africa, and South America. After a long trip to South America in 1980, I moved to Boston where I decided to take a course in anthropology to learn more about the people and places I had seen on my travels. The first course happened to be an introduction to archaeology. Within a few weeks, I was hooked and decided on a career change. After graduation at the Harvard Extension School, I moved back to England to continue graduate studies at University College, London. At the same time, I worked as a part-time substitute elementary teacher and it was not long before children and colleagues learned of my interest in archaeology. Although I did not teach a specific course in archaeology, I often spoke about my particular interest, the Stone Age, and found the children particularly receptive to the subject. I noticed that many became increasingly aware of archaeological topics presented in the media and would often talk to me about what they had seen or read. Some even brought artifacts, such as old coins, into the classroom.

The enthusiasm for archaeology I found among children mirrored my own, so I therefore welcomed the opportunity to write a book on the subject for them. Although books on archaeology for children are becoming more popular in Great Britain, they tend to be restricted to particular aspects—for example, the Romans, Ancient Greece, the Egyptians, or the Stone Age. Some, such as the splendid books of Peter Connolly on Greece and Rome, are presented in great detail based on thorough research; others are of an insufficient length to do anything but give a short synopsis of a subject. Longer time periods may be covered by some publications but detail is lacking. The past is presented as a story based on facts, although the manner in which those facts came to light—that is, the archaeology of the story—is often limited to a very few pages of a book. Encouragingly, in recent publications the actual archaeology itself is beginning to be more widely addressed. English Heritage, the main organization in England responsible for heritage conservation, and the Council for British Archaeology, which promotes interest in and understanding of the archaeological environment of Great Britain and Northern Ireland, both publish books, pamphlets, and education packs for use as source material for curriculum work. It seems to me, and obviously to Oxford University Press, that a volume dealing with the aims and methods of archaeology in some depth will add to and stimulate the growing body of interest in the subject. I had several aims in preparing the contents of my own book:

- To pass on my own enthusiasm for archaeology to children
- To show the range in topic and period covered by archaeology and the different types of archaeologies practiced
- To show the variety of evidence available to and used by archaeologists
- To present archaeological methods and techniques in detail
- To stimulate a problem-solving approach to all subjects by emphasizing the use of such an approach in archaeological investigation
- To provide school teachers with an archaeological resource book

It is my wish to educate and entertain young readers by presenting archaeology as an experience, an adventure, and a process of discovery.

Choosing the Topics

The book is divided into three sections. An introduction to archaeological methods and techniques is presented in the first section. This includes site formation processes, survival and variety of evidence and the information encoded in the evidence, discovery and excavation of sites, and postexcavation work. The concept of relative and absolute dating is discussed and the more common methods are explained. In this way, the readers are introduced to the tools of the trade and the archaeological vocabulary they will encounter as they read on. My main concern for this section is that it not become too dry and lose the reader's attention. It must be carefully worded so that it can be understood with ease;

and I feel, for this reason, that it needs to be particularly well illustrated with photographs, diagrams, and maps.

The second and largest section of the book presents a series of case studies. Each chapter concentrates on one main site that is presented in detail. Other relevant sites may be introduced in illustrations or boxes. The story of the site develops through description of excavations, the evidence revealed, and interpretations of that evidence. I hope that the detective in children will develop as they begin to spot and interpret clues. Sites chosen for this section span periods from the earliest hominid evidence in Africa to the recent garbage project in the United States. They illustrate, too, different aspects of site formation and preservation, excavation techniques, artifact handling, and interpretation. Additionally, they exemplify the range of archaeologies: pre- and protohistoric, Roman, historic, industrial, salvage/rescue, and underwater as well as ethnoarchaeology. Throughout the book the variety of evidence used by archaeologists is underlined.

The final section presents topics that play an important role in archaeology and which I felt would be better treated as topics rather than as individual sites: art, writing, pottery, and burials.

Two further considerations influenced my choice of sites. First was the geographic location of the prospective audience; as the book will be published worldwide, I selected sites that mirrored the global nature of archaeology. A second consideration was influenced by the National Curriculum in England—a curriculum of study, developed by specialists under governmental auspices, that applies to all subjects taught in schools. The National Curriculum for History sets out topics to be covered, targets to be achieved, required assessments, and guidelines for teachers. It aims at developing in children an awareness of past life and change through time as well as introducing them to the range of source material used to discover the past. It further aims to develop analytical and interpretive skills.

Although archaeology is not a subject in its own right, archaeological techniques are suggested as aids in understanding many history topics. The National Curriculum for History also includes the study of a number of non-European ancient civilizations where the role of archaeological evidence is presented. I have therefore included aspects of some of these civilizations—for example, Egypt, Aztecs, Indus, Ancient Greece, and Rome.

The final and most crucial consideration was to choose sites and topics that fit the criteria but that would, above all, attract, maintain the interest of, and stimulate the children. Most readers will be acquainted with or at least have heard about some sites—Stonehenge, Pompeii—and some topics—Egypt, the Aztecs, the Olympic Games, Ice Age hunters. Other sites and topics may be less well known, if at all—for example, underwater archaeology, ethnoarchaeology, railways. Although the book will cover both well-known and less well-known sites and topics, I hope the description of the archaeological investigations leading to subsequent and often conflicting interpretations will provide the young readers with a greater understanding of archaeology at work.

Writing the Book

Preparation of each chapter involves much the same background research as a similar book for adults. I feel it is essential that the most recent research be described where possible. In trying to keep abreast of current literature on each site, I have compiled a mass of notes, which need to be carefully edited. Indeed, the editing is a far greater problem than the background research as there is always much more information than chapter space. Based as I am at the Institute of Archaeology in London, I have been most fortunate in having most of my chapters refereed by in-house specialists. No one has refused to check a chapter and all have made positive contributions and suggestions as well as encouraging my work. As a result, I can pick up and correct mistakes or omissions, and I can feel assured that my facts are accurate.

Also to be considered was the age of the prospective audience in selecting the vocabulary to be used. It was necessary to achieve a balance between using a vocabulary that promotes the reception of sometimes difficult concepts or technical descriptions while still challenging the mind of the reader. Each chapter is reviewed by Oxford University Press's editors for style and vocabulary. Between the academic and style referees, I hope to achieve an acceptable balance of content and vocabulary. The children's response and royalties will tell.

Beyond the Book

I have found the experience of writing the book stimulating, exciting, fulfilling, and educating. I am gaining an insight into the intricacies of book production and publishing. Periods of stress related to time and word limits as well as the choice of illustrations have also reared their ugly heads. Indeed, I had not realized how much time was required to choose, agree on, and receive illustrations, then to prepare captions for them—time I had not considered when submitting my first few estimations of how long it would take to complete a first draft. Neither had I realized the lapse of time between final draft and publication.

Preparation, research, and writing each chapter has also reminded me of the vitality, range, and excitement of archaeology that attracted me in the first place. After years of doctoral research, it was a pleasure to be able to widen my horizons once again and discover that there was more to archaeology than the Lower Palaeolithic of Iberia!

But now that the book nears completion, what next? I hope the book will stimulate and foster in others the enthusiasm for archaeology that I feel. I have encountered such enthusiasm among the participants in adult education courses I currently teach and will use the book as a basis for one of my next classes. With schools, however, it is different. Whereas my job is to concentrate on the topic, school teachers do not usually have enough time to pursue specific aspects of it in great detail. In England, particularly, I have noticed the increasing burden laid on teachers since the introduction of the National Curriculum, which allows little time for more exotic topics. I am convinced that the problem-solving aspect of archaeological investigation can be employed in most other subjects and can aid the intellectual development of children. But when do teachers have the time to discover and understand those techniques? Similarly, the presentation of ancient civilizations may be limited by the teacher's knowledge, workload, and available research time. Ancient Egypt, Rome, and Greece are well-known and popular topics taught with regular monotony. But what about Sumeria, Babylonia, Assyria, Benin, and the Indus, for example? Why do they not enjoy the same popularity? Quite simply, because teachers know far less, if anything at all, about them, nor do they have time to undertake the necessary research required to present them in the same detail as Egypt, for example. I am in the process of setting up a pilot project for a series of seminars and workshops for teachers to raise their level of awareness and interest in the possible approaches to presenting these topics in the classroom. In the future, I would like to see similar workshops as part of student teacher training. Cooperation between archaeologist and teacher can lead to exciting classroom work.

Introducing Research through Chocolate
A Fifth-Grade Class Gets a Taste of Anthropology

ANN CHRISTINE FRANKOWSKI

Every day teachers and students confront cultural diversity: school popu-lations are heterogeneous, curricula stress multiculturalism, and the surround-ing social world heeds global concerns as frequently as local issues. It seems natural, then, that anthropology, whose very essence is the cross-cultural study of humankind, is the discipline to provide educators with the core of concepts and methods of analysis needed to understand and explain cultural diversity. For at least four decades, there have been calls for implementing anthropology in the elementary school curriculum (Dynneson 1977; Kalso 1973; Lauderdale 1977; Messick 1983; Rosenfeld 1968; Soldier 1990), but little has changed since Rosenfeld wrote:

> It should be noted that anthropologists . . . have seemed content to remain unnoticed in public school settings. Few feel an urgent desire to foster the inclusion of their particular passion in the learnings of children. One might conclude . . . that anthropology would clutter the curriculum. Schoolmen seem to see no need for it; and the anthropologist feels he had best remain aloof. (1973, 128)

Anthropology remains invisible in the very area where it would have its most positive and lasting impact: the education of children. The field of anthropol-ogy is relatively unknown, suffering under the stereotypes of archaeology and paleontology. People do not know who anthropologists are and what they do and hence see no need to incorporate their research into education. In 1963, Mandelbaum wrote of the value of teaching anthropology to college students, and his ideas pertain to elementary school students as well:

> It should give students a wider acquaintance with other peoples, a better understanding of diversity and similarity among cultures, and of cultural stability and change. It should open the way to a deeper appreciation of their own culture, and should provide incentive and intellectual equipment with which they will continue to develop their knowledge after they leave the classroom. (1963, 7)

It is precisely these goals that make anthropology relevant in today's pre-collegiate education. Its holistic approach and integration of concepts corre-late with education's focus on coordinating curricula. Anthropology should not compete with existing subjects, especially as state governments continually mandate new programs on already overburdened school districts. Instead, it can supplement units in social studies, language arts, science, and related disciplines. Anthropologists need to be aware of educational research to see how the two fields best intersect. To do so, anthropologists must, as Lindquist states, "labor on the local front. . . . Professional anthropologists, to be effective in public education, must become immersed in local education, for there is no better way of analyzing the needs of school systems" (1973, 530).

The disciplines of anthropology and education complement each other as both teach skills and concepts transferrable into everyday life. As more and more issues pertaining to diversity surface, anthropology can provide ways that foster positive interaction between administrators, teachers, students, and parents. As neighborhoods become more culturally varied (for example, the influx of immigrants and refugees, shifts in rural-urban demographics) and as more school-based management programs are implemented, these same ways can affect school/community interaction as well.

Role of Research

Teachers today find it important to introduce their students to thinking skills and problem-solving techniques. Creativity is nurtured and a "hands-on" approach to learning results in a student's increased understanding and appreciation of educational constructs and processes. One key to successful learning is the use of primary research. By teaching basic research tools, educators provide a framework for helping students organize ideas, investigate the problem, and complete the task. Students and teachers then work together to develop the topic, devise a strategy, and conduct the study.

> If we are to help students function as true researchers, it will be necessary to tackle problems for which we, as teachers, do not have ready answers. . . . In real research, the teacher must give up holding the final solution and take on the role of fellow investigator, never quite sure what the data will bring. Key to this changed role of the teacher is assisting students in posing genuine research questions: questions to which there are no predetermined answers and for which data [are] available. (Starko and Schack 1992, xiii)

Research outlines aid teachers in organizing class projects and assist in keeping both students and faculty on task. In the case study presented in this chapter, Marlene Iris (1992) followed an eight-step program: (1) Students and teachers work together to develop a manageable topic and therefore together they own the project. (2) Students collect and (3) sift through the data, brainstorm, and select a problem on which the whole class can work. (4) Students collect, (5) analyze, and (6) synthesize the data. (7) Students create a product—a book, videotape, play, board display, fair—that explains and illustrates their topic. (8) Finally, students critique their research.

In conducting independent research, students incorporate their own identities and interests into the curriculum while at the same time they learn what has been prescribed by it. The teacher's role as facilitator is crucial. Teachers must be cognizant of the subject matter, the expectations and needs of the students, the tools required to meet research objectives, and the impact of the project on the school itself. As Starko and Schack succinctly state:

> Recognizing that the world they will face as adults will be filled with challenges beyond our imagination today, we cannot begin to give students all the information they will need to be successful. We can, however, give them the tools to think critically, to discover and organize new information. Research methodology provides some of those tools. (1992, xiv)

Case Study: The Chocolate Project

The following case study demonstrates how anthropological concepts and methods were integrated into a research project focused on *chocolate*. Concepts were explained in the context of the subject, and investigative activities helped to illustrate ideas with practical applications. The focus of this class was to develop critical research skills and to conduct primary research.

This project was conducted by a group of fifth-grade students in an Enrichment Triad (E.T.) program over one school calendar year. It was coordinated and supervised by one E.T. teacher, Ms. Marlene Iris, assisted by a committed school staff and a cadre of parent volunteers, including an anthropologist. The students as a class decided the topic of study. They were already familiar with independent learning; in fourth grade, they completed a comprehensive study of a neighboring community.

This case study is organized in three parts: units of exploration, conceptual applications, and research activities. Each unit is summarized as to its main thrust. It is then followed by a discussion of concepts developed to relate anthropology to that unit. The third part centers on research activities that stress the "hands-on" or three-dimensional aspects of learning.

Anthropology through History

Students were introduced to the history of chocolate through a chronological perspective incorporating anthropological concepts. This model provided a framework that would help class members grasp the connection between a historical sequence of events and the integration of cultural factors.

The history of chocolate began in pre-Hispanic middle America (Morton and Morton 1986; Sherman 1984). Farmers cultivated the cacao tree and produced a bean that found prominence in several cultures across this region. Christopher Columbus was not impressed when he was introduced to chocolate by Nicaraguans in 1502, nor were Ferdinand and Isabella when they tasted the product on his return. Several years later, in 1519, Hernán Cortés saw its value in Aztec culture and its potential use by explorers as an aid in conquest, and he brought home with him to Spain both beans and the technology necessary for cocoa production. In pre-Hispanic Mexico, cocoa beans were used for currency, barter, ransom, and tribute. Chocolate, which the Aztec god Quetzalcoatl had given to his people, was a popular beverage bestowing wisdom, understanding, energy, and strength on those who consumed it; and it was Montezuma, the Aztec ruler, who introduced Cortés to chocolate.

Cortés himself found the drink too bitter. His king, Charles V, added sugar, an expensive ingredient at that time, making chocolate popular among Spain's wealthy elite. As Spanish explorers traversed the globe, they introduced cocoa plantations. The consumption of chocolate became more widespread when, in the seventeenth century, it was brought to Italy, France, and England. Drinking chocolate became the rage in these European countries, with price restricting its intake mostly to the upper class. Chocolate houses began appearing in London, open only to males. Chocolate was popular among Mexicans as well. Stories abound as to how aristocratic women had chocolate served to them at mass; when the Bishop attempted to curtail this behavior, he was poisoned—in his morning chocolate!

In the eighteenth century, Carolus Linnaeus named the cocoa bean Theobroma or "Food of the Gods." Dunne and Mackie tell us that the first historical record of chocolate sold in colonial America was at a Boston apothecary in 1712 (1992, 77). This century saw Americans and Europeans experimenting with chocolate processing. In the nineteenth century, the Swiss began to refine the taste of chocolate, but not until the middle of the 1800s was chocolate seen as something other than a beverage. The twentieth century brought to consumers the rapid expansion of chocolate as a confectionery; the popular Hershey "kiss" was invented in 1907 (its streamer added in 1921), and the chocolate bar, introduced at the turn of the century, was heavily popularized during World War I.

Conceptual Applications: Students worked through understanding the definition of culture and its use in explaining diversity: how people are different (and similar) over time, across the globe, and within their own communities. The cross-cultural variability in taste was an interesting avenue to explore. We learn from our culture through familial and peer socialization what tastes good. In the United States, Americans are provincial in their taste: 90 percent of all chocolate consumed is milk chocolate. For centuries, in cooking meat and poultry, Mexicans have added chocolate whereas people in other cultures neither use chocolate nor favor any sweets. These examples are but a few we explored to demonstrate diversity and to introduce the concepts of ethnocentrism and cultural relativism.

The study of chocolate lends itself to discussions of change and culture contact—from its abstract "dynamic" qualities and concepts of acculturation, assimilation, and diffusion to its tangible examples: the word *chocolat* stems from the Nahuatl *xocoatl* or *chocolatl*; chocolate's popularity changed from an unsweetened beverage to candy; the limited geographic area (within twenty degrees of the equator in tropical forests) producing beans and countries building processing plants result in a product that extends over several societies. Cultural contact and diffusion are key issues and span centuries—from the impact of indigenous meso-American cultures on each other and Spanish conquistadors on the Aztecs, to the modification by Europeans and Americans of chocolate processing, and finally to the effect industrial nations have on Third World cultivators of cocoa beans.

The traditional notion of the cultural universal can be explored as well. The role of the European court and its use of power relate chocolate to the political process. Chocolate and its value in dowry exchange integrate kinship and economics. Currency, tribute, trade, ransom, and the environment all impinge on the economic sector. Taxation of chocolate played a pivotal role in filling governmental coffers, and its high cost restricted consumers. A discussion of rituals and values demonstrates religious aspects of culture: chocolate entered the world as a gift from a deity, Toltecs extended cocoa branches as tokens during religious ceremonies, and in the sixteenth and seventeenth centuries Spanish and Italian monks controlled European chocolate production.

The concept of stratification is well illustrated, and students find this especially interesting. The fact that on one continent chocolate is a beverage restricted to the upper class and on another it is sometimes consumed by slaves and plantation cultivators is another example illustrating diversity. In discussing stratification, students examine social class (which can be extended to caste), gender, wealth, achieved and ascribed status, and ethnicity. Students ponder values as well, questioning the sale of humans and their price; a slave in pre-Hispanic Mexico commanded 100 cocoa beans, a rabbit sold for eight. Students can then examine their own social situation in relation to what they found in the cultural data; one example is to see how their own purchasing power and values affect what chocolate they buy. Can they afford to spend twenty dollars a pound for handmade candy, or are they more likely to buy a fifty-cent bar at the supermarket?

No matter what concepts are selected, it is important to demonstrate their cultural integration. The study of politics is not divorced from religion, nor kinship from economics. Chocolate, at some level, is connected directly or indirectly, formally or informally, to many aspects of culture, and in this project, provides the vehicle for understanding what culture is and how it operates.

Research Activities: A cultural anthropologist presented data on chocolate to the class. Students focused on "taste" from a cross-cultural perspective to family and individual preferences. They tasted types of chocolates and were encouraged (but warned) to try unsweetened cocoa at home. Folklore can be introduced; the theme of chocolate exists in jokes, tongue twisters, and jump rope rhymes. Students also could be encouraged to read history, cookbooks (which often contain a great deal of interesting cultural material), novels, short stories, and poems. An art project such as chocolate sculpture is feasible.

From Bean to Mouth

Students reviewed the process of chocolate making, from the collecting of raw materials to the finished product. Candy production, by definition, spans several cultures; beans are harvested in a number of countries in Africa and the Americas, and production employs technological procedures refined over time by Mexican, Spanish, French, Swiss, and American inventors. The class was introduced to the economic aspects of production, comparing a small business to a large-scale production company. Depending on a student group's sophistication, teachers can explore issues relating to the ramifications of international economic exchange policies, equitable pay scales for workers in Third World countries, environmental impact on land use, and effect of cash crop production on local diets. They can even pose the question of whether people living in countries growing cocoa beans can afford to purchase a finished product.

Conceptual Applications: The international components of chocolate production and its cross-cultural linkages provide the core for discussing anthropological concepts on a global scale. Students who have participated in "invention conventions" may be able to examine the relationship of innovation, invention, and change. Concepts from economic anthropology dovetail into this section: reciprocity, redistribution, and market exchange, economic survival and exploitation, corporate culture and the role of secrecy, methods of agriculture and effective land use, the relevance of capital and currency, and culturally specific industrial and governmental standards for product testing and production. Students enjoy finding and comparing chocolate themes on artifacts in the sphere of popular culture; such items include tee shirts, mugs, buttons, post-a-notes, and greeting cards.

Research Activities: Students were asked to assess a videotape on chocolate candy production and were encouraged to search for articles and books on all aspects of chocolate. The Chocolate Manufacturers Association of the U.S.A. was contacted for information, and depending on the research focus of a particular class, other groups such as the Food and Drug Administration and its counterparts in other countries could be contacted as well.

From Factory to Hand

In this unit, the class focused on the channels of candy distribution from the factory to the retailer and compared warehouse markets with chain and independent grocers, and "mom and pop" candy stores with gas stations and vending machine outlets. Students studied the role of the food broker, the profitability of candy (actual cost of item in relation to its selling price), inexpensive ways to market candy, alternative strategies to distribute candy (fund-raising), and the cost of advertising. Five top candy companies and their products were rated as to their national popularity.

Conceptual Applications: Social organization and social control formed the nucleus of this unit. What social groups and individuals are designated to maintain the flow of candy in a society? Who decides which candy, in what sizes, gets distributed to what locations for which clientele to buy? Is the operator of a newsstand treated differently from a chain store grocer? Are there differences in candy distribution between states? neighborhoods? ethnic communities? age groups? What happens when a candy bar does not sell? Why is there price variability in advertising, and who pays? How powerful is the consumer? In this unit, interviewing skills and the concept of sequencing with its relationship to social organization were reinforced.

Research Activities: A candy distributor spoke to the class and fielded questions. He brought numerous examples of candy bars, which the students willingly tasted, compared, and evaluated as to individual and group preferences. The fifth-graders learned to devise flow charts as an explanatory tool.

Candy Manufacturers in International Scope

Students contacted candy manufacturers in several countries to obtain data. Working mostly in groups of two, students composed and sent letters asking a variety of questions focusing on each company's history, genealogical links, and examples of success; its types of products and the number and location of its manufacturing units; its place on the international candy scene; its selection process for naming products; its field-testing procedures and consumer statistics. Companies responded, often sending packets of information and candy samples. A vice president of a major East Coast candy company arranged a conference call to talk with the class. He not only sent candy that his company already marketed locally but also provided new items being field-tested at that time on the West Coast.

Conceptual Applications: Contacting candy companies in the United States and Western Europe once again reinforced the cross-cultural scope of the project. Some children learned early about rejection as not all companies responded and not all questions were asked during the conference call. Other children dealt with anger and envy when one peer consumed more than his share of candy sent to the class by one manufacturer.

Research Activities: The activities in this unit centered on finding addresses of candy companies in order to send letters soliciting information. Students combed household cupboards, magazine advertisements, telephone books, and supermarket displays. As a class, they devised a list of questions and then, individually and in small groups of two and three, sent letters to companies, demonstrating yet another example of "writing across the curriculum." The conference call provided an ideal way for the children to have personal contact with an executive of a major candy company and to ask pertinent questions at the same time. The students field-tested candy not available locally, performing an activity that they themselves would eventually do at their own school with their own product. Students whose schools have computers can use the Internet as yet another avenue from which to obtain data.

Designing, Field-Testing, Marketing, and Selling the Product

Designing a Product: At this point in the project, students knew they wanted to make and market a chocolate candy product. Because few of these fifth-graders had ever made candy, the first step was to acquaint the children with the "hands-on" experience of chocolate making. A chocolate laboratory was created in which the children experimented with painting and forming molds, adding flavoring, and creating hand-built forms. They soon realized that painting is time-consuming, chocolate hardens quickly, and raw materials are expensive. Students formed their own candy company, "KBSS" (Kids Business Super Success), designing their candy with cost and production time in mind. The finished product needed to be easy to handle, inexpensive to make, and large enough in size and deliciously tempting to appeal to an elementary school student-consumer. The class decided that a base of Rice Krispies treats covered in chocolate and decorated with sprinkles would be tasty, attractive, and inexpensive. The school purchased the chocolate and parents supplied other ingredients, paper products, and assistance.

Conceptual Applications: The role of politics and group decision making as well as the imposition of economic factors on the creative process form the core of the conceptual applications in this unit. How does the informal structure work, and who leads in formulating the group's decision? Students discovered that their choice of product had to be negotiated through a decision-making process involving each other, their teacher (who had to agree to release funding for the chocolate), their administrators (from whom they needed permission and a location to make and sell their product), and their families (who were key contributors of resources). They learned that to network effectively they needed to consider a host of limitations. Within the confines of working with chocolate, these fifth-grade confectioners applied problem-solving skills to create a product that would have appeal to a particular age subset of their culture in their school community. They designed a candy with both aesthetic and economic referents in mind.

Research Activities: It takes involvement in only one chocolate laboratory composed of fifth-graders to appreciate Olney's words, "When working with chocolate, always wear brown" (1982). The initial laboratory scheduled in late December of the school calendar year provided the students with "hands-on" learning. Sample molds; milk and bittersweet chocolate; red, green, and white coatings; and a variety of flavorings (crushed peppermint sticks, Heath bar crunch nuggets, and bits of malted milk balls) gave students materials to get the "taste" of working with chocolate.

In the second chocolate laboratory conducted in early spring, the students made their prototypes for field-testing. Initially they had decided to market the chocolate-coated Rice Krispies ball as a "pop" on a stick. However, the candy proved to be too sticky for the children, whose hands were either covered in chocolate or marshmallow Krispies, to insert the stick and keep the product looking "clean." Students quickly solved the problem by designing "balls." Two of the chocolate-covered Rice Krispies candies were coated with sprinkles—one plain chocolate and one multicolored—and the third prototype was left unsprinkled. Students worked in one of three groups either forming, dipping, or sprinkling the treats.

Field-Testing the Product: Students field-tested their prototypes, sampling a small group of children from second, third, and fourth grades. The class devised survey sheets that elicited information on grade, age, gender, and candy preference. Subjects selected their preference on visually aesthetic qualities and then were rewarded for their efforts by tasting one of the three prototypes.

Conceptual Applications: After comparing sampling methods from a scientific perspective, the students soon realized that kinship has a stronger influence in selecting informants when it comes to field-testing candy than any abstract scientific principle. Younger siblings pressured their older sisters and brothers to be included in the sample. "Participatory kinship" was a factor with which to reckon. Once this problem was reconciled (and explained in the larger scope of sampling) and after students confronted the concepts of objectivity and research bias as they related to questioning their informants, the class field-tested their prototypes. Survey sheets were analyzed and the decision finalized: the class would make, advertise, and sell candy with a Rice Krispies/marshmallow base, coated in milk chocolate, and dipped into multicolored sprinkles.

Research Activities: Students selected a research sample and field-tested their culinary prototypes, attempting to be as nonbiased as possible despite the impact of sibling pressure and the researchers' own strong preferences. They compiled and analyzed survey sheets to ascertain the prototype most favored by their research subjects.

Marketing the Product: Students wrestled with the question of how best to market their new candy sensation. They created an extensive publicity campaign, advertising the "Chocolate Chummy," a name selected to appeal to both sexes and all age groups and to elicit "friendly" feelings about the candy. The children advertised their product, price, and date of sale by hanging posters, singing jingles during morning and afternoon announcements, and traveling throughout the school with the "Chocolate Chummy Train," whose "engineers" were outfitted with train whistles and railroad caps. The extremely varied socioeconomic backgrounds of the school children were a major factor in the product's low price, and the fifth-graders decided to donate all proceeds to charity.

Conceptual Applications: Numerous concepts are illustrated in this unit. Economic factors, financial backgrounds of students' families, and a sense of community surfaced quickly when students had to decide the candy's selling price. The class wanted everyone to be able to afford to buy at least one Chummy. Values coupled with economic concerns became real-life, pertinent issues. Students considered the school as an institution and the role it plays in marketing. Permission to advertise had to be secured at every level, whether it involved cajoling the teacher in charge of school announcements or driving the train through the pods and corridors. To an extent, students realized that networking helped; the school principal and classroom teacher were supportive of each other and of the project, and the continual presence of parent volunteers gave credence to the activity. Students needed to discover what factors would sell the Chocolate Chummy to a varied elementary school body—one diverse in age (kindergarten through adult staff) and socioeconomic backgrounds. This class had a sufficient number of incipient feminists who were quick to eliminate any use of male pronouns in the advertising campaign. Other questions were considered: What poster designs would capture the appeal of an elementary school "subculture"? Would singing jingles be effective? Would fifth-grade students who saw themselves fitting in somewhere between "cool" and "awesome" put their social reputations on the line if they pushed the Chummy Train through the school building? A final question was alluded to, but never explored: What if the marketing strategy failed?

Research Activities: A marketing specialist addressed the students, giving pointers on strategy. The class then planned its own marketing campaign. Working within the confines of time, money, school policies, and their own creative abilities, the children made and hung posters, composed commercials and jingles, and devised the theatrical Chocolate Chummy Train, a direct and personal contact that would make the product more real and exciting to its audience.

Selling the Product: The students, teacher, and parent volunteers spent an afternoon making and individually wrapping Chocolate Chummies. On the day of the sale, the students were cautiously optimistic. The class was not prepared for the outcome. The advertising campaign was so successful that once the train started, students lined up with hands full of change to buy candy for themselves and their families. In a very short time it became apparent that there would not be enough candy to satisfy the demand. Several instructional assistants became dogmatic and aggressive (in other words, "mean" and "bossy") and attempted to take over selling the candy. When several students began to cut the Chummies in half, these same assistants proceeded to take over that job as well, maintaining that the fifth-graders were "unsanitary." The train was halted, and students, tearful and angry, went back to the E.T. classroom to support each other and reevaluate the situation. It was decided that the train would run again after the class made more Chummies; students could buy only a limited amount of candy; team leaders were to approach instructional assistants and explain student ownership of the project; a parent volunteer would accompany each group of students to interface with staff. More candy was made (students were becoming quite proficient at this particular culinary skill) and successfully sold during the second and final excursion of the Chocolate Chummy Train.

Conceptual Applications: Concepts of power and conflict became real to these fifth-graders as they brought their project to completion. They soon found that regardless that this was "their" project, they still could be undermined by people in positions more powerful than theirs. Students knew that the staff members have authority, but they did not expect these individuals to cause conflict. The children realized the value of negotiation and eventually understood this whole event in light of the political process. The important role of politics was seen also on a neutral level: cafeteria workers had to be placated if their facilities were to be used, the principal had to approve the project, teachers had to agree to dismiss students from class to make the Chummies. The formation of laws (rules) and their adherence was another dimension: what policies are specific to the school? cafeteria? county? food production? Students discovered that candy could be sold only after lunch and in the pods, not in the cafeteria. Students also formulated their own rules for the composition of working teams, cooking, standards of cleanliness, clean-up, and other task assignments. Importantly, students learned that rules are enforced, and they themselves often have to police each other.

Research Activities: Students again made candy, not once but twice. They perfected and modified their advertising campaign. In selling candy, they handled the mundane aspects of displaying and distributing the chocolate, providing for change in money boxes, and developing ways to sell candy speedily. Students also learned to mediate a conflict, enabling the children to salvage the project and to complete successfully their year-long goal.

Anthropology through Charity

Once the money was collected and the project evaluated, students met to decide which charity would benefit from their work. After some deliberation, the class voted to donate their proceeds to the Humane Society.

Conceptual Applications: The students wished to donate to a charity housed in their own community, a place where they could see results, stressing the strong localized ties that many young people have. This task involved decision making among peers, demonstration of personal values, and a discussion of social expectations as seen through the eyes of ten- and eleven-year-olds.

Research Activities: Students studied brochures from various charities and pleaded their cases before their classmates. After the Humane Society was selected, its representative was invited to the school. When accepting the check, this official brought animals to visit the class, providing a warm and pleasant ending to a year-long research project.

Discussion

In this case study, anthropology slipped in the back door only because an anthropologist-cum-parent volunteer wanted to implement concepts from the discipline and reinforce ideas taught in the previous year. The project served as a working model to connect academic concerns with practical applications, and as an intellectual exercise to see how far a researcher could "stretch" chocolate. Anthropology may need to make many more such trips through the proverbial back door, brought in not only by anthropologists themselves but also by elementary school teachers who are not required to teach the subject matter. In these cases, anthropologists need to be aware of what is being taught and offer guidelines to assist these teachers in introducing anthropology. Lindquist maintains that

> nothing can take the place of the individual anthropologist laboring on the local level, probing, offering his services, and assisting where possible. Regardless of the perfection of revisions in our school systems, the curricula are temporal phenomena that must undergo constant alterations. Anthropologists interested in local education must face squarely the problems connected with implementation and the continuous up-dating of curriculum content. (1973, 532)

He strongly asserts that "nothing, absolutely nothing, can take the place of interested, civic concern by the anthropologist, as citizen and scientist, on the local level" (1973, 533).

The broad scope of anthropology and its breadth of diversity provide a framework for students to link concepts across disciplines, to extrapolate from the abstract to the concrete, and to organize real data into meaningful units. Anthropology furnishes skills and a way of thinking that is lasting; it transcends the classroom and extends into daily life. It helps students become accountable to themselves and their surroundings. It provides a model for students to understand both diversity and homogeneity and serves as a basis for reflection on their own cultural world. Teachers plant ideas in students' minds and nurture their development, but it is the anthropologists who must be responsible for content and must vest in what Mead calls "cultural custodianship" (1963, 606).

How much will students remember from the chocolate project? There is no doubt that for most of these fifth-graders the quintessential experience was their encasement in chocolate—forming, dipping, and sprinkling Chummies. Conducting several months of research had to leave its mark. Students took with them a true understanding of research, a sense of exploration, and, we hope, enough anthropology to make them better citizens in their culturally diverse world.

References

Dunne, Patrick, and Charles L. Mackie. 1992. "Clio's Table. Chocolate the Divine." *Historic Preservation* May–June:74–77.

Dynneson, Thomas. 1977. "Review and Update: Pre-Collegiate Anthropology Materials." *Anthropology and Education Quarterly* 8(1):28–30.

Iris, Marlene. 1992. Chocolate Project. Class File. Bollman Bridge Elementary School, Jessup, Maryland.

Kalso, Milton. 1973. "Contributions from Anthropology to Elementary Social Studies Curricula." *Social Studies* 64(6):254–257.

Lauderdale, Ann G. 1977. "Anthropology Learning Centers: An Enrichment Program." *Anthropology and Education Quarterly* 8(1):23–25.

Lindquist, Lawrence W. 1968. "The Civic Responsibility of Anthropologists to Public Education." *Human Organization* 27(1):1–4. Reprinted in Ianni, Francis A. J., and Edward Storey, eds. 1973. *Cultural Relevance and Educational Issues, 528–533.* Boston: Little, Brown.

Mandelbaum, David G. 1963. "The Transmission of Anthropological Culture." In *The Teaching of Anthropology,* edited by David G. Mandelbaum, Gabriel W. Lasker, and Ethel M. Albert, 1–21. Berkeley: University of California Press.

Mead, Margaret. 1963. "Anthropology and an Education for the Future." In *The Teaching of Anthropology,* edited by David G. Mandelbaum, Gabriel W. Lasker, and Ethel M. Albert, 595–607. Berkeley: University of California Press.

Messick, Rosemary G. 1983. "Implementing the Anthropology Strand in Elementary School Programs." *Social Studies Review* 23(1):45–50.

Morton, Marcia, and Frederic Morton. 1986. *Chocolate: An Illustrated History.* New York: Crown Publishers.

Olney, Judith. 1982. *The Joy of Chocolate.* Woodbury, New York: Barron's Educational Series.

Rosenfeld, Gerard L. 1968. "Anthropology as Social Studies in the Elementary School." *Teachers College Record* 69(8):767–770. Reprinted in Ianni, Francis A. J., and Edward Storey, eds. 1973. *Cultural Relevance and Educational Issues, 528–533.* Boston: Little, Brown.

Sherman, Elaine. 1984. *Madame Chocolate's Book of Divine Indulgences.* Chicago: Contemporary Books.

Soldier, Lee Little. 1990. "Making Anthropology Part of the Elementary Social Studies Curriculum." *Social Education* 54(1):18–19.

Starko, Alane J., and Gina D. Schack. 1992. *Looking for Data in All the Right Places: A Guidebook for Conducting Original Research with Young Investigators.* Mansfield Center, Conn. Creative Learning Press.

Using the Construct of Culture
to Teach about "The Other"

Jane J. White

The Recognition of Difference

Discovering for the first time that there are people who do not look, sound, or even think like we do is a rude awakening that has been well described in folklore, medical advice, and anthropological theory. As American middle-class mothers well know, there comes a time when their eight- to twelve-month-old infants suddenly begin to react to strangers with suspicion: cold stares; stiff, resistant body language; howls; and perhaps frantic attempts to regain the security of their mothers (Kagan 1979). Confronted with this "stranger anxiety," new mothers are advised to remain calm because this is "just a phase" that their infants are going through as they learn to differentiate between themselves, the familiar, and "the other."

Decades of stories also abound about "the ugly American," U.S. citizens who seem to have great difficulty functioning effectively in other countries. Edward Hall first wrote the book *The Silent Language* in 1959 to help naive, unsophisticated Americans who worked abroad. He found that Americans did not grasp the fundamental idea that people in other countries do not always do things the way Americans do (nor do they particularly want to). The Americans were not conscious of the complex but silent patterns that governed their handling of time; their spatial relationships; their attitudes about work, play, or gender roles; or rules about hierarchy and association, subsistence, and hygiene.

The confused, disoriented reaction of people when they are suddenly immersed in an alien way of life is quite literally called *culture shock* (Kottak 1991, 4–5). Tourists returning from abroad often complain of how different ways of life assault their physical systems—the bad smells, the appalling sights, the weirdness of the sounds that constitute a different musical system—but other ways of life may pose an even greater shock to our intellectual systems, our belief systems, and our ways of making meaning out of life.

Accounting for the Unknown
in Anthropology and Education

Anthropology came into being as a science when Europeans began emerging from their isolation from the rest of the world during the fifteenth century. When early explorers began sending back accounts of peoples who were quite different from those in the known European world, European scholars were faced with the problem of making sense out of an ever-growing accumulation of unsettling information. The accounts of primitive savages of Hawaii and New Zealand that resulted from Captain Cook's voyages; the "woolly Red Indians" brought back from North America and displayed at royal courts, public fairs, and expositions; and the lurid reports that poured in from missionaries describing pagan, depraved, and lust-filled cannibals clearly did not fit into the established categories of thought about humans who were supposed to be at the center of a rational and moral universe (as defined by European norms). Did the presence of these others mean that humans were fundamentally bestial, savage, lost but for the grace of God?

The first decision made by Europeans was whether the newly encountered Africans, native Americans, Polynesians, and Australian aborigines were humans or beasts. Did these creatures possess souls? It was not until 1537 that a papal bull stated unequivocally that non-Europeans, specifically American Indians, were officially human beings (Bohannon and Curtin, 1971, 45). Thus, rather than being exterminated as wild animals, they were souls who could be saved for the Church.

The Organizing Construct of Culture

The organizing construct of culture was "invented" in 1871 by E. B. Tylor. The first sentence of his book entitled *Primitive Culture* defined culture as "that complex whole which includes knowledge, belief, art, morals, law, custom and any other capabilities and habits acquired by man as a member of society" (p. 1). This was truly a revolutionary and powerful concept because it explained how groups of people who have occupied a common territory over time act and think in the same ways. Instead of ways of knowing and acting being handed down because they are innate, they are transmitted culturally. For the first time, the explanation of nurture was used to counteract the explanation of nature. The construct of culture also is powerful because it is a holistic explanation—a large set of interacting and interlocking practices, processes, and beliefs that are interdependent and interconnected.

Malinowski ([1922] 1984) established that culture could be scientifically studied. When he lived for several years with a village of Trobriand Islanders—people who had been described as exotic, puzzling, primitive, and illiterate—he found that scientific systematic notes of their daily mundane details of routines and activities revealed an order and pattern.

Postulation of the concept of culture meant that the observer's goal was to discover the insiders' categories of meaning. Rather than judging them in terms of the observer's own standards and beliefs, the ways of the indigenous population were to be empirically described as the insiders perceived them to outside members of other cultures. With the notion of culture, enculturation, cultural differences, culture contact, and cultural conflict can also be constructed and considered as possible ways to explain events in the world around us.

Teaching the Concept of Culture in Elementary Schools

Can children and their teachers use this notion of culture to help them sort out some of their reactions to people who are different? Can the notion of a group-learned way of life handed down (but ever changing) to members within the boundaries of their society more accurately and efficiently help children understand how and why people look, act, sound, believe, and think the ways they do?

Today, in 1996, the first concept listed in *Expectations of Excellence: Curriculum Standards for Social Studies* developed by the National Council for the Social Studies is "culture." Thus, the construct of culture is not used just to explain why people who live far away or long ago are different. In this newest standard, culture is presented as a powerful academic concept that also describes, legitimates, and explains why people within our own society are different. This definition also tries to show that students as citizens should feel, think, and act tolerantly about people from different cultures.

It is laudable but relatively easy for a national educational society to issue a set of benchmarks. Easy to proclaim but how does it get done? As a researcher, I am interested in what really goes on in classrooms. What knowledge is constructed in classrooms about culturally different people? How is the knowledge constructed? Rather than just being a mere vocabulary word that is memorized and then discarded, is the concept of culture *used* by a teacher and/or students to pose and answer legitimate questions about how life works?

How Sixth-Grade Students Talk about Culturally Different Artifacts

In 1971, I studied the ways small groups of my sixth-grade students made meaning out of concrete objects from another culture when I, their teacher, was not present. Six groups with three students each were tape-recorded as they talked about six Hausa (Nigerian) artifacts for fifteen minutes.

I found that the sixth-graders solved the problem of making meaning out of the artifacts by making six types of comments that followed a general sequence:

1. First they label or put names on the object or part of the object: "I bet that is a good luck charm."

2. Students ask questions of each other: "How could it be a hoe with this kind of blade?"

3. Students describe aspects of the object. They often use adjectives: "It's pretty light," or "It's all rusty."

4. Students relate the object to some activity or process. They tell how it was made or how it might have been used: "Well, I think they burned it to get this design."

5. Students make more abstract inferences. They distance themselves by not using the name of the artifact. They use the word *because* in their statement: "They must have had cattle because they have leather." "And they know how to sew." "And how to butcher calves." These specific comments were made about an object the students could not label. Even though they could not name it, they could still infer many things about the culture from it. "Flurries" of interaction using higher-cognitive processes like this example characteristically came near the end of artifact discussions.

6. Sometimes students generalize. They make summary statements relating several inferences: "I think that the people of Nigeria know how to use the stuff that was around them to survive in their climate." Students do not always get to this point in their discussion but when they do, they use these types of statements to bring closure to their interaction.

Developmentally Appropriate Meanings of the Concept of Culture

Even though these naturalistic observations showed one example of how students could talk their way into understanding, we must also ascertain other strategies children utilize or do not utilize at different ages. Piaget and Weil (1951) studied the development of children's ideas and feelings toward their homeland vis-à-vis the development of their differentiation of other countries. The researchers articulated three stages of *decentering* as children integrate new data and progress to a new stage of reciprocity:

1. Unconscious egocentrism: In this stage, a child (about age six) assumes that his or her perceptions of the world are the only ones possible. Children in the study could not deal with the logical and spatial relationship between the part to the whole, between Geneva and Switzerland.

2. Subordination of a child's concepts and emotions to slightly larger collective units: By age eight or nine, children could spatially place Geneva within Switzerland but could not identify themselves as simultaneously Genovese and Swiss.

3. Sociocentricity: By age eleven and older, children in the study could integrate the spatial and logical relationships between their town and country. They could understand that foreigners feel toward their countries the way the children felt about their own (reciprocity).

In 1976, I videotaped twelve kindergartners, twelve third-graders, and twelve sixth-graders interviewing a person culturally different from themselves. The children had been instructed to act like detectives and they had fifteen minutes to ask all the questions they wanted to about this person and her country. Although there were individual differences among children of the same age level, I found different processes for making meaning at the ages of five to six, eight to nine, and eleven to twelve.

The kindergartners expressed themselves as if they lived in the here and now. They talked about the concrete items they saw in front of them. There were no questions about anything that did not appear on the table or any abstract concepts. Kindergartners literally needed to touch. One of their favorite ways of asking questions was nonverbally. They would hold up pictures and artifacts and just wait to be told about them. Kindergartners attempted to translate the new things they saw in terms of items from their own culture. The word "like" was used frequently. For example, a wall hanging was "like a towel." When they saw familiar objects, the kindergartners would relate personal stories of how they knew about that object—an animal they had seen at the zoo; something their mother had cooked.

The third-graders frequently manipulated the artifacts and asked naming and identifying questions, such as "What is this?"; they also tended to go beyond these types of questions if an object did not fit with their expectations. A question that third-graders constantly asked was, "How was it made?" and "What is it made of?" These third-graders also started to ask *why* questions: "Why does tea grow on high mountains?" Sometimes I would find third-graders and sixth-graders displaying a pattern that I characterize as intellectual playfulness as they asked long series of "what if" questions." For example, "If there is a flood, what happens to the houses?"

Sixth-graders were like the kindergartners and the third-graders in that they worked to identify artifacts and spontaneously related foreign things and events to their own personal experiences. Like the third-graders, they asked technical questions and carried out longer dialogues with follow-up questions. However, with sixth-graders, I often had the impression that the rich environment of artifacts got in the way of their conversation. The sixth-graders were not bound by the here and now. They asked questions about abstract concepts. For example, "Have you had wars in your country?" "Is there education?" They also actively contrasted cultures by relating the way of life in Sri Lanka to the way of life in India, for example.

The presence of different cultural materials stimulated sixth-graders to ask and learn more about their own culture. On discovering that there were two official languages in Sri Lanka, a sixth-grader turned to me and asked, "Do we have two languages?" These sixth-graders gave evidence that they had decentered and were exhibiting reciprocity. They were able to think of possible problems from the informant's point of view, such as "Did it take you long to learn two languages? Was it hard?" When shown writing in a different alphabet, a third-grader had not decentered. She interpreted the symbols as inadequate attempts to form the ABC's that she knew. However, a sixth-grader said, "It might be hard for us to write like your language and yet it's hard for you to write our language, yet it might seem easy to us."

Sixth-graders acted much more like adults socially. They disliked silent intervals and they made many polite comments. "Oh, that's very interesting." "Your people are very skilled."

At the end of every interview I asked each child to summarize what he or she had learned. The majority of kindergartners either cheerfully ignored the question or mentioned only one or two items. The third-graders responded by mentioning artifacts they had seen as if in a list. The ordering of the list frequently corresponded to the order in which the topics had been discussed. Sixth-graders, though, presented reordered and reorganized information.

What Does and Does Not Work: Teaching about Different Cultures in Classrooms

Using Artifacts, Stories, and Literature

Four years of observations in classrooms in a working-class, urban, white elementary school (White 1980) revealed that a one-on-one conversation is much easier to conduct than classroom lessons. When a first-grade teacher brought in artifacts (clothing) from Pakistan, the students rejected and jeered at the different clothes, which they said looked like diapers. This teacher was more successful when she later brought in other Pakistani artifacts and asked the children to guess how the Pakistanis might have used them. Although the students' responses were ethnocentric, they did not reject the notion of the "other." This teacher was most successful when, at the end of the lesson, she told a story based on her personal experiences involving camels' wearing bells around their necks.

Many other teachers have found literature highly effective in teaching about "the other" because it allows children to assume the perspectives of the culturally different characters. Pat Robeson, a fifth-grade teacher in a magnet school in Prince George's County, describes a classroom lesson based on literature that she taught in 1991 (White and Robeson, 1992). The lesson focused on two children in South Africa and their journey to Johannesburg to visit their grandmother, as described in *Journey to Jo'burg*. The book allowed the students to compare their culture to another, from the perspective of children their own age.

Using Problem Solving: The Students as Researchers

In my dissertation research, I recorded an unplanned but very productive conversation when a sixth-grade teacher, who had been showing students *National Geographic* pictures of the Yąnamonö, suddenly asked them to solve a problem, forcing her students to become researchers. A question like "What would you have to do to live in a tropical forest near the Amazon?" can lead to problem solving as students seek information to answer their own questions.

Initially responding like American travelers, these students pragmatically made preparations for protection such as defending against disease and procuring provisions. Sixth-grade students were able to shift the level of meanings being constructed from specific answers to generalized solutions. These students used the notion of culture in a new way when they worked through many ideas of how they would adapt as a group to a new environment.

Ironically, just when precollegiate teachers are being encouraged to use the construct of culture, many anthropologists are rejecting it (Winkler 1994; Marcus, this volume). But students can learn from critiques of the discipline. In a lesson I observed in Charles County, Maryland, in 1993, middle school students studied their own stereotypes and later conducted research on issues of representation. Two visitors from North Africa asked the students to brainstorm images they had of Africa. They also asked them to list images they did not think they would see in Africa. One of the visitors then showed slides from his recent trip to Africa and asked students to identify stereotypes they had and how they thought they were formed. The teachers also handed out a sheet that showed the results of a survey of African images of Americans.

Students gave written responses to the questions about their stereotypes of Africa, compared with the slides. In discussing what they expected to see, what they did not expect to see, and what they did see, they decided that many of the false images of both peoples were transmitted through TV and movies. The students then set up and conducted research on how different Americans were represented in TV commercials. They counted and graphed representations and associations by age, gender, and ethnicity and drew conclusions about how different Americans are presented. Overtly teaching and using concepts of culture, stereotypes, and ethnocentrism helped these students to reflect on social processes that had previously been hidden to them.

Conclusion

A major problem for anthropology is how to describe other people's cultures—their standards for perceiving, believing, evaluating, and acting (Hymes 1974, 104). Teachers and students share this problem. Through the use of artifacts, personal experience stories, literature, and pictures, teachers can craft activities in which student emotions, assumptions, beliefs, and knowledge are elicited. Then, being mindful of what is developmentally appropriate, teachers can introduce the construct of culture to help students explore, question, struggle with, and reflect on their notions of other peoples. Although it is not easy to overcome the barriers and problems of confronting "the other," students often learn more about themselves and their way of life though comparison with other ways of life. Students must learn to find alien ways believable if they are to be competent world citizens as well as capable of sophisticated transactions within their own multicultural society.

References

Bohannan, Paul, and Philip Curtin. 1971. *Africa and Africans*. Garden City, N.Y.: Natural History Press.

Hall, Edward T. [1959] 1966. *The Silent Language*. Greenwich, Conn: A Fawcett Premier Book.

Hymes, Dell. 1974. "The Use of Anthropology: Critical, Political, Personal." In *Reinventing Anthropology,* edited by D. Hymes. New York: Random House.

Kagan, Jerome. 1979. "Overview: Perspectives on Human Infancy." In *Handbook of Infant Development,* edited by J. Osofsky. New York: Wiley.

Kottak, Conrad Phillip. 1994. *Anthropology: The Exploration of Human Diversity.* 6th ed. New York: McGraw-Hill.

Malinowski, Bronislaw. [1922] 1984. *Argonauts of the Western Pacific.* Prospect Heights, Ill.: Waveland Press.

National Council for the Social Studies. 1994. *Expectations of Excellence: Curriculum Standards for Social Studies.* Washington, D.C.: National Council for the Social Studies.

Piaget, Jean, and d'Annemarie Weil. 1951. "Le Developpement chez l'enfant, de l'idee de patrie et des relations avec l'etranger" ["Development in Children of the Idea of the Homeland and of Relations with Others"]. *Bulletin International des Sciences Sociales* 3:539–560.

Tylor, E. B. 1871. *Primitive Culture.* 2 vols. London: John Murray.

White, Jane J. 1971. "Using Artifacts in the Teaching of Social Studies." Master's thesis presented to the Elementary Education Faculty of the University of Wisconsin-Madison.

———. 1980. "An Ethnographic Study of the Construction of Knowledge about Different Cultures in an Elementary School." Doctoral dissertation presented to the faculty of the Graduate School of Education, University of Pennsylvania.

White, Jane J., and Patricia Robeson. 1992. "How Exemplary Teachers Overcome Problems in the Teaching of Anthropology." Paper presented at the Invited Symposium, 91st Annual Meeting of the American Anthropological Association, San Francisco.

Winkler, Karen. 1994. "Anthropologists Urged to Rethink their Definitions of Culture." *Chronicle of Higher Education,* 14 December, A18.

"Shut My Mouth Wide Open"
A Conversation with Successful Teachers of African American Students

GLORIA LADSON-BILLINGS

The expression "shut my mouth wide open" is an African American folk saying that captures the unity of opposites that is characteristic of African and African American world views (Nichols 1986). Clearly, in a Western view of the world, if your mouth is open, it cannot be shut. However, you can be so shocked, dismayed, or overwhelmed by a statement, action, or event that your mouth can literally be wide open while at the same time all forms of verbal communication are shut off.

This chapter describes a conversation with teachers who are effective with African American students. The teachers' mouths are open because they have plenty to say. Yet they are shut because heretofore very few people have been interested in what they have to say. My work attempts to share some of their knowledge so that more teachers can be successful not only with African American students but with all students.

Studying Successful Teachers of African American Students

I began working with teachers who are successful with African American students in 1952 when I entered kindergarten myself in a segregated, working-class black public school in Philadelphia. After attending integrated secondary schools, this working relationship resumed when I entered a historically black college, continued when I began teaching in a desegregated school, and took on new meaning when my first child entered public school.

In 1988, I began systematically to examine the pedagogical excellence of teachers who are successful with African American students (Ladson-Billings 1991). I had a strong belief that despite the high dropout rates and the poor test scores (Irvine 1990) there were (and are) teachers who are successfully teaching African American students. It was less clear to me what the successful teaching would look like or how success would be defined.

I began by approaching African American parents who attended a black Baptist church in the San Francisco Bay area. Initially, this choice of church-goers was a matter of convenience. I subsequently discovered that 72 percent of

African American youths who graduate from high school attend church regularly, as opposed to only 14 percent of African American high school dropouts (American Baptist Churches 1989). Thus, the likelihood of finding parents of successful African American students was higher among this selected group. I asked these parents to identify elementary- and intermediate-level teachers they believed had promoted success for their children. In the course of our discussions, we had to grapple with what the parents meant by "success." The parents made it clear that in addition to academic success, they were interested in teachers who could foster the social and cultural success that helped their students maintain a positive identification with the African American community (Ladson-Billings 1991).

After the parents generated a list of teachers, I contacted school principals and asked them to identify successful teachers of African American students. The principals indicated that their selections were based on student achievement test scores, classroom management, classroom observations, and their perceptions of student attitudes about school.

Those teachers who appeared on both lists constituted the sample. Eight of the nine teachers agreed to participate in the study. Five of the eight teachers in the study are African American; three are white; all are female.

Each teacher agreed to participate in a tape-recorded ethnographic interview (Spradley 1979) lasting from forty-five minutes to two hours. Although each participant was asked the same questions, their interests, backgrounds, and experiences determined how detailed the responses to individual questions were. Some teachers talked extensively about their growing up and early school experiences; others talked more about their philosophy and their beliefs about teaching and students.

I then observed each of the classrooms and videotaped the teachers in action; these videotapes were reviewed and critiqued by all the teachers, who formed what I termed a *research collaborative*. The decision to have the teachers view each others' tapes was both methodological and cultural. Berliner (1989) suggests that the nature of expert behavior is so automatic that experts cannot really explain how and why they do what they do. I hypothesized that although individual experts may not be able to explain themselves, a collective of experts may be able to explain and name each other's expert actions and behaviors.

Second, the notion of a *collective* was consistent with an Afrocentric perspective (Asante 1987, 6) that places "African ideals at the center of any analysis that involves African culture and behavior." During the course of these collective meetings, the teachers began to articulate what I have termed a *culturally relevant* pedagogy. The teachers agreed that because they see what they do as normative, it had not occurred to them to identify it as anything other than teaching. It was only after we began discussing how other teachers teach African American students that they could see a need to differentiate their teaching from that of their less successful peers.

Talkin' That Talk

In late May of 1990, seven of the eight teachers met to discuss their thoughts and feelings about their teaching, their students, and the research project and process. It is important to underscore why this kind of talk is unusual and worthy of exploration. Despite the research suggesting that most class time is taken up by talk and that most of that talk is by teachers (Good and Brophy 1987), teachers have relatively few opportunities or incentives to discuss what, how, or why they do what they do.

The teachers in this study have approximately sixty minutes per day during which they are not engaged with students—during the fifteen-minute recess period and the forty-five-minute lunch period—and that time is often taken up by other work. Teachers are criticized for not conducting themselves in a more professional manner—that is, they do not discuss aspects of their work and share expertise. However, it is more likely that this tendency not to talk about professional concerns is because of time constraints on meaningful discussion. The whole process of establishing rapport and overcoming initial apprehensions takes time, even among teachers who know one another. Additionally, there are few incentives for teachers to spend time discussing their thoughts and ideas about teaching.

This study provided a forum in which the teachers could talk freely and candidly about their teaching, their students, the school, and the community. Although three of the teachers are white, the tone and tenor of the conversation is decidedly African American. There is much overlap in the speech, with one person beginning a thought or idea and another person jumping in to complete and or embellish that thought or idea. In a Western view, this kind of behavior might be interpreted as rude or inappropriate. However, much like the Hawaiian talk-story (Au 1980), this overlapping turn-taking represents a kind of "with-it-ness" that indicates the listener, who becomes the "interrupter," is so engaged in what the speaker is saying that she is capable of completing the thought or idea and extending it with some of her own thoughts and ideas.

Another type of speech overlap that is apparent in this conversation is the kind of call and response that is an important feature of the African American worship experience. Instead of sitting quietly while the preacher delivers the sermon, African American congregations are expected to participate in the worship service by commenting aloud their approval, agreement, and understanding of the preached word. Throughout this conversation, the teachers are heard to say "yes" and "un-huh" in agreement with and support of the speaker. This overlap is another form of "with-it-ness." There were instances of disagreement in the conversation, but different teachers took on the role of mediator and found ways to bring those statements of disagreement together. This mediation often contained clarifying statements and provided ways for speakers to understand divergent viewpoints.

Another feature of the speakers in this conversation is that their speech is embedded in contexts. Gee (1989) suggests that the storytelling of white middle-class youngsters is much like news reporting, with discrete events told in chronological sequence. African American youngsters, however, often surround their stories with deeply textured, complex scenes and events that may seem tangential or unrelated to the story. Teachers who hear both these types of stories indicate that the white, middle-class student's story is clear and concise and makes sense whereas the African American student's story is confusing, off the topic, and nonsensical. The teachers' speech in this conversation is similar to the African American students' stories, filled with stories and anecdotes and digressions from the interviewer's questions.

The teachers also choose not to speak in portions of the conversation, with the transcript containing instances of long pauses and silences. I was anxious for the teachers to talk, but as a member of this particular cultural and speech community, I understand that silence is a mighty weapon in African American communication. It is used very effectively by African American boys in the classroom to challenge the teacher's authority (Kunjufu 1984).

Humor is another feature in this conversation. Throughout the tapes there are moments of levity and outbursts of laughter. The teachers' humor represents both the ease that they felt with each other and their willingness to demystify their practice.

Talkin' and Testifyin'

As a way to begin, I gave each of the teachers a questionnaire that contained twenty-eight statements taken from the dimensions of culturally relevant teaching (see Ladson-Billings 1990, 1991). The statements were cast in simple declarations and the teachers were asked to rate each of them from 1 to 5 in terms of how closely it represented their thinking. The ranking produced seven themes with which we began the conversation: teaching as an art; the importance of the teacher-student relationship; discipline; building community; success; communication; and knowledge and competence.

For brevity, I have turned "provocative pedagogical propositions" from these conversations into summaries and analysis: For me as a teacher educator, these successful teachers' beliefs have serious implications for how I teach my courses and how students are supervised.

Teaching as an Art

I don't think there any rules for teaching. . . . I don't think you can put down hard and fast rules and say this is the way you have to do a certain thing in the classroom.

You don't just get directions for being a good teacher. . . .

It just can't be a job, either. . . .

For the statement "Teaching is an art rather than a science," six of the seven teachers rated it 5 ("Most represents my thinking") and one rated it 4.

Its reciprocal, "Teaching is a technical task, not an artistic one" was rated 1 by five of the teachers, and 2 by the remaining two. There was nothing in the conversation that suggested it was impossible to teach someone to teach, but they did refer to the need for creativity.

The Importance of the Student-Teacher Relationship

I think that the relationship is a major part of teaching. That's the most important part, being able to be heart to heart with a child.

I think it's . . . very important that they [the students] know that you care about them. You're not going to get very much accomplished without that.

Discipline

Many of the boys are labeled troublemakers and hard to control and that isn't necessarily so. At least I haven't found that, because some students who I have received from other teachers who had problems with them . . . well, they get to me and there isn't any problem. So I think it's really how you perceive children.

You know, usually I enjoy the kids that get into trouble. It sounds crazy but there's a life in the classroom with them.

There is so much more you can do besides hassle a child because he didn't put his name on the top of a paper.

I think . . . children also have to learn that they have to handle the problem, not that we need to send them off to someone.

The importance of relationship emerges in the discussion of discipline as well as in commitment to the students. One of the primary concerns these teachers have about teaching African American youngsters is in establishing a good relationship. Their not so successful counterparts are more interested in maintaining order and control (Ladson-Billings and King 1990). The teachers were reluctant to discuss discipline as a separate entity because they insisted that it was a part of a larger network of interactions that take place in the classroom.

Building Community

I expect a lot from the whole class. . . . We start off as a class, getting our community together, but there's a lot of room for competition, too.

I think they view themselves as a team. You know we all have to make it. . . . When one child doesn't understand a concept or a skill, the students are more than willing. . . . I don't have to ask.

[You want them to] meet the challenge . . . not [by] trying to prove that they're above the community.

I think it's important to get children to see what they can actually do in the community. A lot of the kids say, "I'm going to move out of [this community]. I hate this community." Well, what is the community? When you talk about the community including the churches and the parents, then they say, "I don't want to leave that" . . .

The theme of building community transcends the classroom. The teachers intentionally build a classroom community that they expect will have an ultimate payoff in the larger community. Rather than conceive of the school as a fortress against the hostile forces of the community, they stress that the school is a part of the community and hostile forces are something that invaded the community. Their role as teachers is to help students learn to function effectively in a community. It begins in the classroom and moves into the neighborhood.

Success

I've never had a child that wasn't successful . . . because I make sure they can be successful.

As a classroom teacher I feel that it's my responsibility to make sure the child[ren] succeed.

If the thing [that teachers asked a child to produce] isn't the way the teacher perceives it, then, of course, the kids have got the problem, the teacher doesn't. . . . And somehow by the time they get to the fifth grade some of our kids are just so depressed about their lack of work or success.

[In my classroom] it's everybody, let's pitch in and make sure this person succeeds because we all have to do it.

Often I have a child who has real difficulty getting something. I won't put a grade on the report card. It kills me. . . . I tell the parent I can't give your child an 'F.' Your child did not understand this and I must have done something that kept your child from getting this. . . . Let's come back to this later.

The theme of success emerged when the teachers responded to the questionnaire statements: "I try to have students see their successes as class successes and failures as class failures" (all 4s and 5s) and "No matter how you try, failure is inevitable for some" (range 1–3). The teachers placed great emphasis on their role in assuring the success of each student, viewing success as including the students' social, artistic, organizational, and performance-based abilities.

Communication

It's important for teachers to be able to listen too. Sometimes we don't take the time to listen to what children have to say . . . it's amazing how much talking they want to do . . . and it's not gossip. They're not bringing tales from home or that sort of stuff. It's just very interesting things that they know and want to tell you about . . . things that they've discovered. It's important on the part of the teacher to be able to listen.

I've discovered that with writing, some students say, "I just don't have anything to say." And I say, "Are you sure it's not that you don't have anything to say or that you have so much to say you don't know where to start?" And that's what it is and so if you just let them write and write and write and get it all out and then organize it, it works just as well as trying to make them be perfect.

The theme of communication came out of the teachers' discussion about developing relationships and discipline. Their discussion focused on allowing students opportunities to communicate. The teachers have a sense of the power relationships that exist in the classroom and they realize that their own authority allows them to communicate whenever and however they choose. They recognize that the students' voices are rarely encouraged in the classroom.

Knowledge and Competence

It's recognizing that children have knowledge. I think we need to recognize that they don't come like a blank page to the classroom. I think acknowledging the children's competence means a lot.

It's showing them more than information.

They come with knowledge, more than we think.

And I think it's important to have students recognize for themselves how much they bring.

In the conversation about the statements, "Teaching involves pulling knowledge out of the students" (4s and 5s) and "Teaching involves putting knowledge into the students" (1s and 2s), the teachers believed that the students already know something and have something to contribute to the intellectual environment. This position is very different from those who see African American students as deprived, deficient, and "at risk." Once again the teachers' focus is on the students and their knowledge as opposed to themselves (and their own knowledge). However, the teachers also did not question their own pedagogical judgments and abilities.

Talk Is Cheap?

What implications for teacher education can we draw from conversations with these successful teachers? Based on what they know and think, how should other teachers be prepared if they are to accept the challenge of teaching African American and other students of color?

1. If teaching is an art, what aspects of teacher preparation are directed toward cultivating that art? The typical preparation program involves a sequence that includes foundations courses, methods courses, and field experiences (Edmundson 1990). At what juncture do we insert the art of teaching? In

general, teaching itself lacks status on the campuses where most teachers are prepared, with good research and scholarship being more likely to result in tenure and promotion than good pedagogy. Nor are education majors required or encouraged to observe exemplary professors or cooperating teachers and seriously analyze their pedagogy. The teachers in this research collective felt that their teacher preparation program gave them no insights into how to teach African American students. They believe their artistry was cultivated over time and, in some instances, through the mentorship of an experienced colleague.

2. How do teacher education programs reinforce the centrality of the teacher-student relationship? Prospective teacher candidates gave two kinds of responses to the question, "Why do you want to be a teacher?" The first response, typically from elementary teacher candidates, goes something like, "I just love children." The second response, typically from a secondary candidate goes something like, "I love mathematics (or whatever)." Neither type of response suggests a real grasp of the significance of the teacher-student relationship. "I love children" shows a lack of experience with them as beings with whom one must bargain and negotiate; whom one must coax, respect, and accept; and who it may be difficult to love or even like. Even if the love of children is real, it is not a sufficient prerequisite for teaching, as opposed to working in, say, child care, recreation, or a social service agency for children. When asked to explain "Why teaching?" as opposed to other work with children, many of our children-loving education candidates cannot articulate the specialness of the teacher-student relationship or connect it with the social purposes of schooling.

Similarly, the "I love my subject matter" respondents seem to have forgotten that they must somehow teach that subject to 150 adolescent people who often do not have the slightest interest in it, in groups of approximately thirty, five times a day for forty-five to fifty minutes. Again, the love and knowledge of one's subject matter, although essential, will not prepare a teacher to connect effectively with students who are undergoing the stresses and strains of growing up.

3. What role does student discipline play in teacher preparation programs? Most prospective teachers have anxieties about their ability to manage the classroom and discipline students. One approach to discipline in teacher preparation programs is to require students to take a specific course in classroom management. This course may combine research findings and cases that students are supposed to assimilate and adapt for their own classroom settings. A second approach simply suggests that if the curriculum is good enough, there will be no discipline problems.

Neither of these approaches is consistent with what the successful teachers in this study suggest. From their perspective, discipline is a part of the teacher-student relationship, and as the teacher invests time getting to know students and allows them to know her, the boundaries of the relationship are established and discipline and management result from it. If teacher education programs do not adequately address the relationships between students and teachers, can they successfully address discipline?

4. How do teacher education programs build community? This question raises special challenges, considering that many colleges and universities maintain tenuous and sometimes acrimonious relationships with the communities in which they are located, and that universities themselves often resemble a tangle of divisions and hierarchies among schools, departments, subject matters, and so on. Consider only the land use and admission battles fought by urban campuses with their communities, the "town-gown" problems of suburban or rural campuses, the medical school kingdoms, the relative invisibility of schools of education, and the differing statuses and physical separation of various subject matter disciplines within most education departments.

5. How do teacher education programs prepare teachers to encourage and engender success? Although the teachers in this study talk about ways of ensuring that all students are successful and define success in a variety of areas, the students in their classrooms do perform better on standard measures of achievement than students in other classrooms at the same grade level in their district. Current activity in teacher education and teacher assessment suggests some movement toward more flexible measures of success (Shulman 1989).

6. Although courses in communication often are a part of teacher education programs, the notion of communication that includes reciprocity and mutuality (King and Mitchell 1990) as conveyed by the teachers in the collective is missing in the curriculum. Teachers must understand the need for clarity (Cruikshank 1985) and other tenets of good communication in the classroom, but teacher education must in addition help prospective teachers understand the significance and power of student communication and language. The literature on how students experience school and the curriculum is scant (Erickson and Schultz 1991), but as apparent from the findings in this study, successful teaching is connected with developing student communication in the classroom context. Teacher education must add to our understanding of student communication.

7. Knowledge and competence are obvious priorities in teacher education programs. However, how knowledge is created, transmitted, distorted, politicized, and used for specific purposes is not always made evident in teacher education (King and Ladson-Billings 1990). Are teacher education programs willing to take ideological positions that students are free to examine critically to better understand their own ideological and moral positions? Or are they going to persist in the guise of objectivity and neutrality (Sirotnik 1988), producing prospective teachers who uncritically accept existing curriculum content and existing social arrangements. Again, this issue must be addressed by teacher education programs.

8. Finally, will teacher education ever place real value on the work of practitioners? Can we still claim to support the work of teachers when their voices are regarded as distant echoes in the preparation of novice teachers? When will we go into classrooms to truly listen and learn rather than to talk and tell? What are the possibilities for equal status collaborations between

teachers and university professors? How can we more fairly reward the work of cooperating and master teachers?

Walking the Talk?

Despite education's current interest in cultural diversity, the literature on preparation of teachers for African American students is almost nonexistent (Ladson-Billings 1991). However, teachers who successfully work with African American students can be found in the nation's schools, public and private. For teacher education to improve the way it prepares teachers for diversity, forums are needed in which successful teachers can talk openly about their pedagogy. As Clifford Geertz (1973, 5) suggests, "If you want to understand what a science is, you should look in the first instance not at its theories or its findings, and certainly not at what its apologists say about it; you should look at what the practitioners of it do."

References

American Baptist Churches. 1989. Handout. Valley Forge, Penn.

Asante, M. K. 1987. *The Afrocentric Idea*. Philadelphia: Temple University Press.

Au, K. H. 1980. "Participation Structures in a Reading Lesson with Hawaiian Children: An Analysis of a Culturally Appropriate Instructional Event." *Anthropology and Education Quarterly* 112:91–115.

Berliner, D. 1989. "Implications of Studies of Expertise in Pedagogy for Teacher Education and Evaluation. In *New Directions for Teacher Assessment*, 39–67. Proceedings of the 1988 Educational Testing Service Invitation Conference. Princeton, N.J.: Educational Testing Service.

Cruickshank, D. 1985. "Applying Research on Teacher Clarity." *Journal of Teacher Education* 36:44–48.

DuBois, R., and M. Li. (1971). *Reducing Social Tension and Conflict: The Group Conversation Method*. New York: YMCA Press.

Edmundson, P. 1990. "A Normative Look at the Curriculum in Teacher Education." *Phi Delta Kappan* 71(9):717–722.

Erickson, F., and J. Schultz. 1991. "Students' Experience of the Curriculum." In *Handbook of research on curriculum*, edited by P. Jackson. New York: Macmillan.

Gee, J. 1989. "Literacy, Discourse and Linguistics: An Introduction." *Journal of Education* 171(1):5–17.

Geertz, C. 1973. *The Interpretation of Cultures*. New York: Basic Books.

Good, T., and J. Brophy. 1987. *Looking in Classrooms*. 4th ed. New York: Harper & Row.

Irvine, J. 1990. *Black Students and School Failure*. Westbury, CT: Greenwood Press.

King, J., and Ladson-Billings, G. 1990. "The Teacher Education Challenge in Elite University Settings: Developing Critical Perspectives for Teaching in a Democratic and Multicultural Society." *European Journal of Intercultural Studies*, 1(2):15–30.

King, J., and Mitchell, C. 1990. *Black Mothers to Sons: Juxtaposing African American Literature and Social Practice.* New York: Peter Lang.

Kunjufu, J. 1984. *Countering the Conspiracy to Destroy Black Boys.* Chicago: Afro-American Images.

Ladson-Billings, G. 1990. "Culturally Relevant Teaching: Effective Instruction for Black Students." *The College Board Review,* no. 155, Spring, pp. 20–25.

Ladson-Billings, G. 1991. "Like Lightning in a Bottle: Attempting to Capture the Pedagogical Excellence of Successful Teachers of Black Students." *The International Journal of Qualitative Studies in Education* (in press).

Ladson-Billings, G. 1991. "Who Will Teach *Our* Children: Preparing Teachers to Successfully Teach African-American Students." Manuscript.

Ladson-Billings, G., and King, J. 1990. *Cultural Identity of African-Americans: Implications for Achievement.* Monograph prepared for Mid-Continental Regional Educational Laboratory (McREL). Aurora, CO.

Nichols, E. 1986. "Cultural Foundations for Teaching Black Children." In Oswald M. T. Ratteray (Ed.). *Teaching Mathematics, Vol. I: Culture, Motivation, History and Classroom Management* (pp. 1–7). Washington, D.C.: Institute of Independent Education.

Shulman, L. 1989. "The Paradox of Teacher Assessment." *New Directions for Teacher Assessment* (pp. 13–27). Proceedings of the 1988 ETS Invitational Conference. Princeton, N.J.: Educational Testing Service.

Sirotnik, K. 1988. "Studying the Education of Educators: Methodology." *Phi Delta Kappan,* 70(3):241–247.

Spradley, J. 1979. *The Ethnographic Interview.* New York: Holt, Rinehart and Winston.

Teaching Anthropological Methods to Teachers
The Transformation of Knowledge

NORMA GONZALEZ AND CATHY AMANTI

As we explore yet another of the multifaceted aspects of the teaching of anthropology, the admonition of the Spindlers (1990, 108) takes on critical importance: "Learning about human cultures must occur empathetically and emotionally as well as conceptually or cognitively." This chapter addresses the applied level of teaching anthropology. The method of teaching anthropology and ethnographic methods to teachers that is described here is not meant for the transmission of anthropological knowledge for its own sake but to effectuate real and tangible change in the relationships between teachers, households, and students. Anthropological knowledge becomes in itself a pedagogical tool. What we describe is a collaborative effort between anthropologists and educators that seeks to establish a radically revised dialogue between teachers and the households from which their students emerge. This collaborative effort has functioned on three levels. At the first level, teachers have been exposed to anthropological theory and methodology in participant/observation, interviewing techniques, eliciting oral histories, questionnaire construction, and field note writing. At the second level, teachers have entered their students' homes as field-workers. This effort by teachers to "know" their students does not come through secondhand information in the form of inservices or "experts" but from the actual experience of entering their own students' households.

Outfitted with an anthropological perspective, teachers went to the homes of their students, not with an agenda to "teach" the parents or to inform them about classroom concerns but as "learners," as anthropologists seeking to construct a template for understanding the quotidian lives of their students (see Moll, Amanti, Neff, and González 1992). At the third level, teachers met together in study groups to debrief collectively about their experiences in the fieldwork situation. In addition, teachers actively constructed curriculum units that tapped into the "funds of knowledge" they had identified in the households. Within this process, not only do students learn from teachers, but more important, teachers learn from the concrete, lived experiences of students and their families.

The basic anthropological construct of cultural relativism is an important foundation for teachers approaching their students' households. As much of the educational literature has continued to portray the households of poor and minority students as somehow deviating from norms constructed around mainstream practices, families are often viewed as suffering from some form of "deficit." This "deficit" is often singled out as the root of the academic difficulties of these children. An approach to households that does not focus on the "dysfunctional" aspects of household dynamics can radically alter the perception of how students live their daily lives. Going one step further than the model of cultural relativism, which does not assign any evaluative judgment to cultural practices, teachers were asked to think about their students' households as actually being rich in "funds of knowledge." These funds of knowledge are inventories of information that are contained within every household and include an impressive array of skills, survival strategies, and home practices that may be utilized by the classroom teachers to contextualize academic content areas. The "funds of knowledge" found within households in our sample of Native American, African American, and Mexican-origin households in Tucson, Arizona, often reflect the historically accumulated adaptive strategies rooted in southwestern ecology and subsistence activities and are the social capital on which households draw (Vélez-Ibañez, Moll, González, and Neff 1991).

In addition to learning anthropological methods, the teachers benefited from several fortuitous factors that facilitated the shift to teacher/researcher. First, a child's teacher has ready access to the home in a position of honor and respect, an entrée that is not available to many anthropologists entering the field for the first time. The households evidenced no suspicion of motives and no reluctance to share essential and often very private information. The common link of concern for the child formed the foundation for productive communication. Second, the teachers had been observers (if not participants) within the community and neighborhood, usually for several years. The store of informal data they had acquired from being part of the neighborhood served to make concrete the everyday experiences of their students as the teachers began their fieldwork process.

Their ethnographic training became a true nexus of theory and practice. As the teachers developed theoretically, ethnography became a pedagogical tool that spilled over into many areas. First, the teachers came to know the community empathetically and emotionally. The affective ties that were initiated during the household visits forged a link between home and school that has remained a solid basis for continued connections. As teachers came to see and feel and taste the household sights and sounds and smells, they were planting seeds of reciprocity the households were eager to nurture (see Vélez-Ibañez and Greenberg 1992). Teachers were able to see their students in context, viewing them as multidimensional, vibrant, and contoured beings, embedded within the construction of a household identity. They fleshed out the static categories of "kinship" and "labor history" and "oral history" with genuine and tangible links to the child. They found out about grandfathers who had fought in the Mexican Revolution; uncles whose ranches were visited on weekends in Mexico; mothers whose knowledge of candy making, and the intricate sugar processing that accompanied it, surpassed their own; and grandmothers whose ethnobotanical knowledge of medicinal herbs and curative properties of plants were reservoirs waiting to be tapped. They learned that the ethnographers' probing unlocked rich repositories of fertile resources. They came away from interviews continually amazed at the multiplicity of factors that the classroom strips away from their students in presenting unidimensional portraits of the child and of the family. They learned that "culture" is not a static grab bag, a dumping ground for the surface markers of quinceañeras, tamales, and cinco de mayo celebrations. Instead, they learned how households network in informal market exchanges. They learned how cross-border activities made "mini-ethnographers" of their students. And more important, they learned that culture is neither monosemic nor normative, that it is constantly negotiated as human agents contest fluid domains. They identified processual approaches (see Rosaldo 1989) to viewing households, rooted in praxis and the lived contexts of their students (see González et al. 1993).

The teachers' ethnographic visits often had an emancipating effect within the households. Parents animatedly recounted for teachers the personal narratives of their mothers and fathers, and their own discourse reflected the odysseys that led them to be where they are. One mother, after relating her own educational history, began to reflect on her story and later informed the teacher that she would be returning to school. Another father, as a retired landscaper, seeing that an open relationship could be established with the school, offered his landscaping skills to the principal, an offer that was eagerly accepted. One teacher reported that in a single day the parents of three of the children whose families she had interviewed came in to inquire about school matters that had puzzled them and to enlist her help in finding transportation to a school conference. The reflexive process involved in narrating their own unique and singular life course was a welcome communicative event for many parents who often conversed with the teachers for hours, engrossed in the mutual intersubjectivity of the ethnographic interview.

Finally, as the ostensible pedgagogical goal of the interview, teachers were able to sort the household knowledge and retrieve the information that could be meaningfully incorporated into their curricular agenda. Within the study groups, the teachers' experience articulated theory. Ethnographic work allowed the teachers to expand snippets of their experience as the basis for their own theoretical development. As has been noted (Segal 1990, 122), reflexively oriented work needs to "begin with the understanding that systematic thinking about [one's] own experiences is a valid source of some knowledge and insight." Ethnographic experience became a collaborative endeavor; rather than the result of a lone researcher's venturing out into the field, it was a multi-authored and polyphonic discourse constructed out of the participant/field-worker/teacher/anthropologist experience. As teacher-researchers and university-based researchers shaped the discursive properties of ethnographic construction, the intersubjective nature of the process became salient. Mentoring functions switched quickly back and forth as participants manipulated their own spheres of expertise. Within this interactive and constitutive process, the role of the teacher was defined in nontraditional ways. As participants evolved within an inquiry-based ethnographic process, teacher agency and teachers' voices jointly constructed and negotiated a multivocal approach to studying the field. To highlight the voice of one teacher in this process, Cathy Amanti, a sixth-grade teacher who was involved in the pilot project and who recently received a master's degree in anthropology, highlights her own journey into the domain of ownership of anthropological field methods and critical reflection:

> *I taught sixth grade in a bilingual classroom before taking a leave of absence to pursue graduate work in anthropology. I was attracted to participating in this project at that time because I knew my students were bringing valuable information to school based on their background experiences and I also knew that I was not taking advantage of this resource. I hoped that by going into my students' homes I would somehow find the key that would help me develop strategies to make use of the wealth of experiences they have had to increase their engagement and success in school.*
>
> *I participated as a teacher in the pilot phase of this project. After several training sessions and armed with questionnaires developed by project staff, I became immersed in the daily lives of my students and their families as a novice ethnographer. The impact this had on me as a teacher went far beyond my expectations. Two areas where the impact was profound were my approach to curriculum and my relationship with my students.*
>
> *In the area of curriculum development, as a teacher of predominantly Mexican and U.S. Mexican students, I believed in the importance of acknowledging and including aspects of my students' culture in my classroom practice. Teachers are admonished to build on students' prior knowledge but are given no guidelines for how to elicit this knowledge. In addition, the multicultural curriculum available in schools perpetuates an outdated notion of culture as special and isolated ritual events and artifacts, the kind featured in* National Geographic. *Its focus on holidays, "typical" foods, and "traditional" artifacts covers a very narrow range of my students' experiences and ignores the reality of life in the borderlands, which often falls outside the norms of traditional Anglo or Mexican culture.*
>
> *The experience I had participating in this project helped me expand my concept of culture. This expanded notion turned out to be the key that helped me develop strategies for including in my classroom practice the knowledge my students were bringing to school. It was the kind of information elicited through the questionnaires that was the catalyst for this transformation. I sought information on labor, family and residential history, literacy, daily activities, and parenting roles. But I was not looking for static categories or judging the households' activities in these areas according to any standards—my own or someone else's. I simply sought to elicit and describe the context within which my students were being socialized. This meant that if the father of one of my students did not have a "job," I did not stop the inquiry there. The structure of the questionnaires*

encouraged me to continue probing to discover any type of activity the father and mother were doing to ensure the well-being of the household.

If we were simply eliciting labor history associated with categories of work in the formal economic sector, we would risk both missing and devaluing a great deal of the experiences of our students and their families. This has clear implications for the way we, as educators, should approach culture. If our idea of culture is bound up with notions of authenticity and tradition, how much practice will we ignore as valueless and what will this say to our students? But if our idea of culture is broadened to include the ways we organize and make sense of all our experiences, we have many more resources to draw on in the classroom.

The other area of classroom practice this project impacted was my relationship with my students. This was partly a result of the kind of information I elicited when using the questionnaire on parenting roles. It proved invaluable to me as having an understanding of family, and parent-child interactions gave me a context for my students' behavior and made it more comprehensible to me. I think the result of gaining this information is that I became more understanding and responsive to the students whose families I interviewed. In some instances, I even reinterpreted behavior that I might previously have categorized as misbehavior in a different light.

After interviewing three of my students' families, I developed, in collaboration with other teachers participating in the project and other project staff, an inquiry-based curriculum unit that allowed my students' funds of knowledge to come into play. The theme of the unit was candy because during an interview I had observed one of my students selling a neighbor candy he had brought back from Mexico. As the unit developed, my students focused on the differences between Mexican and U.S. candies. As they were researching, investigating, hypothesizing, and drawing conclusions, they were also able, for the first time, to articulate their knowledge and feelings about living on the border between two countries and cultures. The result was enthusiastic participation in the learning process by the entire class.

While I was planning and implementing my curriculum unit, this project supported me in experimenting and exploring ways to restructure my pedagogical practices by incorporating the knowledge I had gained about my students. In this restructuring process, I sought pedagogical methods that were more sensitive and that allowed me to acknowledge the multiple bodies of knowledge present in my students' homes. But it was the process of designing and implementing the actual curriculum that has transformed me in another and completely unexpected way. Most curriculum is imported into the classroom rather than developed on site to respond to the needs of a particular population of students. As I developed my curriculum for the project, I also drew on my own previous teaching experience and pedagogical funds of knowledge. This had an empowering effect on me in that the process affirmed my abilities as a teacher. The result is that I now feel less dependent on educational "experts" to tell me how to teach or solve my pedagogical problems. I believe that with the anthropological tools I now have to bridge the gap between my classroom and my students' lives, combined with my own pedagogical knowledge, I am in a better position than anyone to judge how best to teach my students and provide them with the kind of learning environment they need. This attitude contradicts a great deal of educational research. I am now critical of the way teachers are portrayed in much of this research, including in educational ethnographies. Teachers are often stereotyped in the same manner in which they are accused of stereotyping their students. They are cast as having an adversarial relationship with their students. This portrayal of teachers, common to both macro and micro ethnographic approaches, provides rationalization for an expanding educational bureaucracy and concomitant loss of control by teachers over their working conditions. It also justifies the imposition of change in schools while excluding teachers from the process. But the teacher work force is not monolithic. All the teachers working on this project have participated under great time constraints, visiting their students' homes during evenings and weekends. They are not taking on this burden because of any criticism leveled against them but because they are advocates for their students rather than their adversaries. This project represents a radical departure from the norm in educational research. It acknowledges and includes the knowledge of teachers in constructing the research process. It allows teachers to be co-researchers rather than mere recipients of its conclusions. This has both strengthened and grounded the work we are doing.

It has been noted (Segal 1990, 122) that "the interaction between field and fieldworker is the locus for gathering distinctively anthropological data. . . . It is a dialogue between self and environment. The objective is to teach the student how to begin having this conversation." In the ethnographic training of teachers, the conversation that was begun evolved into several unanticipated outcomes. It spun first of all around the joint construction of ethnographic knowledge. It then spun around the issue of teachers as researchers. It touched on the Freirian (1970, 1984) notion of dialogue as an emancipatory educational process as teachers and households teased out a consciousness of the historical character of their experiences. As Savage (1989) has indicated, ethnography can be seen as a tool for social action and can enable persons to transform the limitations of their cirumstances. In the powerful dialogue that this ethnographic training can engender, parents can find a passageway to the schools via the teacher. As the teacher validates the households' experience as one from which rich resources or funds of knowledge can be extracted, parents themselves come to authenticate their skills as worthy of pedagogical notice. Within a different exchange in this dialogue, teachers began to perceive the transformative power that critical reflection can have on their own theoretical development. This is not to say that the process has been unproblematic. We have learned about the pitfalls of uneven participation, of superficial application of anthropological categories, of teachers' time constraints in writing field notes, and of the difficulty of translating household funds of knowledge into meaningful curriculum units. The point, however, is not whether teachers have learned to become good ethnographers.

We suggest that the potential of teaching ethnographic methods to teachers lies in the unleashing of a dialogue of empowerment for households and for teachers, and ultimately for the children they serve. In describing communities of learners, it has been remarked that "people learn best when they are actively exploring, thinking, asking their own questions, and constructing knowledge through discovery" (Ayers 1992, 20). This process encapsulates the ethnographic fieldwork of teachers. As teachers become co-learners along with their students, and parents along with their children, the challenging sense that knowledge is open-ended and active seeps into the dialogical process. The probing disposition of mind that fosters learning as a lifetime experience can produce the meaningful reflexive and discursive processes inherent in creating environments for learning.

References

Ayers, W. 1992. "Work That Is Real: Why Teachers Should Be Empowered." In *Empowering Teachers and Parents: School Restructuring through the Eyes of Anthropologists*, edited by G. Alfred Hess, Jr. Westport, Conn.: Bergin and Garvey.

Freire, P. 1970. *Pedagogy of the Oppressed,* translated by M. B. Ramos. New York: Seabury Press.

———. 1984. *The Politics of Education*, translated by D. Macedo. Amherst, Mass.: Bergin and Garvey.

González, N., L. Moll, M. Floyd-Tenery, A. Rivera, P. Rendon, R. González, and C. Amanti. 1995. "Funds of Knowledge for Teaching in Latino Households." *Urban Education* 29(4): 443–470.

Moll, L., C. Amanti, D. Neff, and N. González. 1992. "Funds of Knowledge for Teaching: Using a Qualitative Approach to Connect Homes and Classrooms." *Theory into Practice* 31(2):132–141.

Rosaldo, R. 1989. *Culture and Truth: The Remaking of Social Analysis.* Boston: Beacon Press.

Savage, M. 1989. "Can Ethnographic Narrative Be a Neighborly Act?" *Anthropology and Education Quarterly* 19:3–19.

Segal, E. 1990. "The Journal: Teaching Reflexive Methodology on an Introductory Level." *Anthropology and Education Quarterly* 21:121–127.

Spindler, G., and L. Spindler. 1990. "The Inductive Case Study Approach to Teaching Anthropology." *Anthropology and Education Quarterly* 21:106–112.

Vélez-Ibañez, C., and J. Greenberg. 1992. "Formation and Transformation of Funds of Knowledge among U.S. Mexican Households." *Anthropology and Education Quarterly* 23:313–335.

———, L. Moll, N. González, and D. Neff. 1991. "Promoting Learning and Educational Delivery and Quality among 'at Risk' U.S. Mexican and Native American Elementary School Children in Tucson, Arizona." Pilot Project Final Report to W. K. Kellogg Foundation.

ABOUT THE CONTRIBUTORS

Cathy Amanti is a multi-grade intermediate teacher in a bilingual classroom at Hollinger Elementary school in Tucson, Arizona. She is currently involved in the bilingual teacher cadre for the Tucson Unified School District.

Robert Borofsky teaches cultural anthropology at Hawaii Pacific University. He teaches courses in cultural anthropology, ethnography of the Pacific, and the culture of nursing. He has recently received two teaching awards.

Lawrence Breitborde is the vice president and dean of the college at Knox College. In the past, he taught courses on social and linguistic anthropology, multilingualism, and Africa. In 1985, he received the Teacher of the Year award at Beloit College.

Alice Brues taught physical anthropology for twenty-three years at the University of Colorado. Her favorite course, not surprisingly, is human races. She is currently contemplating writing a children's book on the subject.

Erve Chambers teaches at the University of Maryland. His teaching interests are in applied anthropology and the anthropology of tourism. He is a recent recipient of the University of Maryland's Lilly-CTR Fellowship for Teaching Excellence.

Dennis Cheek is the coordinator of mathematics, science, and technology and lead contact for the social studies, Rhode Island Department of Elementary and Secondary Education. He has taught students from grade 5 through graduate school in the United States, Great Britain, and Germany. His special interests are in curriculum development projects and policy studies.

Mark Nathan Cohen is a University Distinguished Teaching Professor at the SUNY College at Plattsburgh where he has taught physical anthropology and archaeology since 1971. He has received the SUNY Chancellor's Award for Excellence in Teaching and the Freshman Honor Society's award for teaching. He was recently nominated for the Carnegie (formerly CASE) Professor of the Year award.

Jean DeBernardi is a linguistic and cultural anthropologist at the University of Alberta. She teaches courses in social and cultural anthropology and religion, specializing in South China and Southeast Asia.

James Deetz is the David A. Harrison III Professor of New World Studies at the University of Virginia where he teaches courses in general archaeology and historical archaeology in addition to directing field schools on the Virginia tidewater. In addition, he also holds an honorary professorship at the University of Cape Town.

Carol Eastman is senior vice president and executive vice chancellor at the University of Hawaii. Before turning to administration, she taught language classes (Swahili and other Bantu languages), language and culture, and anthropological and linguistic theory and method.

Carol Ember teaches anthropology at Hunter College of the City University of New York, teaching courses in cultural anthropology, research design, statistics, cross-cultural research, and psychological anthropology.

Melvin Ember taught anthropology at Hunter College until 1987, when he became president of the Human Relations Area Files at Yale University. While at Hunter College, he taught courses in cultural anthropology, social organization, political organization, research design, and statistics.

Brian Fagan has been associated with the University of California at Santa Barbara since 1967. He teaches undergraduate and graduate courses in general archaeology and world prehistory. He has been involved in multimedia and interactive approaches to teaching for many years.

Michele Foster has recently moved from the University of California at Davis to The Claremont Graduate School where she teaches courses in the anthropology of education and African American English. In 1994, she was awarded the Outstanding Faculty Award by Delta Sigma Theta at the University of California at Davis.

Ann Christine Frankowski teaches at both the University of Maryland, Baltimore County, and at the School of Continuing Studies, Johns Hopkins University. She teaches courses on childhood and adolescence, anthropological research methods, and cultures of Asia and the Pacific Rim.

Ernestine Friedl is the James B. Duke Professor Emeritus at Duke University. While at Duke, she taught courses ranging from urban sociology to "The Negro in the Old and New World," later specializing in the anthropology of gender, modern Greece, and the Mediterranean. She received the Distinguished Teacher Award from the Queens College Alumni Association.

Richard Furlow has taught anthropology at a number of institutions and is currrently dean of Social and Behavioral Sciences at the College of DuPage. He has a strong interest in conveying anthropological ideas to the general public and is working on exporting the community college concept to India.

Norma González has taught anthropology to elementary school teachers at the University of Arizona for the past five years. Her teaching specialty is in field methods for educators.

Marvin Harris is graduate research professor at the University of Florida. He teaches courses in culture theory, modernization, and cultural ecology.

William Haviland has been teaching introductory cultural, physical, and archaeological anthropology at the University of Vermont since 1965. He regularly teaches courses on Native North Americans, Native Americans of Vermont, and Native Americans of South America.

Karl Heider teaches cultural anthropology at the University of South Carolina, teaching courses in visual anthropology (ethnographic, fiction film), nonverbal behavior, Oceania and Indonesia.

Nancy Hickerson teaches linguistic anthropology at Texas Tech University. She teaches ethnolinguistics and theory, North and South America.

Rodney Kirk has taught cultural anthropology at Central Michigan University since 1969. His particular teaching interests include Latin America (rural reform in Mexico and Chile) and Latinos in the United States. He has recently been involved in creating a required "race and cultural diversity" course for his university.

Conrad Kottak chairs the department of anthropology at the University of Michigan, specializing in anthropology and development; ecological anthropology; media, society, and culture; and research methods. He has received two recent teaching awards: the State of Michigan Teaching Excellence Award and the College of Literature, Science and Arts Excellence in Education at the University of Michigan.

Gloria Ladson-Billings is in the School of Education at the University of Wisconsin-Madison. She teaches teachers about multiculturalism and anthropology.

Leonard Lieberman teaches physical anthropology at Central Michigan University, teaching introductory level courses as well as specialized courses in human variation. He also runs a physical anthropology laboratory.

George Marcus chairs the department of anthropology at Rice University where he teaches courses in cultural critique and Polynesia.

David McCurdy teaches cultural anthropology at Macalester College. His special teaching concerns are cognitive anthropology, systematic ethnography, and India. He was awarded the Macalester College Outstanding Teaching Award in 1995.

George Michaels is an instructional consultant at the University of California at Santa Barbara. He teaches quantitative methods and has been involved in using multimedia in teaching archaeology.

Norah Moloney taught elementary school in England, Canada, and Australia before turning special attention to archaeology. She is currently teaching general archaeology at the Institute of Archaeology, University College, London, as well as teaching teachers how to use archaeology in the elementary level classroom.

Yolanda Moses is president of City College of City University of New York and president of the American Anthropological Association (1996–1998). Before becoming a full-time administrator, she taught courses in education, women in society, and contemporary Caribbean and African culture.

Carol Mukhopadhyay teaches cultural anthropology at San Jose State University. Her special interests are in social organization, cognitive-economic anthropology, methods and theory, gender roles, and South Asia.

Serena Nanda chairs the department of anthropology at John Jay College of Criminal Justice, part of the City University of New York system. Her teaching interests are in gender, ethnicity and law, and India. She is also involved in an interdisciplinary, theme-based undergraduate liberal arts program.

Fred Plog was, until his death in 1992, associated with New Mexico State University, where he served as chair of the department of anthropology. His teaching specialties were in economic anthropology, culture change, archaeological theory and method, archaeological survey, and the prehistory of the American Southwest.

Stephen Plog has taught anthropology and archaeology at the University of Virginia since 1978. His teaching interests are in archaeological method and theory, North American prehistory, the archaeology of the American Southwest, and tribal social organization.

Aaron Podolefsky is dean of the College of Social and Behavioral Sciences at the University of Northern Iowa. His teaching interests continue to be in applied anthropology, law and legal anthropology, and New Guinea.

Frank E. (Gene) Poirier chairs the department of anthropology at Ohio State University. He teaches introductory physical anthropology, human evolution, and nonhuman primate socioecology. He has received several Arts and Sciences Teaching Awards, a teaching award from the Black Greek Council, and an Alumni Award for Distinguished Teaching.

Patricia Rice is an Eberly Professor for Outstanding Teaching at West Virginia University and a Research Fellow at the Institute of Archaeology, University College, London. Her teaching interests are in prehistoric and primitive art, archaeology, and physical anthropology. She has been awarded several college and university Outstanding Teaching Awards, and in 1991 was named the Carnegie (formerly CASE) Professor of the Year for West Virginia.

Deborah Rubin teaches introductory anthropology courses as well as courses on anthropological theory at the University of the Pacific. She has recently organized workshops at annual AAA meetings on the topic "Teaching about

Race and Gender"; in 1994, she received the Outstanding Teacher of the School of International Studies Award at her university.

Ruth Selig is an anthropologist-educator who serves as the assistant to the provost at the Smithsonian Institution. Before her Smithsonian appointment, she taught in both public and private schools in Boston and Washington, D.C. She was involved in establishing the Anthropology for Teachers program at George Washington University as well as *AnthroNotes,* where she continues to write articles.

George Spindler is professor emeritus of anthropology and education at Stanford University but continues to teach ethnographic methods at Stanford and the University of California at Davis with his wife, Louise Spindler. He has received the Lloyd W. Dinkelspiel award at Stanford for his contributions to undergraduate education, and the distinguished career award from the American Education Research Association. He was recently elected to the National Academy of Education.

Louise Spindler is professor emeritus of anthropology and education at Stanford University but continues to teach ethnographic methods at Stanford and the University of California at Davis with her husband, George Spindler. She was recently elected to the National Academy of Education.

Philip L. Stein is the dean of academic affairs at Los Angeles Pierce College where he also teaches physical anthropology and a laboratory that accompanies the course.

Karen E. Tice is a senior associate at Formative Evaluation Research Associates (FERA) in Ann Arbor, Michigan. Her main interests are in disseminating information about practicing anthropology, and she teaches qualitative data collection and analysis to FERA's multidisciplinary staff.

John van Willigen teaches applied anthropology at the University of Kentucky. His other teaching interests are in human sexuality and food and culture. Early in his career, he was awarded the Standard Oil Award for Effective Teaching and more recently won the Chancellor's Teaching Award at his university.

Jane White teaches at the University of South Carolina. Her teaching interests are in the ethnography of education and teaching anthropology to education majors and teachers.

Corinne Shear Wood is professor emeritus at the University of California-Fullerton, where she taught physical anthropology, medical anthropology, human adaptation, and culture and nutrition.

INDEX

ISBN 1-55934-711-2

90000